Inter-American Development Bank

Latin America in Graphs

Demographic, Economic and Social Trends

Published by the Inter-American Development Bank
Distributed by The Johns Hopkins University Press

• 1994-95 •
Edition

Latin America in Graphs

Demographic, Economic and Social Trends (1974-1994)

© Copyright 1995 by the Inter-American Development Bank

Inter-American Development Bank
1300 New York Avenue, N.W.
Washington, D.C. 20577

Distributed by
The Johns Hopkins University Press
2715 North Charles Street
Baltimore, Maryland 21218-4319

ISBN: 0-940602-79-2

INTRODUCTION TO LATIN AMERICA IN GRAPHS, 1974-1994

This document has been prepared by Statistics and Quantitative Analysis in the Integration and Regional Studies Department. It contains a selection of graphs for each of the 26 Developing Member Countries of the Inter-American Development Bank. There are as well graphs for four economic regions and for Latin America (i.e., aggregates of the member countries). The objective is to represent trends in important Demographic, Social and Economic variables over the period 1974-1994. Using standardized variables and graphs across countries makes comparing them with each other and the regional and Latin American aggregates possible.

The graphs have been grouped into six major sections covering the following topics:

1. **Population and Vital Statistics**
    Growth of School-age population
    Population by major age groups
    Fertility and number of births
    Population Pyramid 1990, 2000 and 2010

2. **Education**
    Net Enrollment Rates by Level
    Public Current Expenditure by Level
    Survival Rates in Primary Education
    Efficiency in Primary Education
    Illiteracy Rates
    Average years of Schooling

3. **National Accounts**
    GDP Per Capita
    GDP and Population Growth Rates
    Contribution to change in total supply
    GDP Growth by Major Sectors of Origin
    Degree of Openness of the Economy
    Investment and Domestic Saving Rates

4. **Balance of Payments**
    Current Account Balance as a percent of GDP
    Current Account Components as a percent of GDP
    Exports and Imports of Goods, FOB
    Private and Goverment Capital Flows
    Investment in the Private sector as a percent of GDP
    Stock of International Reserves

5. **Energy**
    Production and Consumption of Energy
    Production of Primary Energy
    GDP and Energy Consumption
    Energy Surplus
    Supply of Primary Energy by Major Fuel, 1992
    Energy Requirement Per Capita

6. **External Debt**
    Net External Debt Per Capita
    Structure of Disbursed External Debt, End 1992
    Multilateral Debt as a Percent of Disbursed
        External Debt
    Interest Payments as a Percent of Exports
    Implicit Interest Rate Versus LIBOR
    Debt and Accumulated Current Account Deficits

For each topic, except Education, the six selected standardized graphs are shown in succession for Latin America, for four economic regions and for the 26 countries. Graphs on Education are available for Latin America and the 26 countries, but not for the economic regions. In the case of Latin America and the four regions, a common scale is used in the graphs to facilitate comparisons.

Descriptions of the graphs and country notes are given at the beginning of each section.

All of the data are taken directly from the Bank's Economic and Social Data Base (ESDB). Many of the series are published in Basic Socio-Economic Data and in the Statistical Profiles of the country chapters and the Statistical Appendix of *Economic and Social Progress in Latin America, 1994 Report*. Data for 1994 are estimates provided by the IDB country economists as concerns National Accounts and Balance of Payments. External Debt data for 1994 are World Bank estimates.

This publication was prepared and coordinated by Jacques Anas with the participation of Robert Vos for Education, Uziel Nogueira for Energy Statistics, Fernando Orrego, Augusto Angulo and Ivo Maric, under the general supervision of Michael McPeak.

TECHNICAL NOTE

1. CHOICE OF SCALE FOR THE GRAPHS

The choice of scale is an important issue insofar as it may influence the reader's judgement regarding the magnitude(s) of the variables shown. Using a common scale for each graph across countries is impractical because of variations in the magnitudes of the variables among countries and the presence of extreme cases. At the aggregate level of Latin America and the Economic Regions, however, the variance of magnitudes is much lower.

As a consequence, all graphs for Latin America and four Economic Regions are shown with a common scale. When possible, a common scale also was used at the country level to help readers make direct comparisons between countries and to avoid misleading representations (e.g., multilateral debt as a percent of total debt, fertility rate, etc.). In other cases, the Latin American indicator was sometimes used as an "anchor" series, allowing for direct intercountry comparisons (e.g. GDP per Capita).

2. ECONOMIC AND GEOGRAPHICAL AREAS

LATIN AMERICA: The aggregate of the 26 IDB developing member countries.

CACM: Central American Common Market, including Costa Rica, El Salvador, Guatemala, Honduras and Nicaragua.

CARICOM: Caribbean Common Market, including 12 countries of the Caribbean region. In this publication, Caricom Indicators are calculated from the six Caricom country members of the IDB: Bahamas, Barbados, Belize, Guyana, Jamaica and Trinidad and Tobago

ANDEAN PACT: Bolivia, Colombia, Ecuador, Peru and Venezuela.

MERCOSUR: Argentina, Brazil, Paraguay and Uruguay.

EUROPEAN UNION: Austria, Belgium, Denmark, Finland, France, Germany, Greece, Ireland, Italy, Luxembourg, Netherland, Portugal, Spain, Sweden and The United Kingdom.

3. ENERGY STATISTICS AND CONCEPTS

International Energy Statistics and Balances have been regularly compiled and published since 1952 by the United Nations Statistical Division. The basic principle is to express all forms of energy in a common energy measure (joule, oil or coal equivalent). The main forms of energy are: solid fuels (coal, lignite, coke etc.), liquid fuels (crude petroleum, petroleum products from distillation, condensate, etc.), gaseous fuels (natural gas, coke-oven gas, etc.), electricity (primary and secondary) and traditional fuels (or biomass). The main concepts used in the graphs are:

Primary Energy: refers to the production or imports of energy before any domestic transformations (for example primary electricity includes geothermal, hydro, nuclear, solar, tide, wind and wave but excludes thermal).

Energy Consumption: (traditionally called energy requirement) represents the total energy needed to satisfy the final domestic consumption by industry and construction, by transport and by households and other consumers. It is equal to the final consumption augmented by the "losses" ocurred during the process of transformation (conversion losses, consumption by the energy sector and non-energy uses) and in transport and distribution. The non-energy uses are a "loss" of energy resources, mainly petroleum, for the country but an input for the chemical industry and other users. The losses may represent an equivalent of 25% of the final consumption and reach 100% in some countries of the region. The energy consumption is satisfied by the supply of domestic production of primary energy augmented of net imports (and reduced by bunkers and the variation of primary stocks).

Imports and exports: include trade in primary and secondary energy products. Observe that all forms of energy are tradable even if oil is the most traded.

Commercial energy: the expression is commonly used and refers to all forms of energy except biomass energy. In fact, a proportion of biomass energy is commercialized but is not considered as commercial energy in the UN traditional conceptual language.

Biomass energy: defined as fuelwood, bagasse, charcoal, natural wastes and alcohol like ethanol and methanol. Data on fuelwood and charcoal production are from the Food and Agriculture Organization (FAO). Calculation of bagasse production is based on ECLAC methodology and sugar production data are from the Sugar Yearbook. Biomass is also called traditional energy but this expression can be confused with conventional energy.

TABLE OF CONTENTS

	PAGE
1. Population and Vital Statistics:	
Description of the graphs	2
Latin America graphs	3
Economic regions graphs	5-8
Country graphs	9-34
2. Education:	
Description of the graphs	36
Latin American graphs	37
Country graphs	39-64
3. National Accounts:	
Description of the graphs	66
Latin American graphs	67
Economic regions graphs	69-72
Country graphs	73-98
4. Balance of Payments:	
Description of the graphs	100
Latin American graphs	101
Economic regions graphs	103-106
Country graphs	107-132
5. Energy:	
Description of the graphs	134
Latin American graphs	135
Economic regions graphs	137-140
Country graphs	141-166
6. External Debt:	
Description of the graphs	168
Latin American graphs	169
Economic regions graphs	171-174
Country graphs	175-200

Statistics as of January 1995

POPULATION AND VITAL STATISTICS

POPULATION AND VITAL STATISTICS

Data are from the 1992 round of population estimates and projections prepared by the United Nations Population Division. In the case of Belize, which was not included in the UN estimates exercise because of its low level of population, national sources have been used. Projections are shown in the graphs until 2010. They correspond to the medium variant, considered the "most likely" scenario. Descriptions of the graphs follow:

1. GROWTH OF SCHOOL-AGE POPULATIONS (ANNUAL AVERAGE)

Growth rates are shown for the school-age populations 0 to 4, 5 to 9, 10 to 14 and 15 to 19. In many countries the graphs show a stabilisation or even a decrease of those populations in the two coming decades. This will produce a lower demand on the school system with a lag which is visible on the graph.

2. POPULATION BY MAJOR AGE GROUPS (STRUCTURE)

The graph shows the past evolution and the projection to 2010 of the population structure by major age groups 0-14, 15-60 and 60+. In the United Nations nomenclature, age 60 and over is generally used to define the elderly.

3. FERTILITY AND NUMBER OF BIRTHS

The objective of the graph is to show that a decrease in the fertility rate does not necessarily imply a reduction in the number of births. The evolution of the number of women of child-bearing age is also a determinant and depends on past fertility rates. This explains a possible lag of two to three decades before the drop in fertility may have a significative impact on the number of births. The age pyramids are useful for following those women cohorts.

4. POPULATION PYRAMIDS 1990, 2000 AND 2010

The population pyramid gives, as a percent of the total population, the number of males and females for each age-group.

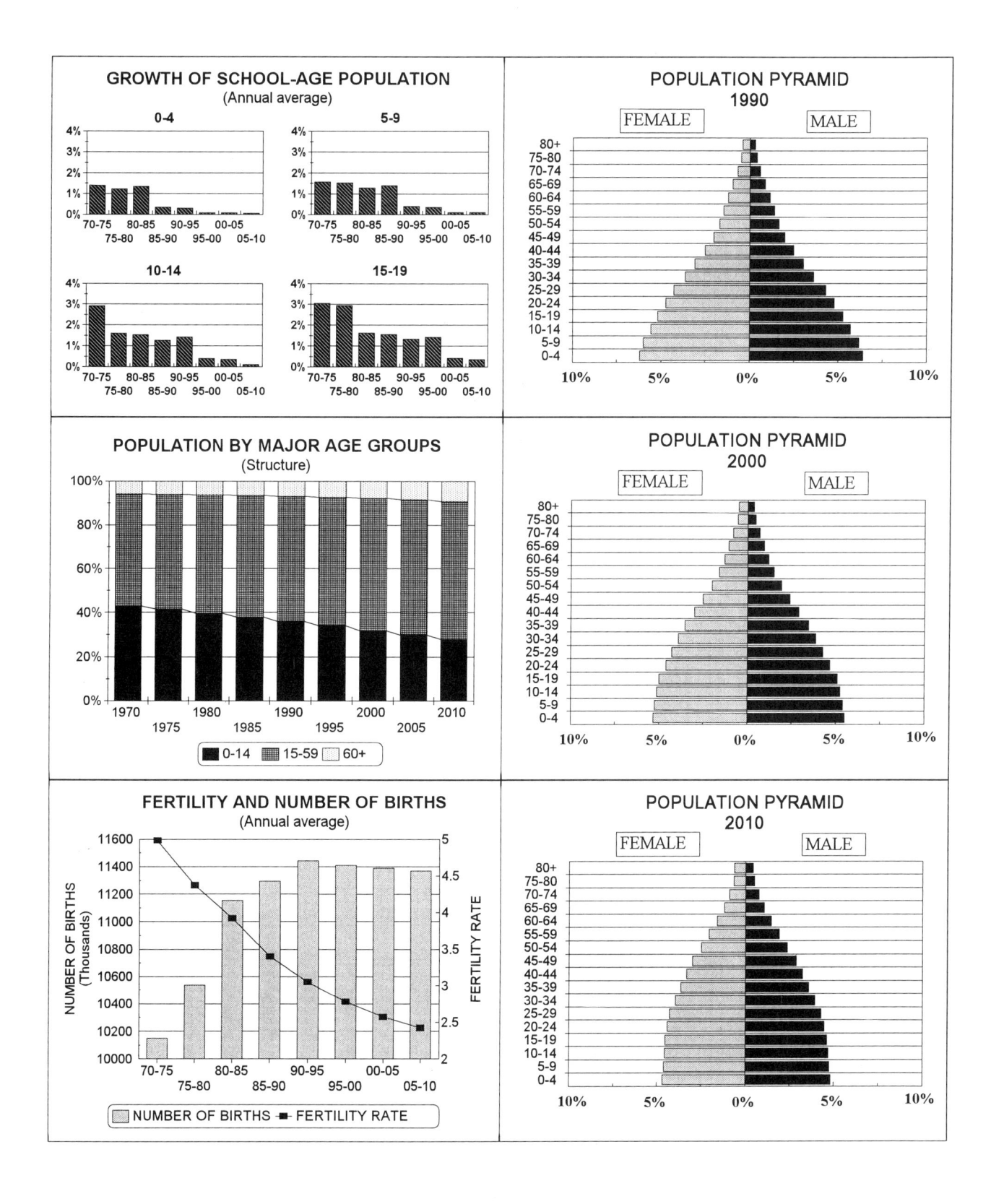

LATIN AMERICA
Population and Vital Statistics

Statistics and Quantitative Analysis/IDB

ANDEAN GROUP
Population and Vital Statistics

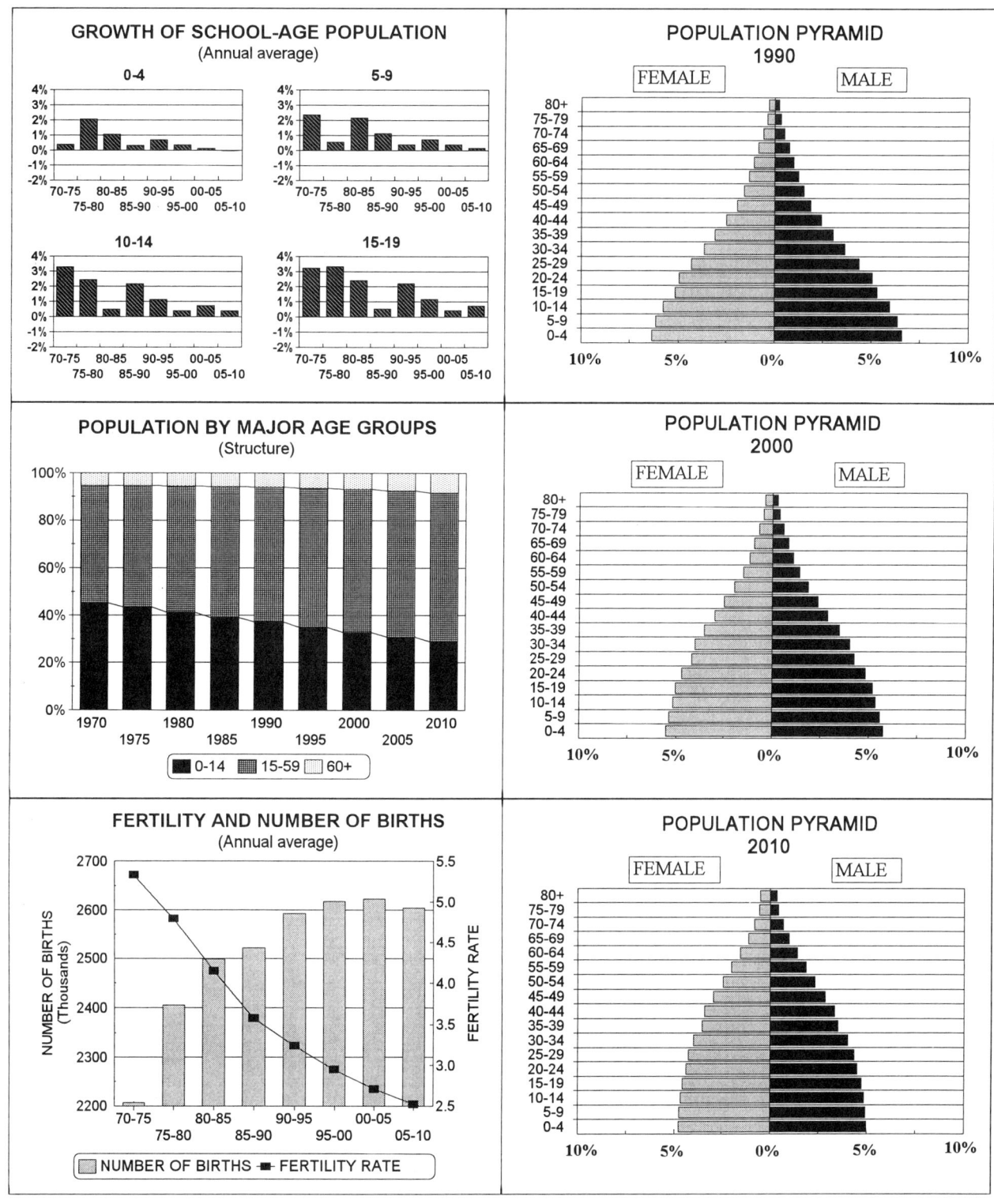

GROWTH OF SCHOOL-AGE POPULATION
(Annual average)

- 0-4
- 5-9
- 10-14
- 15-19

POPULATION BY MAJOR AGE GROUPS
(Structure)

Legend: 0-14, 15-59, 60+

FERTILITY AND NUMBER OF BIRTHS
(Annual average)

Legend: NUMBER OF BIRTHS, FERTILITY RATE

POPULATION PYRAMID 1990
FEMALE | MALE

POPULATION PYRAMID 2000
FEMALE | MALE

POPULATION PYRAMID 2010
FEMALE | MALE

Countries included: Bolivia, Colombia, Ecuador, Peru and Venezuela.

Statistics and Quantitative Analysis/IDB

CACM
Population and Vital Statistics

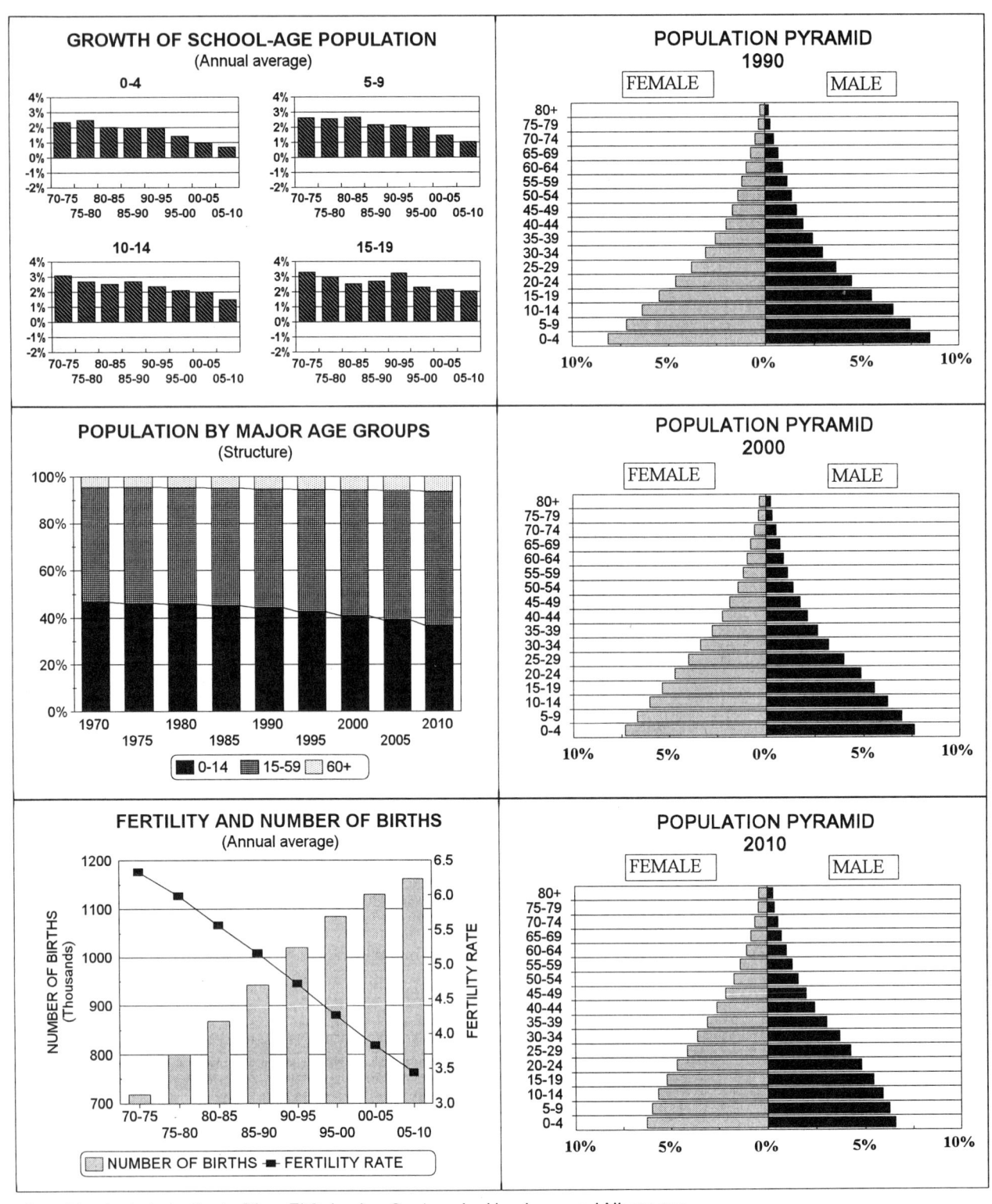

GROWTH OF SCHOOL-AGE POPULATION
(Annual average)

0-4

5-9

10-14

15-19

POPULATION BY MAJOR AGE GROUPS
(Structure)

■ 0-14   ▨ 15-59   ▢ 60+

FERTILITY AND NUMBER OF BIRTHS
(Annual average)

NUMBER OF BIRTHS — FERTILITY RATE

POPULATION PYRAMID 1990
FEMALE / MALE

POPULATION PYRAMID 2000
FEMALE / MALE

POPULATION PYRAMID 2010
FEMALE / MALE

Countries included: Costa Rica, El Salvador, Guatemala, Honduras and Nicaragua.

Statistics and Quantitative Analysis/IDB

CARICOM
Population and Vital Statistics

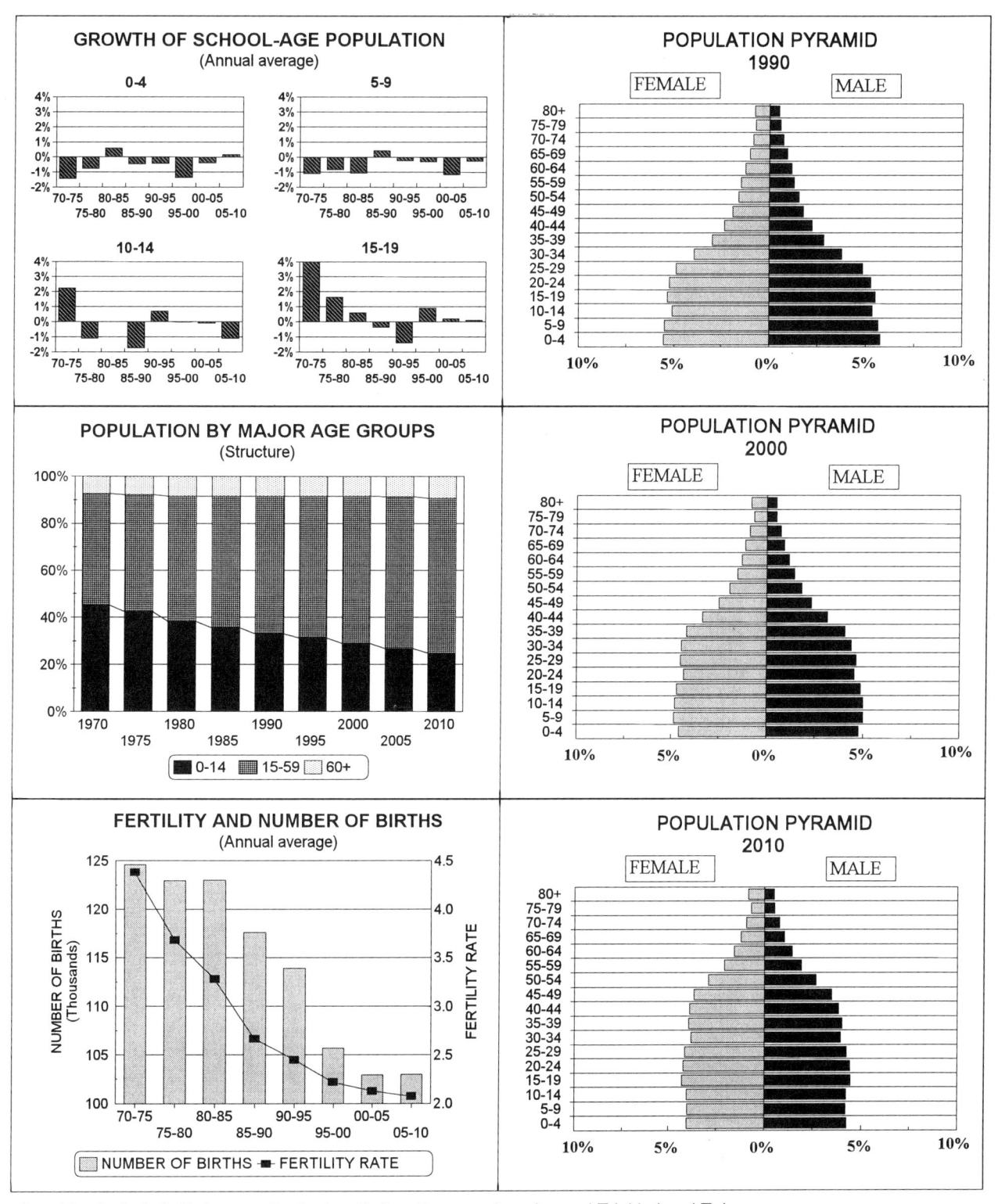

GROWTH OF SCHOOL-AGE POPULATION
(Annual average)

POPULATION PYRAMID 1990

POPULATION BY MAJOR AGE GROUPS
(Structure)

POPULATION PYRAMID 2000

FERTILITY AND NUMBER OF BIRTHS
(Annual average)

POPULATION PYRAMID 2010

Countries included : Bahamas, Barbados, Belize, Guyana, Jamaica and Trinidad and Tobago.

Statistics and Quantitative Analysis/IDB

MERCOSUR
Population and Vital Statistics

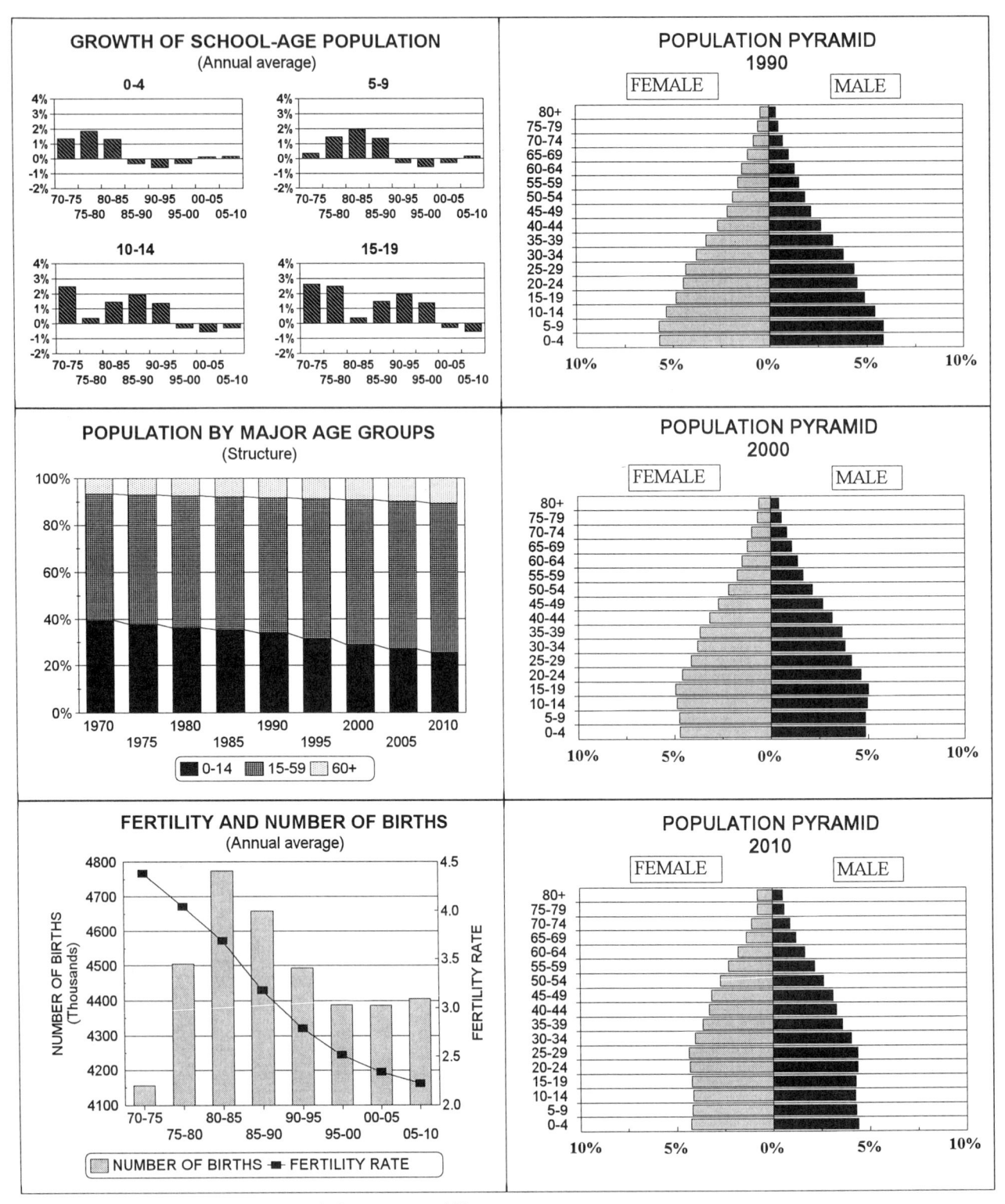

GROWTH OF SCHOOL-AGE POPULATION
(Annual average)

- 0-4
- 5-9
- 10-14
- 15-19

POPULATION BY MAJOR AGE GROUPS
(Structure)

Legend: 0-14, 15-59, 60+

FERTILITY AND NUMBER OF BIRTHS
(Annual average)

Legend: NUMBER OF BIRTHS, FERTILITY RATE

POPULATION PYRAMID 1990
FEMALE | MALE

POPULATION PYRAMID 2000
FEMALE | MALE

POPULATION PYRAMID 2010
FEMALE | MALE

Countries included: Argentina, Brazil, Paraguay and Uruguay.

Statistics and Quantitative Analysis/IDB

ARGENTINA
Population and Vital Statistics

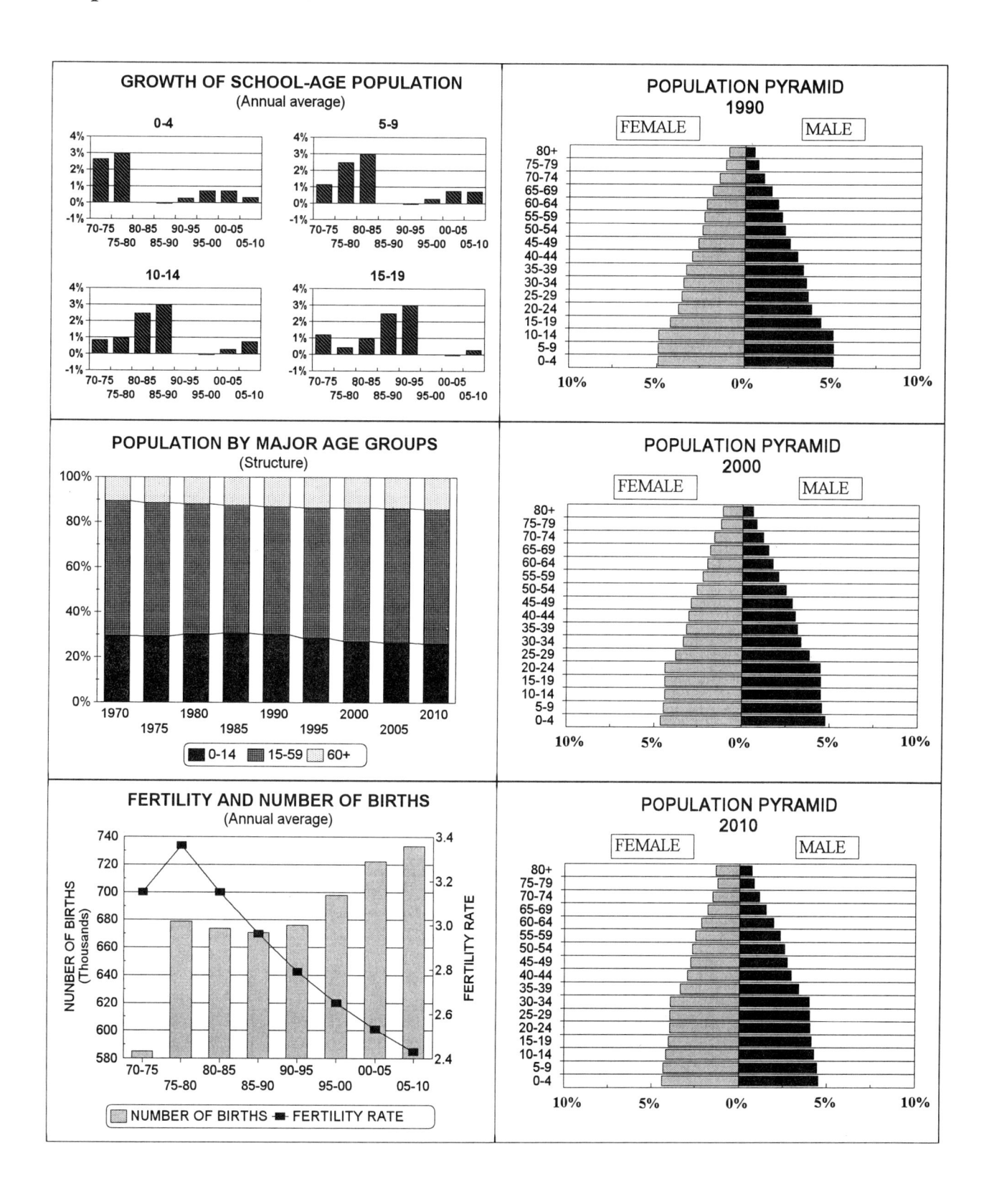

Statistics and Quantitative Analysis/IDB

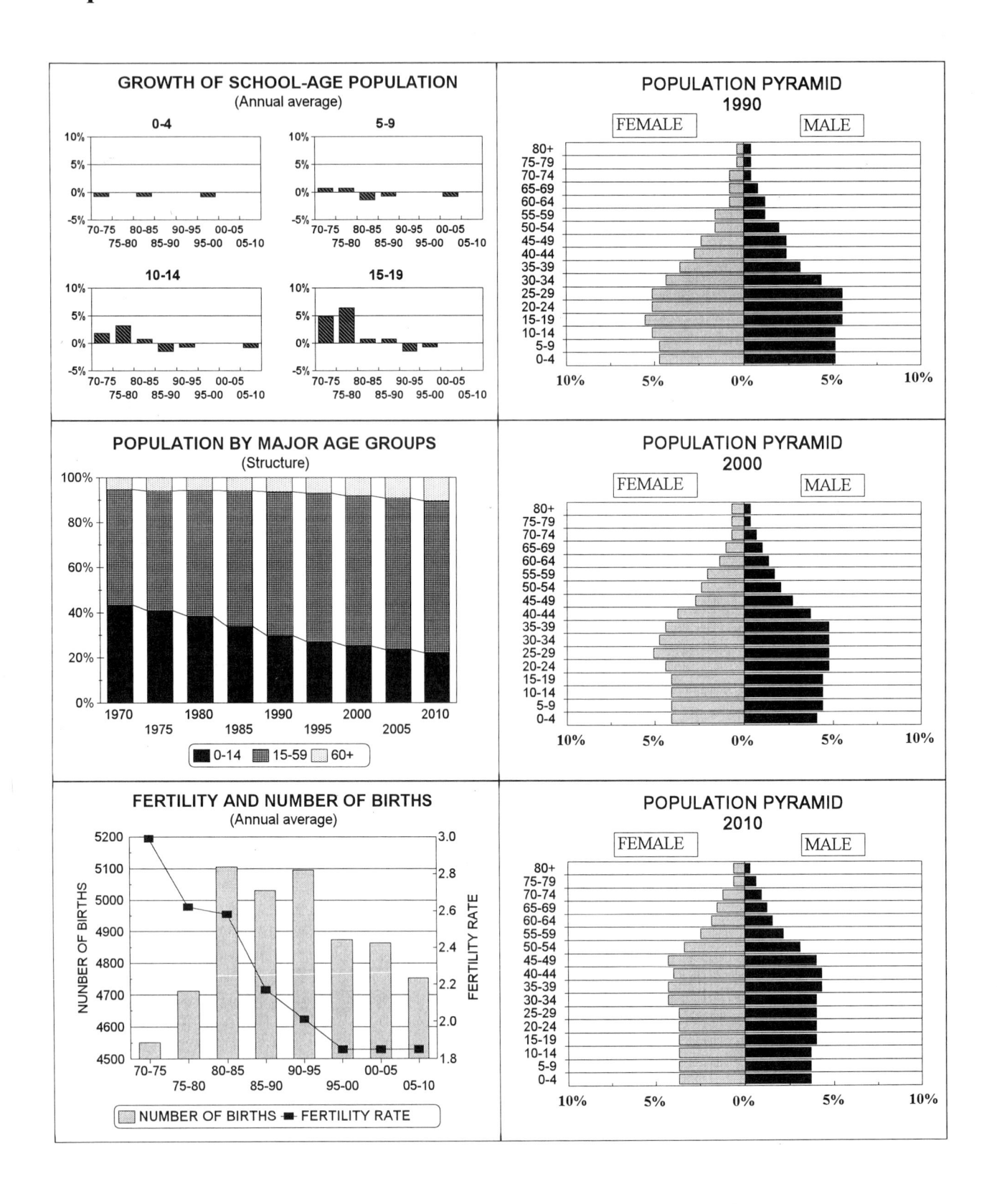

BAHAMAS
Population and Vital Statistics

GROWTH OF SCHOOL-AGE POPULATION
(Annual average)

POPULATION PYRAMID 1990

POPULATION BY MAJOR AGE GROUPS
(Structure)

POPULATION PYRAMID 2000

FERTILITY AND NUMBER OF BIRTHS
(Annual average)

POPULATION PYRAMID 2010

Statistics and Quantitative Analysis/IDB

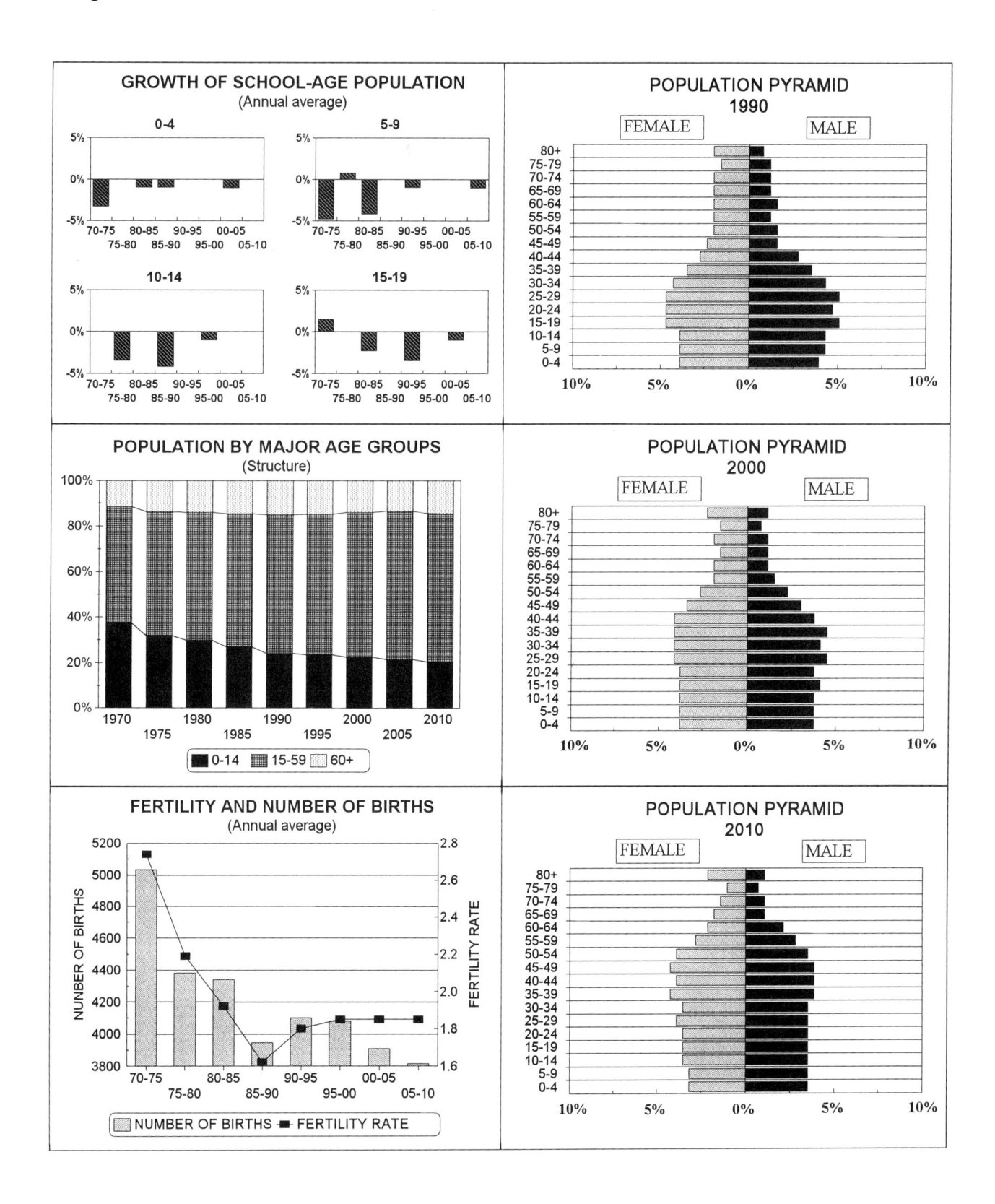

BARBADOS
Population and Vital Statistics

GROWTH OF SCHOOL-AGE POPULATION
(Annual average)

- 0-4
- 5-9
- 10-14
- 15-19

POPULATION PYRAMID 1990

POPULATION BY MAJOR AGE GROUPS
(Structure)

0-14 | 15-59 | 60+

POPULATION PYRAMID 2000

FERTILITY AND NUMBER OF BIRTHS
(Annual average)

NUMBER OF BIRTHS — FERTILITY RATE

POPULATION PYRAMID 2010

Statistics and Quantitative Analysis/IDB

BELIZE
Population and Vital Statistics

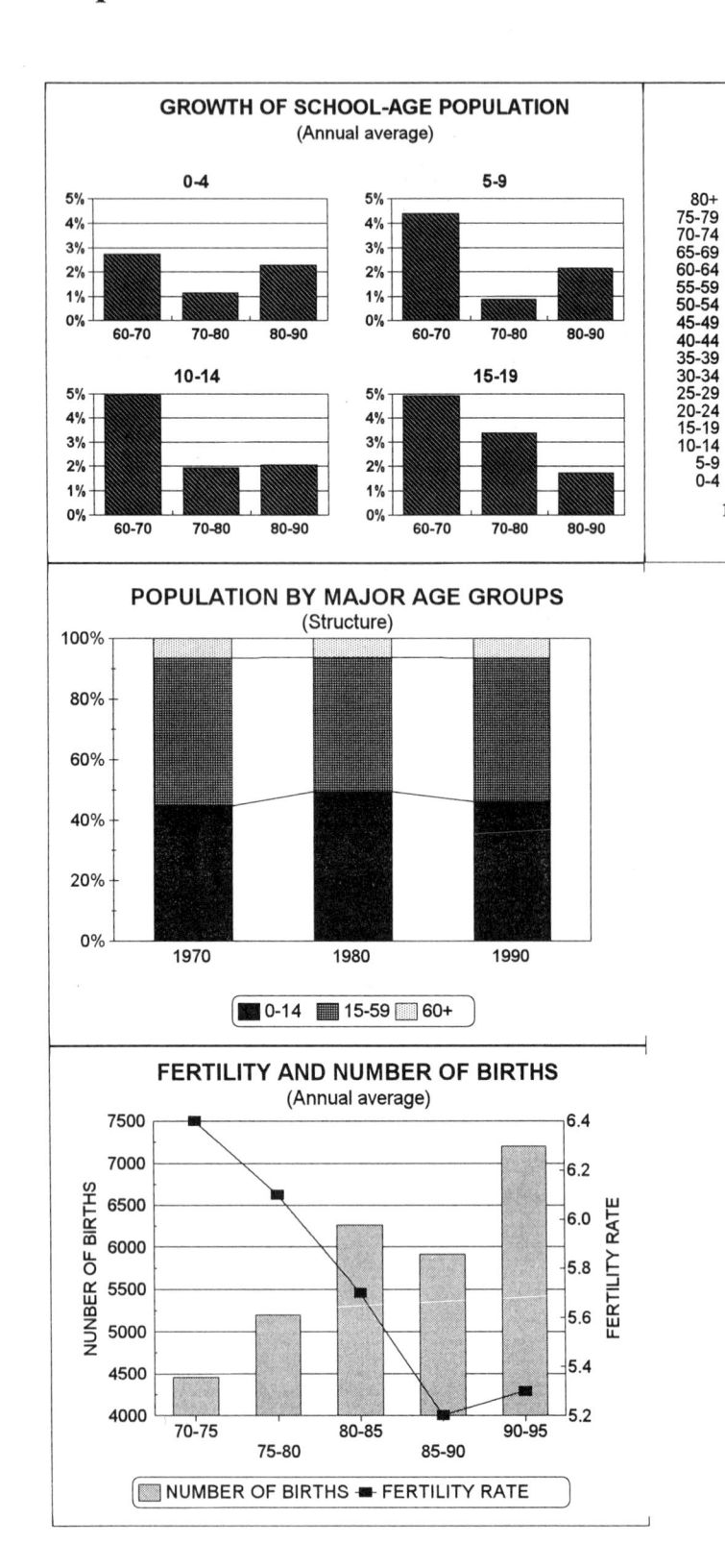

GROWTH OF SCHOOL-AGE POPULATION
(Annual average)

POPULATION PYRAMID
1991

POPULATION BY MAJOR AGE GROUPS
(Structure)

FERTILITY AND NUMBER OF BIRTHS
(Annual average)

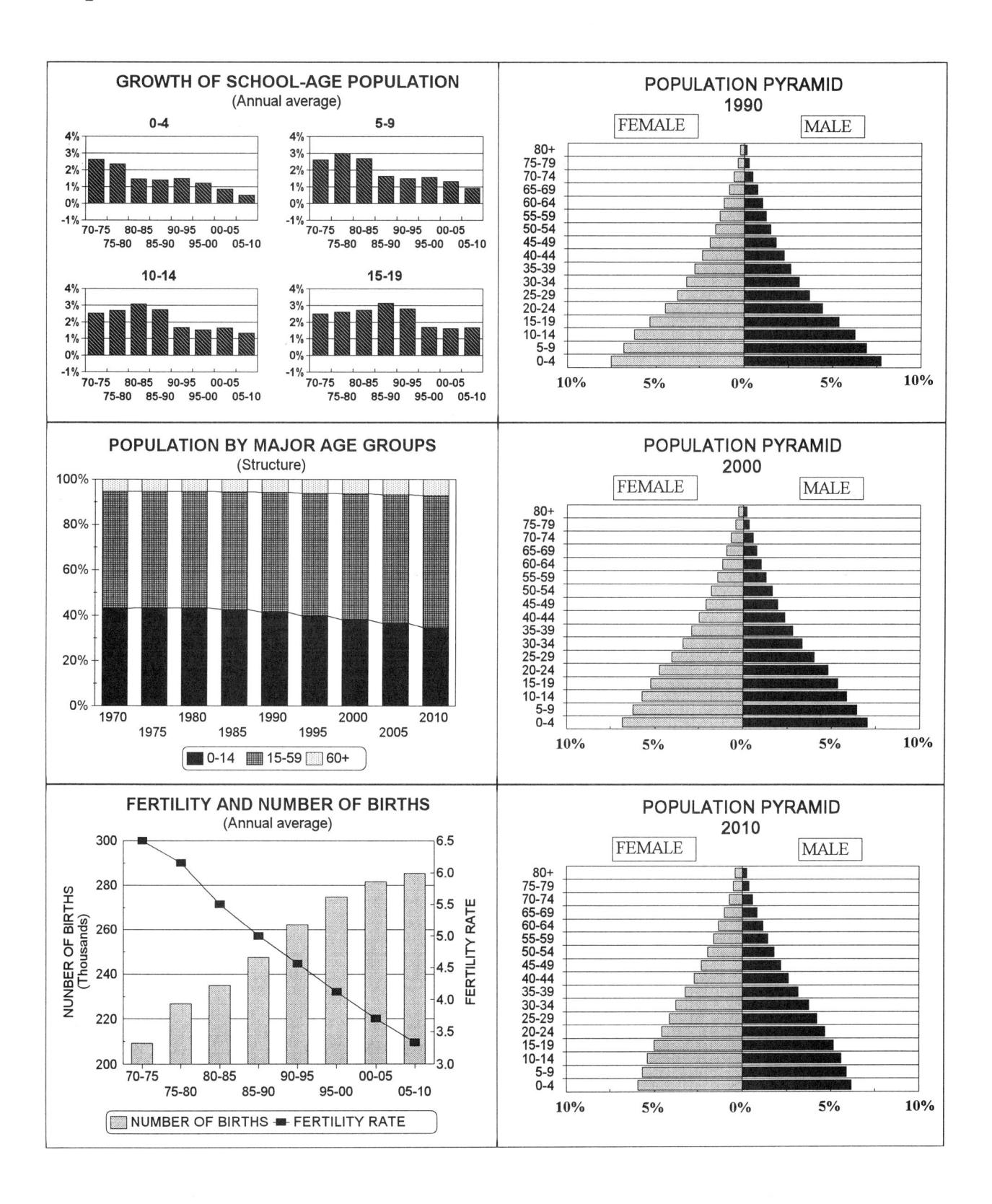

BOLIVIA
Population and Vital Statistics

GROWTH OF SCHOOL-AGE POPULATION
(Annual average)

- 0-4
- 5-9
- 10-14
- 15-19

POPULATION BY MAJOR AGE GROUPS
(Structure)

Legend: 0-14, 15-59, 60+

FERTILITY AND NUMBER OF BIRTHS
(Annual average)

Legend: NUMBER OF BIRTHS, FERTILITY RATE

POPULATION PYRAMID 1990
FEMALE | MALE

POPULATION PYRAMID 2000
FEMALE | MALE

POPULATION PYRAMID 2010
FEMALE | MALE

Statistics and Quantitative Analysis/IDB

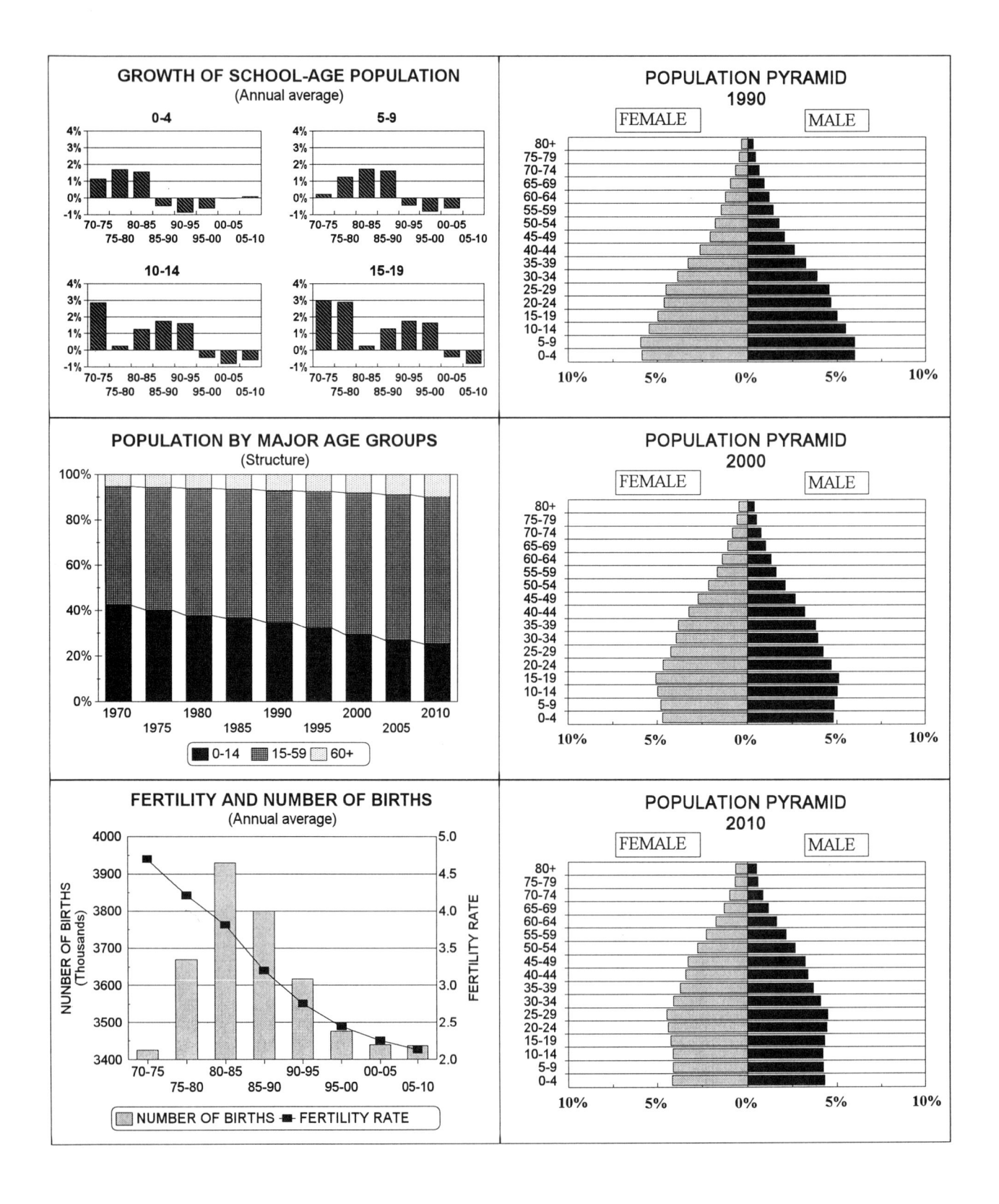

BRAZIL
Population and Vital Statistics

GROWTH OF SCHOOL-AGE POPULATION
(Annual average)

POPULATION PYRAMID 1990

POPULATION BY MAJOR AGE GROUPS
(Structure)

POPULATION PYRAMID 2000

FERTILITY AND NUMBER OF BIRTHS
(Annual average)

POPULATION PYRAMID 2010

Statistics and Quantitative Analysis/IDB

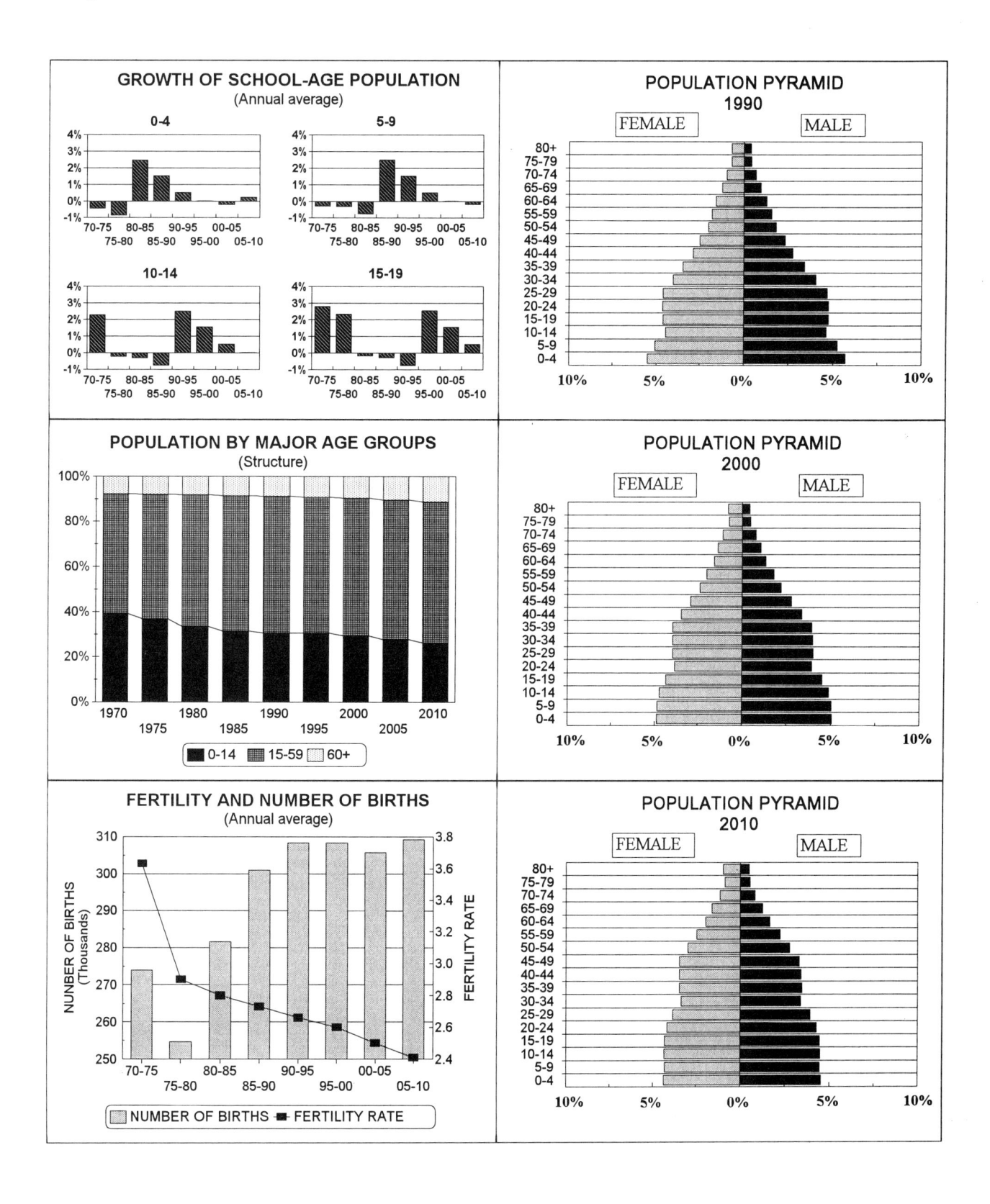

CHILE
Population and Vital Statistics

GROWTH OF SCHOOL-AGE POPULATION
(Annual average)

- 0-4
- 5-9
- 10-14
- 15-19

POPULATION BY MAJOR AGE GROUPS
(Structure)

Legend: 0-14, 15-59, 60+

FERTILITY AND NUMBER OF BIRTHS
(Annual average)

Legend: NUMBER OF BIRTHS, FERTILITY RATE

POPULATION PYRAMID 1990
FEMALE | MALE

POPULATION PYRAMID 2000
FEMALE | MALE

POPULATION PYRAMID 2010
FEMALE | MALE

Statistics and Quantitative Analysis/IDB

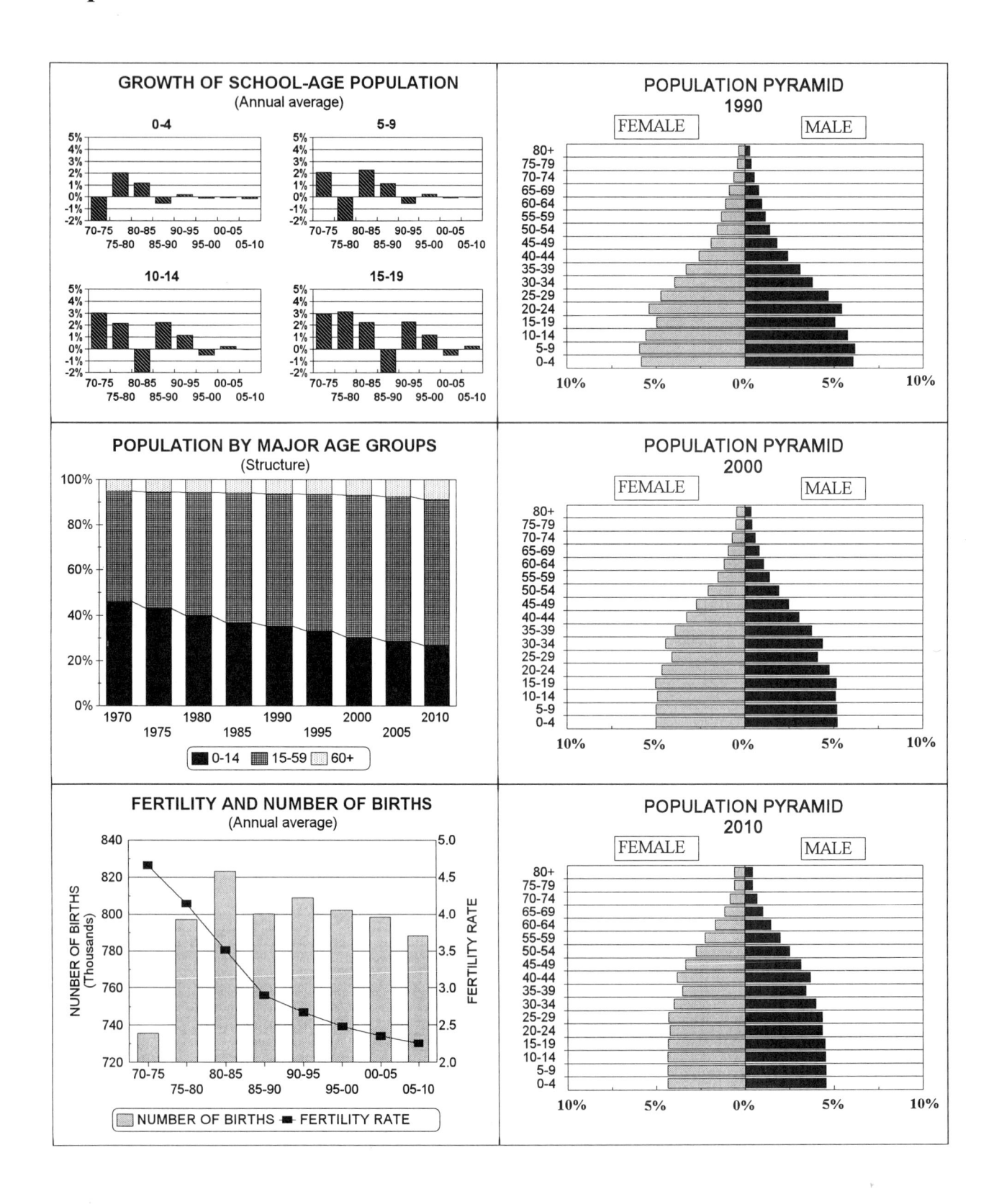

COLOMBIA
Population and Vital Statistics

GROWTH OF SCHOOL-AGE POPULATION
(Annual average)

0-4

5-9

10-14

15-19

POPULATION BY MAJOR AGE GROUPS
(Structure)

0-14 | 15-59 | 60+

FERTILITY AND NUMBER OF BIRTHS
(Annual average)

NUMBER OF BIRTHS — FERTILITY RATE

POPULATION PYRAMID 1990
FEMALE | MALE

POPULATION PYRAMID 2000
FEMALE | MALE

POPULATION PYRAMID 2010
FEMALE | MALE

Statistics and Quantitative Analysis/IDB

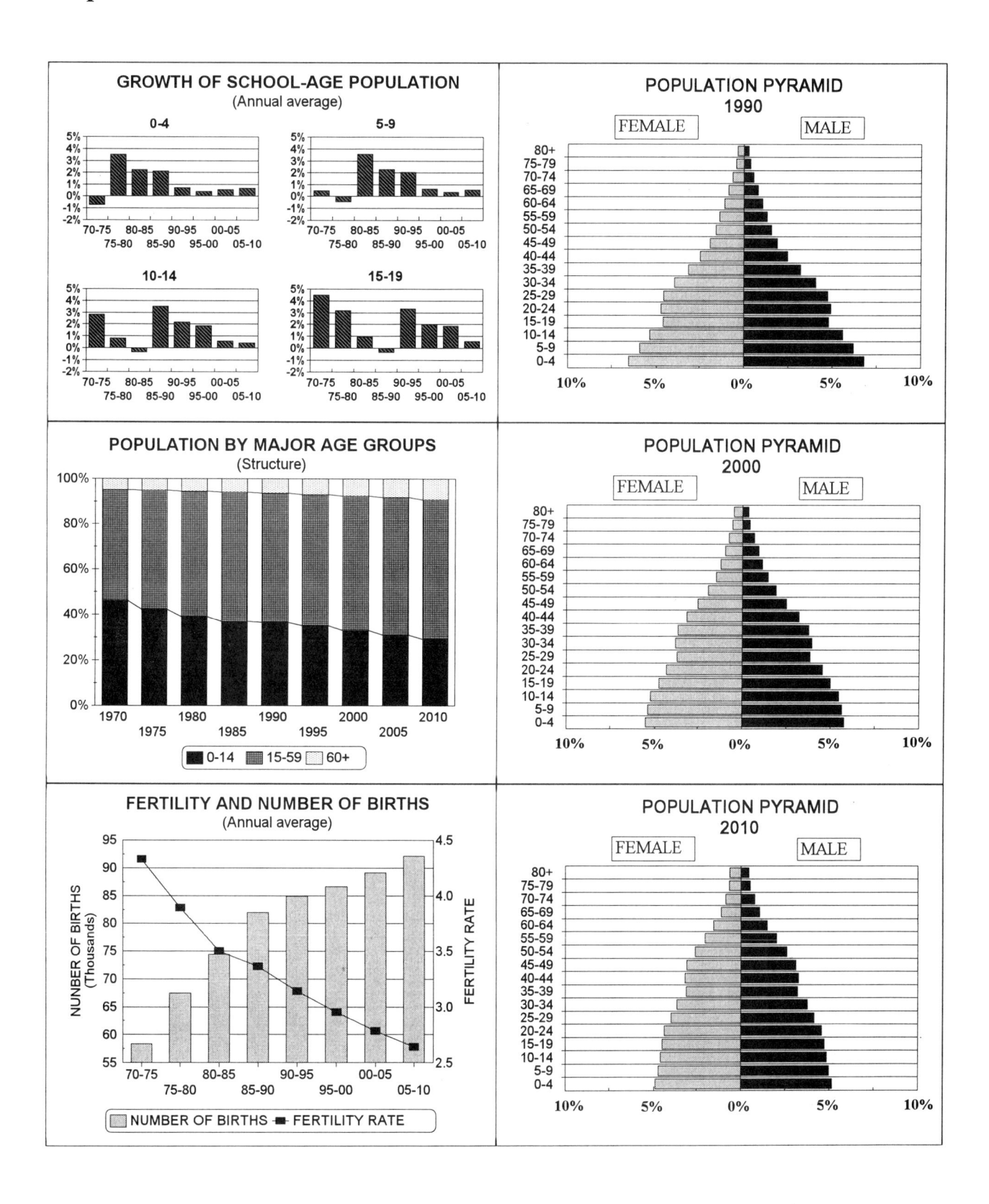

COSTA RICA
Population and Vital Statistics

Statistics and Quantitative Analysis/IDB

DOMINICAN REPUBLIC
Population and Vital Statistics

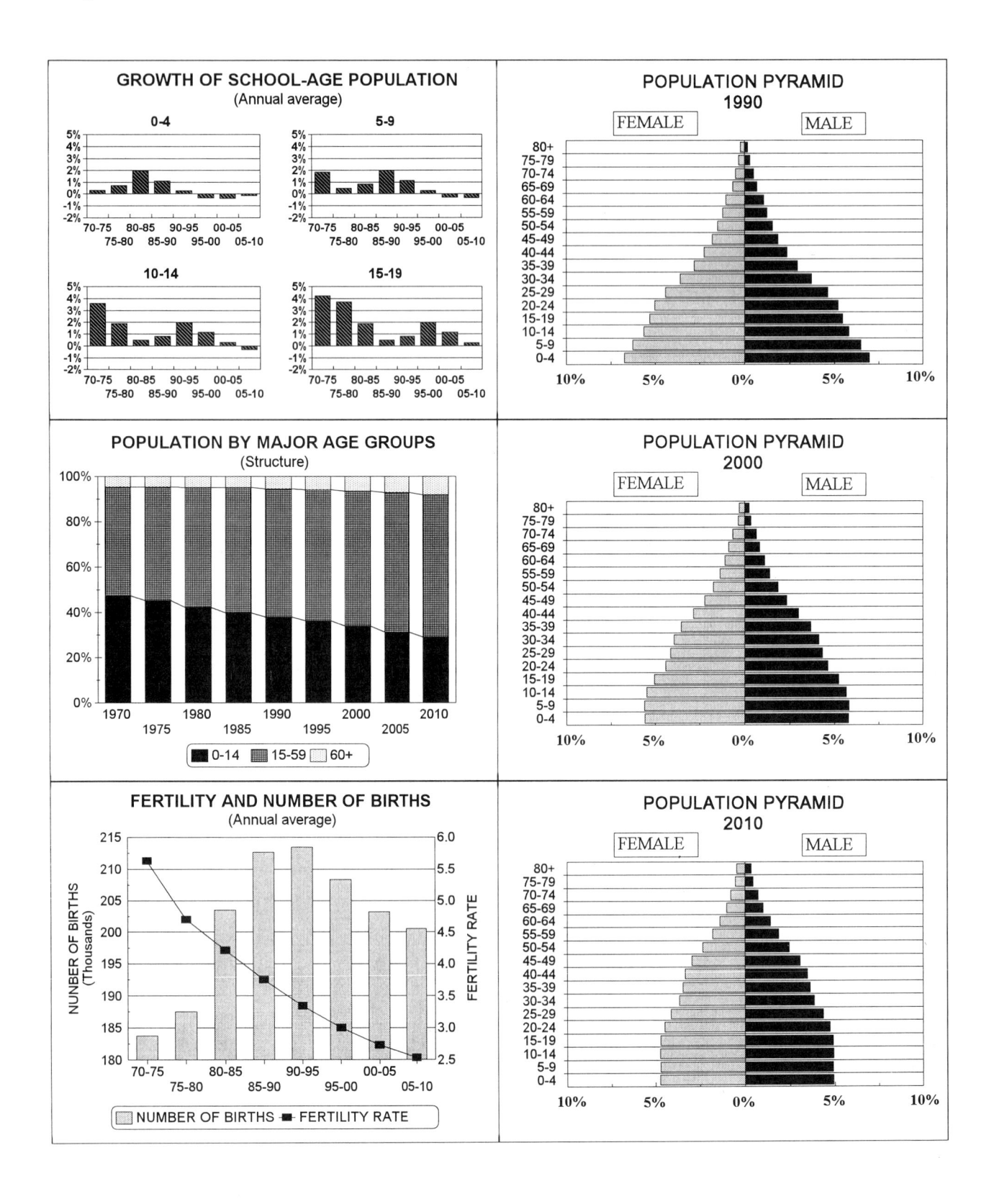

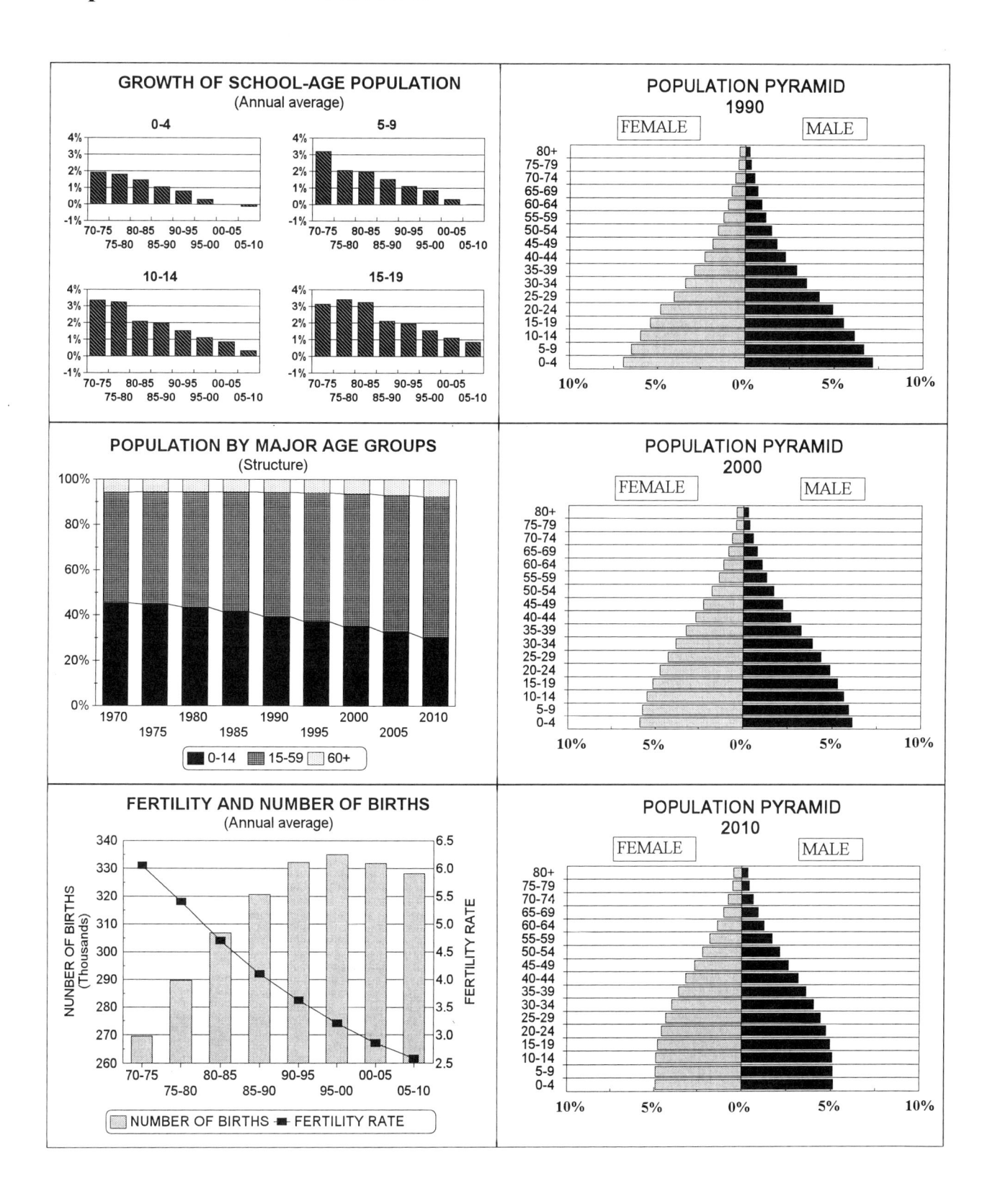

ECUADOR
Population and Vital Statistics

Statistics and Quantitative Analysis/IDB

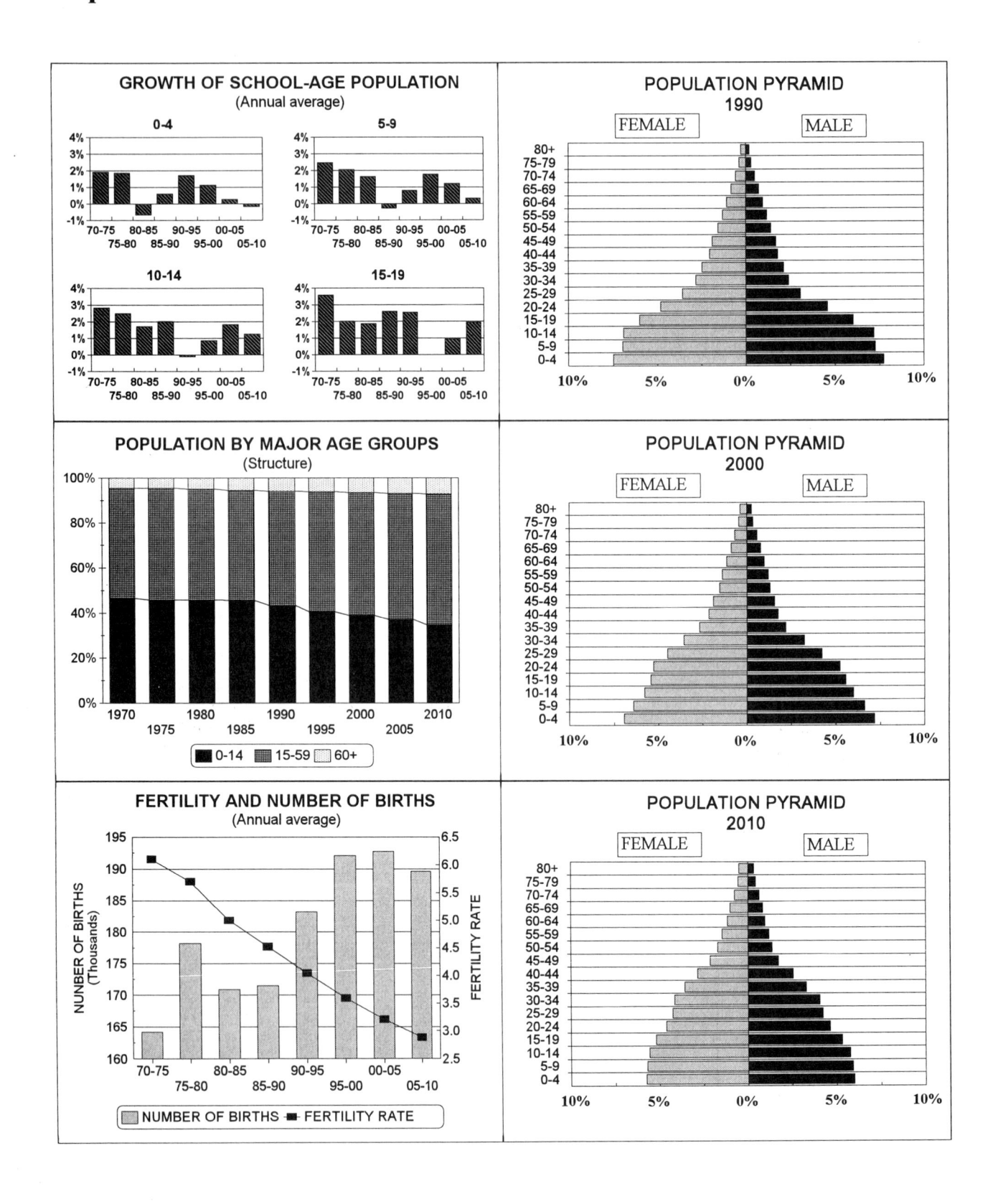

EL SALVADOR
Population and Vital Statistics

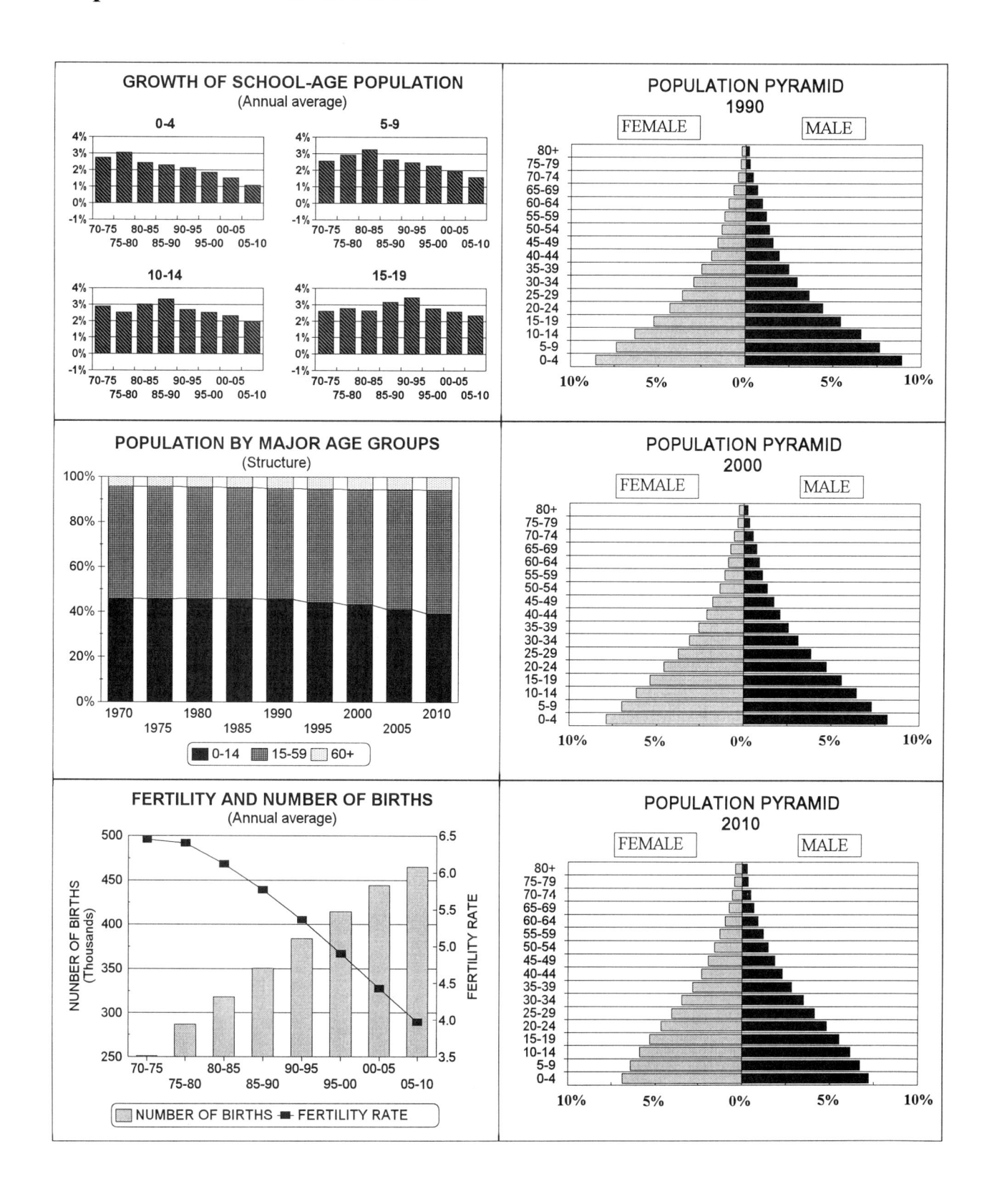

GUATEMALA
Population and Vital Statistics

GROWTH OF SCHOOL-AGE POPULATION
(Annual average)

0-4

5-9

10-14

15-19

POPULATION BY MAJOR AGE GROUPS
(Structure)

■ 0-14   ▨ 15-59   ▢ 60+

FERTILITY AND NUMBER OF BIRTHS
(Annual average)

NUMBER OF BIRTHS ■— FERTILITY RATE

POPULATION PYRAMID
1990
FEMALE / MALE

POPULATION PYRAMID
2000
FEMALE / MALE

POPULATION PYRAMID
2010
FEMALE / MALE

Statistics and Quantitative Analysis/IDB

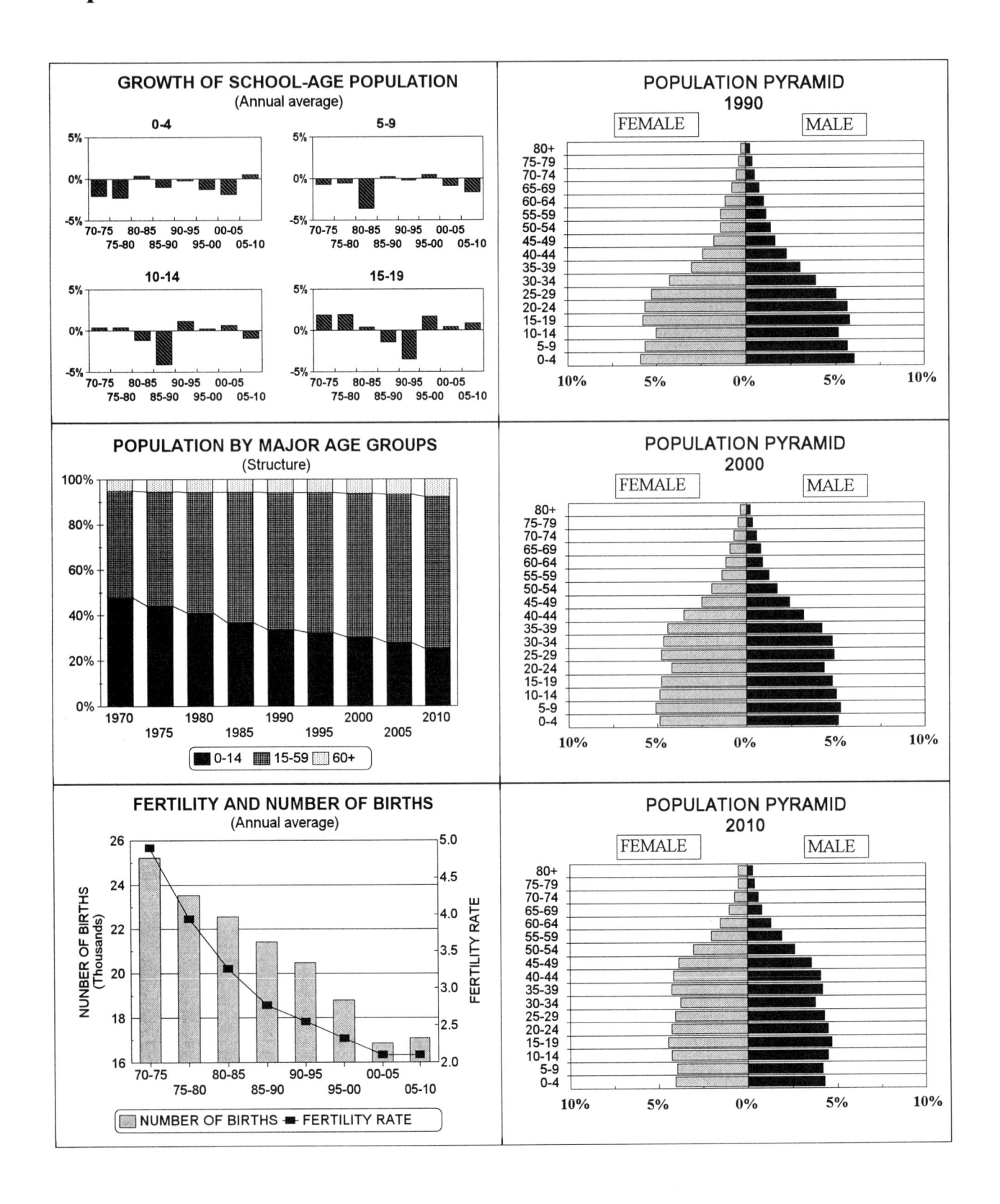

GUYANA
Population and Vital Statistics

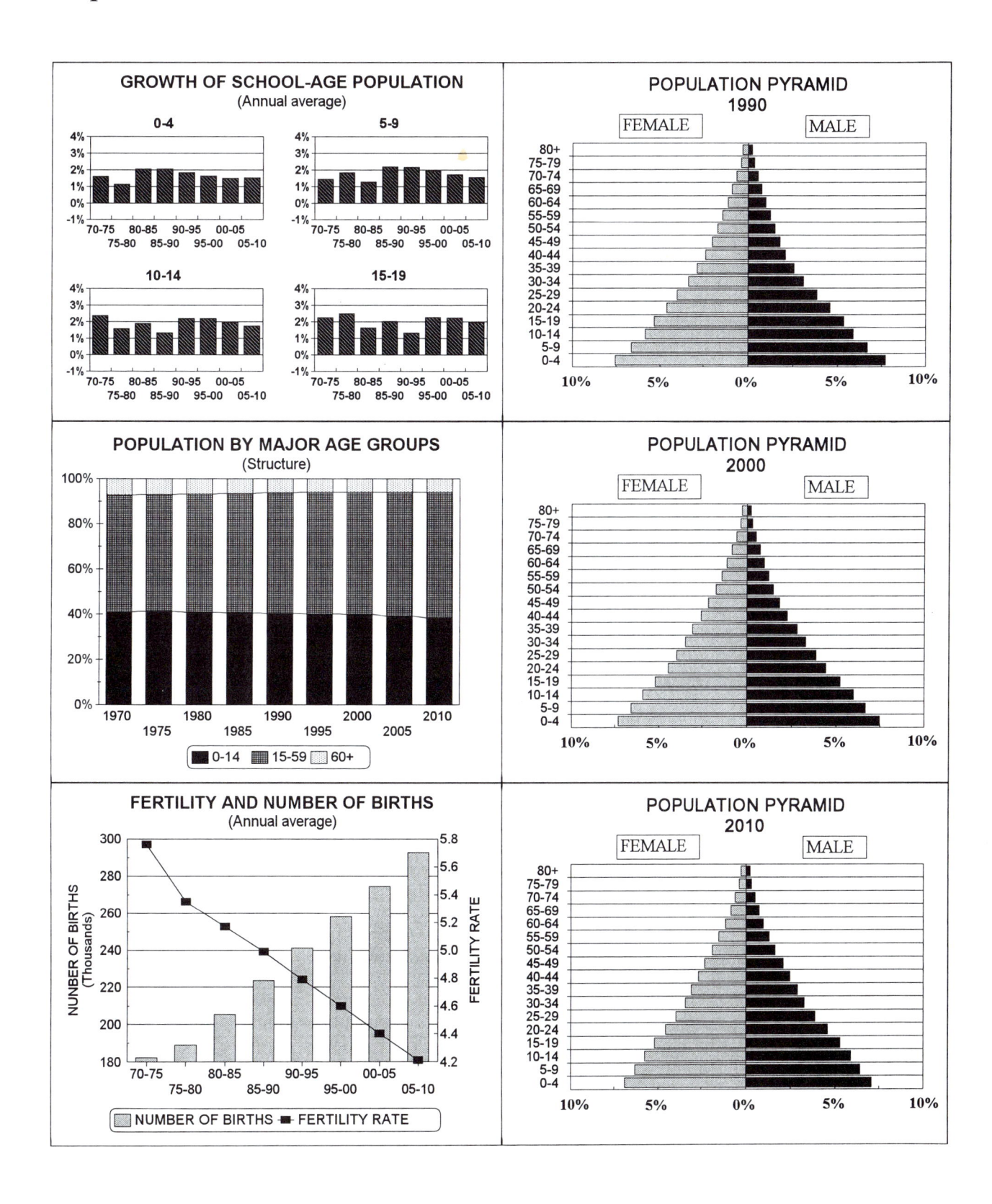

HAITI
Population and Vital Statistics

Statistics and Quantitative Analysis/IDB

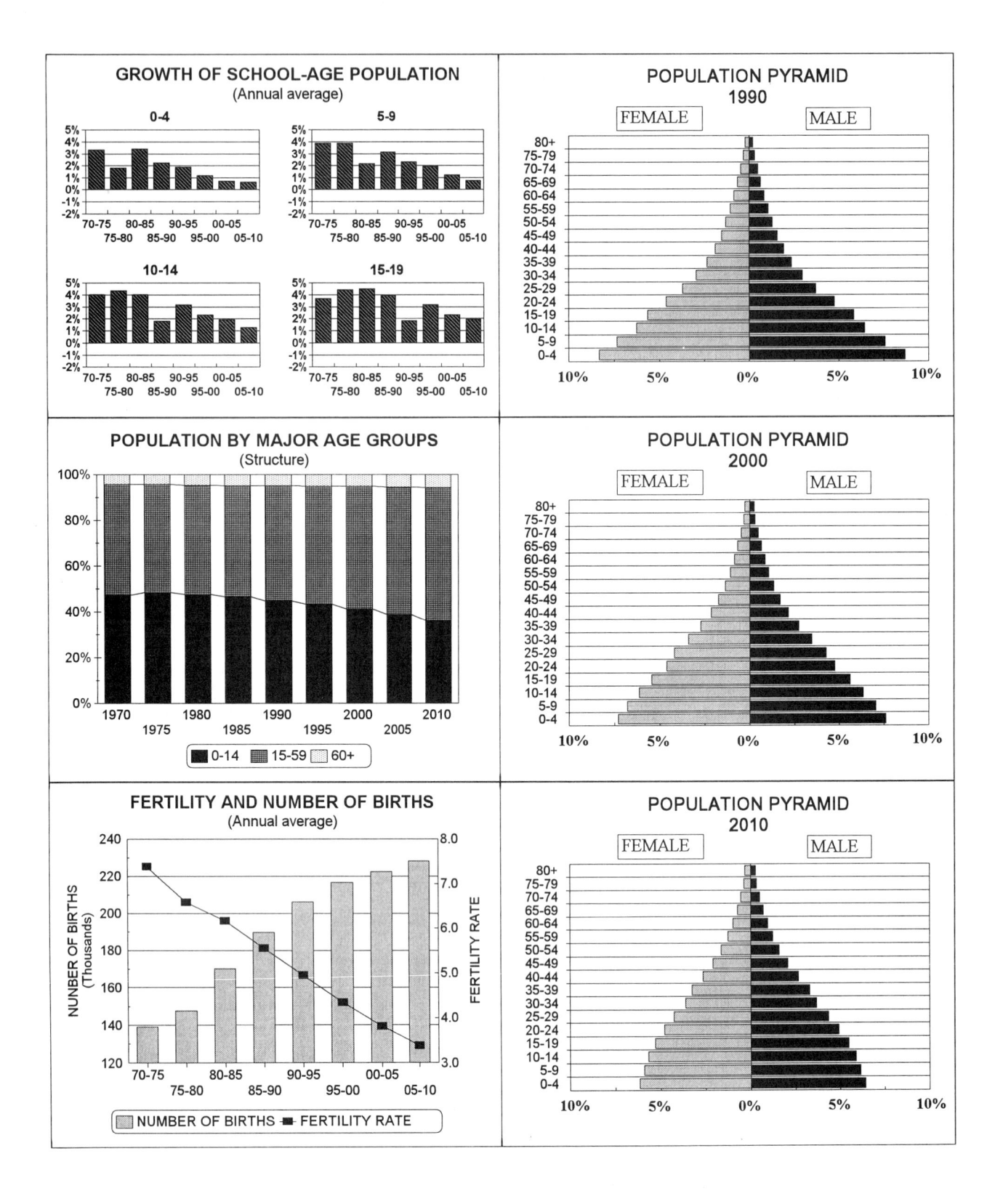

HONDURAS
Population and Vital Statistics

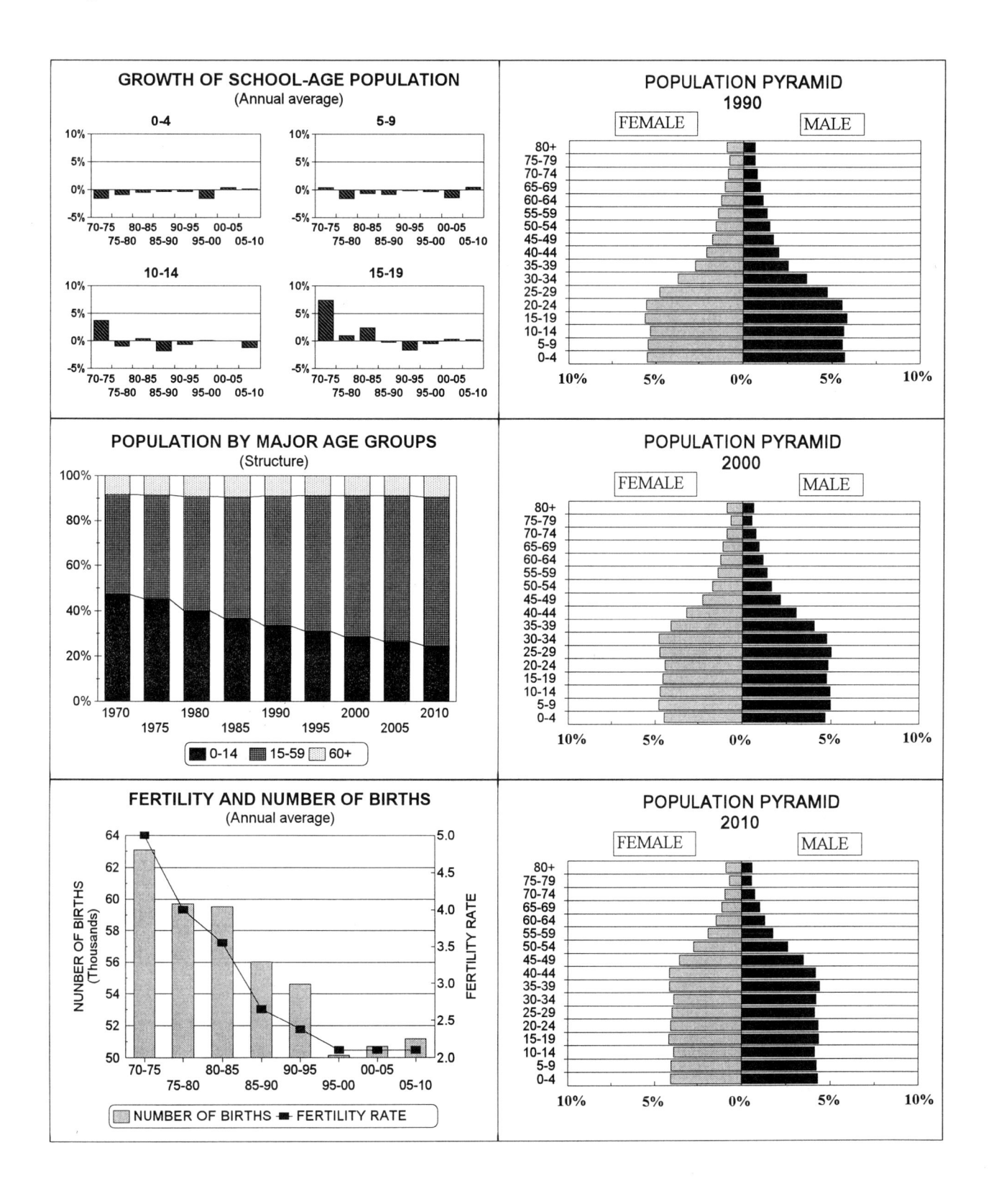

JAMAICA
Population and Vital Statistics

GROWTH OF SCHOOL-AGE POPULATION
(Annual average)

0-4

5-9

10-14

15-19

POPULATION PYRAMID 1990
FEMALE | MALE

POPULATION BY MAJOR AGE GROUPS
(Structure)

■ 0-14 ▨ 15-59 ▦ 60+

POPULATION PYRAMID 2000
FEMALE | MALE

FERTILITY AND NUMBER OF BIRTHS
(Annual average)

▨ NUMBER OF BIRTHS ■ FERTILITY RATE

POPULATION PYRAMID 2010
FEMALE | MALE

Statistics and Quantitative Analysis/IDB

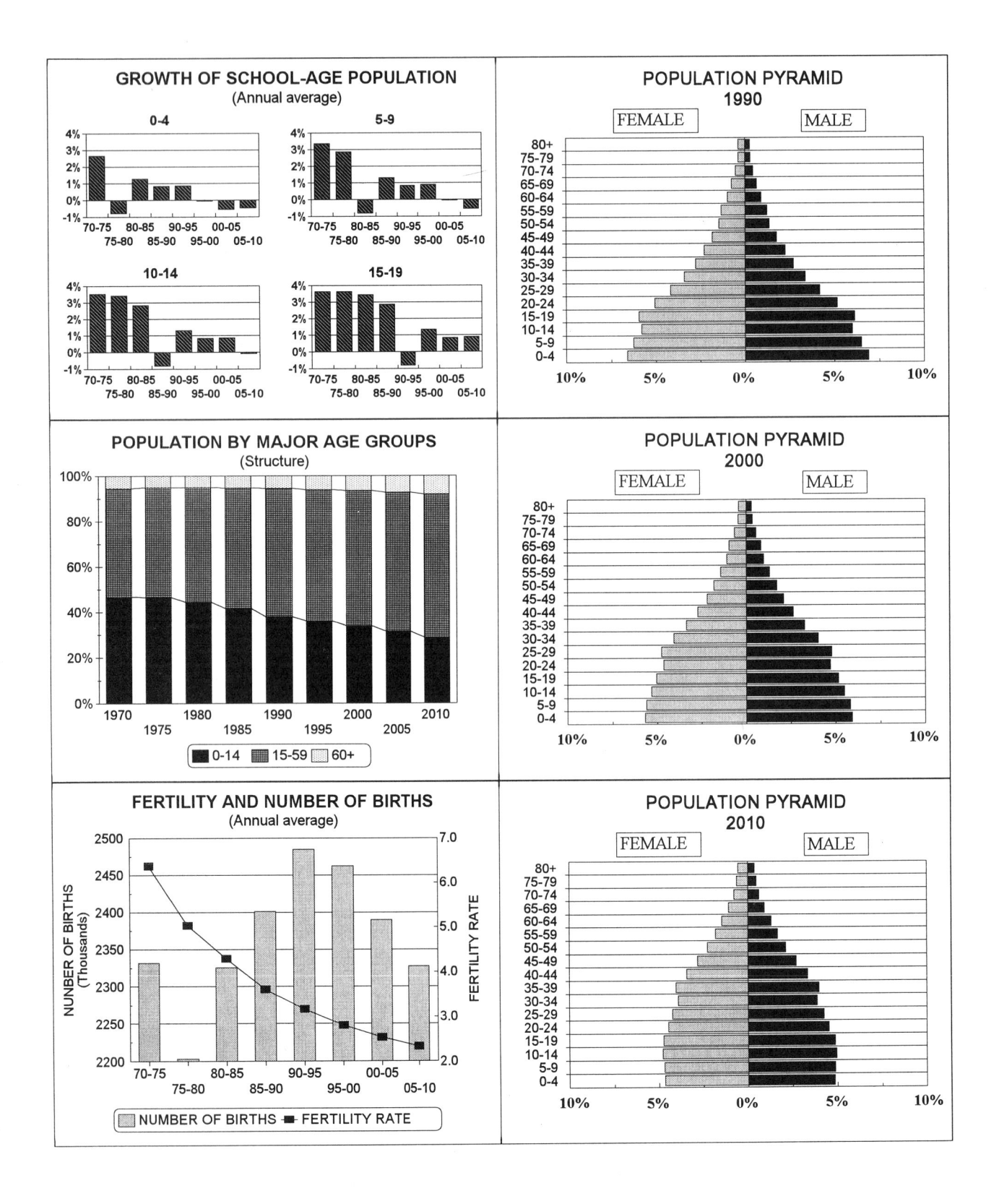

MEXICO
Population and Vital Statistics

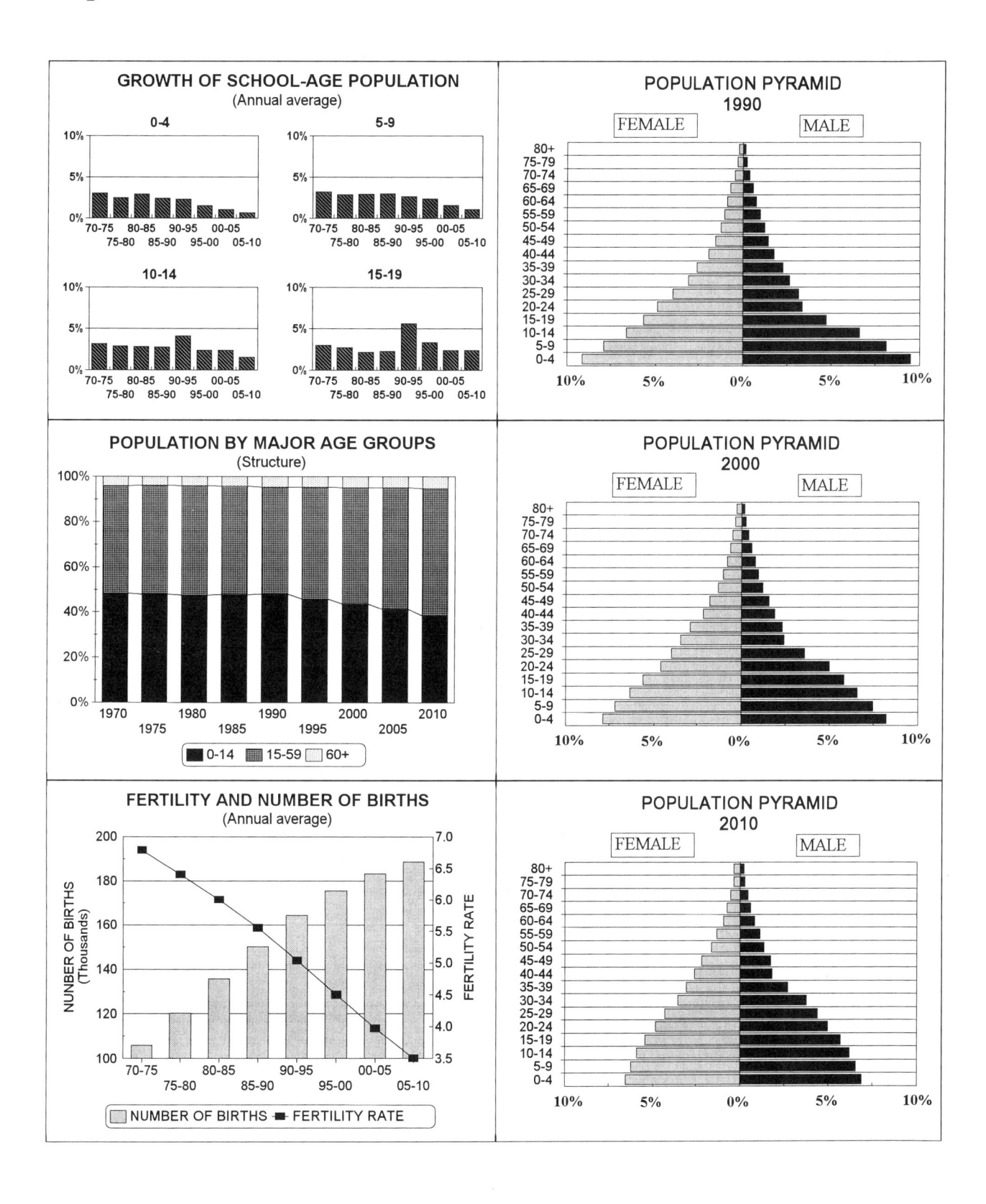

NICARAGUA
Population and Vital Statistics

GROWTH OF SCHOOL-AGE POPULATION
(Annual average)

POPULATION PYRAMID 1990

POPULATION BY MAJOR AGE GROUPS
(Structure)

POPULATION PYRAMID 2000

FERTILITY AND NUMBER OF BIRTHS
(Annual average)

POPULATION PYRAMID 2010

Statistics and Quantitative Analysis/IDB

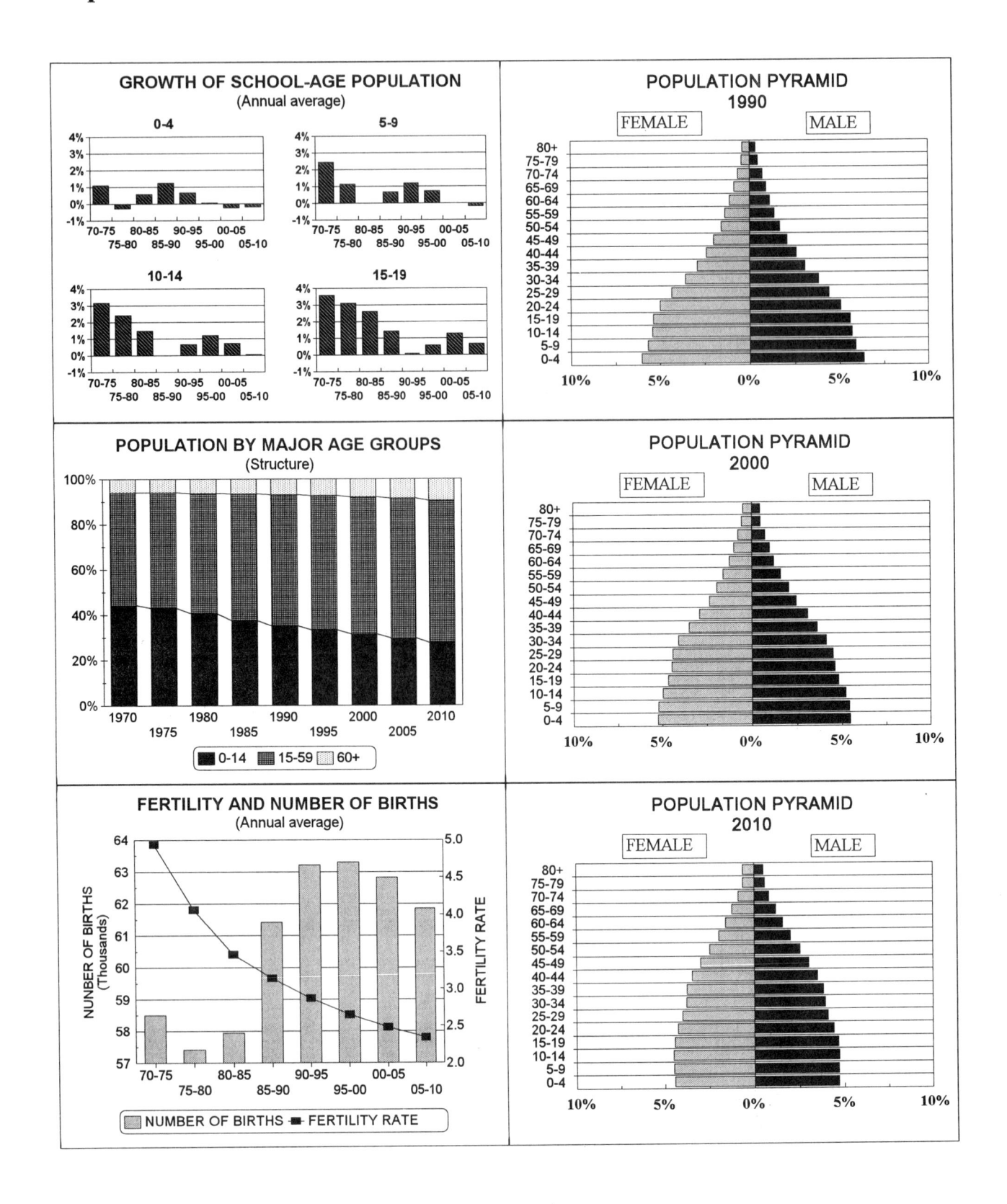

PANAMA
Population and Vital Statistics

GROWTH OF SCHOOL-AGE POPULATION
(Annual average)

- 0-4
- 5-9
- 10-14
- 15-19

POPULATION BY MAJOR AGE GROUPS
(Structure)

- 0-14
- 15-59
- 60+

FERTILITY AND NUMBER OF BIRTHS
(Annual average)

- NUMBER OF BIRTHS
- FERTILITY RATE

POPULATION PYRAMID 1990
FEMALE / MALE

POPULATION PYRAMID 2000
FEMALE / MALE

POPULATION PYRAMID 2010
FEMALE / MALE

Statistics and Quantitative Analysis/IDB

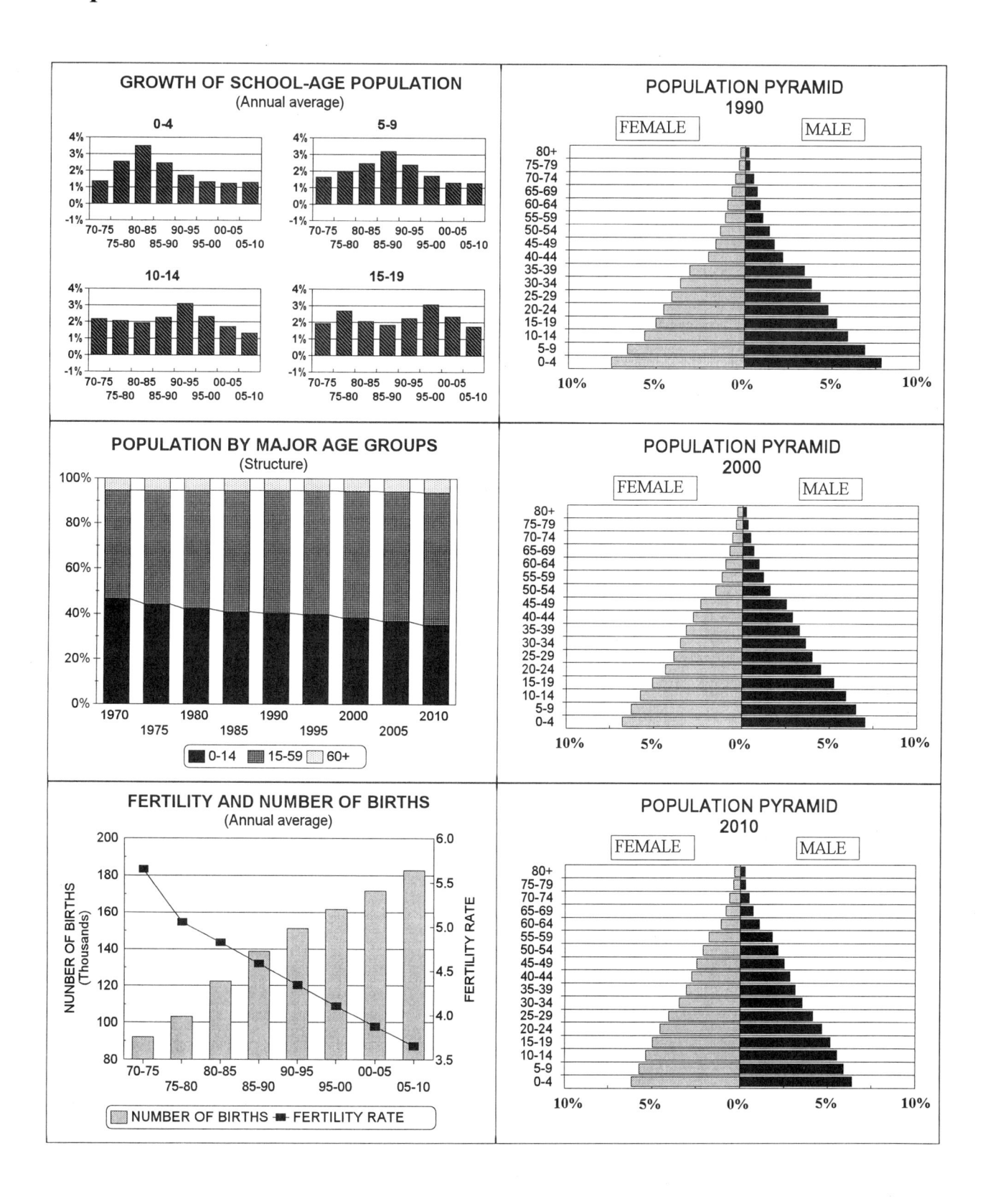

PARAGUAY
Population and Vital Statistics

GROWTH OF SCHOOL-AGE POPULATION
(Annual average)

POPULATION PYRAMID 1990

POPULATION BY MAJOR AGE GROUPS
(Structure)

POPULATION PYRAMID 2000

FERTILITY AND NUMBER OF BIRTHS
(Annual average)

POPULATION PYRAMID 2010

Statistics and Quantitative Analysis/IDB

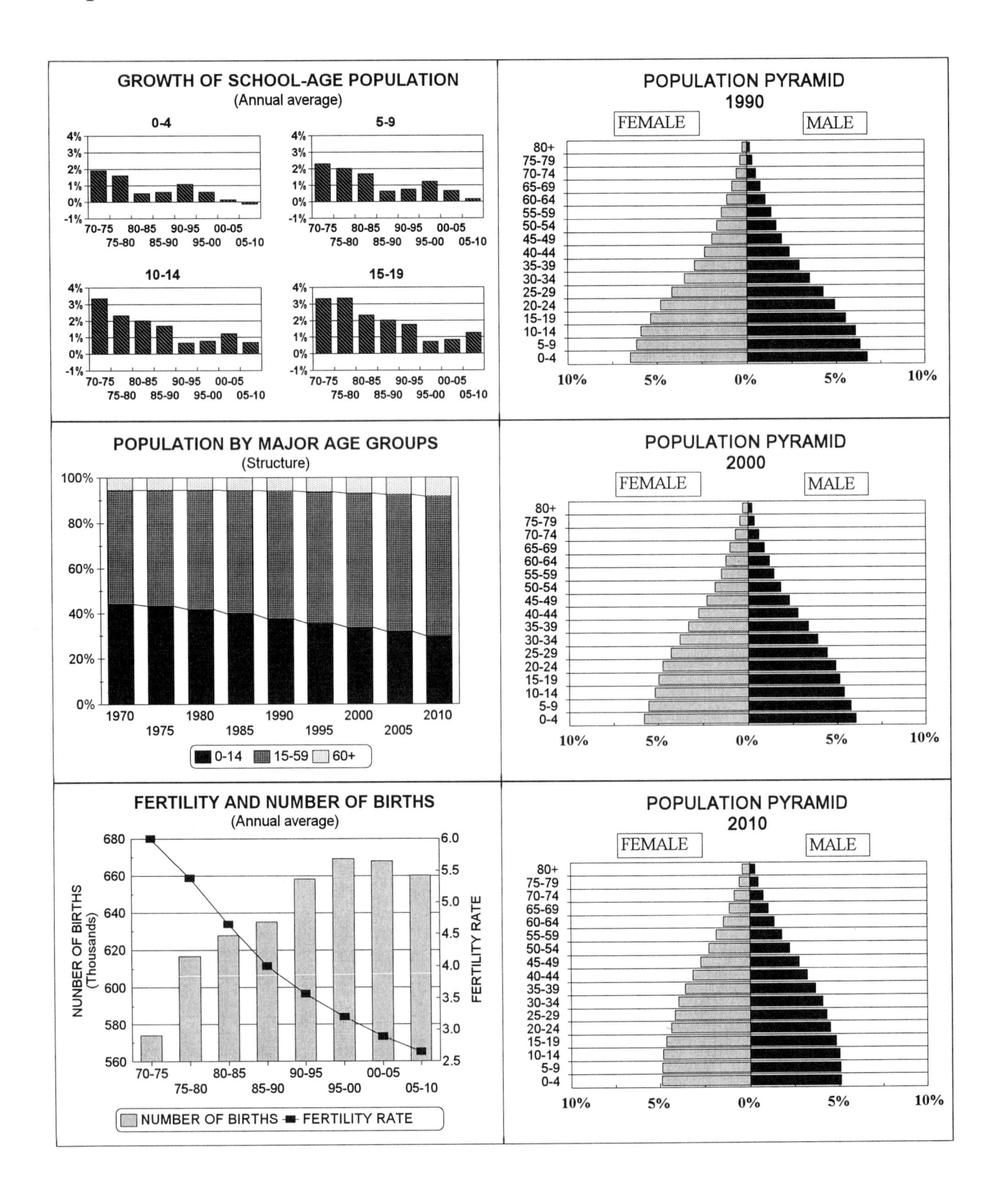

PERU
Population and Vital Statistics

GROWTH OF SCHOOL-AGE POPULATION
(Annual average)

- 0-4
- 5-9
- 10-14
- 15-19

POPULATION PYRAMID 1990
FEMALE | MALE

POPULATION BY MAJOR AGE GROUPS
(Structure)

0-14 | 15-59 | 60+

POPULATION PYRAMID 2000
FEMALE | MALE

FERTILITY AND NUMBER OF BIRTHS
(Annual average)

NUMBER OF BIRTHS | FERTILITY RATE

POPULATION PYRAMID 2010
FEMALE | MALE

Statistics and Quantitative Analysis/IDB

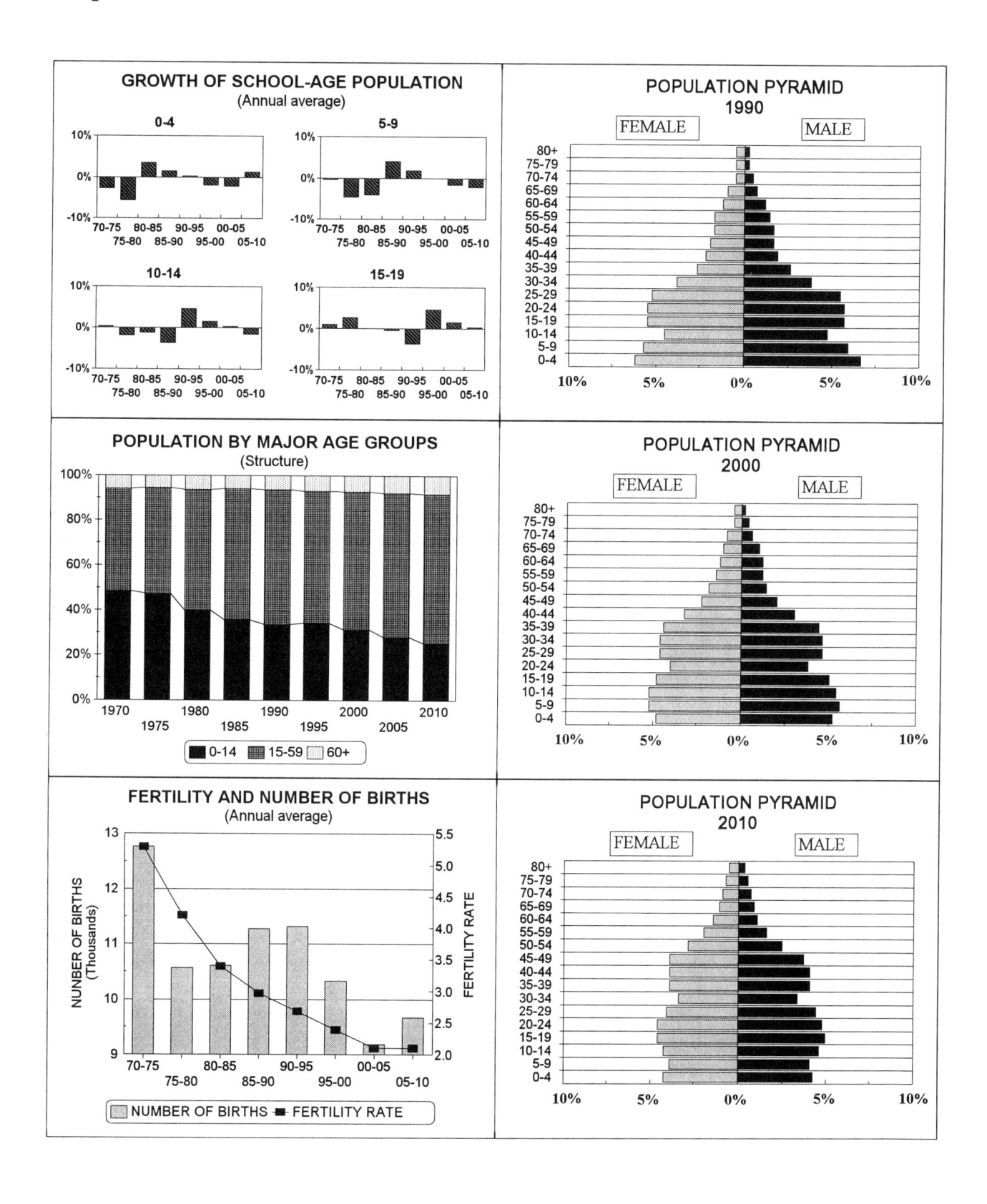

SURINAME
Population and Vital Statistics

GROWTH OF SCHOOL-AGE POPULATION
(Annual average)

0-4
5-9
10-14
15-19

POPULATION BY MAJOR AGE GROUPS
(Structure)

- 0-14
- 15-59
- 60+

FERTILITY AND NUMBER OF BIRTHS
(Annual average)

NUMBER OF BIRTHS — FERTILITY RATE

POPULATION PYRAMID 1990
FEMALE | MALE

POPULATION PYRAMID 2000
FEMALE | MALE

POPULATION PYRAMID 2010
FEMALE | MALE

Statistics and Quantitative Analysis/IDB

TRINIDAD AND TOBAGO
Population and Vital Statistics

GROWTH OF SCHOOL-AGE POPULATION
(Annual average)

- 0-4
- 5-9
- 10-14
- 15-19

POPULATION BY MAJOR AGE GROUPS
(Structure)

- 0-14
- 15-59
- 60+

FERTILITY AND NUMBER OF BIRTHS
(Annual average)

- NUMBER OF BIRTHS
- FERTILITY RATE

POPULATION PYRAMID 1990
FEMALE | MALE

POPULATION PYRAMID 2000
FEMALE | MALE

POPULATION PYRAMID 2010
FEMALE | MALE

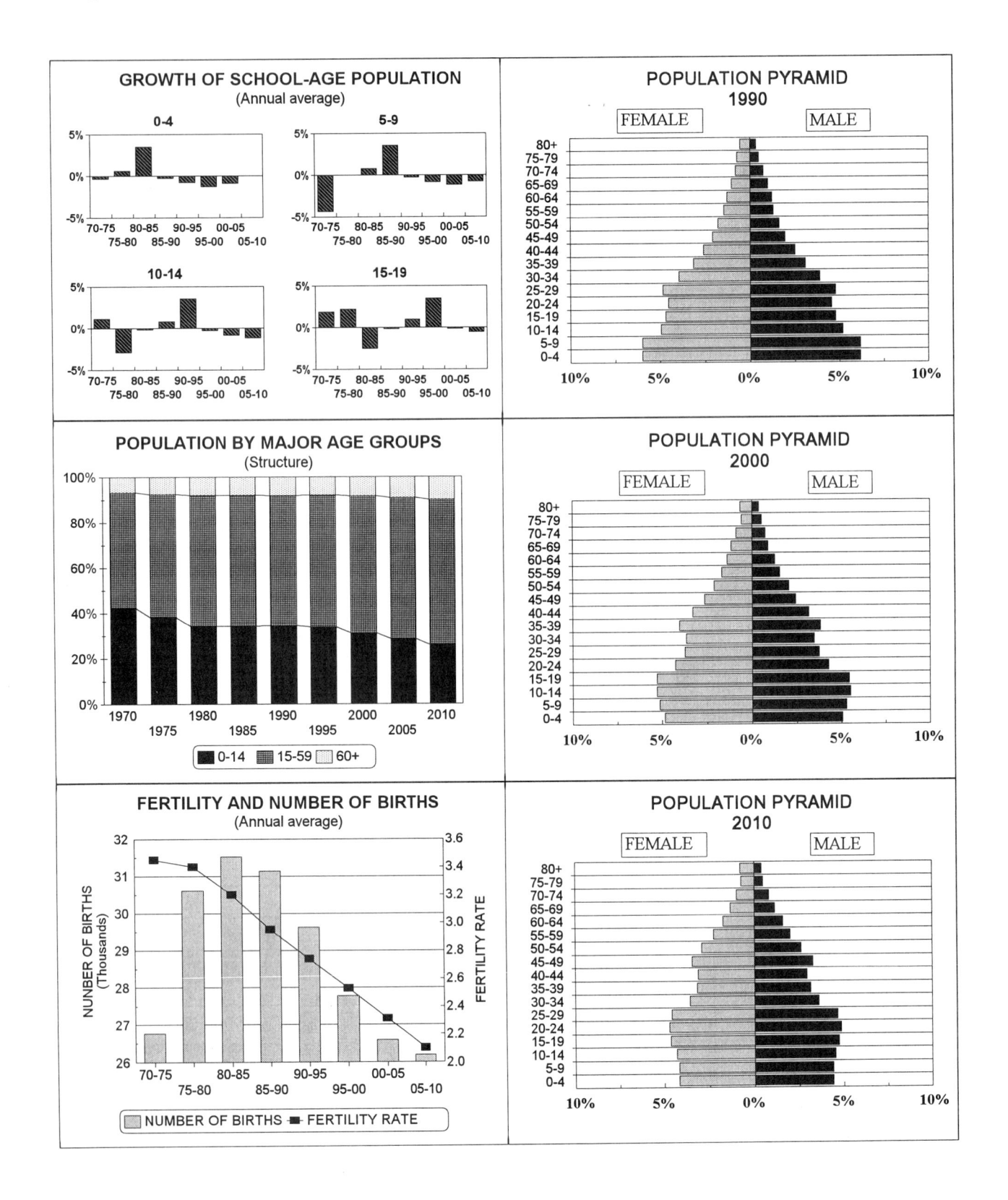

Statistics and Quantitative Analysis/IDB

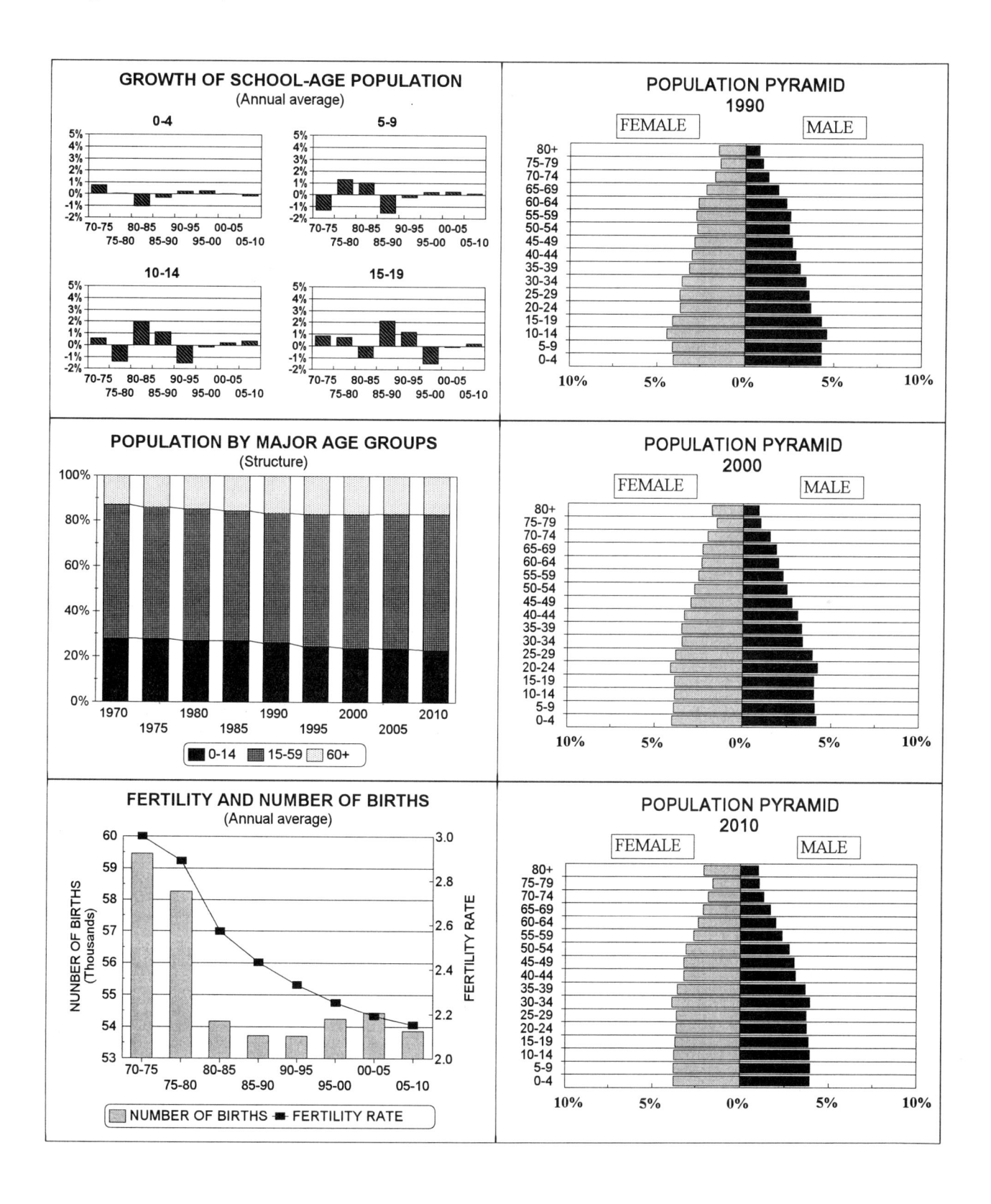

URUGUAY
Population and Vital Statistics

GROWTH OF SCHOOL-AGE POPULATION
(Annual average)

- 0-4
- 5-9
- 10-14
- 15-19

POPULATION BY MAJOR AGE GROUPS
(Structure)

- 0-14
- 15-59
- 60+

FERTILITY AND NUMBER OF BIRTHS
(Annual average)

- NUMBER OF BIRTHS
- FERTILITY RATE

POPULATION PYRAMID 1990

POPULATION PYRAMID 2000

POPULATION PYRAMID 2010

Statistics and Quantitative Analysis/IDB

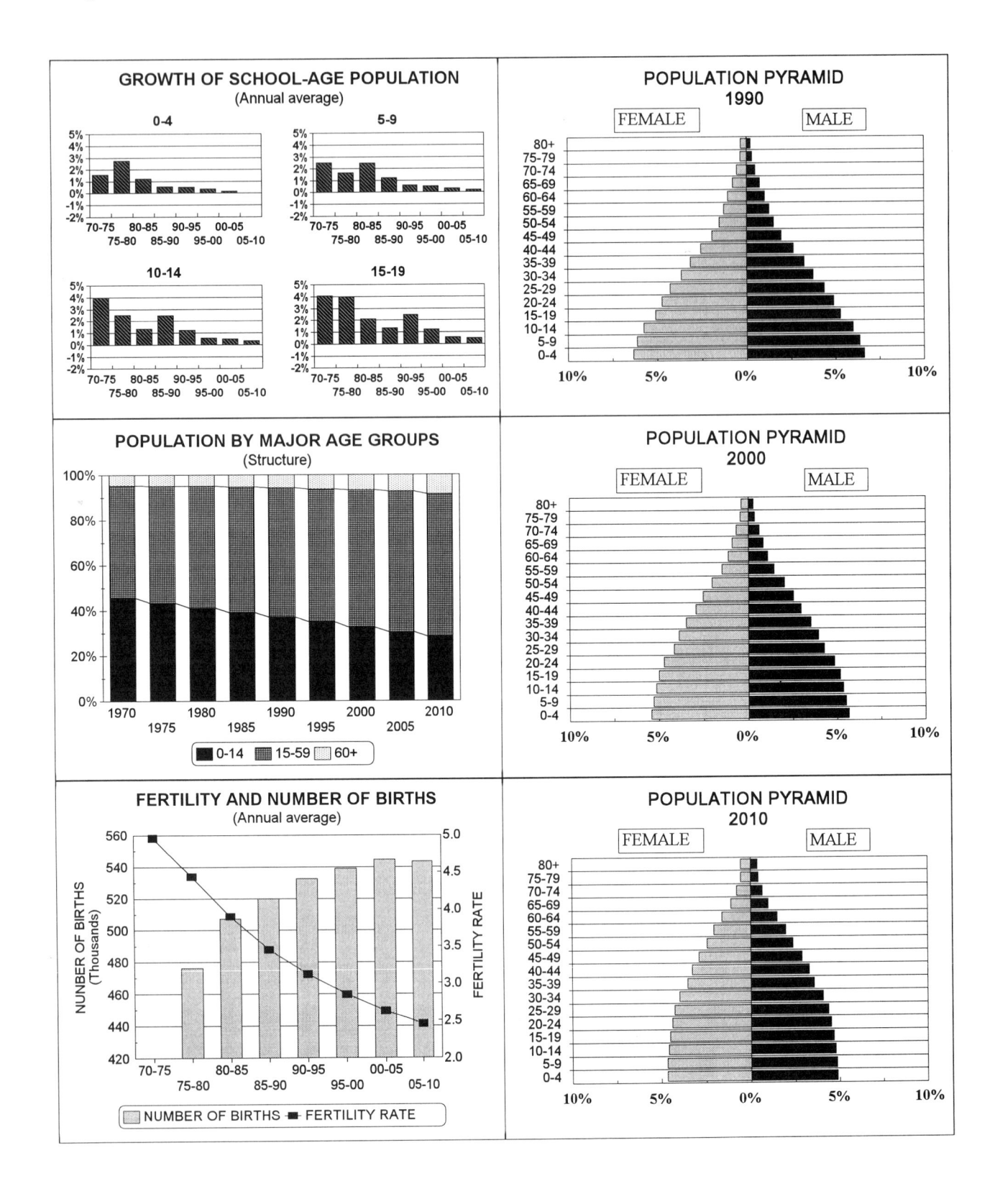

VENEZUELA
Population and Vital Statistics

GROWTH OF SCHOOL-AGE POPULATION
(Annual average)

0-4

5-9

10-14

15-19

POPULATION BY MAJOR AGE GROUPS
(Structure)

0-14 ■ 15-59 ■ 60+ □

FERTILITY AND NUMBER OF BIRTHS
(Annual average)

NUMBER OF BIRTHS — FERTILITY RATE

POPULATION PYRAMID 1990
FEMALE — MALE

POPULATION PYRAMID 2000
FEMALE — MALE

POPULATION PYRAMID 2010
FEMALE — MALE

Statistics and Quantitative Analysis/IDB

EDUCATION

EDUCATION

Data on education are from the United Nations Education, Scientific and Cultural Organization (UNESCO) and national sources. Estimates on average years of schooling are based on calculations by Robert J. Barro and Jong-Wha Lee ("International Comparisons of Educational Attainment", Harvard University and International Monetary Fund, February 1993). The Latin American average is calculated as a simple arithmetic average of the countries of the region. Descriptions of the graphs follow.

1. NET ENROLLMENT RATES BY LEVEL IN 1990

The Net Enrollment Rate is calculated for the primary and secondary level of education by dividing the number of enrollments in the official age range of the schooling level by the whole population in the same age range. Observe that the Gross Enrollment Rate would consider the number of enrolled pupils irrespective of age. For the Tertiary level, the gross enrollment rate is shown in the graph.

2. PUBLIC CURRENT EXPENDITURE BY LEVEL

The graph shows for 1980 and 1990 the structure of the Public Current Expenditure on education by level. However, in some countries, a large proportion of the expenditure on education is not disaggregated by educational levels, so that the structure may be slightly distorted in these cases

3. SURVIVAL RATES IN PRIMARY SCHOOL (BASED ON 1989 COHORT)

This indicator gives the percentage among pupils of the same cohort starting primary school of those who reach grade 2, grade 4 and the final grade. It provides, therefore, an estimate of the dropout level throughout primary school. The estimate is based on the Reconstructed Cohort Method when data on repeaters are available. When data on repeaters are missing, the Apparent Cohort Method is used.

4. EFFICIENCY IN PRIMARY SCHOOL IN 1990

The graph shows the relationship in 1990 between the survival rate in the last grade of primary school and the number of pupils per teacher. Each dot represents one of the 22 Latin American countries for which data are available. A regression line was calculated without outliers, separating countries with higher efficiency than the average (above the line) from countries with lower efficiency (below the line).

5. ILLITERACY RATES IN 1990

The Illiteracy rate represents the proportion of illiterates among the adult population 15 years and over. The rate is shown for total, male and female populations.

6. AVERAGE YEARS OF SCHOOLING (FOR POPULATION AGED 25 AND OVER)

The average years of schooling is an indicator of the average level of education of the stock of human capital of the country. Historical data are from a study based on the perpetual inventory method applied to the population age 25 and over. Estimates for 1995 and projections for 2000 are from IDB

LATIN AMERICA
Education

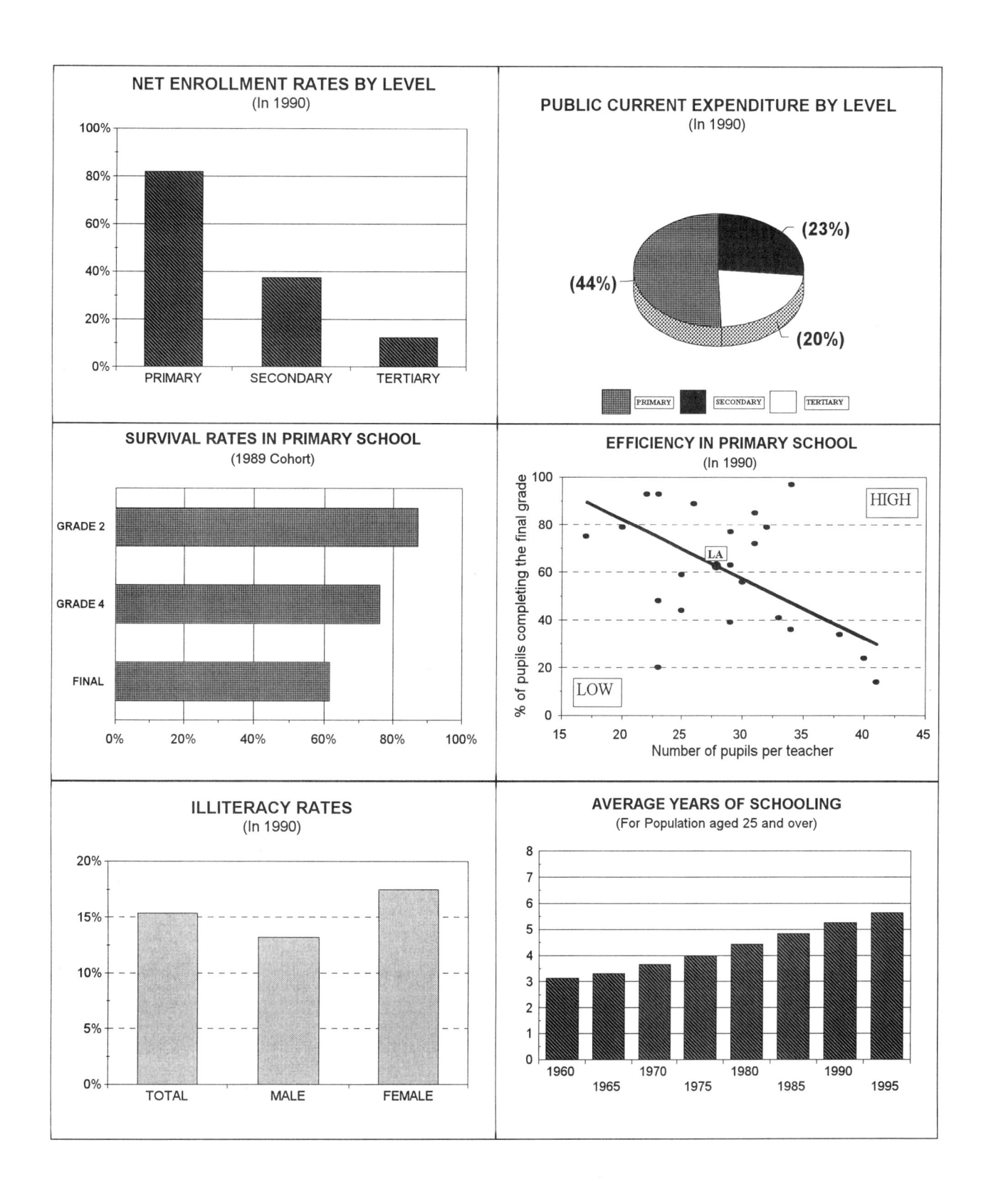

NET ENROLLMENT RATES BY LEVEL
(In 1990)

PUBLIC CURRENT EXPENDITURE BY LEVEL
(In 1990)

- PRIMARY: (44%)
- SECONDARY: (23%)
- TERTIARY: (20%)

SURVIVAL RATES IN PRIMARY SCHOOL
(1989 Cohort)

EFFICIENCY IN PRIMARY SCHOOL
(In 1990)

ILLITERACY RATES
(In 1990)

AVERAGE YEARS OF SCHOOLING
(For Population aged 25 and over)

Statistics and Quantitative Analysis/IDB

ARGENTINA
Education

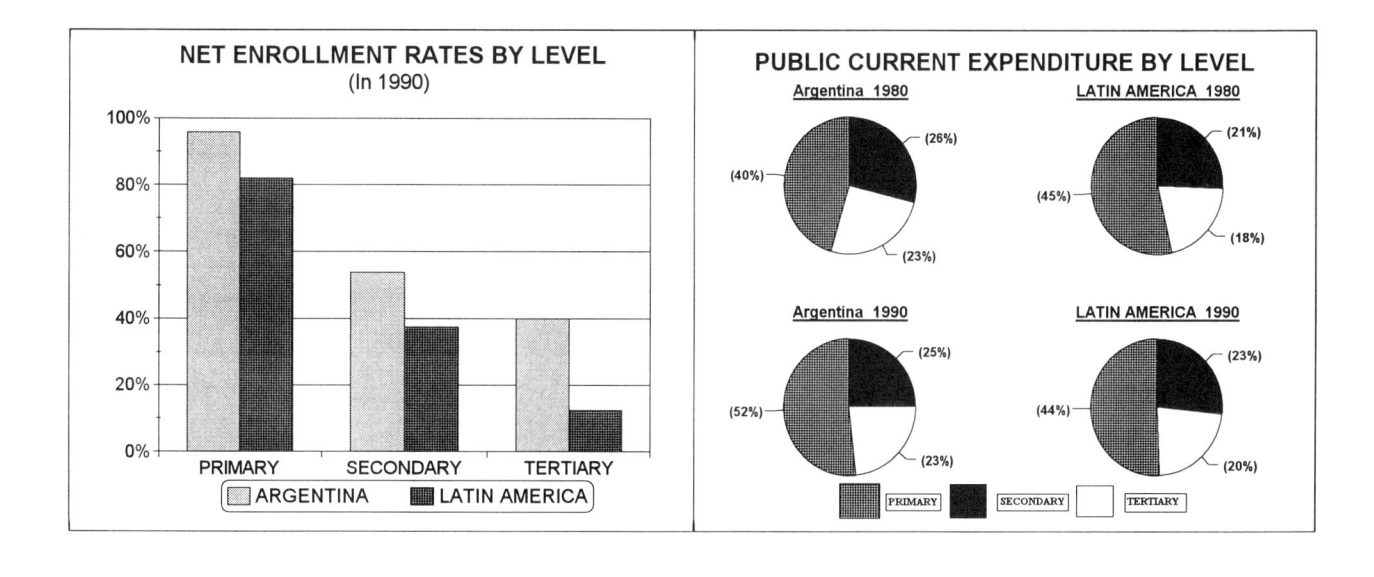

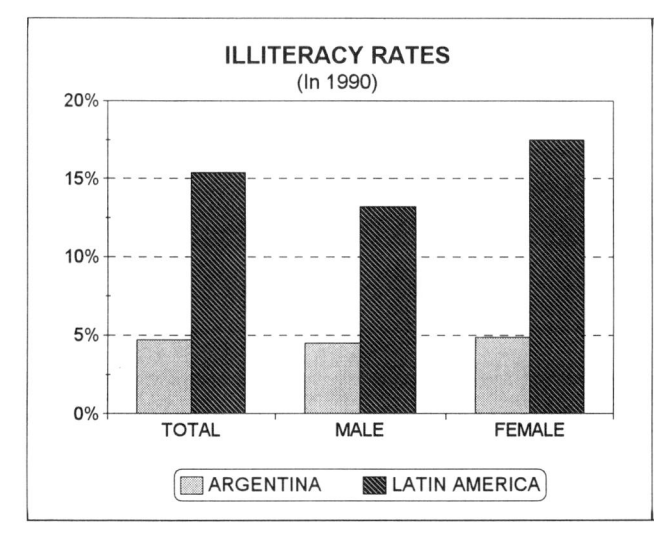

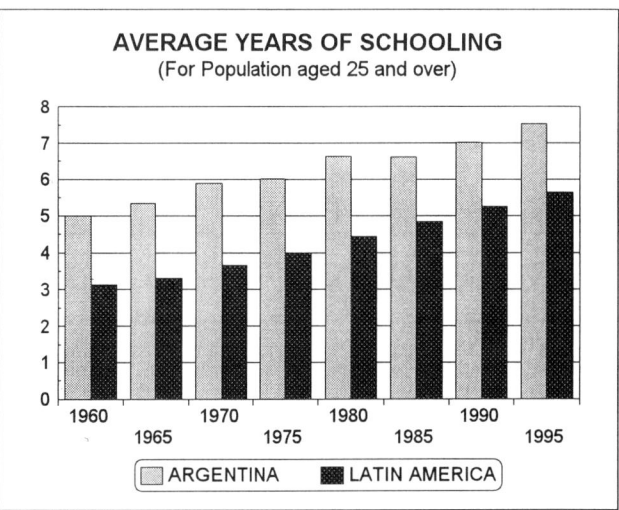

NET ENROLLMENT RATES BY LEVEL
(In 1990)

PUBLIC CURRENT EXPENDITURE BY LEVEL

Argentina 1980: Primary (40%), Secondary (26%), Tertiary (23%)
Latin America 1980: Primary (45%), Secondary (21%), Tertiary (18%)
Argentina 1990: Primary (52%), Secondary (25%), Tertiary (23%)
Latin America 1990: Primary (44%), Secondary (23%), Tertiary (20%)

ILLITERACY RATES
(In 1990)

AVERAGE YEARS OF SCHOOLING
(For Population aged 25 and over)

Statistics and Quantitative Analysis/IDB

BAHAMAS
Education

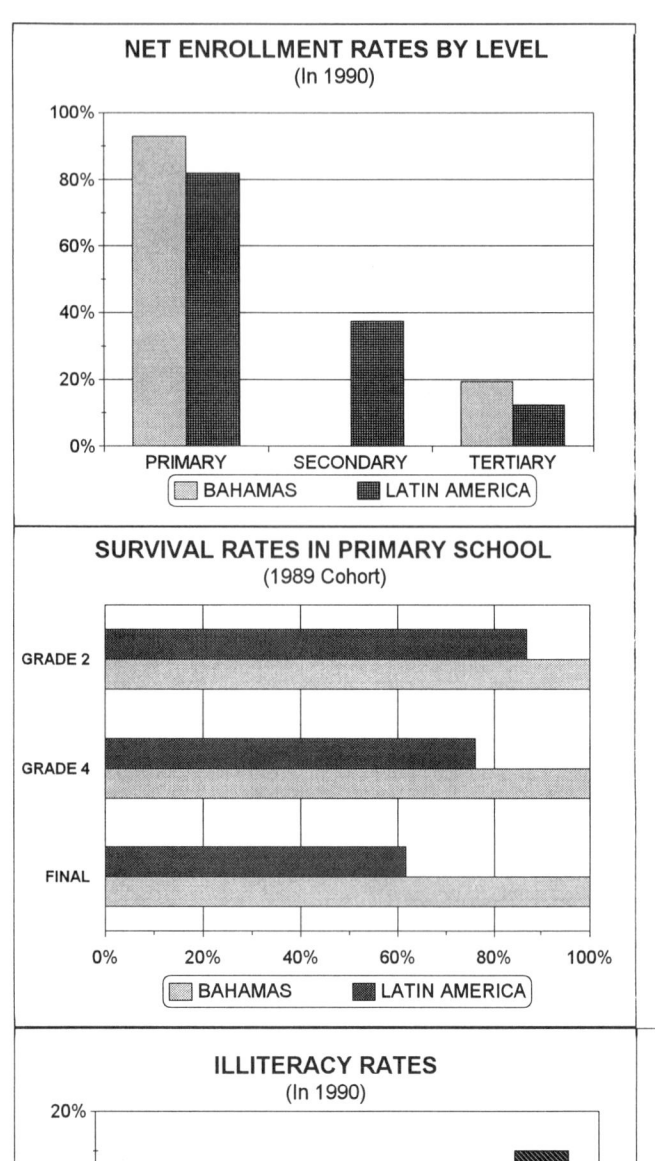

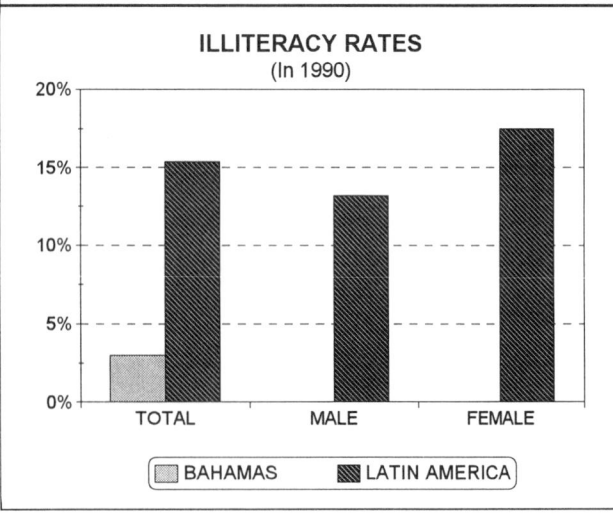

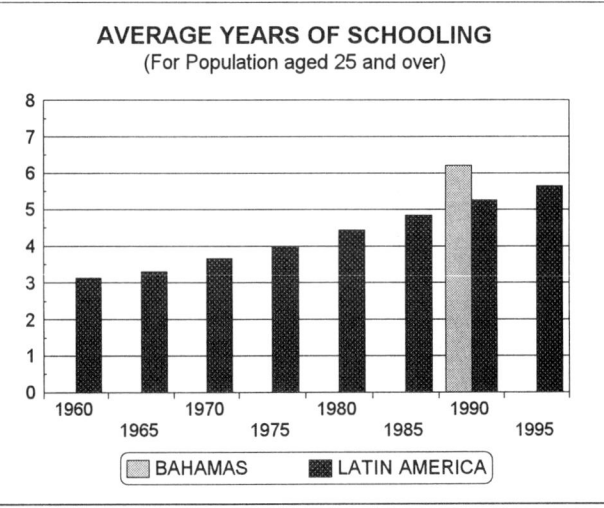

NET ENROLLMENT RATES BY LEVEL
(In 1990)

Level	Bahamas	Latin America
Primary	~93%	~82%
Secondary	—	~37%
Tertiary	~19%	~12%

SURVIVAL RATES IN PRIMARY SCHOOL
(1989 Cohort)

Grade	Bahamas	Latin America
Grade 2	~100%	~87%
Grade 4	~100%	~76%
Final	~100%	~62%

ILLITERACY RATES
(In 1990)

	Bahamas	Latin America
Total	~3%	~15%
Male	—	~13%
Female	—	~17.5%

AVERAGE YEARS OF SCHOOLING
(For Population aged 25 and over)

Year	Bahamas	Latin America
1960		3.1
1965		3.3
1970		3.7
1975		4.0
1980		4.4
1985		4.8
1990	6.2	5.2
1995		5.6

Statistics and Quantitative Analysis/IDB

BARBADOS
Education

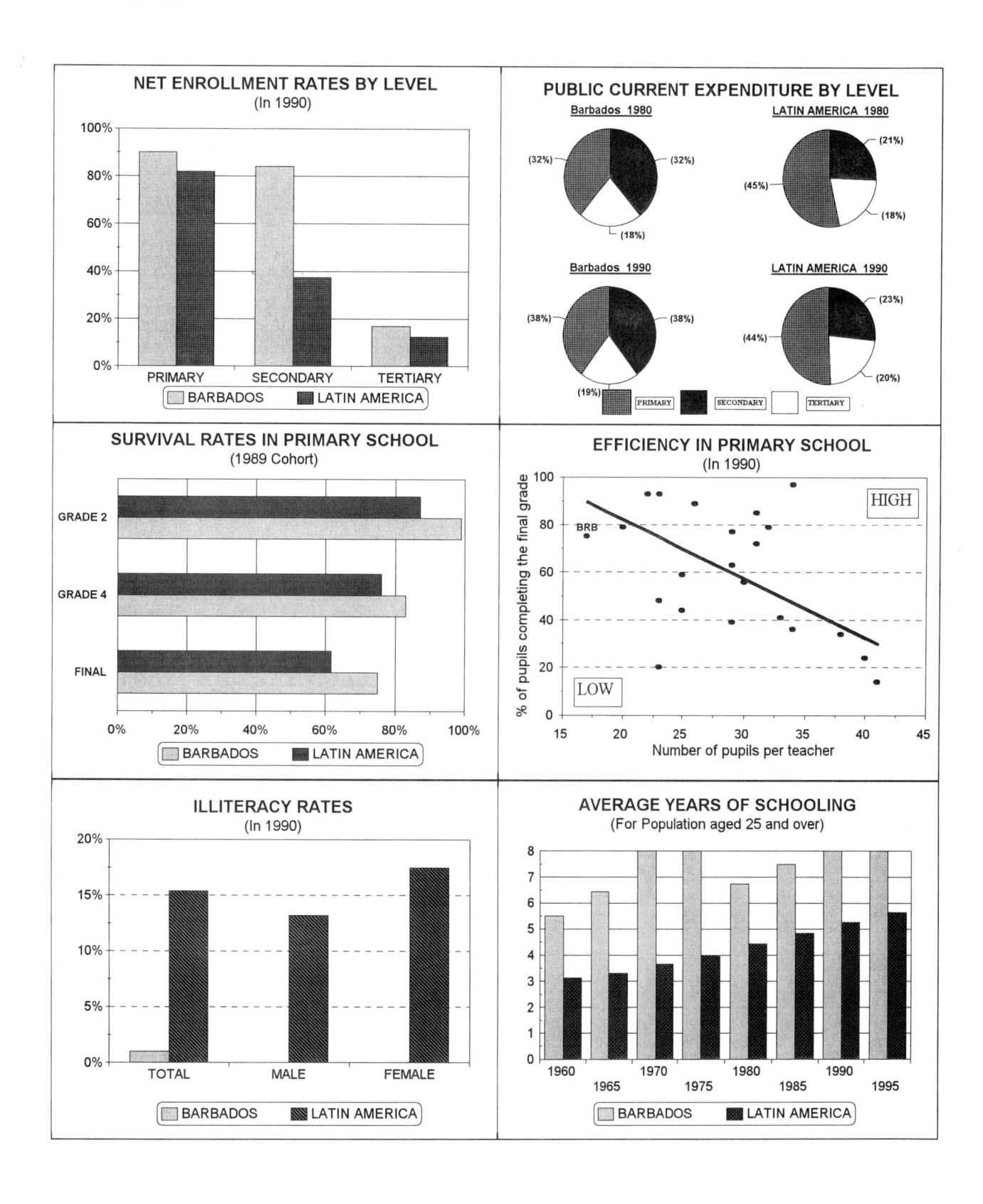

NET ENROLLMENT RATES BY LEVEL
(In 1990)

PUBLIC CURRENT EXPENDITURE BY LEVEL

Barbados 1980: Primary (32%), Secondary (32%), Tertiary (18%)
Latin America 1980: Primary (45%), Secondary (21%), Tertiary (18%)
Barbados 1990: Primary (38%), Secondary (38%), Tertiary (19%)
Latin America 1990: Primary (44%), Secondary (23%), Tertiary (20%)

SURVIVAL RATES IN PRIMARY SCHOOL
(1989 Cohort)

EFFICIENCY IN PRIMARY SCHOOL
(In 1990)

ILLITERACY RATES
(In 1990)

AVERAGE YEARS OF SCHOOLING
(For Population aged 25 and over)

Statistics and Quantitative Analysis/IDB

BELIZE
Education

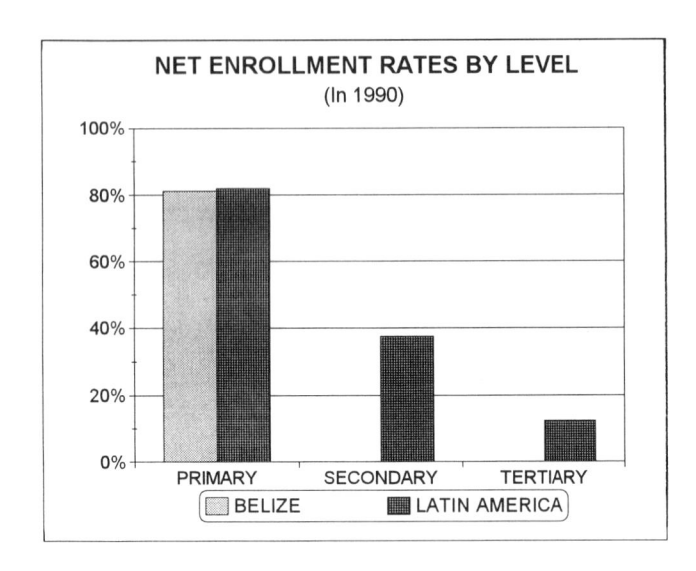

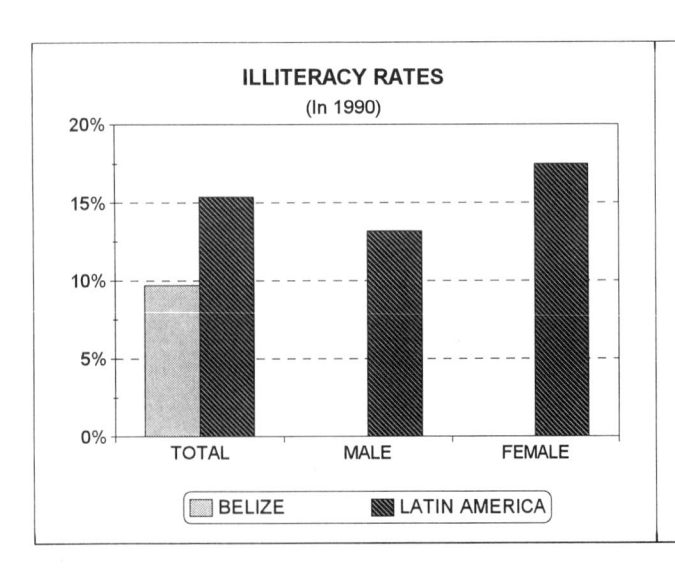

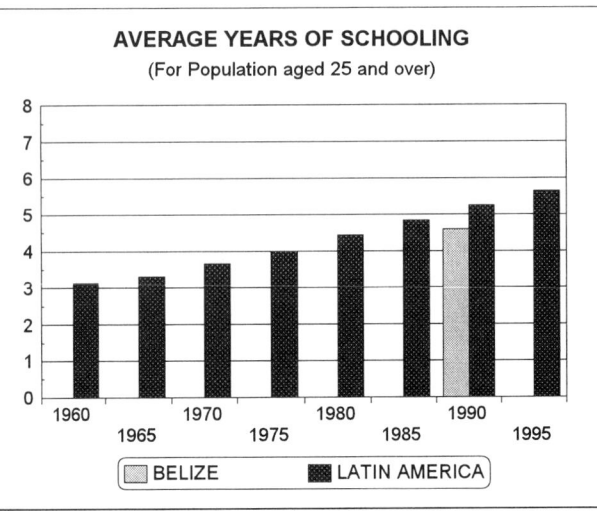

NET ENROLLMENT RATES BY LEVEL
(In 1990)

Level	Belize	Latin America
Primary	~81%	~82%
Secondary	0%	~38%
Tertiary	0%	~13%

ILLITERACY RATES
(In 1990)

	Belize	Latin America
Total	~8%	~15%
Male	0%	~13%
Female	0%	~17%

AVERAGE YEARS OF SCHOOLING
(For Population aged 25 and over)

Year	Belize	Latin America
1960		3.1
1965		3.3
1970		3.7
1975		4.0
1980		4.5
1985		4.9
1990	4.6	5.3
1995		5.7

BOLIVIA
Education

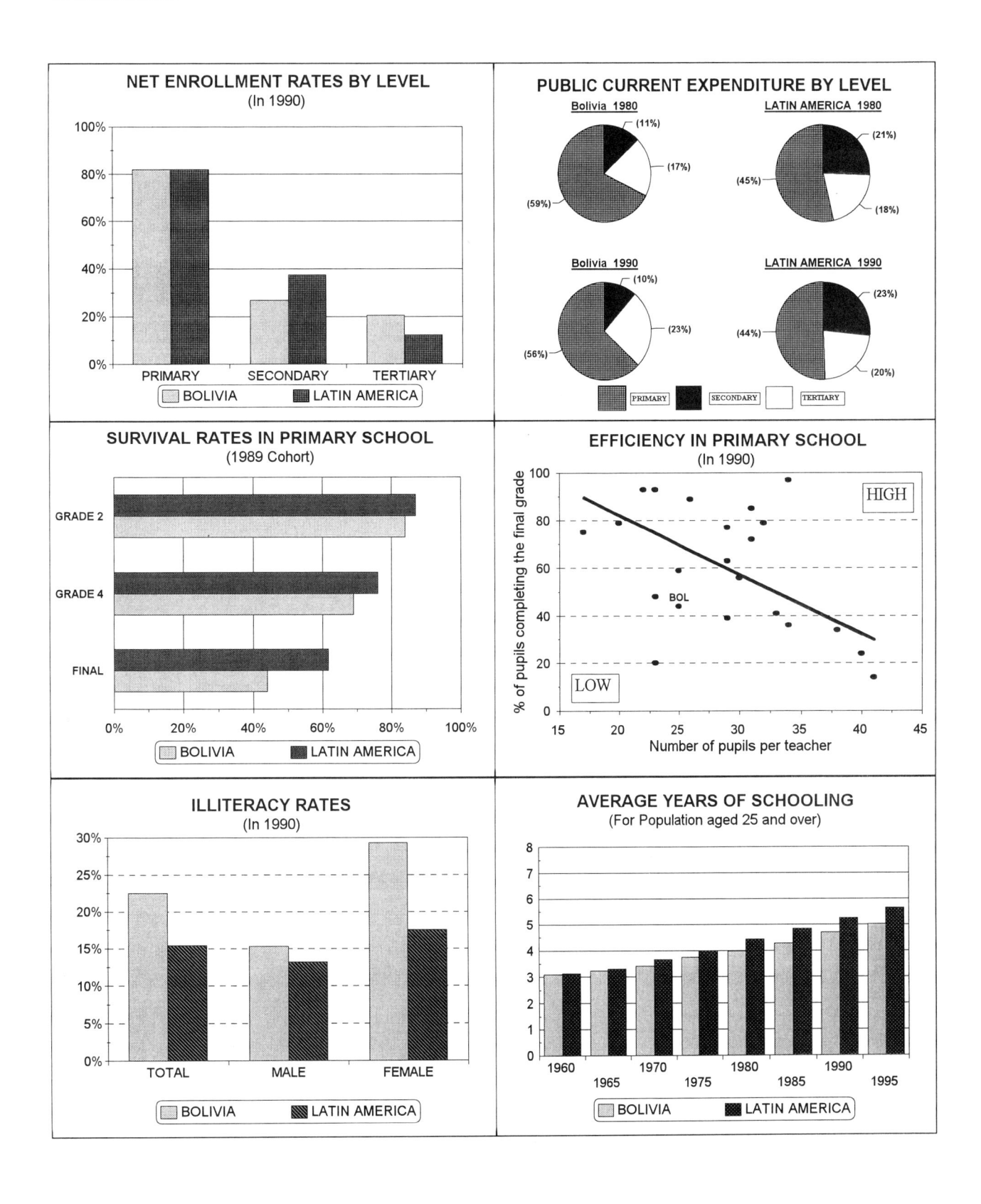

NET ENROLLMENT RATES BY LEVEL
(In 1990)

PUBLIC CURRENT EXPENDITURE BY LEVEL

Bolivia 1980: (11%) Secondary, (17%) Tertiary, (59%) Primary
Latin America 1980: (21%) Secondary, (18%) Tertiary, (45%) Primary
Bolivia 1990: (10%) Secondary, (23%) Tertiary, (56%) Primary
Latin America 1990: (23%) Secondary, (20%) Tertiary, (44%) Primary

SURVIVAL RATES IN PRIMARY SCHOOL
(1989 Cohort)

EFFICIENCY IN PRIMARY SCHOOL
(In 1990)

% of pupils completing the final grade vs. Number of pupils per teacher

ILLITERACY RATES
(In 1990)

AVERAGE YEARS OF SCHOOLING
(For Population aged 25 and over)

Statistics and Quantitative Analysis/IDB

BRAZIL
Education

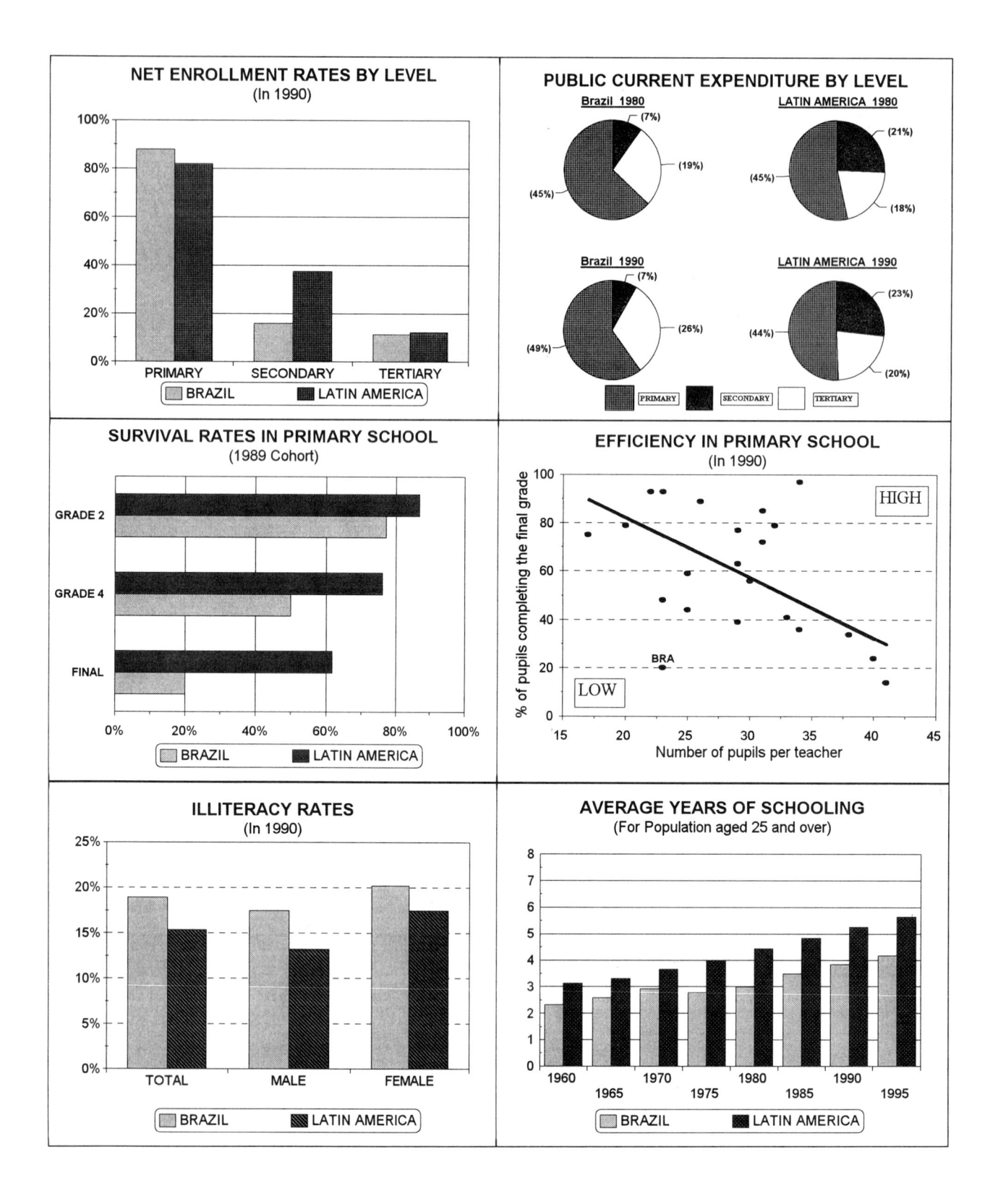

NET ENROLLMENT RATES BY LEVEL
(In 1990)

Level	Brazil	Latin America
Primary	~88%	~82%
Secondary	~15%	~37%
Tertiary	~11%	~12%

PUBLIC CURRENT EXPENDITURE BY LEVEL

Brazil 1980: Primary (45%), Secondary (7%), Tertiary (19%) [remainder 29%]
Latin America 1980: Primary (45%), Secondary (21%), Tertiary (18%)
Brazil 1990: Primary (49%), Secondary (7%), Tertiary (26%)
Latin America 1990: Primary (44%), Secondary (23%), Tertiary (20%)

SURVIVAL RATES IN PRIMARY SCHOOL
(1989 Cohort)

Grade	Brazil	Latin America
Grade 2	~77%	~88%
Grade 4	~50%	~77%
Final	~20%	~62%

EFFICIENCY IN PRIMARY SCHOOL
(In 1990)

Scatter plot: % of pupils completing the final grade vs. Number of pupils per teacher. BRA shown at approximately (23, 20) — LOW efficiency.

ILLITERACY RATES
(In 1990)

	Brazil	Latin America
Total	~19%	~15%
Male	~17%	~13%
Female	~20%	~17%

AVERAGE YEARS OF SCHOOLING
(For Population aged 25 and over)

Year	Brazil	Latin America
1960	2.3	3.1
1965	2.6	3.3
1970	2.9	3.7
1975	2.8	4.0
1980	3.0	4.4
1985	3.5	4.8
1990	3.9	5.2
1995	4.2	5.6

Statistics and Quantitative Analysis/IDB

CHILE
Education

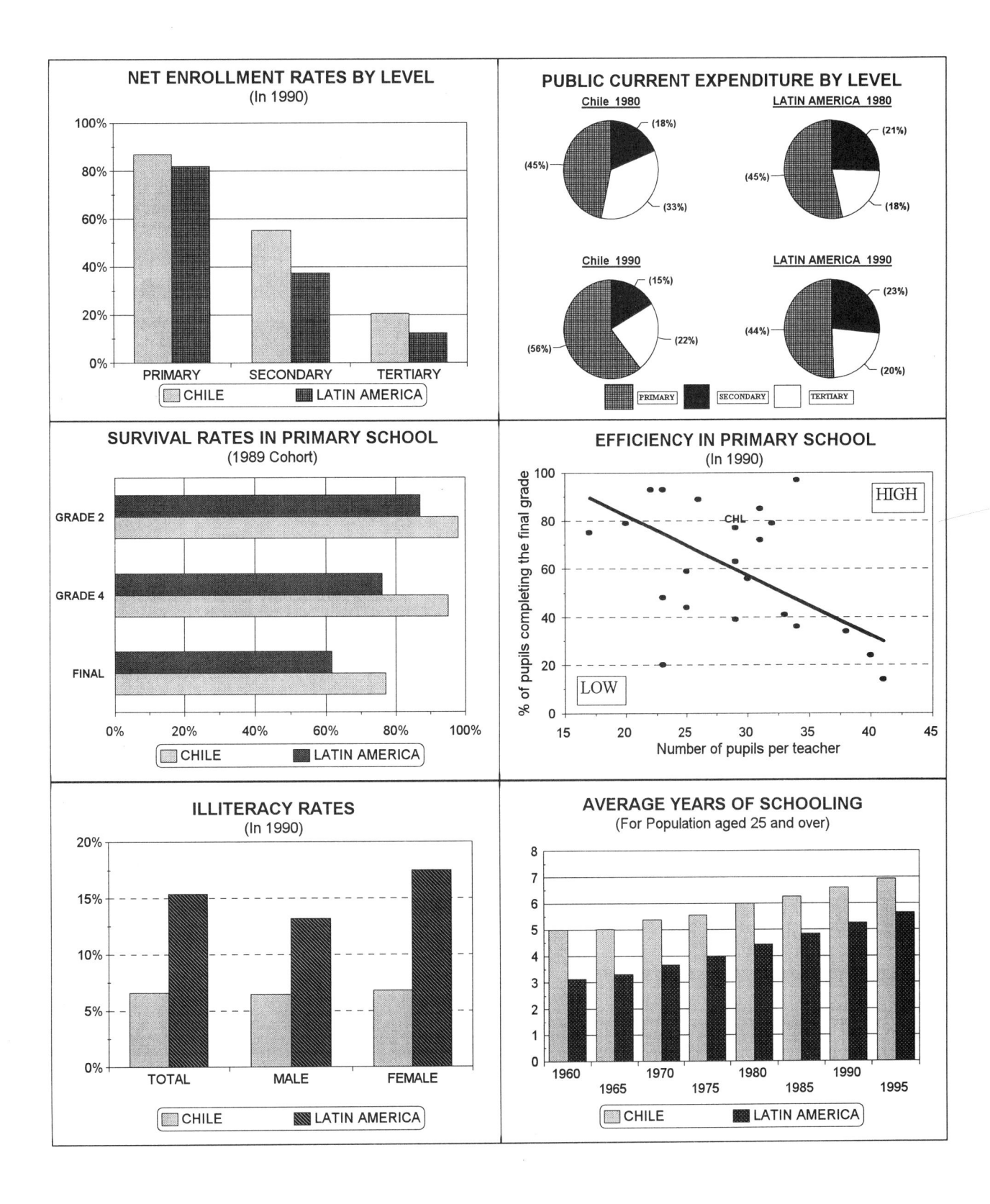

NET ENROLLMENT RATES BY LEVEL
(In 1990)

PUBLIC CURRENT EXPENDITURE BY LEVEL

Chile 1980: Primary (45%), Secondary (18%), Tertiary (33%)
Latin America 1980: Primary (45%), Secondary (21%), Tertiary (18%)*
Chile 1990: Primary (56%), Secondary (15%), Tertiary (22%)
Latin America 1990: Primary (44%), Secondary (23%), Tertiary (20%)

SURVIVAL RATES IN PRIMARY SCHOOL
(1989 Cohort)

EFFICIENCY IN PRIMARY SCHOOL
(In 1990)

ILLITERACY RATES
(In 1990)

AVERAGE YEARS OF SCHOOLING
(For Population aged 25 and over)

Statistics and Quantitative Analysis/IDB

COLOMBIA
Education

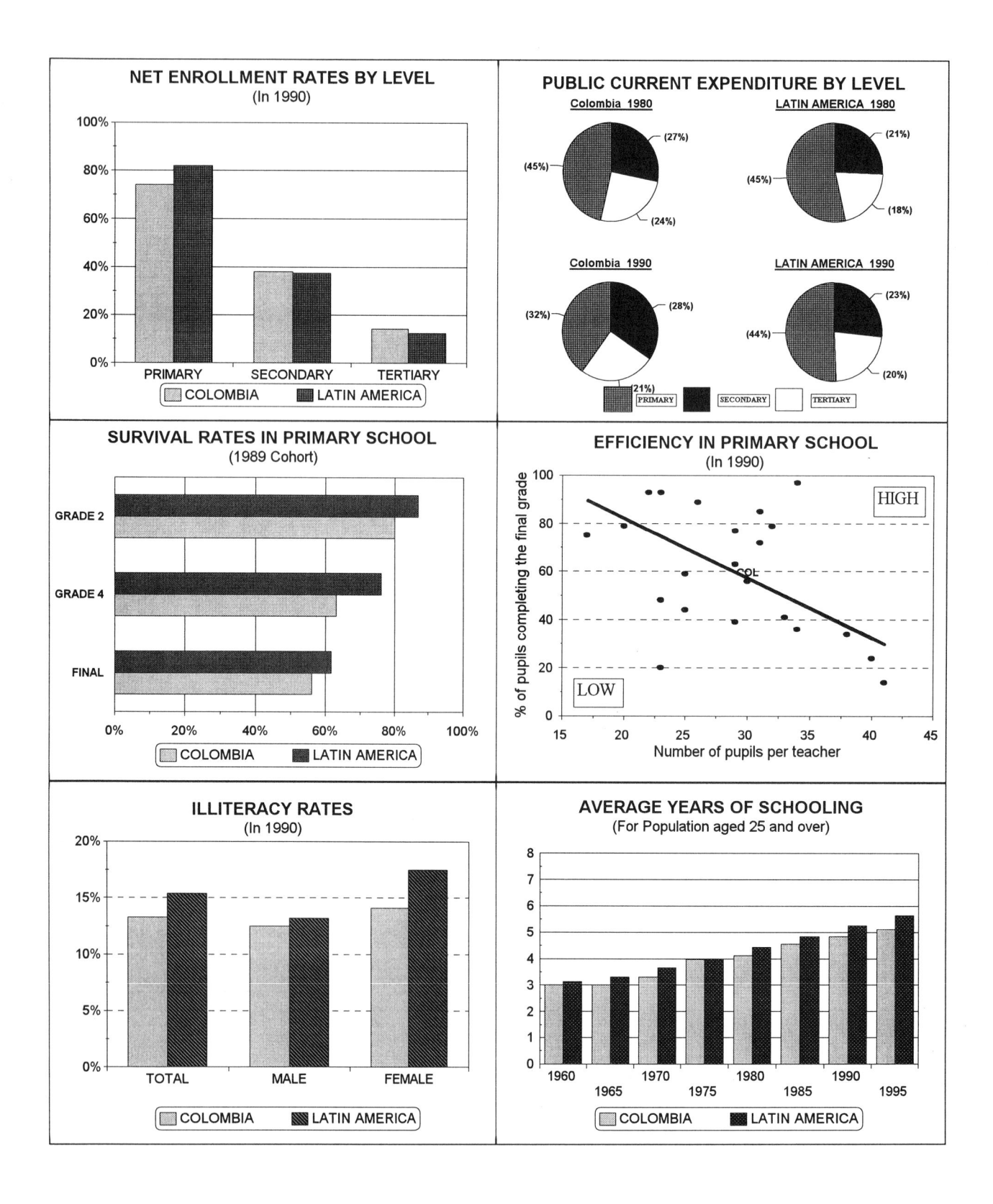

NET ENROLLMENT RATES BY LEVEL
(In 1990)

PUBLIC CURRENT EXPENDITURE BY LEVEL

Colombia 1980: Primary (45%), Secondary (27%), Tertiary (24%)
Latin America 1980: Primary (45%), Secondary (21%), Tertiary (18%)
Colombia 1990: Primary (32%), Secondary (28%), Tertiary (21%)
Latin America 1990: Primary (44%), Secondary (23%), Tertiary (20%)

SURVIVAL RATES IN PRIMARY SCHOOL
(1989 Cohort)

EFFICIENCY IN PRIMARY SCHOOL
(In 1990)

% of pupils completing the final grade vs. Number of pupils per teacher

ILLITERACY RATES
(In 1990)

AVERAGE YEARS OF SCHOOLING
(For Population aged 25 and over)

Statistics and Quantitative Analysis/IDB

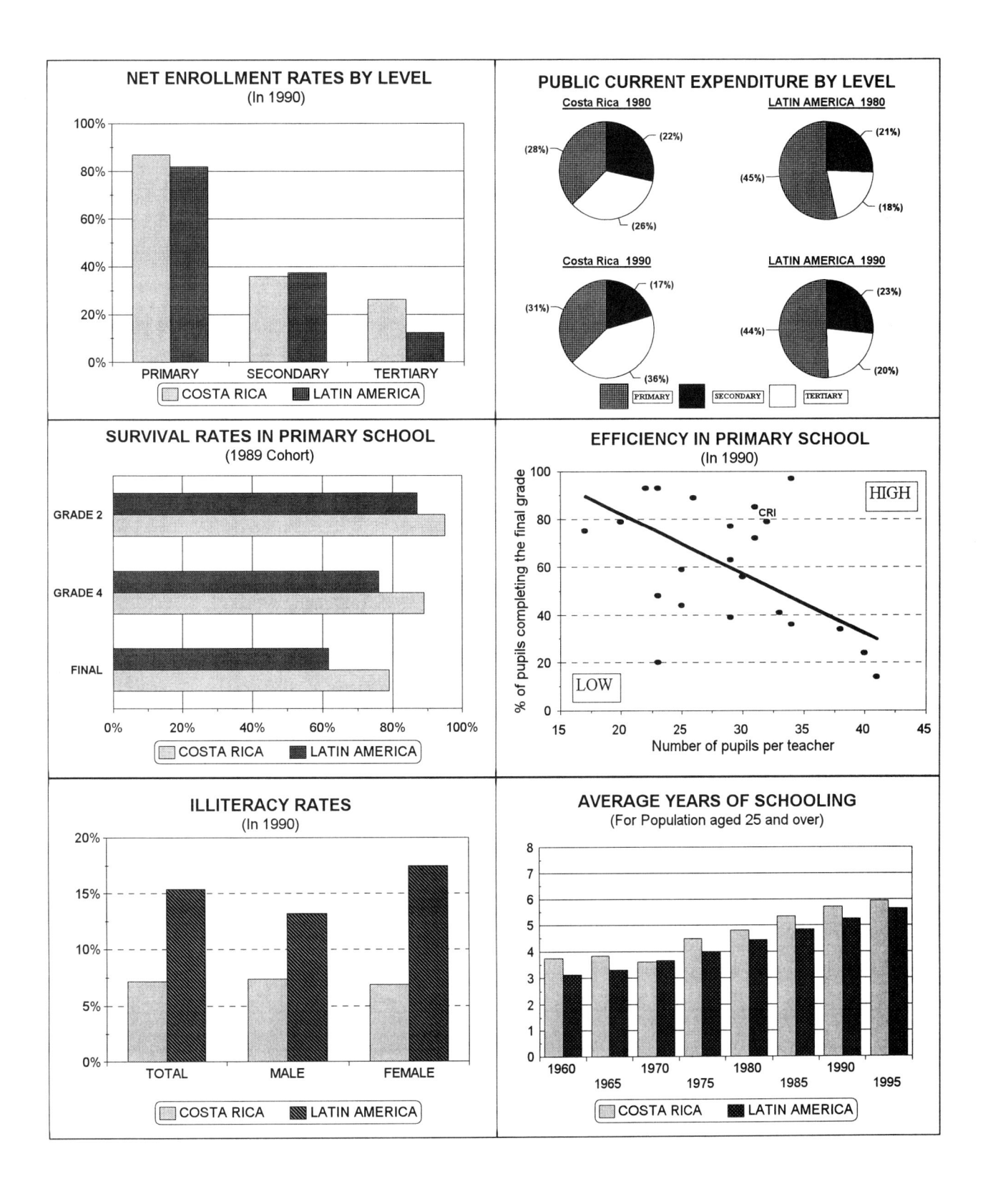

COSTA RICA
Education

NET ENROLLMENT RATES BY LEVEL
(In 1990)

PUBLIC CURRENT EXPENDITURE BY LEVEL

Costa Rica 1980: Primary (28%), Secondary (22%), Tertiary (26%)
Latin America 1980: Primary (45%), Secondary (21%), Tertiary (18%)
Costa Rica 1990: Primary (31%), Secondary (17%), Tertiary (36%)
Latin America 1990: Primary (44%), Secondary (23%), Tertiary (20%)

SURVIVAL RATES IN PRIMARY SCHOOL
(1989 Cohort)

EFFICIENCY IN PRIMARY SCHOOL
(In 1990)

ILLITERACY RATES
(In 1990)

AVERAGE YEARS OF SCHOOLING
(For Population aged 25 and over)

Statistics and Quantitative Analysis/IDB

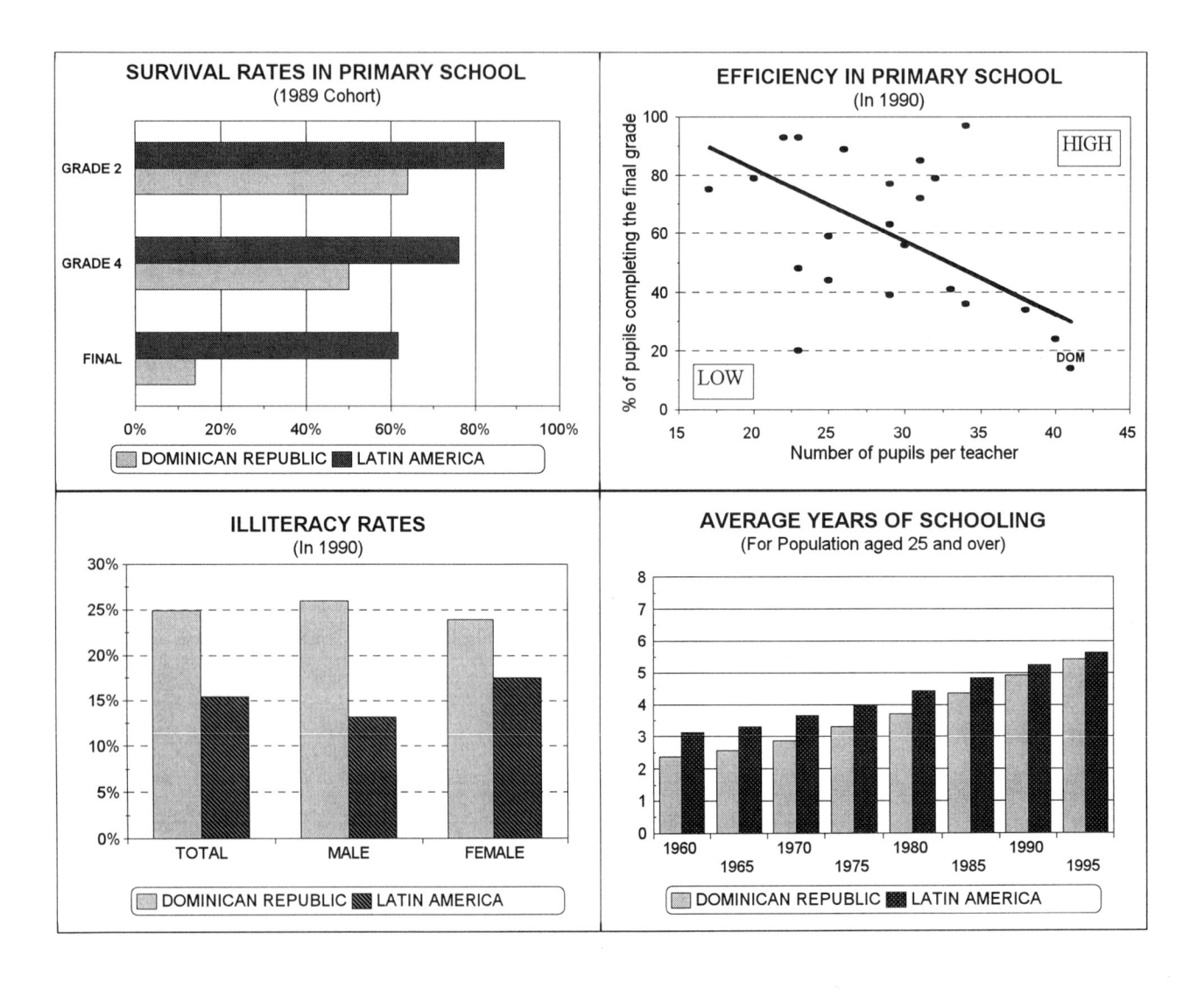

DOMINICAN REPUBLIC
Education

SURVIVAL RATES IN PRIMARY SCHOOL
(1989 Cohort)

DOMINICAN REPUBLIC / LATIN AMERICA

EFFICIENCY IN PRIMARY SCHOOL
(In 1990)

% of pupils completing the final grade vs. Number of pupils per teacher

HIGH / LOW / DOM

ILLITERACY RATES
(In 1990)

	DOMINICAN REPUBLIC	LATIN AMERICA
TOTAL	25%	15.5%
MALE	26%	13%
FEMALE	24%	17.5%

AVERAGE YEARS OF SCHOOLING
(For Population aged 25 and over)

Year	DOMINICAN REPUBLIC	LATIN AMERICA
1960	2.4	3.1
1965	2.6	3.3
1970	2.9	3.6
1975	3.3	4.0
1980	3.7	4.4
1985	4.4	4.8
1990	5.0	5.2
1995	5.4	5.6

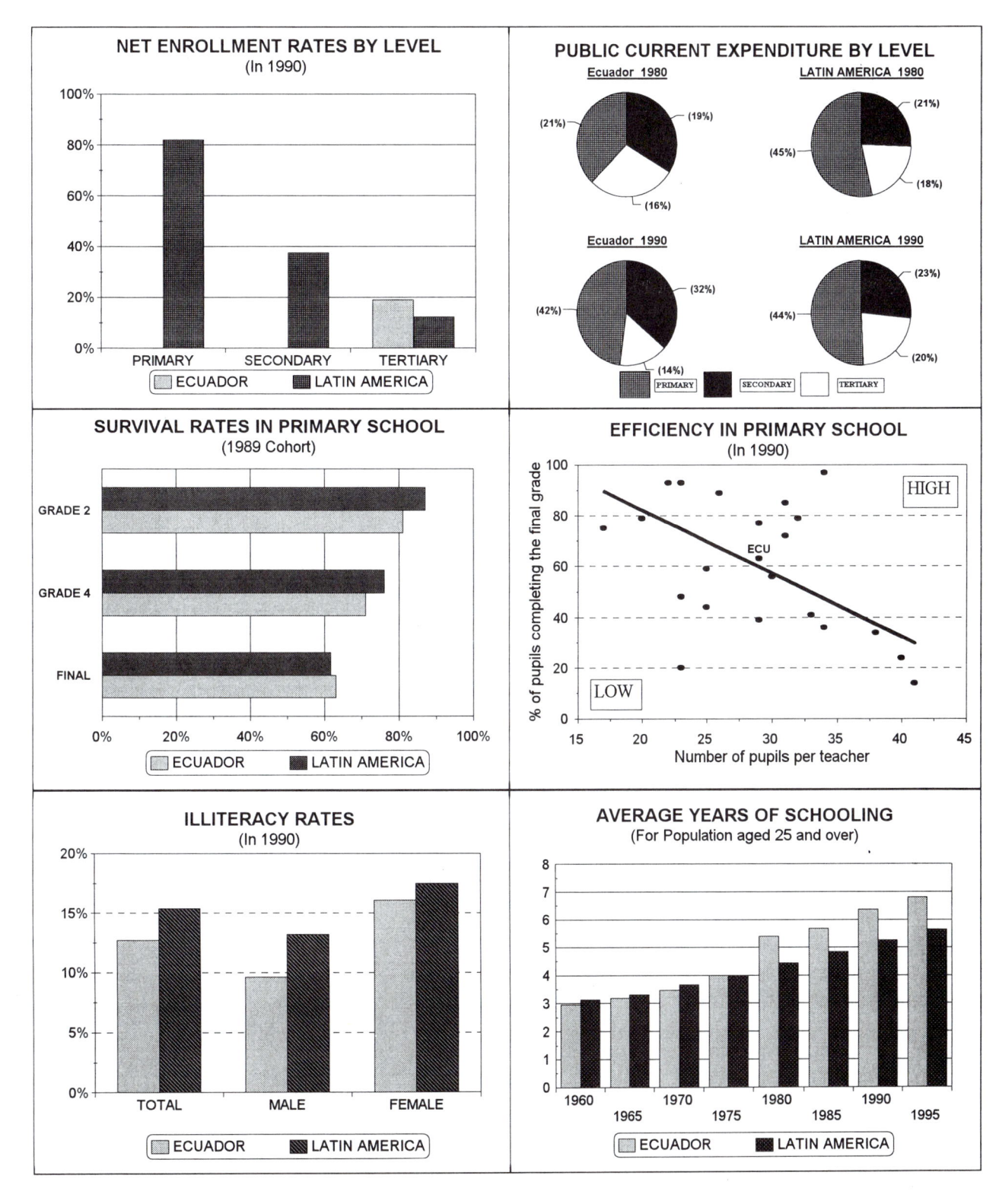

ECUADOR
Education

NET ENROLLMENT RATES BY LEVEL
(In 1990)

PUBLIC CURRENT EXPENDITURE BY LEVEL

Ecuador 1980: Primary (21%), Secondary (19%), Tertiary (16%)
Latin America 1980: Primary (45%), Secondary (21%), Tertiary (18%)
Ecuador 1990: Primary (42%), Secondary (32%), Tertiary (14%)
Latin America 1990: Primary (44%), Secondary (23%), Tertiary (20%)

SURVIVAL RATES IN PRIMARY SCHOOL
(1989 Cohort)

EFFICIENCY IN PRIMARY SCHOOL
(In 1990)

ILLITERACY RATES
(In 1990)

AVERAGE YEARS OF SCHOOLING
(For Population aged 25 and over)

Geographisches Institut
der Universität Kiel
Statistics and Quantitative Analysis/IDB

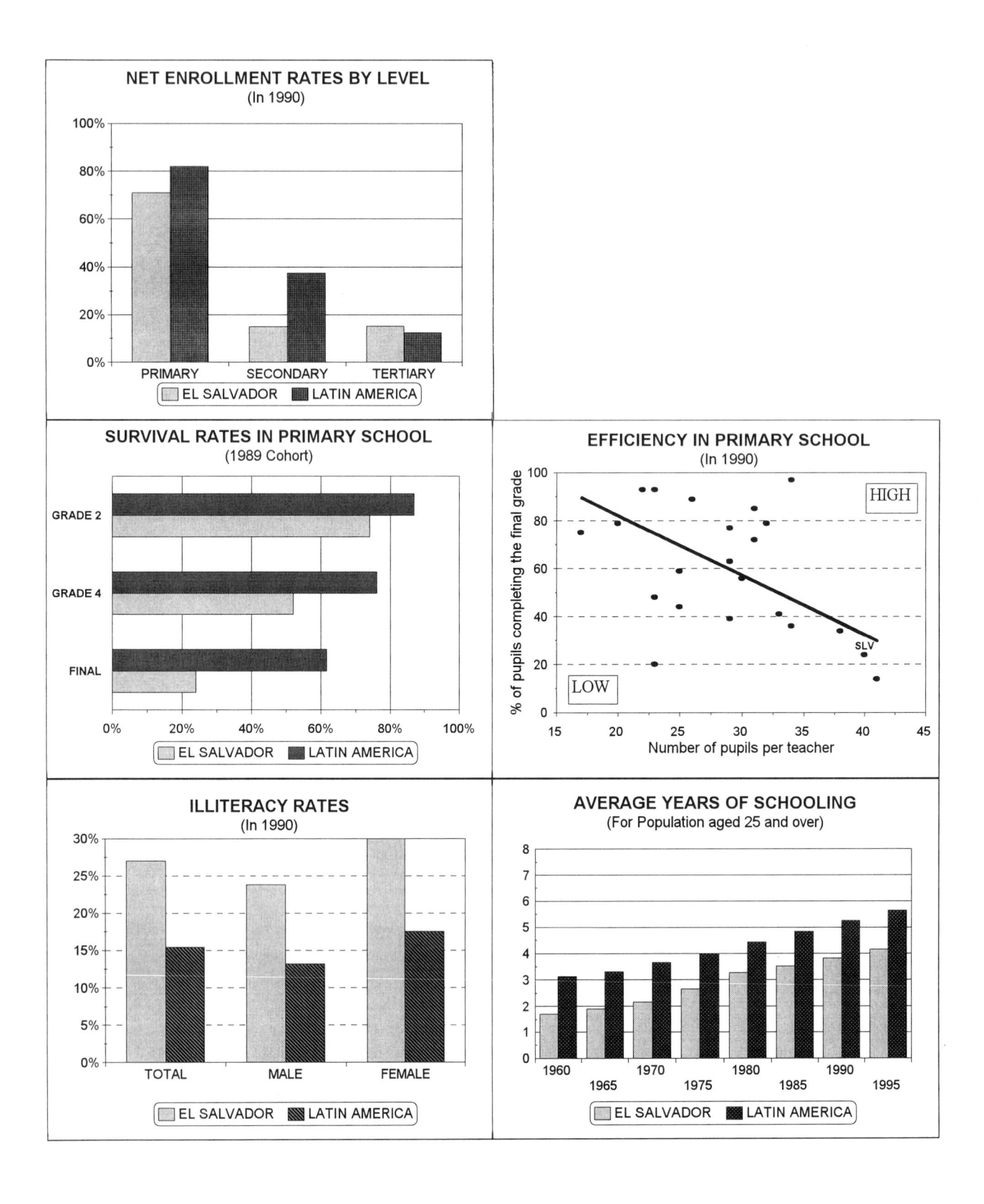

EL SALVADOR
Education

NET ENROLLMENT RATES BY LEVEL
(In 1990)

SURVIVAL RATES IN PRIMARY SCHOOL
(1989 Cohort)

EFFICIENCY IN PRIMARY SCHOOL
(In 1990)

ILLITERACY RATES
(In 1990)

AVERAGE YEARS OF SCHOOLING
(For Population aged 25 and over)

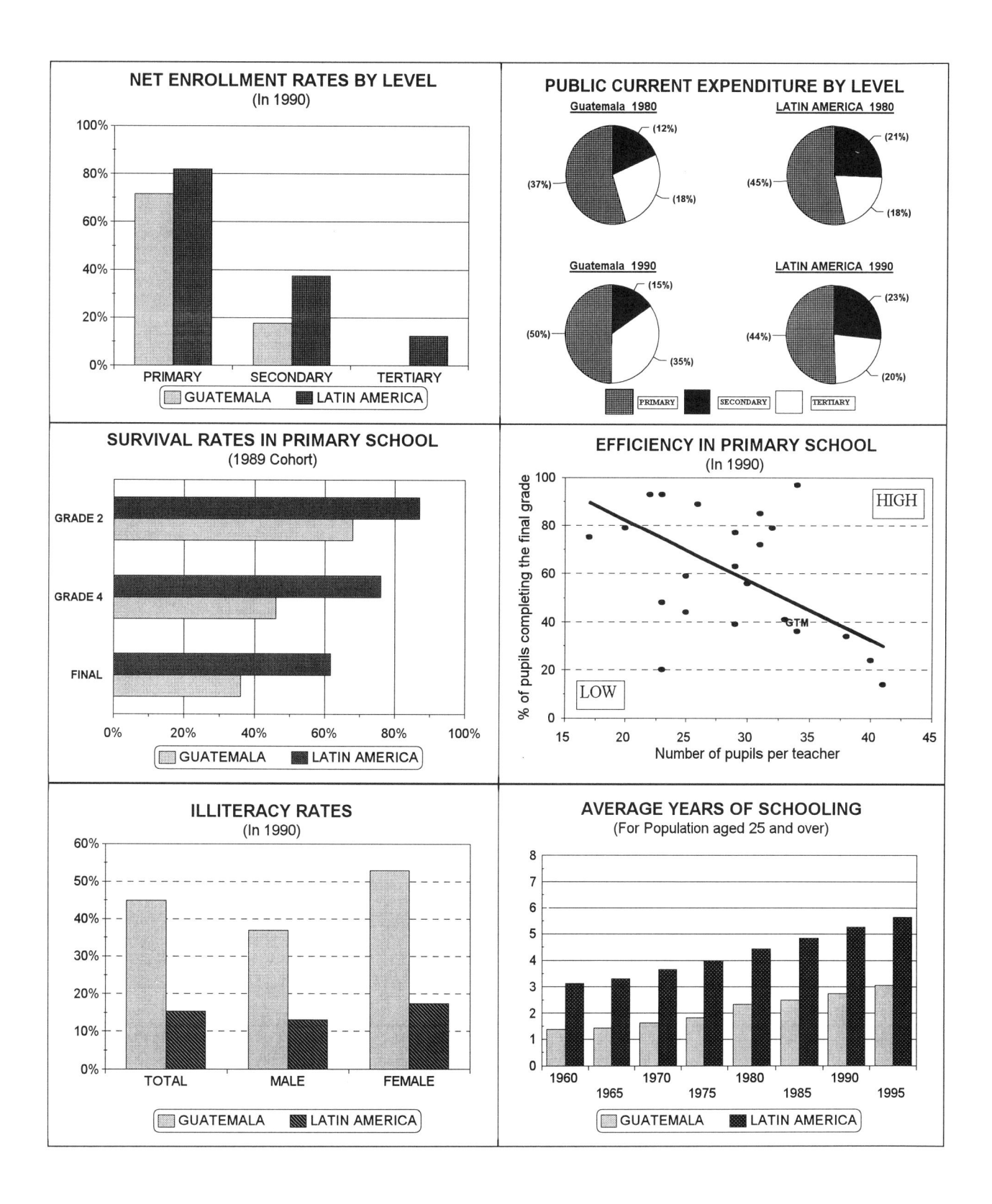

GUATEMALA
Education

NET ENROLLMENT RATES BY LEVEL
(In 1990)

PUBLIC CURRENT EXPENDITURE BY LEVEL

Guatemala 1980: Primary (37%), Secondary (12%), Tertiary (18%)
Latin America 1980: Primary (45%), Secondary (21%), Tertiary (18%)
Guatemala 1990: Primary (50%), Secondary (15%), Tertiary (35%)
Latin America 1990: Primary (44%), Secondary (23%), Tertiary (20%)

SURVIVAL RATES IN PRIMARY SCHOOL
(1989 Cohort)

EFFICIENCY IN PRIMARY SCHOOL
(In 1990)

ILLITERACY RATES
(In 1990)

AVERAGE YEARS OF SCHOOLING
(For Population aged 25 and over)

Statistics and Quantitative Analysis/IDB

GUYANA
Education

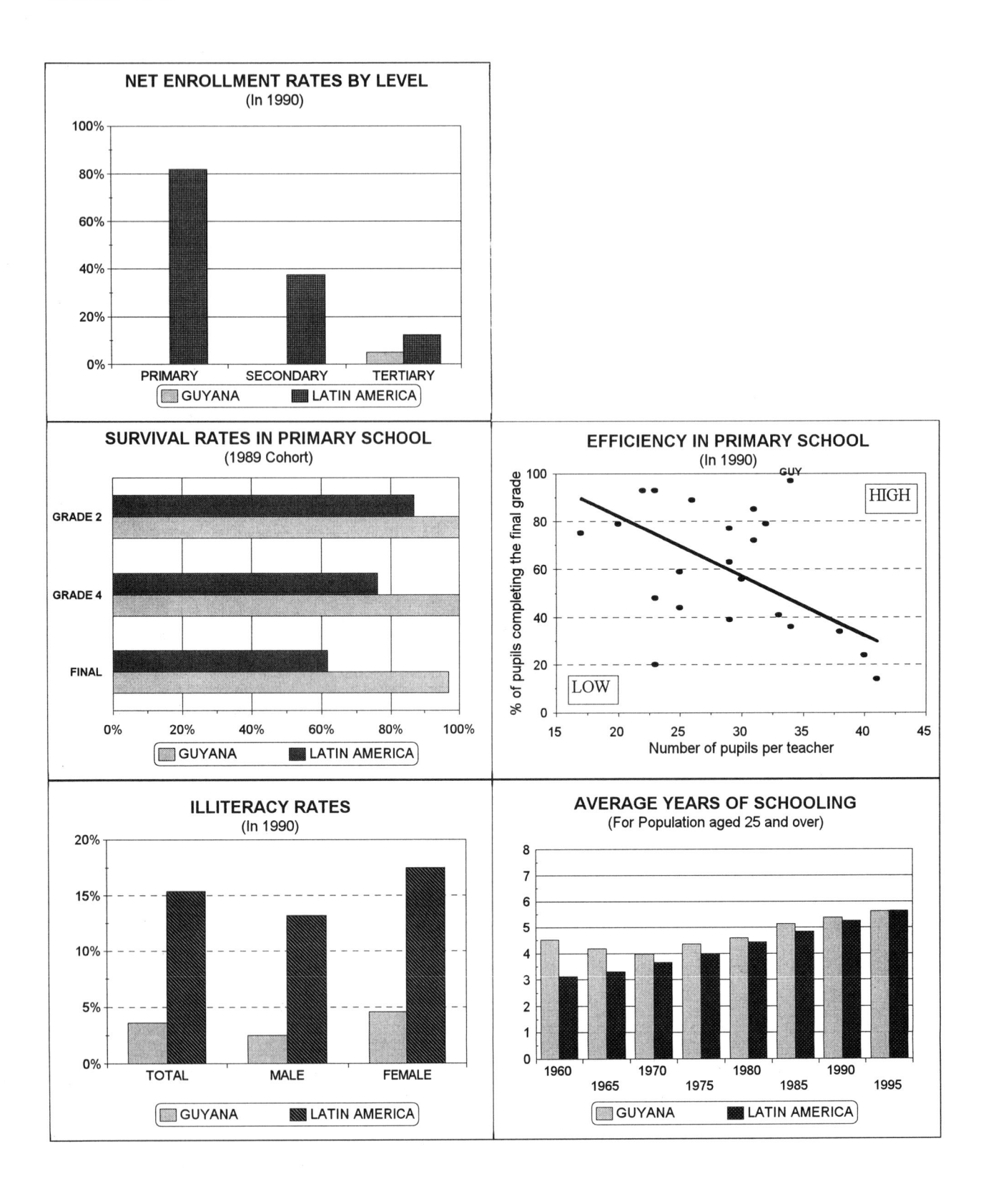

NET ENROLLMENT RATES BY LEVEL
(In 1990)

SURVIVAL RATES IN PRIMARY SCHOOL
(1989 Cohort)

EFFICIENCY IN PRIMARY SCHOOL
(In 1990)

ILLITERACY RATES
(In 1990)

AVERAGE YEARS OF SCHOOLING
(For Population aged 25 and over)

HAITI
Education

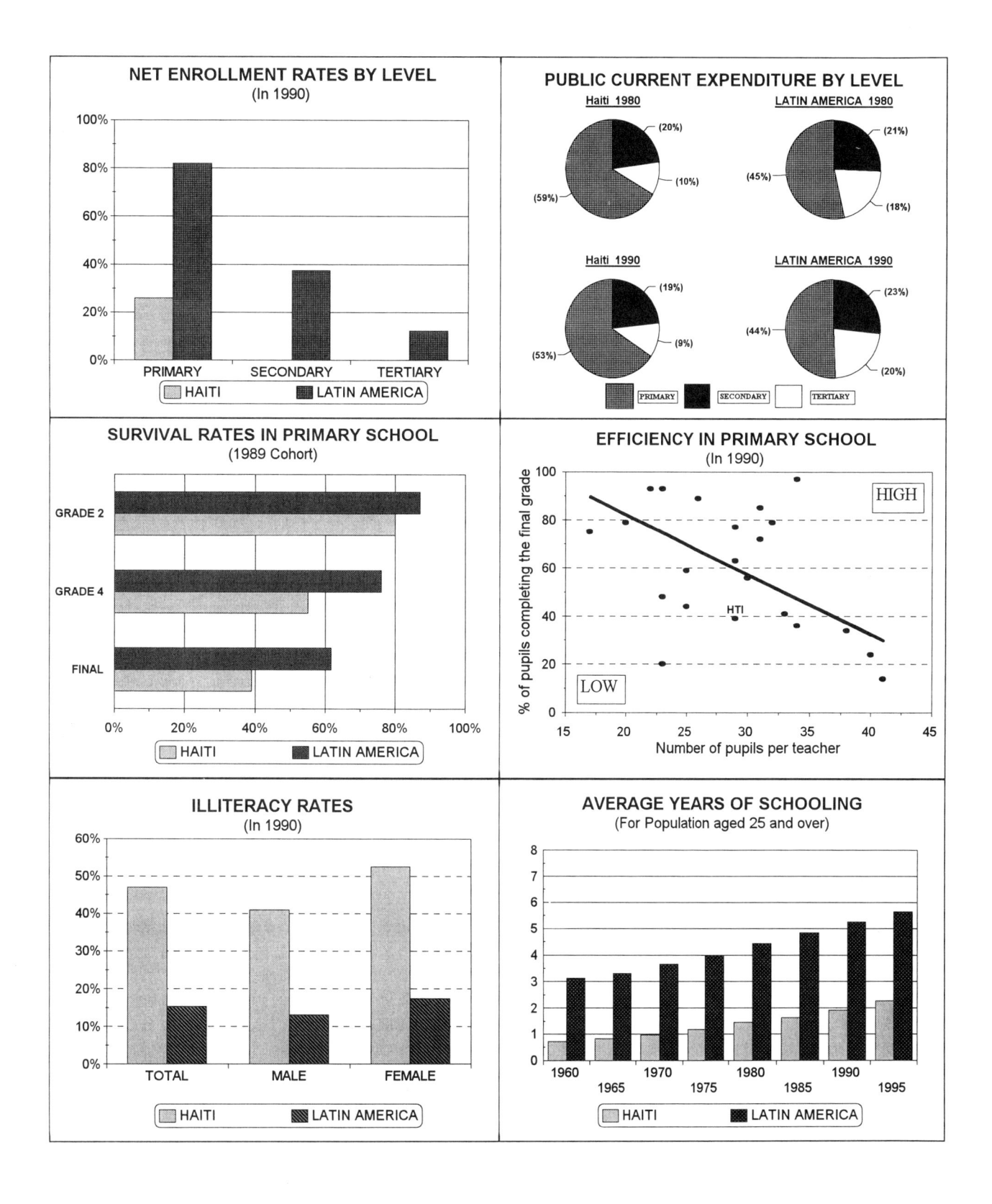

NET ENROLLMENT RATES BY LEVEL
(In 1990)

PUBLIC CURRENT EXPENDITURE BY LEVEL

Haiti 1980: Primary (59%), Secondary (20%), Tertiary (10%)
Latin America 1980: Primary (45%), Secondary (21%), Tertiary (18%)
Haiti 1990: Primary (53%), Secondary (19%), Tertiary (9%)
Latin America 1990: Primary (44%), Secondary (23%), Tertiary (20%)

SURVIVAL RATES IN PRIMARY SCHOOL
(1989 Cohort)

EFFICIENCY IN PRIMARY SCHOOL
(In 1990)

ILLITERACY RATES
(In 1990)

AVERAGE YEARS OF SCHOOLING
(For Population aged 25 and over)

Statistics and Quantitative Analysis/IDB

HONDURAS
Education

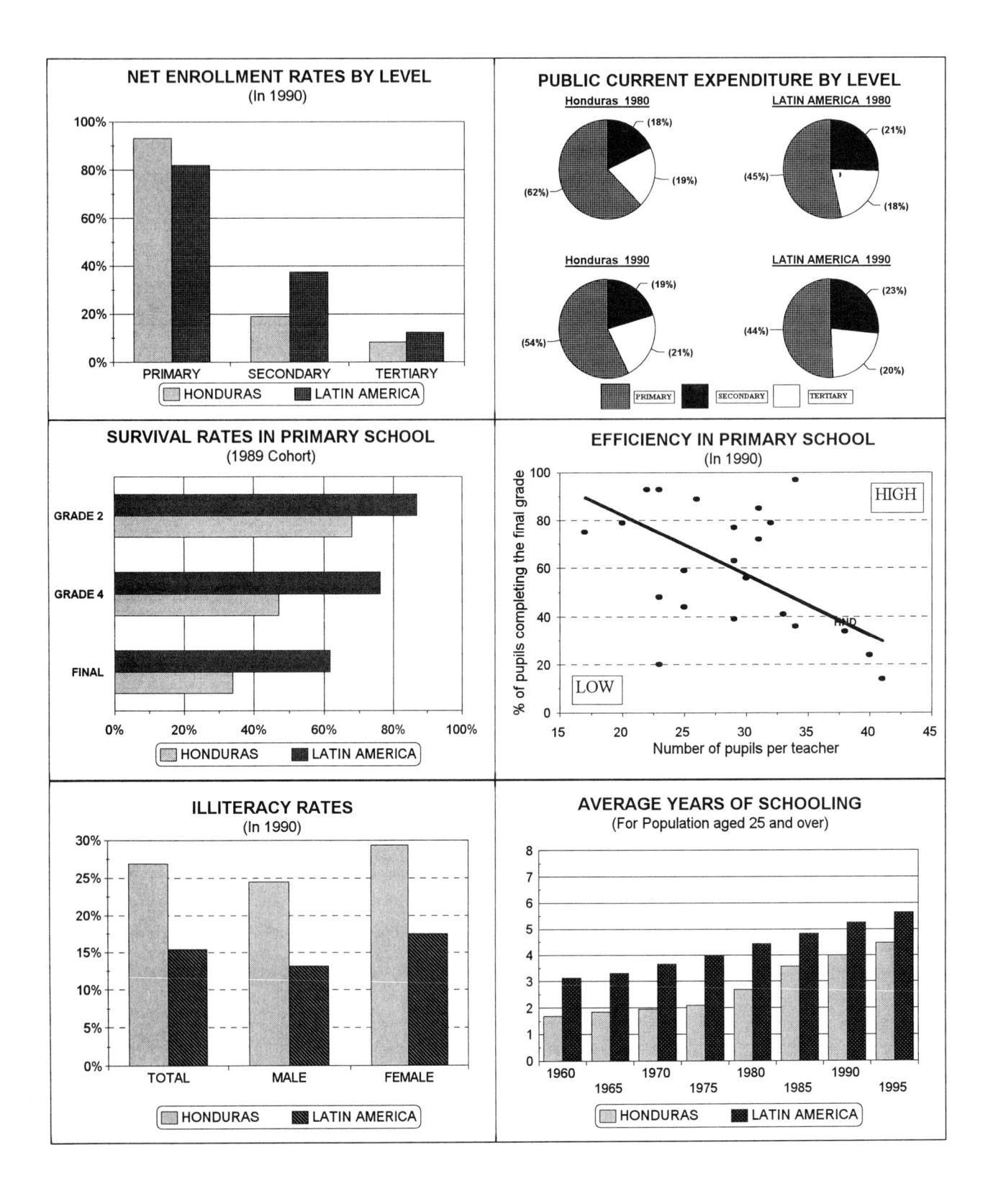

NET ENROLLMENT RATES BY LEVEL
(In 1990)

PUBLIC CURRENT EXPENDITURE BY LEVEL

Honduras 1980: Primary (62%), Secondary (18%), Tertiary (19%)
Latin America 1980: Primary (45%), Secondary (21%), Tertiary (18%)
Honduras 1990: Primary (54%), Secondary (19%), Tertiary (21%)
Latin America 1990: Primary (44%), Secondary (23%), Tertiary (20%)

SURVIVAL RATES IN PRIMARY SCHOOL
(1989 Cohort)

EFFICIENCY IN PRIMARY SCHOOL
(In 1990)

ILLITERACY RATES
(In 1990)

AVERAGE YEARS OF SCHOOLING
(For Population aged 25 and over)

Statistics and Quantitative Analysis/IDB

JAMAICA
Education

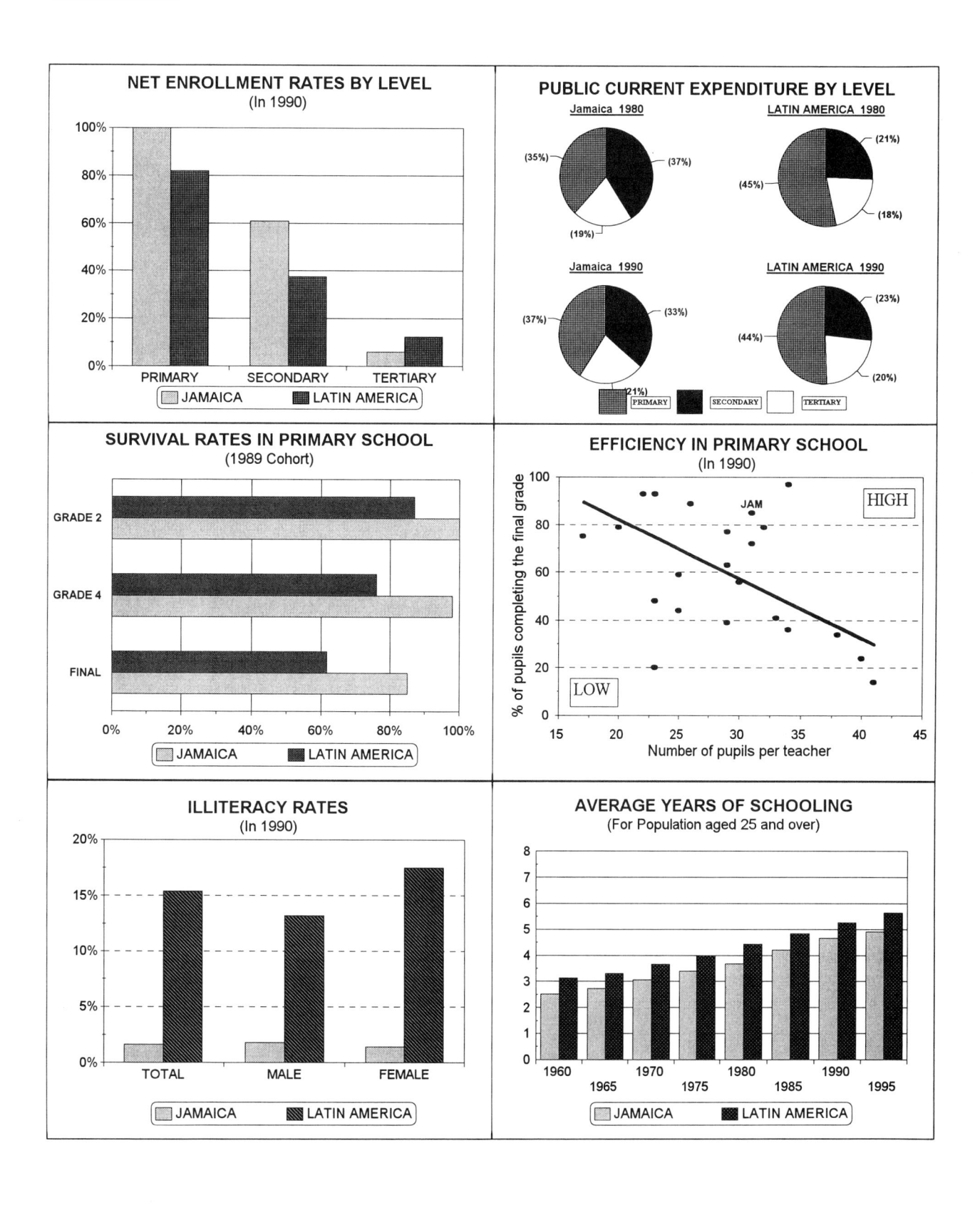

NET ENROLLMENT RATES BY LEVEL
(In 1990)

PUBLIC CURRENT EXPENDITURE BY LEVEL

Jamaica 1980: (35%), (37%), (19%)
LATIN AMERICA 1980: (21%), (45%), (18%)
Jamaica 1990: (37%), (33%), (21%)
LATIN AMERICA 1990: (23%), (44%), (20%)

PRIMARY | SECONDARY | TERTIARY

SURVIVAL RATES IN PRIMARY SCHOOL
(1989 Cohort)

EFFICIENCY IN PRIMARY SCHOOL
(In 1990)

% of pupils completing the final grade vs. Number of pupils per teacher

HIGH / LOW / JAM

ILLITERACY RATES
(In 1990)

AVERAGE YEARS OF SCHOOLING
(For Population aged 25 and over)

Statistics and Quantitative Analysis/IDB

MEXICO
Education

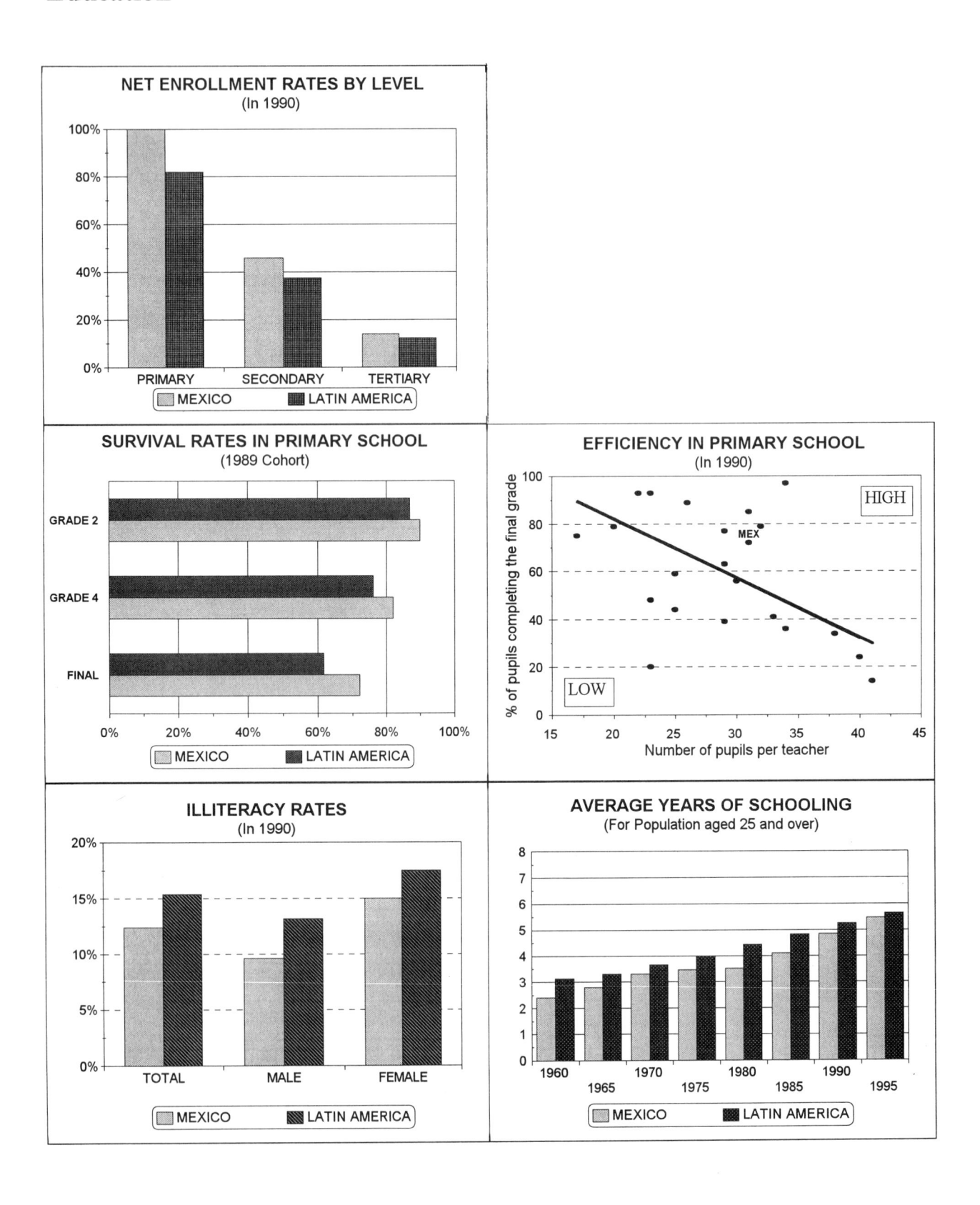

NET ENROLLMENT RATES BY LEVEL
(In 1990)

SURVIVAL RATES IN PRIMARY SCHOOL
(1989 Cohort)

EFFICIENCY IN PRIMARY SCHOOL
(In 1990)

ILLITERACY RATES
(In 1990)

AVERAGE YEARS OF SCHOOLING
(For Population aged 25 and over)

Statistics and Quantitative Analysis/IDB

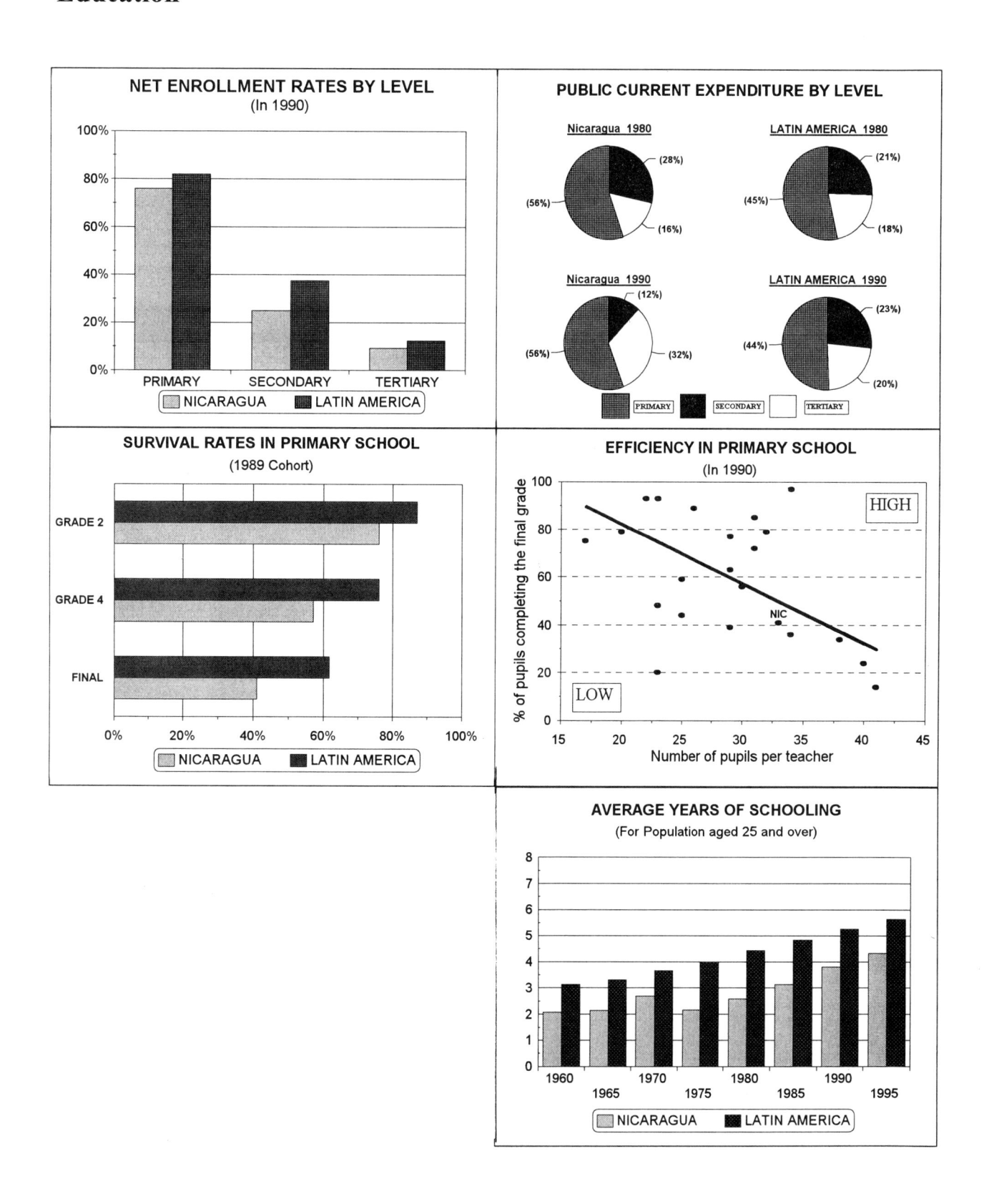

NICARAGUA
Education

NET ENROLLMENT RATES BY LEVEL
(In 1990)

PUBLIC CURRENT EXPENDITURE BY LEVEL

Nicaragua 1980: Primary (56%), Secondary (28%), Tertiary (16%)
Latin America 1980: Primary (45%), Secondary (21%), Tertiary (18%)
Nicaragua 1990: Primary (56%), Secondary (12%), Tertiary (32%)
Latin America 1990: Primary (44%), Secondary (23%), Tertiary (20%)

SURVIVAL RATES IN PRIMARY SCHOOL
(1989 Cohort)

EFFICIENCY IN PRIMARY SCHOOL
(In 1990)

% of pupils completing the final grade vs. Number of pupils per teacher

AVERAGE YEARS OF SCHOOLING
(For Population aged 25 and over)

Statistics and Quantitative Analysis/IDB

PANAMA
Education

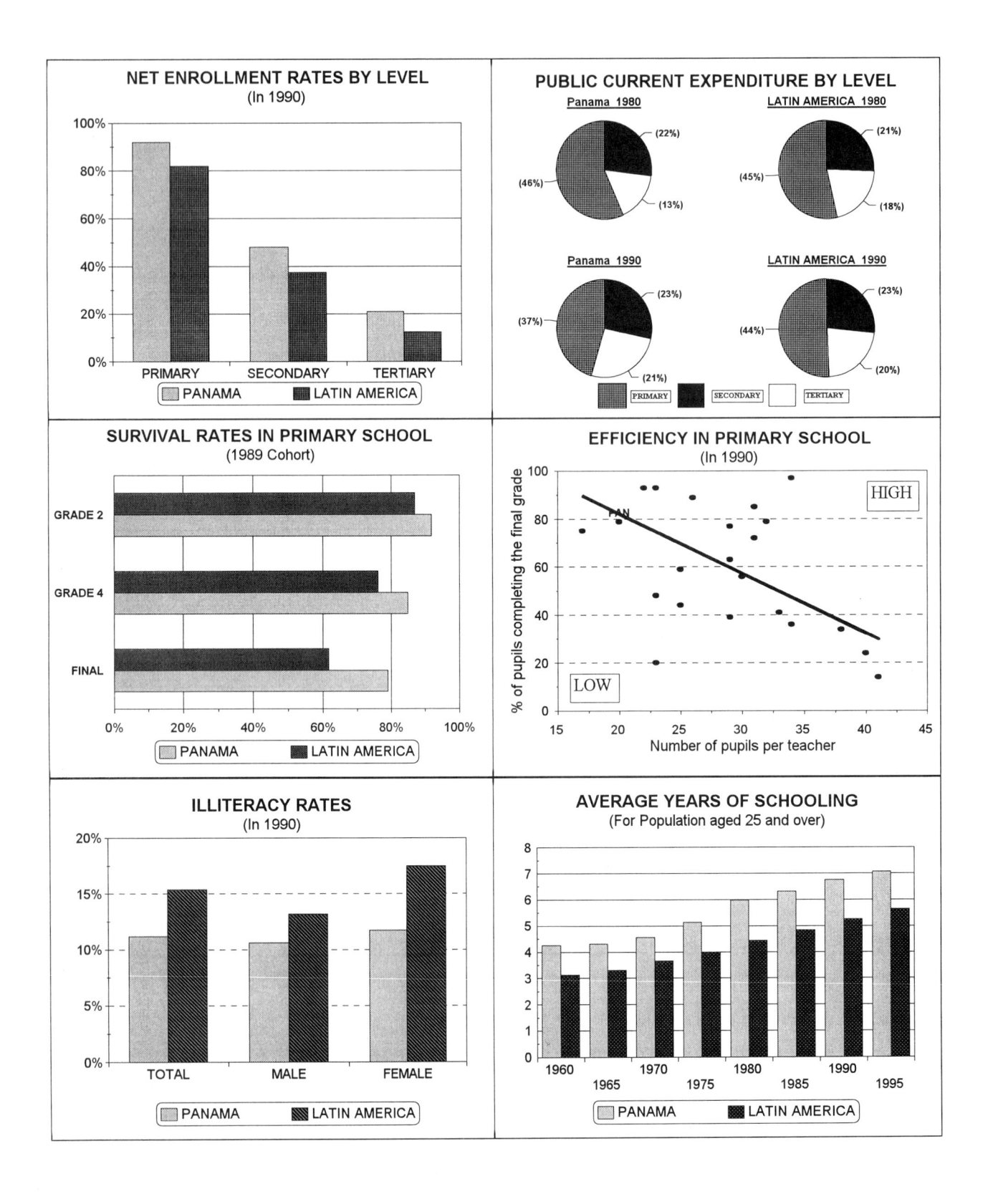

NET ENROLLMENT RATES BY LEVEL
(In 1990)

PUBLIC CURRENT EXPENDITURE BY LEVEL

Panama 1980: (22%), (13%), (46%)
LATIN AMERICA 1980: (21%), (18%), (45%)
Panama 1990: (23%), (21%), (37%)
LATIN AMERICA 1990: (23%), (20%), (44%)

PRIMARY | SECONDARY | TERTIARY

SURVIVAL RATES IN PRIMARY SCHOOL
(1989 Cohort)

GRADE 2, GRADE 4, FINAL — PANAMA / LATIN AMERICA

EFFICIENCY IN PRIMARY SCHOOL
(In 1990)

% of pupils completing the final grade vs. Number of pupils per teacher. HIGH / LOW. PAN marked.

ILLITERACY RATES
(In 1990)

TOTAL, MALE, FEMALE — PANAMA / LATIN AMERICA

AVERAGE YEARS OF SCHOOLING
(For Population aged 25 and over)

1960, 1965, 1970, 1975, 1980, 1985, 1990, 1995 — PANAMA / LATIN AMERICA

Statistics and Quantitative Analysis/IDB

PARAGUAY
Education

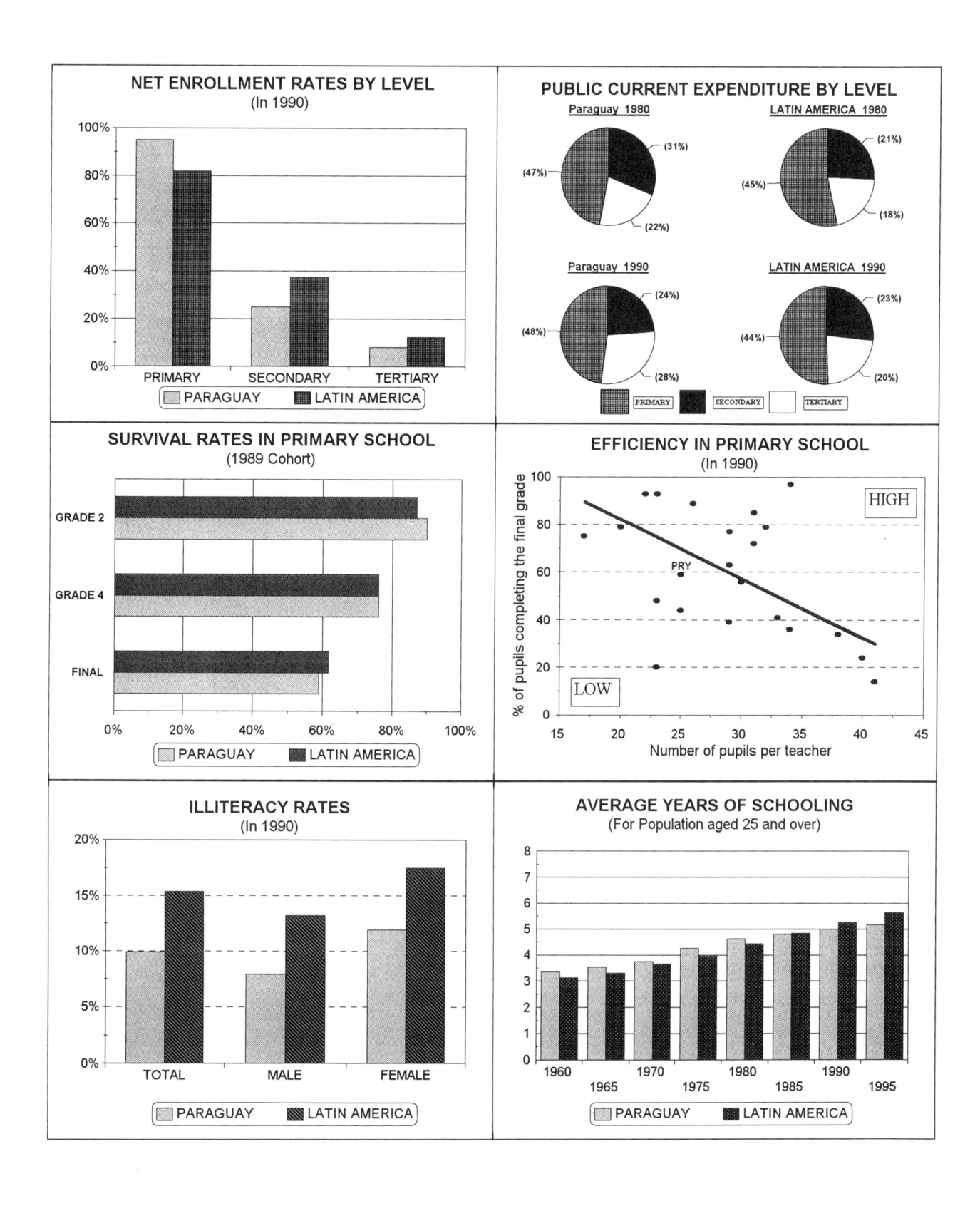

NET ENROLLMENT RATES BY LEVEL
(In 1990)

PUBLIC CURRENT EXPENDITURE BY LEVEL

Paraguay 1980: Primary (47%), Secondary (31%), Tertiary (22%)
Latin America 1980: Primary (45%), Secondary (21%), Tertiary (18%)
Paraguay 1990: Primary (48%), Secondary (24%), Tertiary (28%)
Latin America 1990: Primary (44%), Secondary (23%), Tertiary (20%)

SURVIVAL RATES IN PRIMARY SCHOOL
(1989 Cohort)

EFFICIENCY IN PRIMARY SCHOOL
(In 1990)

ILLITERACY RATES
(In 1990)

AVERAGE YEARS OF SCHOOLING
(For Population aged 25 and over)

Statistics and Quantitative Analysis/IDB

PERU
Education

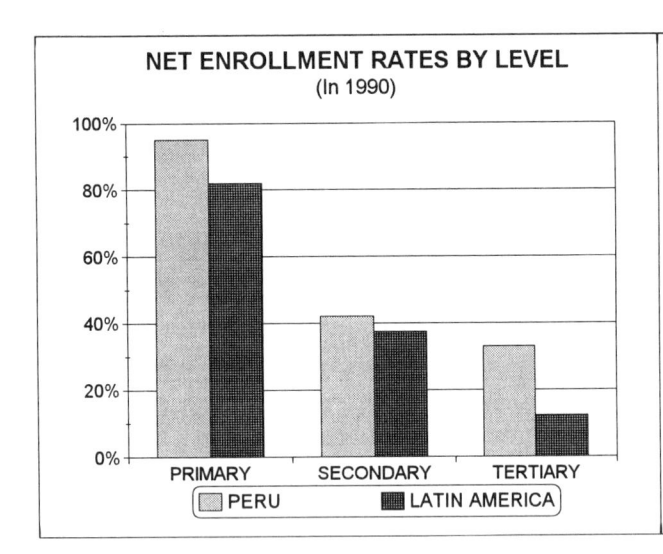

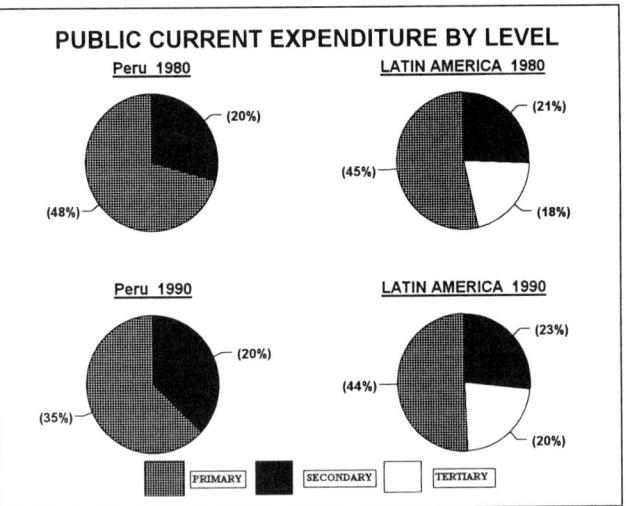

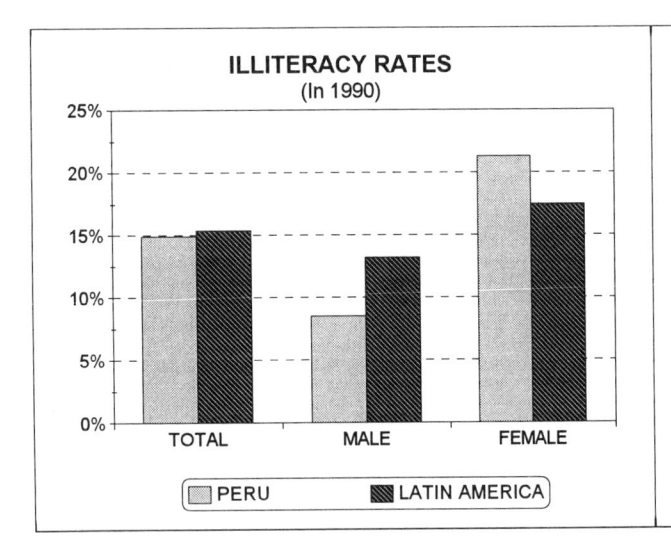

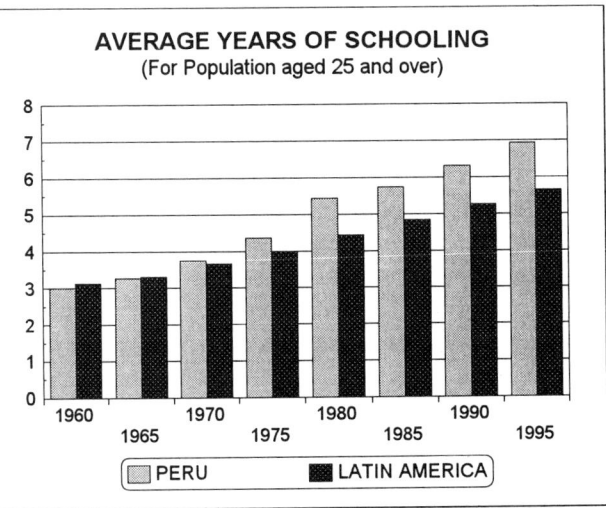

NET ENROLLMENT RATES BY LEVEL
(In 1990)

PUBLIC CURRENT EXPENDITURE BY LEVEL

Peru 1980: Primary (48%), Secondary (20%)
Latin America 1980: Primary (45%), Secondary (21%), Tertiary (18%)
Peru 1990: Primary (35%), Secondary (20%)
Latin America 1990: Primary (44%), Secondary (23%), Tertiary (20%)

ILLITERACY RATES
(In 1990)

AVERAGE YEARS OF SCHOOLING
(For Population aged 25 and over)

Statistics and Quantitative Analysis/IDB

SURINAME
Education

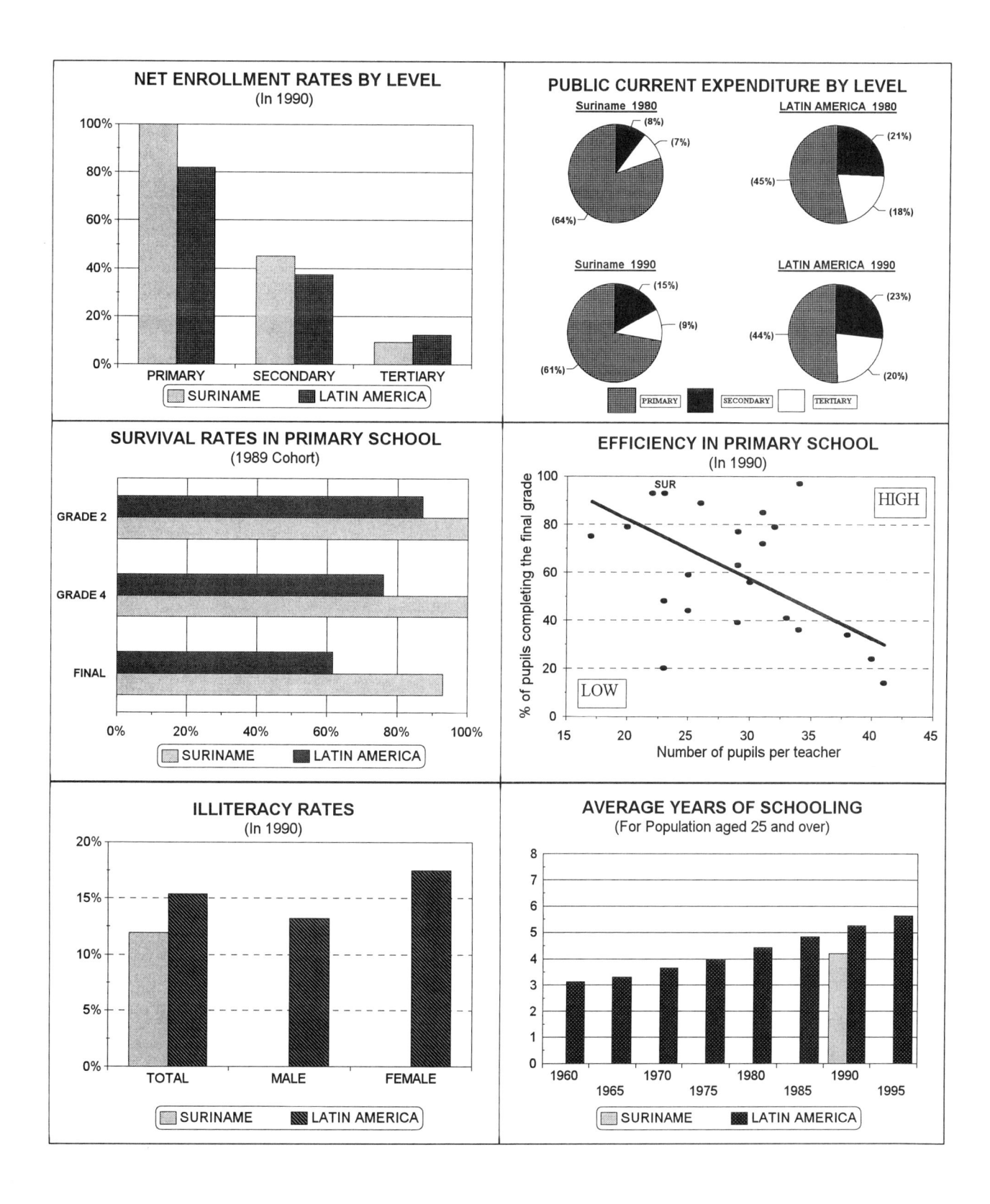

NET ENROLLMENT RATES BY LEVEL
(In 1990)

PUBLIC CURRENT EXPENDITURE BY LEVEL

Suriname 1980: Primary (64%), Secondary (8%), Tertiary (7%)
Latin America 1980: Primary (45%), Secondary (21%), Tertiary (18%)
Suriname 1990: Primary (61%), Secondary (15%), Tertiary (9%)
Latin America 1990: Primary (44%), Secondary (23%), Tertiary (20%)

SURVIVAL RATES IN PRIMARY SCHOOL
(1989 Cohort)

EFFICIENCY IN PRIMARY SCHOOL
(In 1990)

ILLITERACY RATES
(In 1990)

AVERAGE YEARS OF SCHOOLING
(For Population aged 25 and over)

Statistics and Quantitative Analysis/IDB

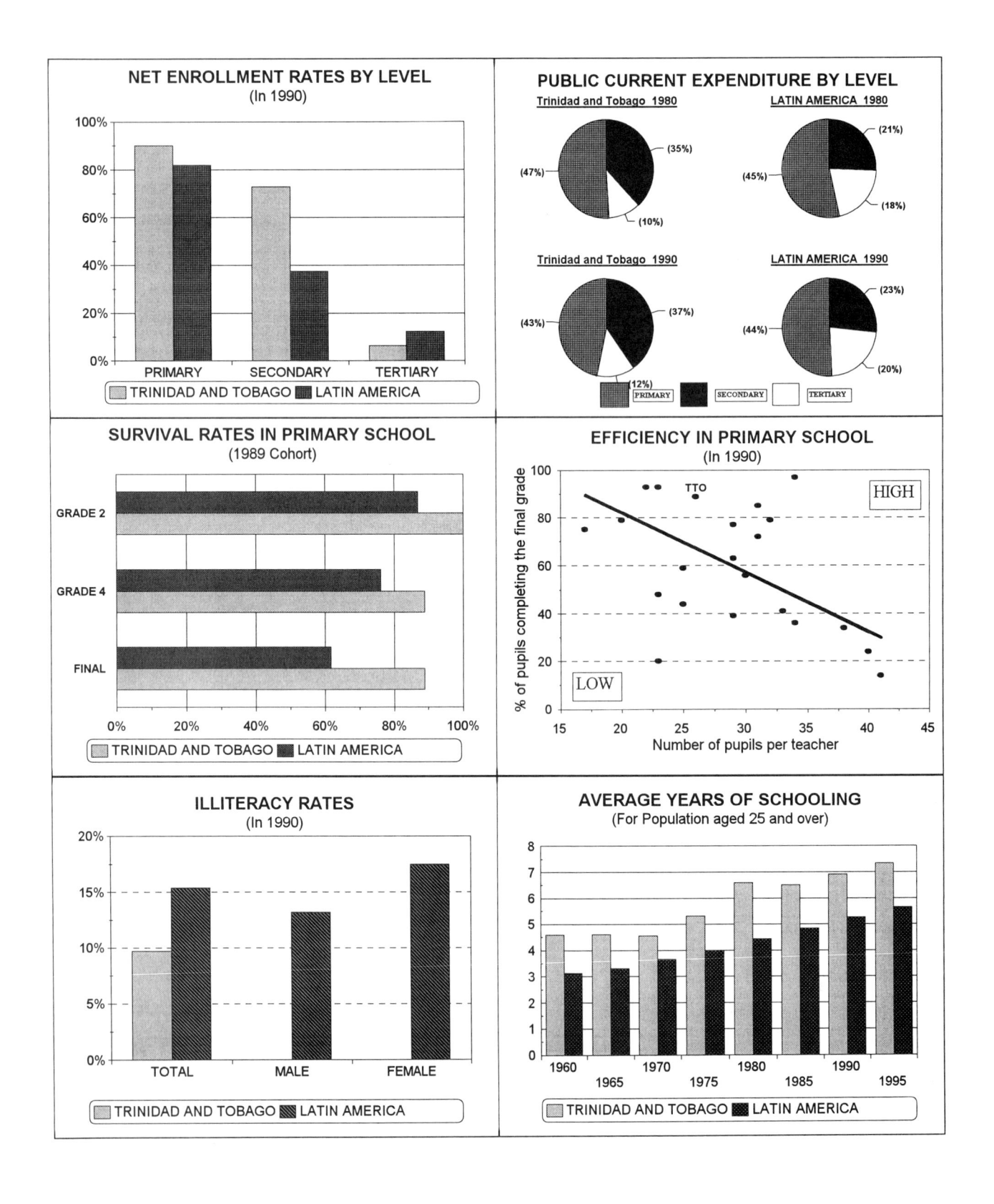

TRINIDAD AND TOBAGO
Education

NET ENROLLMENT RATES BY LEVEL
(In 1990)

PUBLIC CURRENT EXPENDITURE BY LEVEL

Trinidad and Tobago 1980: (47%), (35%), (10%)
LATIN AMERICA 1980: (45%), (21%), (18%)
Trinidad and Tobago 1990: (43%), (37%), (12%)
LATIN AMERICA 1990: (44%), (23%), (20%)

PRIMARY | SECONDARY | TERTIARY

SURVIVAL RATES IN PRIMARY SCHOOL
(1989 Cohort)

EFFICIENCY IN PRIMARY SCHOOL
(In 1990)

% of pupils completing the final grade vs. Number of pupils per teacher

ILLITERACY RATES
(In 1990)

AVERAGE YEARS OF SCHOOLING
(For Population aged 25 and over)

Statistics and Quantitative Analysis/IDB

URUGUAY
Education

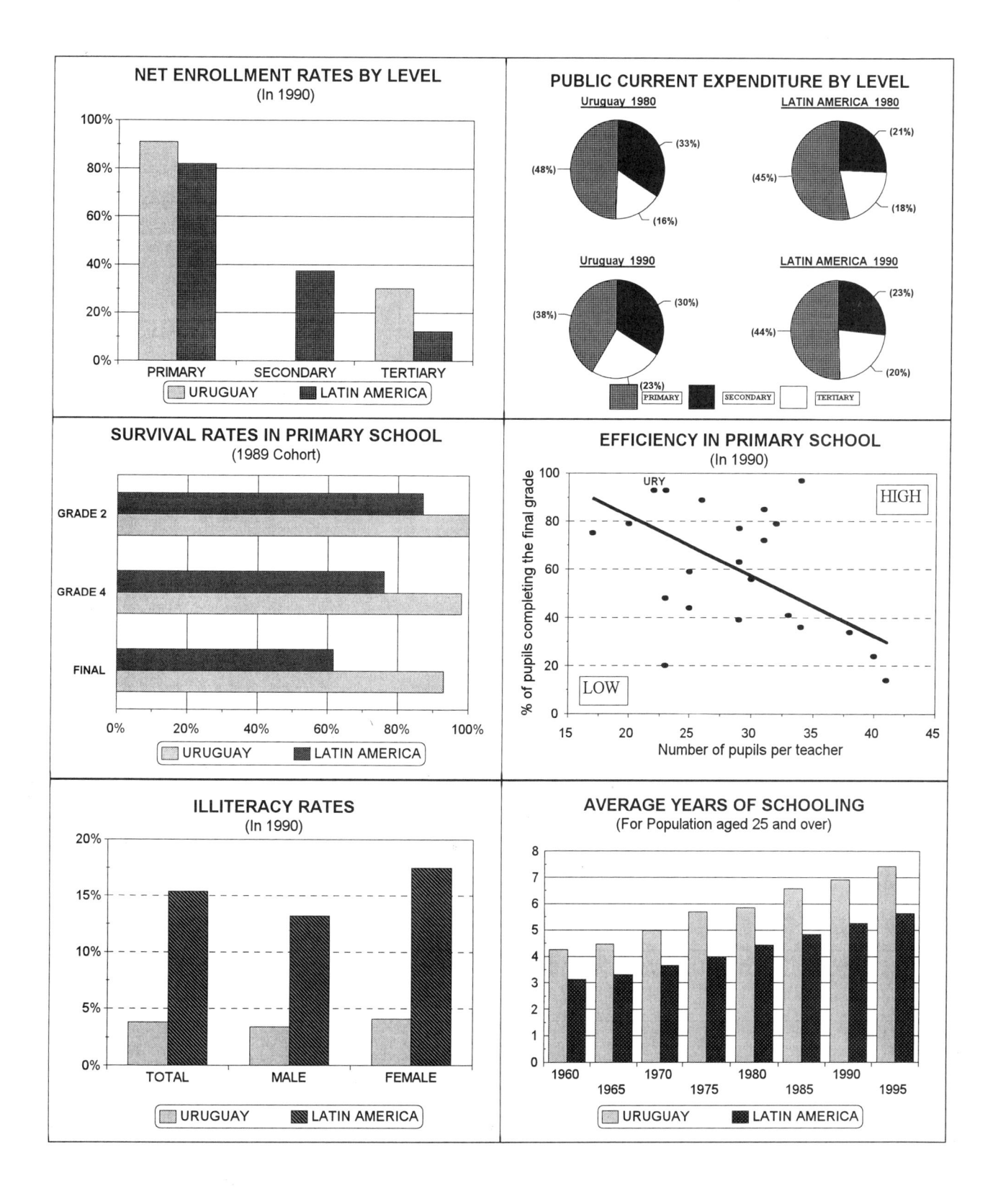

NET ENROLLMENT RATES BY LEVEL
(In 1990)

PUBLIC CURRENT EXPENDITURE BY LEVEL

Uruguay 1980: Primary (48%), Secondary (33%), Tertiary (16%)
Latin America 1980: Primary (45%), Secondary (21%), Tertiary (18%)
Uruguay 1990: Primary (38%), Secondary (30%), Tertiary (23%)
Latin America 1990: Primary (44%), Secondary (23%), Tertiary (20%)

SURVIVAL RATES IN PRIMARY SCHOOL
(1989 Cohort)

EFFICIENCY IN PRIMARY SCHOOL
(In 1990)

ILLITERACY RATES
(In 1990)

AVERAGE YEARS OF SCHOOLING
(For Population aged 25 and over)

Statistics and Quantitative Analysis/IDB

VENEZUELA
Education

NET ENROLLMENT RATES BY LEVEL
(In 1990)

SURVIVAL RATES IN PRIMARY SCHOOL
(1989 Cohort)

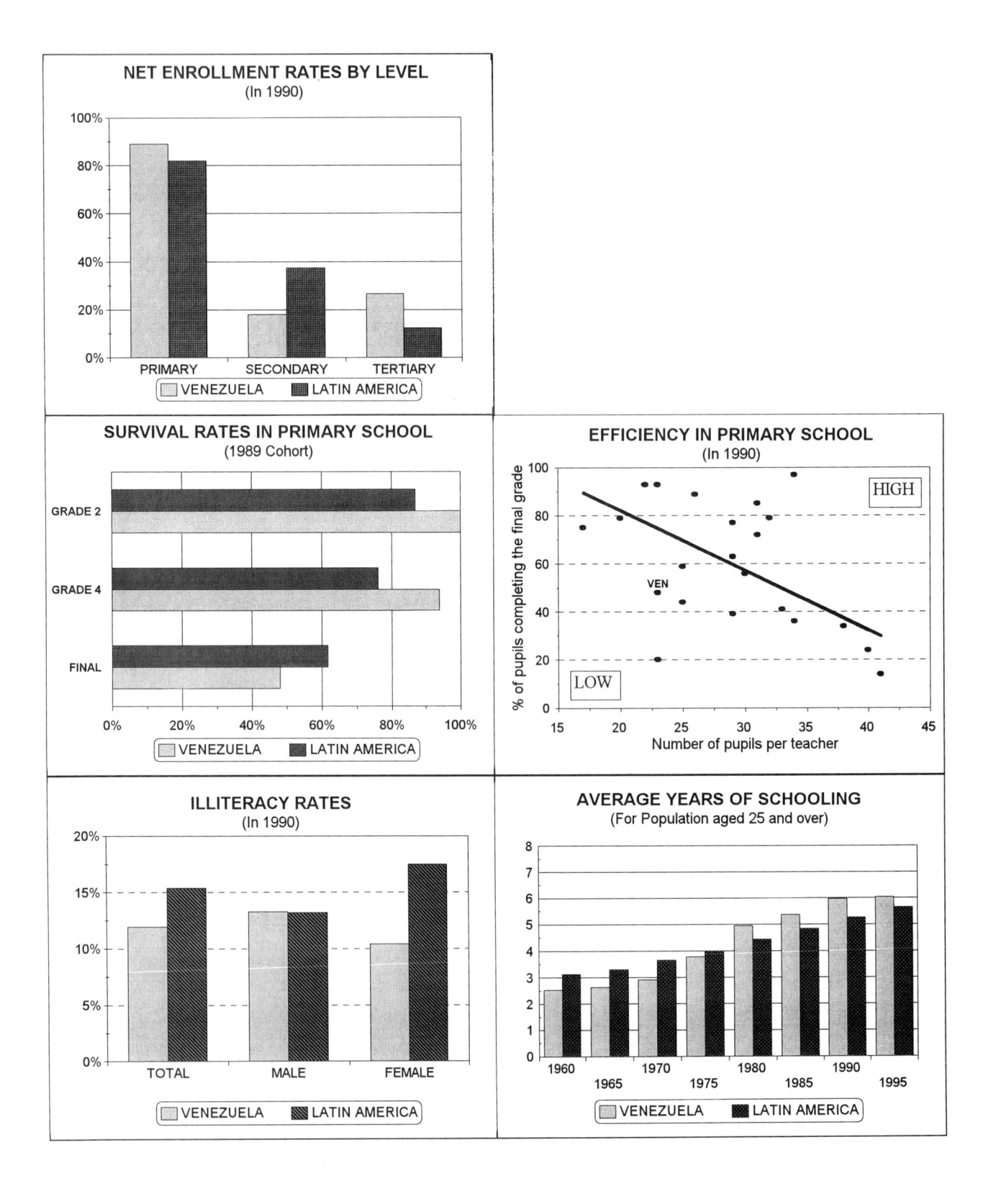

EFFICIENCY IN PRIMARY SCHOOL
(In 1990)

ILLITERACY RATES
(In 1990)

AVERAGE YEARS OF SCHOOLING
(For Population aged 25 and over)

Statistics and Quantitative Analysis/IDB

NATIONAL ACCOUNTS

NATIONAL ACCOUNTS

All graphs are produced using data in 1988 US Dollars calculated by Statistics and Quantitative Analysis from official member country data. Population estimates are from CELADE and the United Nations Population Division. Data for 1994 are IDB estimates. Descriptions of the graphs follow:

1. GDP PER CAPITA

Each country or region level of Gross Domestic Product (GDP) per capita is compared with the average level for Latin America (the aggregate of 26 IDB developing member countries).

2. GDP AND POPULATION GROWTH RATES

The graph shows when the GDP growth rate of the country or region is sufficient, or not, to cover the population growth rate.

3. CONTRIBUTION TO CHANGE IN TOTAL SUPPLY

The graphs give a breakdown of the growth rate of total supply (GDP + Imports) between the contribution of the three components of final demand (Consumption, Investment and Exports). The contribution of a component is calculated as its growth rate multiplied by the share of the component in total demand in the previous year. This allows the identification of the engines of growth on the demand side.

4. GDP GROWTH BY MAJOR SECTORS, 1974=100

Agriculture includes Agriculture and Livestock Production, Forestry and Logging, and Fishing. *Industry* includes Manufacturing, Mining and Quarrying, Construction and Electricity, Gas and Water. *Services* includes Wholesale and Retail Trade, Transport and Communications, Financial, Government and Other Services.

5. DEGREE OF OPENNESS OF THE ECONOMY

The ratios are Exports and Imports of Goods and Non-factor Services to GDP. Since the ratios are calculated in real terms, the graph indicates the changing openness in volume terms, based on 1988 prices.

6. INVESTMENT AND DOMESTIC SAVING RATES

Investment refers to Gross Fixed Capital Formation plus Change in Stocks. Domestic Saving is calculated as the difference between GDP and total consumption in constant 1988 US Dollars but does not include the terms of trade effect (this effect may be thought of as cyclical and therefore temporary). In most cases, the difference between Domestic Saving and Investment is, if not already negative, insufficient to cover factor payments abroad (interest and dividends) even after considering current transfers received. In these cases, the country would need to use External Saving (equal to the current account deficit of the Balance of Payments in constant prices).

Country Notes

Bahamas
Since GDP is the only national accounts series to be estimated in constant prices by the local authorities, only the first two graphs are available for the country.

Belize
Data are available only from 1980.

Brazil
Beginning in 1987, Investment excludes the Change in Stocks.

Guyana
Electricity, Gas and Water are included in Manufacturing

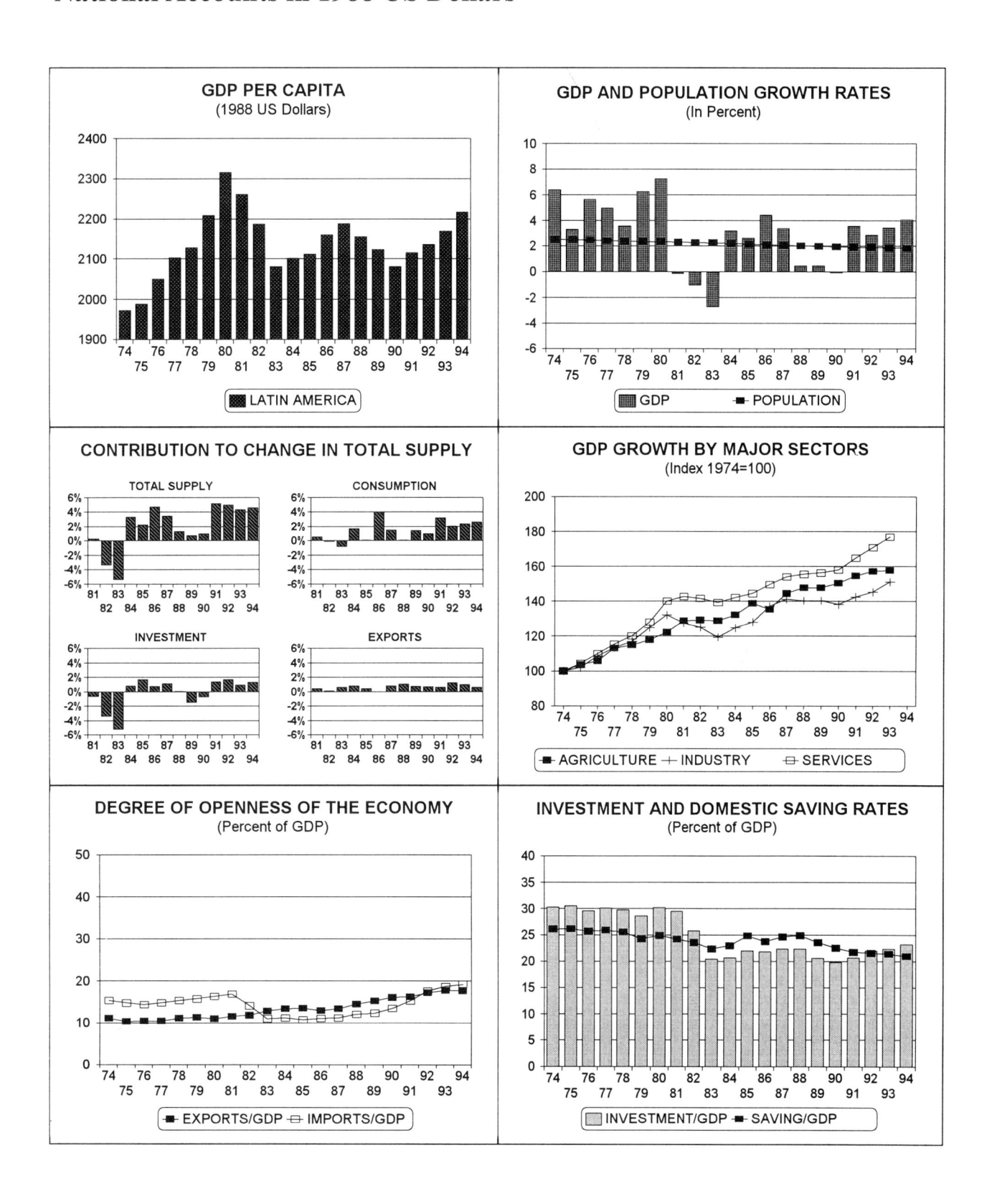

LATIN AMERICA
National Accounts in 1988 US Dollars

Statistics and Quantitative Analysis/IDB

ANDEAN GROUP
National Accounts in 1988 US Dollars

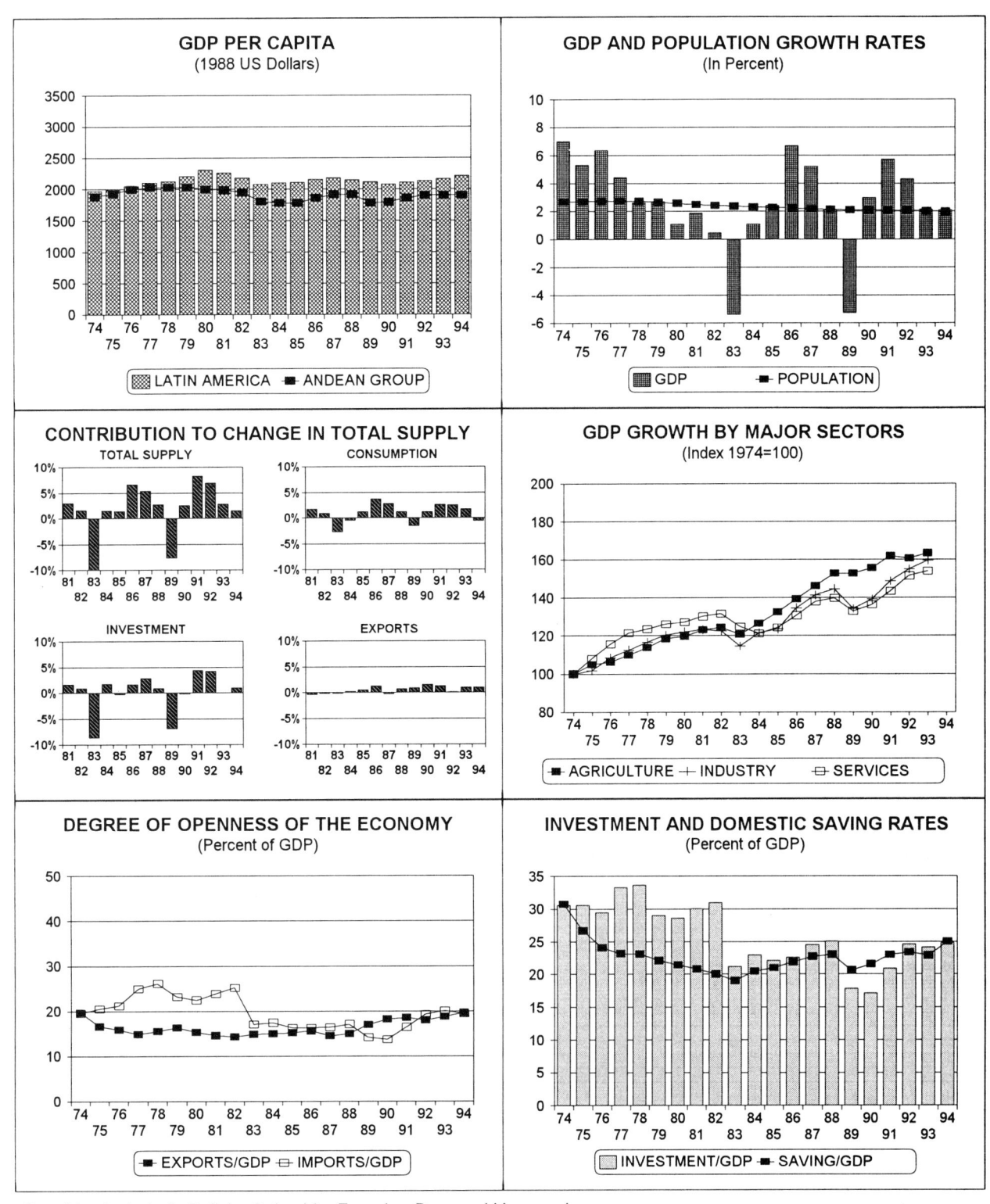

GDP PER CAPITA
(1988 US Dollars)

GDP AND POPULATION GROWTH RATES
(In Percent)

CONTRIBUTION TO CHANGE IN TOTAL SUPPLY

GDP GROWTH BY MAJOR SECTORS
(Index 1974=100)

DEGREE OF OPENNESS OF THE ECONOMY
(Percent of GDP)

INVESTMENT AND DOMESTIC SAVING RATES
(Percent of GDP)

Countries included : Bolivia, Colombia, Ecuador, Peru and Venezuela.

Statistics and Quantitative Analysis/IDB

CACM
National Accounts in 1988 US Dollars

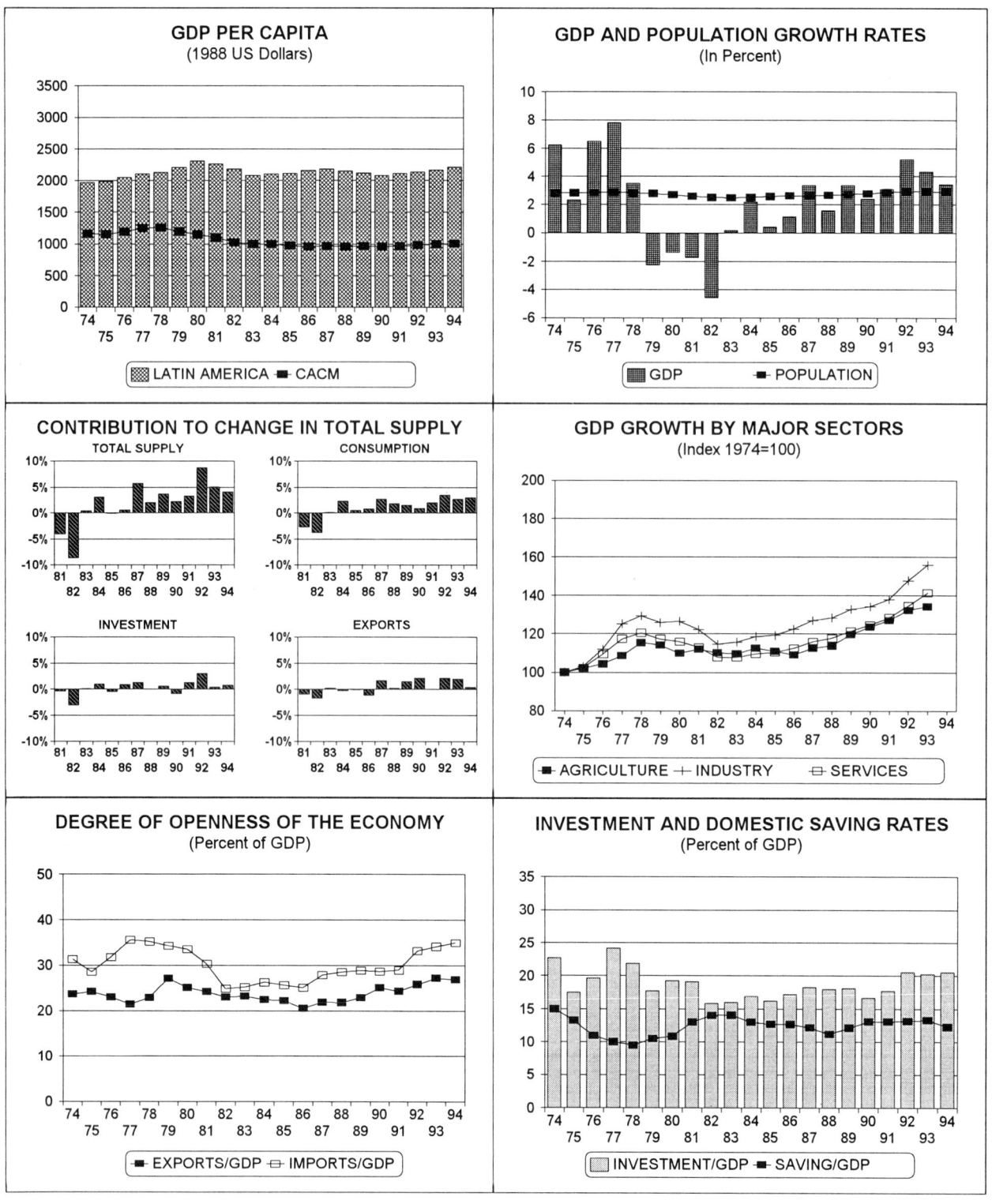

Countries included : Costa Rica, El Salvador, Guatemala, Honduras and Nicaragua.

CARICOM
National Accounts in 1988 US Dollars

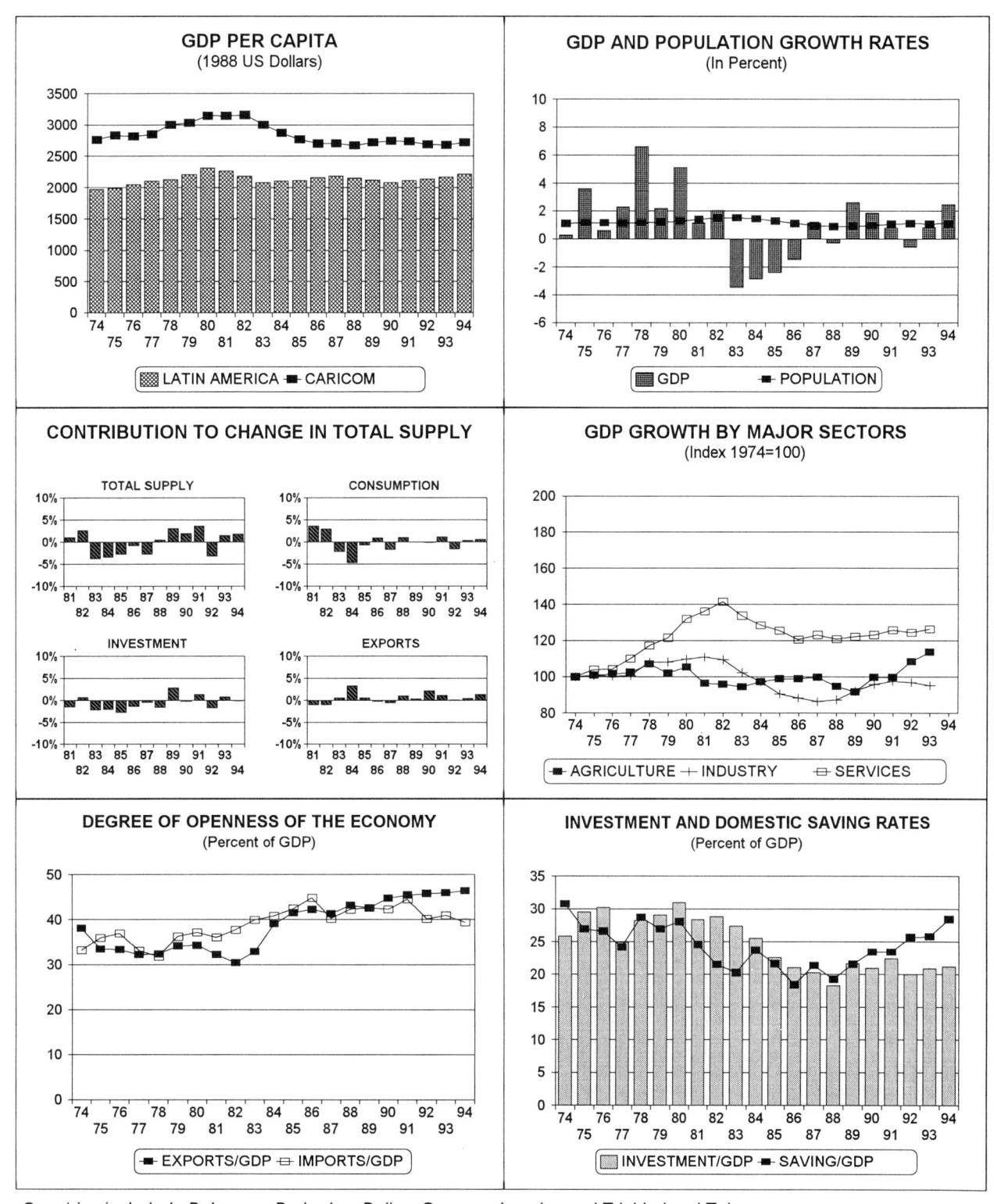

Countries included : Bahamas, Barbados, Belize, Guyana, Jamaica and Trinidad and Tobago.

Statistics and Quantitative Analysis/IDB

MERCOSUR
National Accounts in 1988 US Dollars

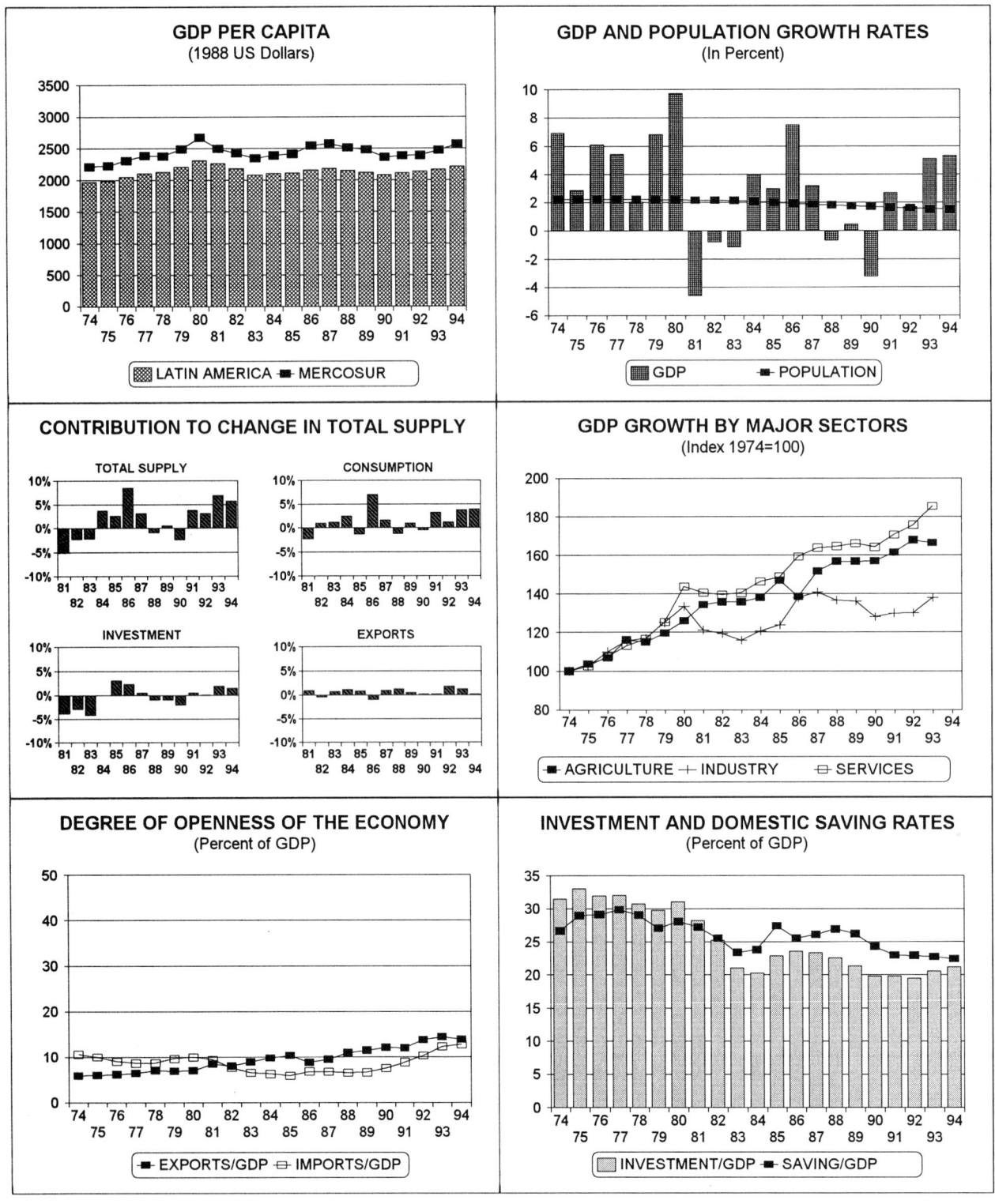

GDP PER CAPITA
(1988 US Dollars)

GDP AND POPULATION GROWTH RATES
(In Percent)

CONTRIBUTION TO CHANGE IN TOTAL SUPPLY

TOTAL SUPPLY

CONSUMPTION

INVESTMENT

EXPORTS

GDP GROWTH BY MAJOR SECTORS
(Index 1974=100)

DEGREE OF OPENNESS OF THE ECONOMY
(Percent of GDP)

INVESTMENT AND DOMESTIC SAVING RATES
(Percent of GDP)

Countries included : Argentina, Brazil, Paraguay and Uruguay.

Statistics and Quantitative Analysis/IDB

ARGENTINA
National Accounts in 1988 US Dollars

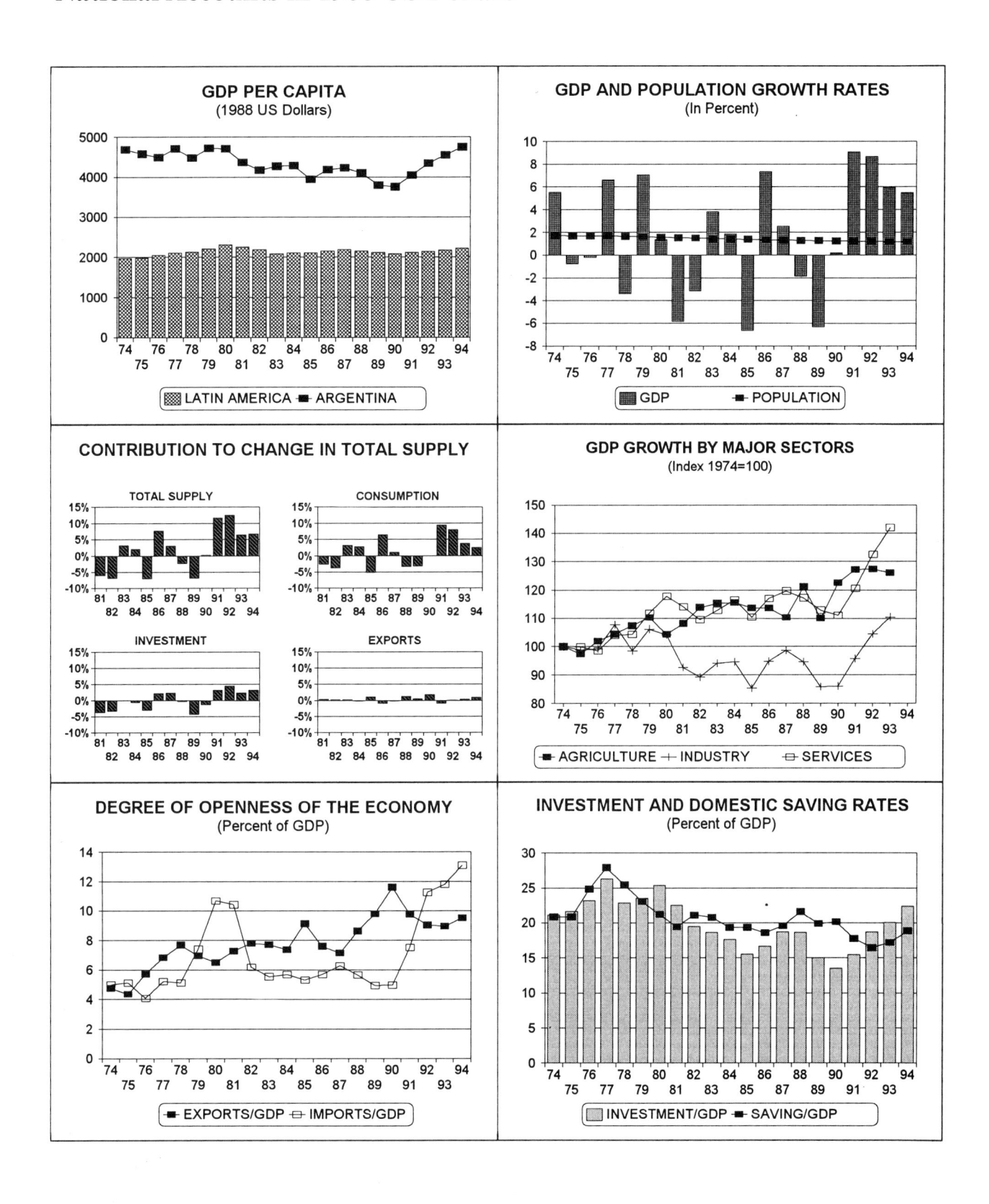

Statistics and Quantitative Analysis/IDB

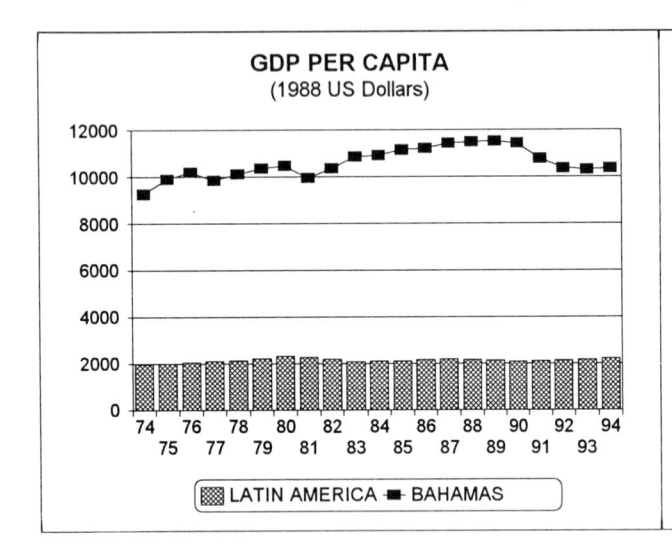

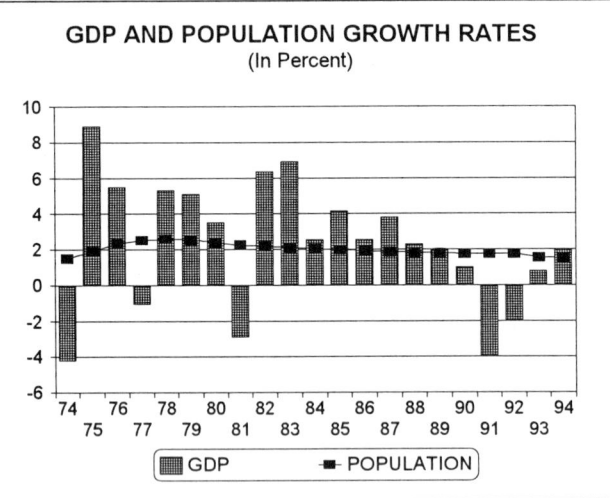

BAHAMAS
National Accounts in 1988 US Dollars

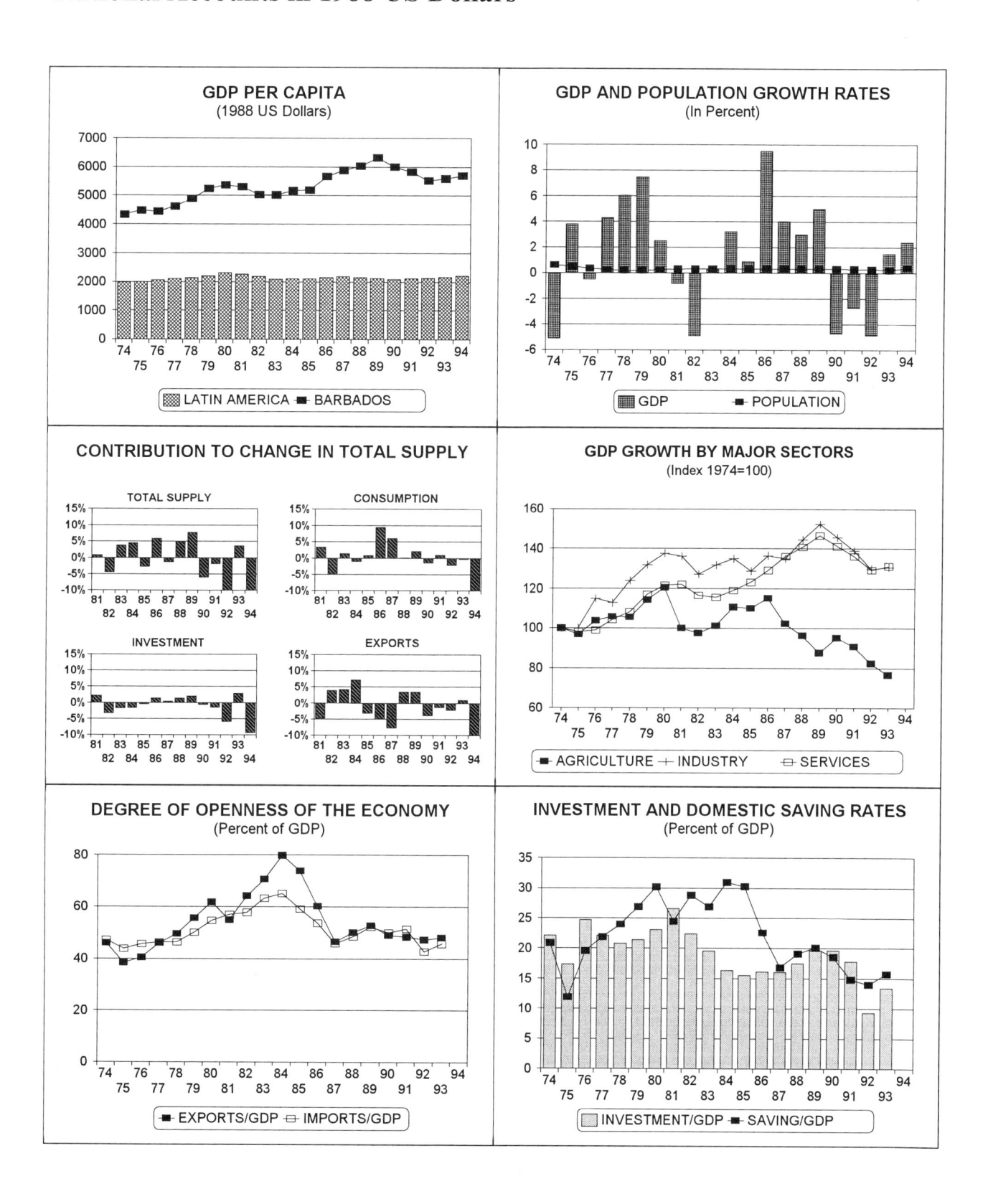

BARBADOS
National Accounts in 1988 US Dollars

Statistics and Quantitative Analysis/IDB

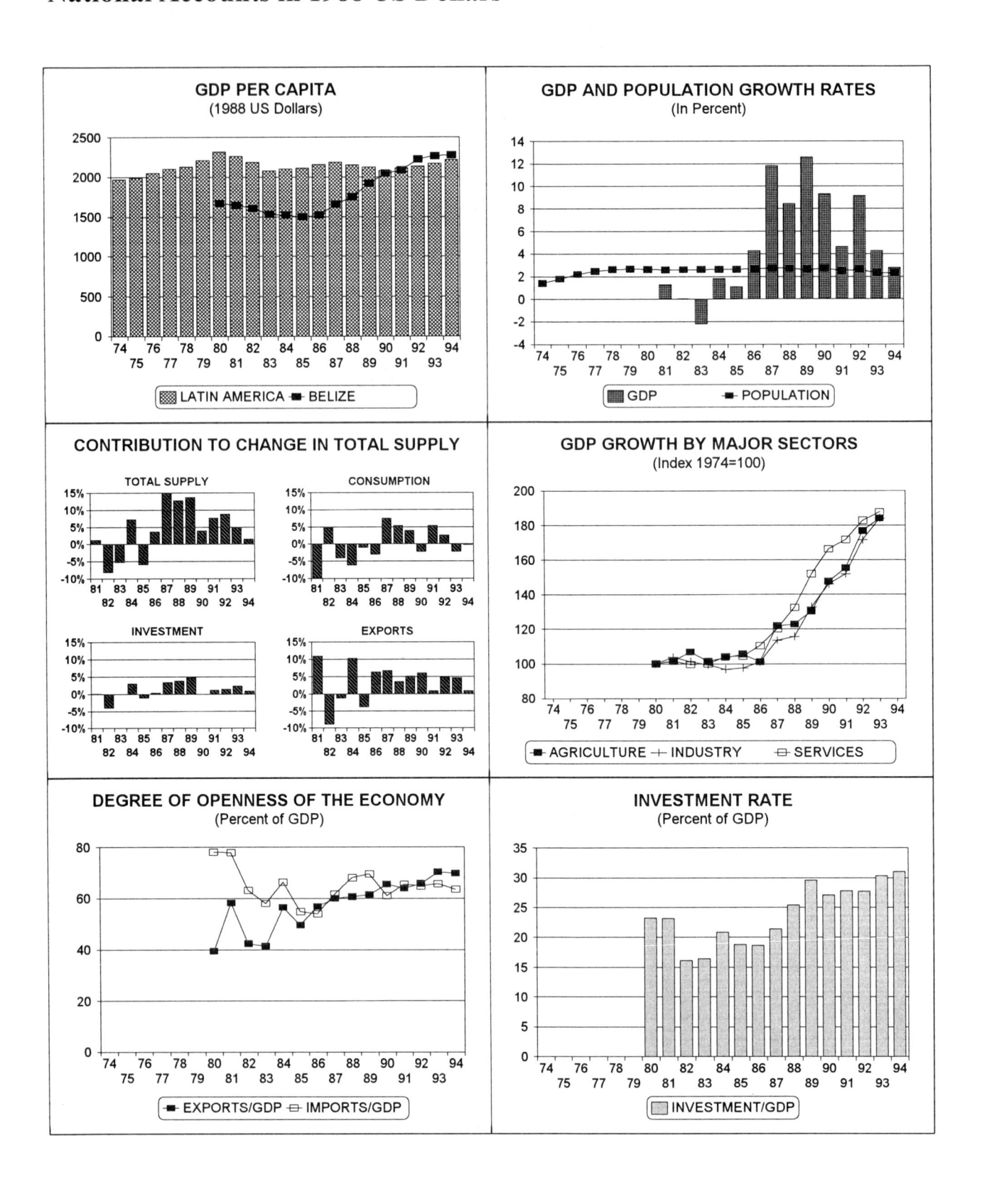

BELIZE
National Accounts in 1988 US Dollars

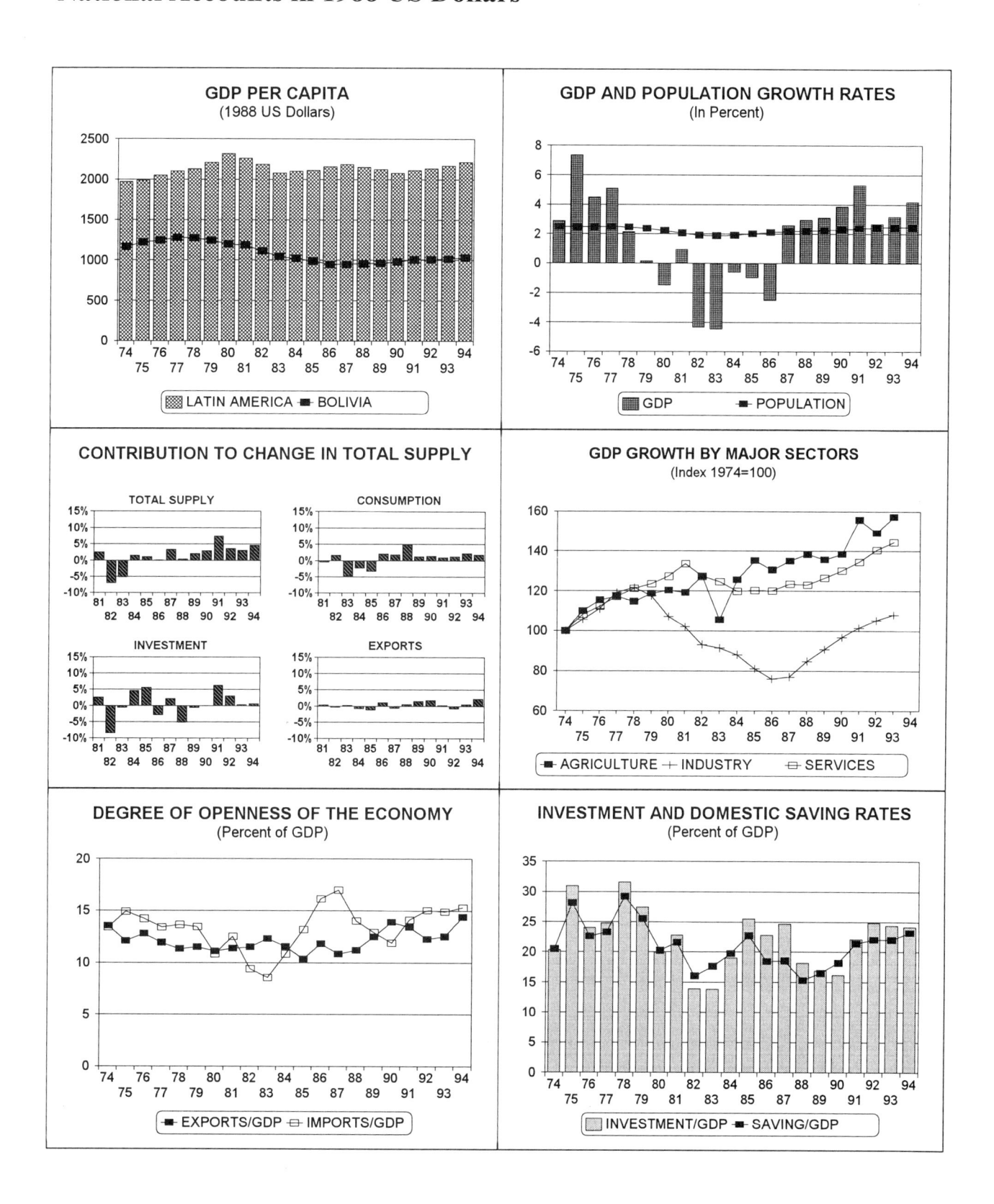

BOLIVIA
National Accounts in 1988 US Dollars

GDP PER CAPITA
(1988 US Dollars)

LATIN AMERICA — BOLIVIA

GDP AND POPULATION GROWTH RATES
(In Percent)

GDP — POPULATION

CONTRIBUTION TO CHANGE IN TOTAL SUPPLY

TOTAL SUPPLY | CONSUMPTION
INVESTMENT | EXPORTS

GDP GROWTH BY MAJOR SECTORS
(Index 1974=100)

AGRICULTURE — INDUSTRY — SERVICES

DEGREE OF OPENNESS OF THE ECONOMY
(Percent of GDP)

EXPORTS/GDP — IMPORTS/GDP

INVESTMENT AND DOMESTIC SAVING RATES
(Percent of GDP)

INVESTMENT/GDP — SAVING/GDP

Statistics and Quantitative Analysis/IDB

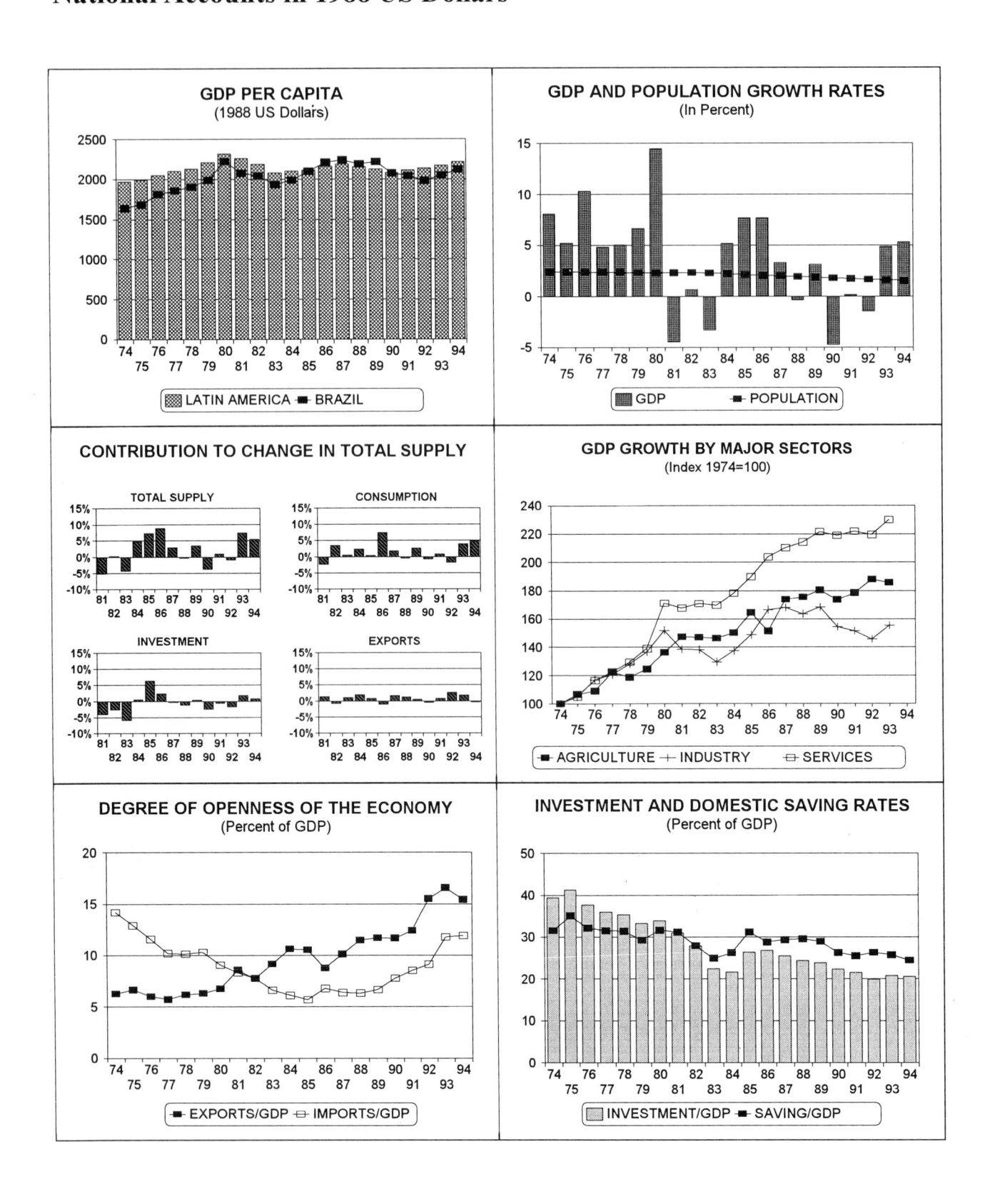

BRAZIL
National Accounts in 1988 US Dollars

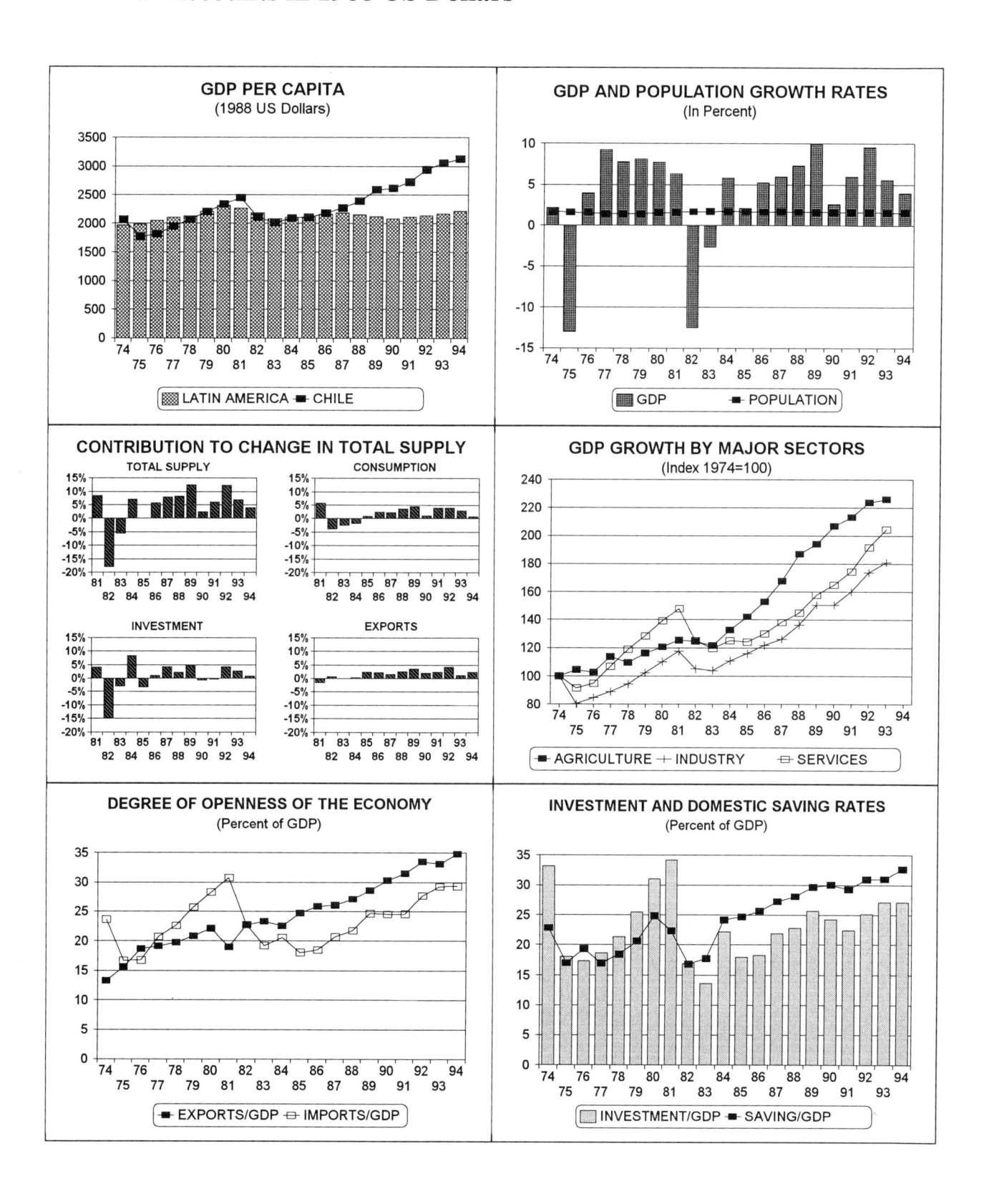

CHILE
National Accounts in 1988 US Dollars

Statistics and Quantitative Analysis/IDB

79

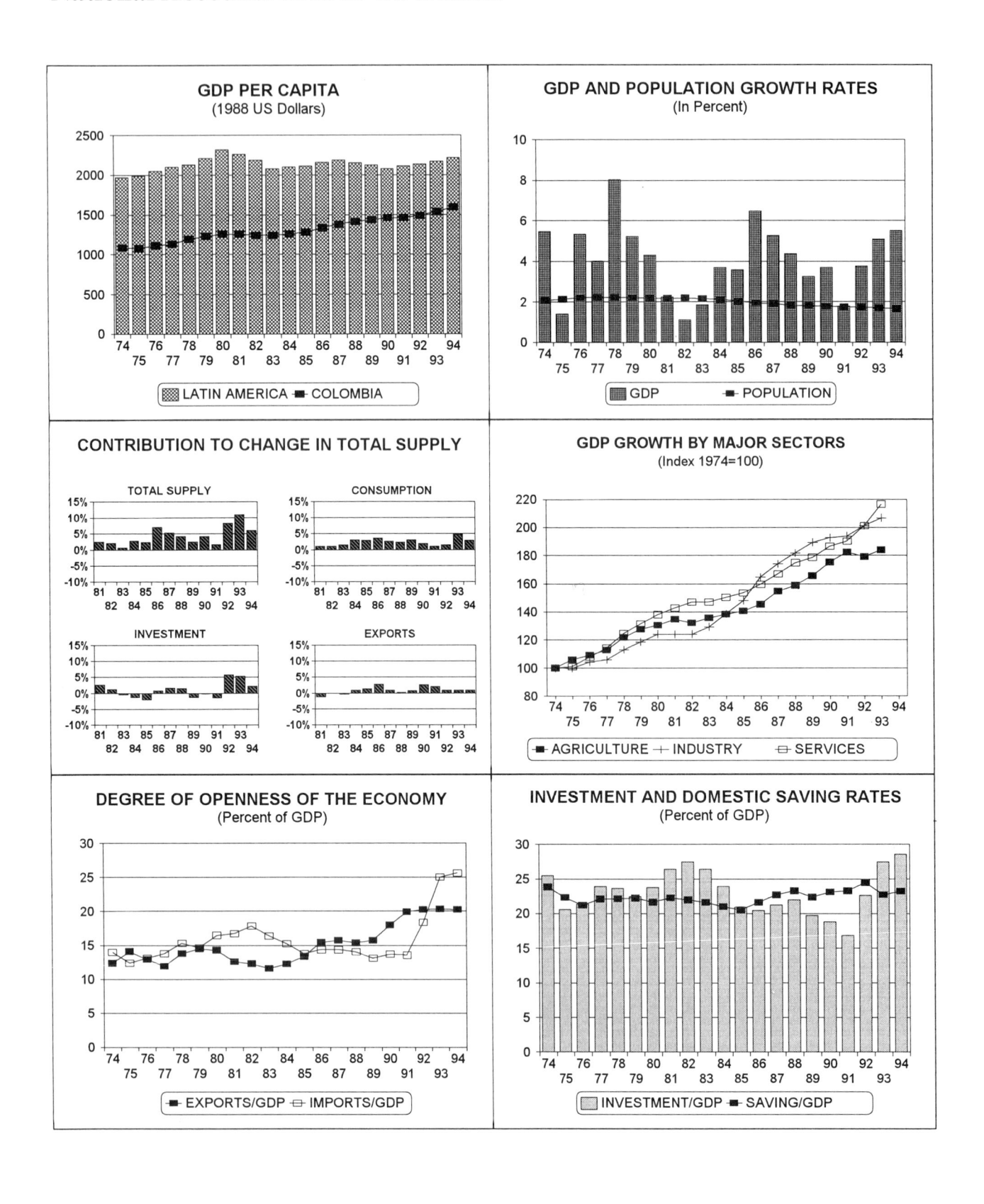

COLOMBIA
National Accounts in 1988 US Dollars

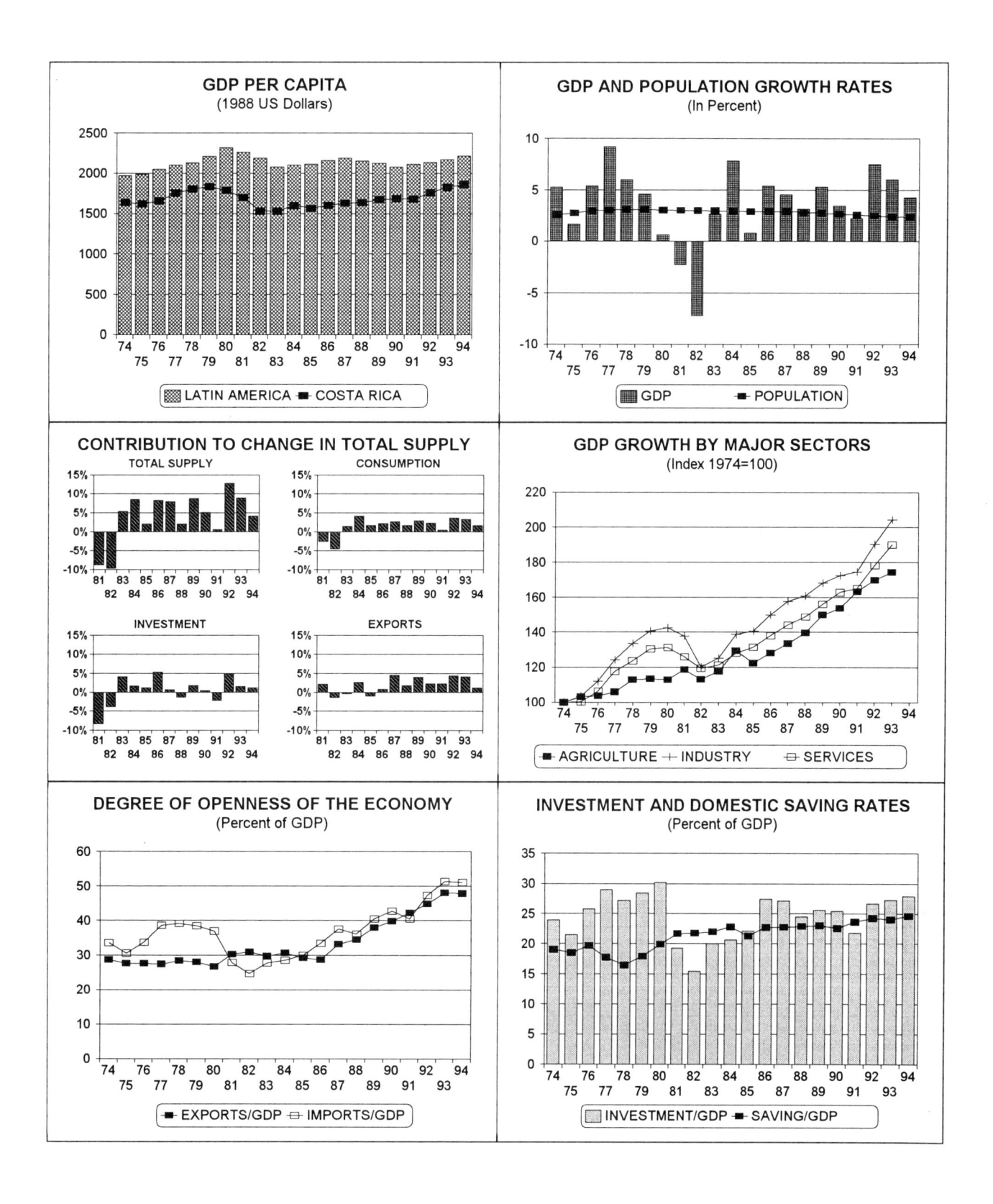

COSTA RICA
National Accounts in 1988 US Dollars

GDP PER CAPITA
(1988 US Dollars)

GDP AND POPULATION GROWTH RATES
(In Percent)

CONTRIBUTION TO CHANGE IN TOTAL SUPPLY

GDP GROWTH BY MAJOR SECTORS
(Index 1974=100)

DEGREE OF OPENNESS OF THE ECONOMY
(Percent of GDP)

INVESTMENT AND DOMESTIC SAVING RATES
(Percent of GDP)

Statistics and Quantitative Analysis/IDB

DOMINICAN REPUBLIC
National Accounts in 1988 US Dollars

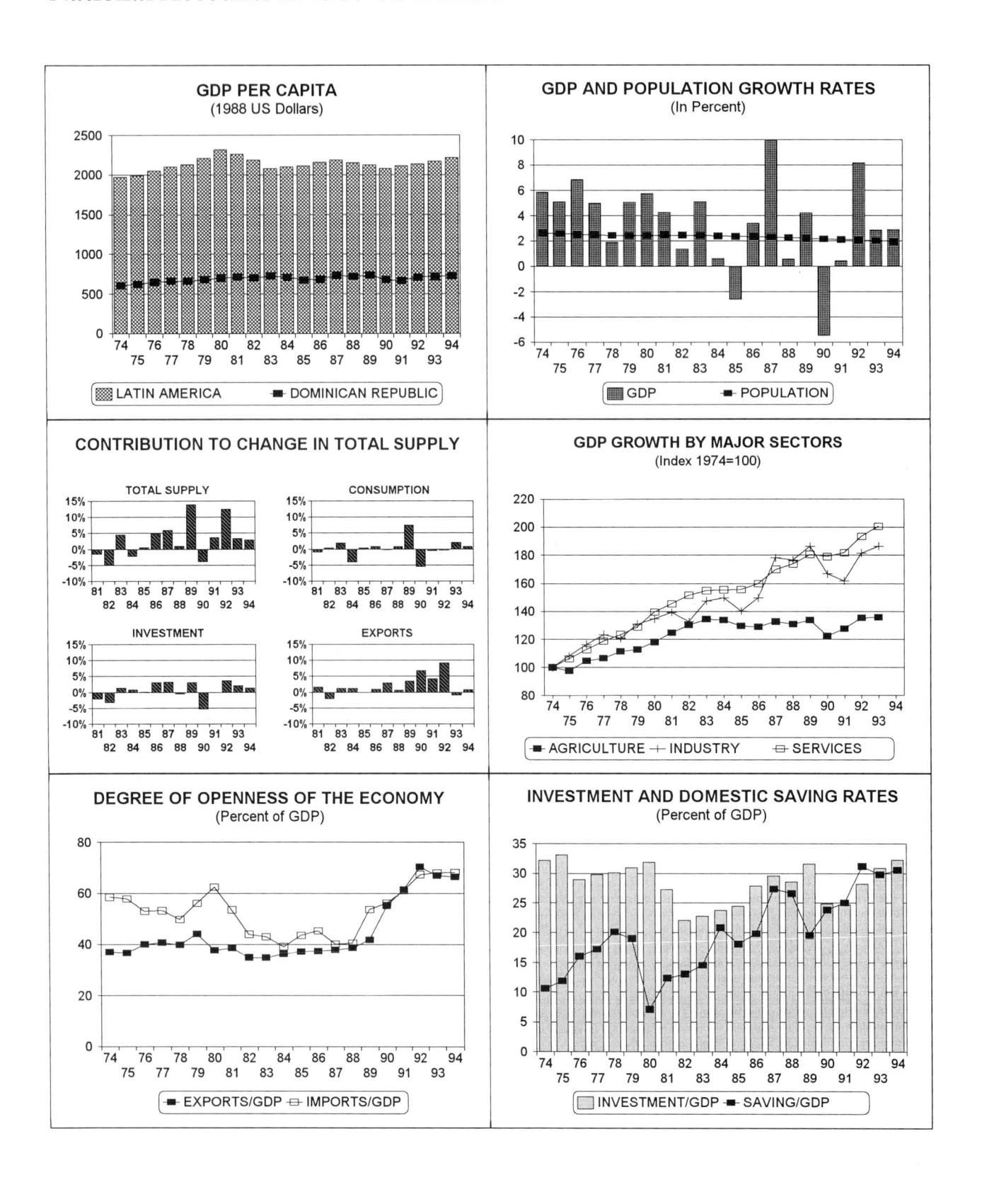

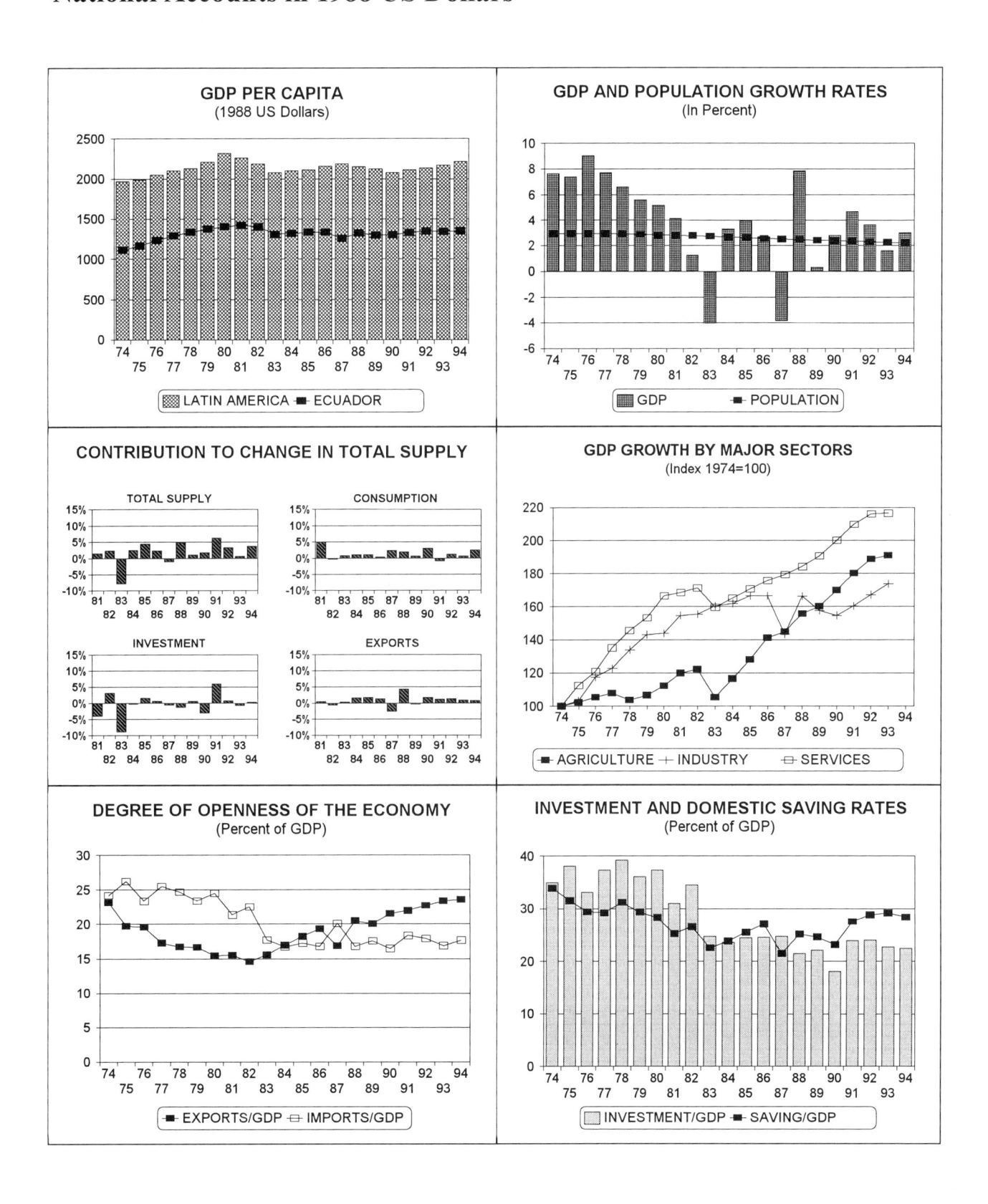

ECUADOR
National Accounts in 1988 US Dollars

Statistics and Quantitative Analysis/IDB

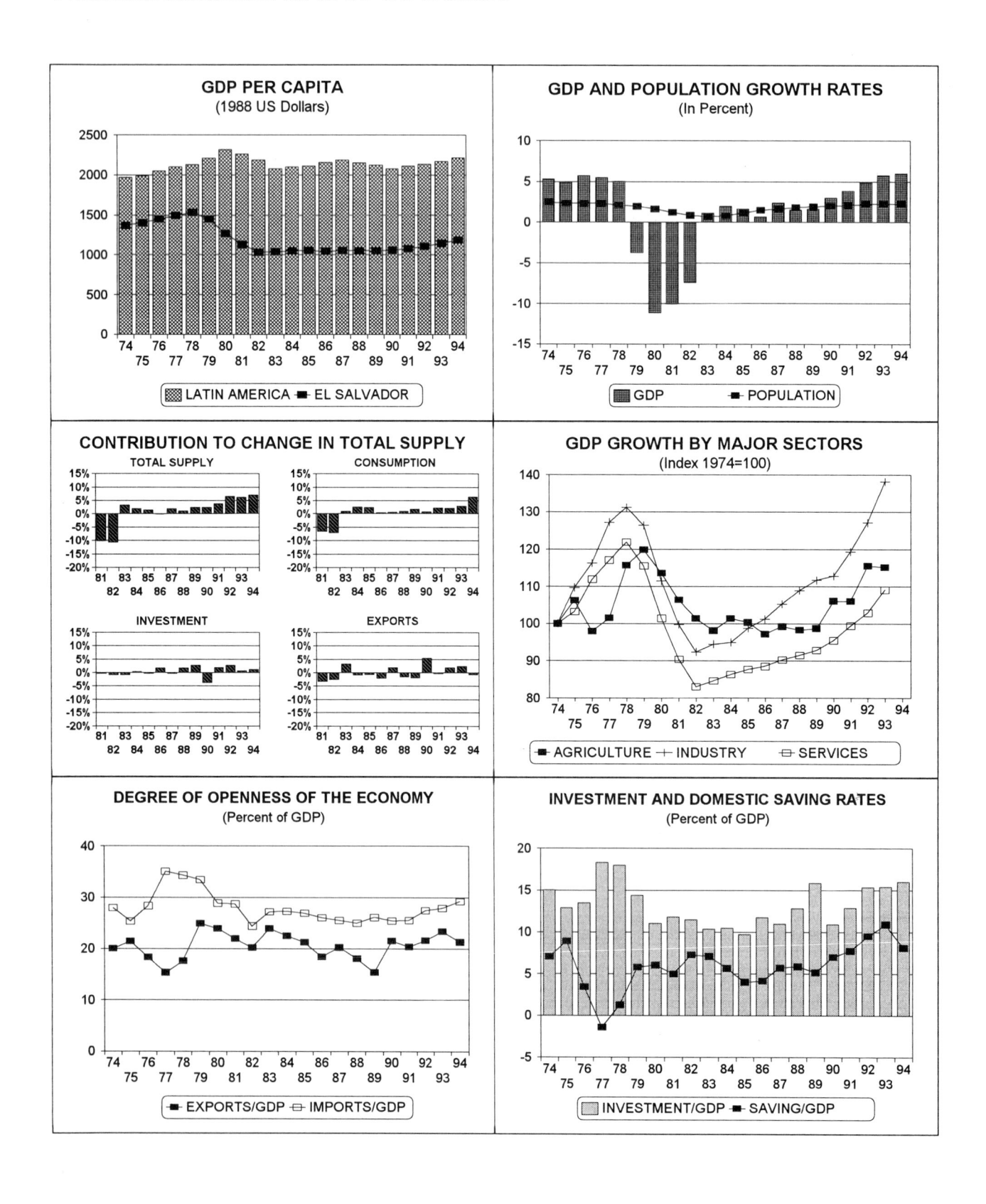

EL SALVADOR
National Accounts in 1988 US Dollars

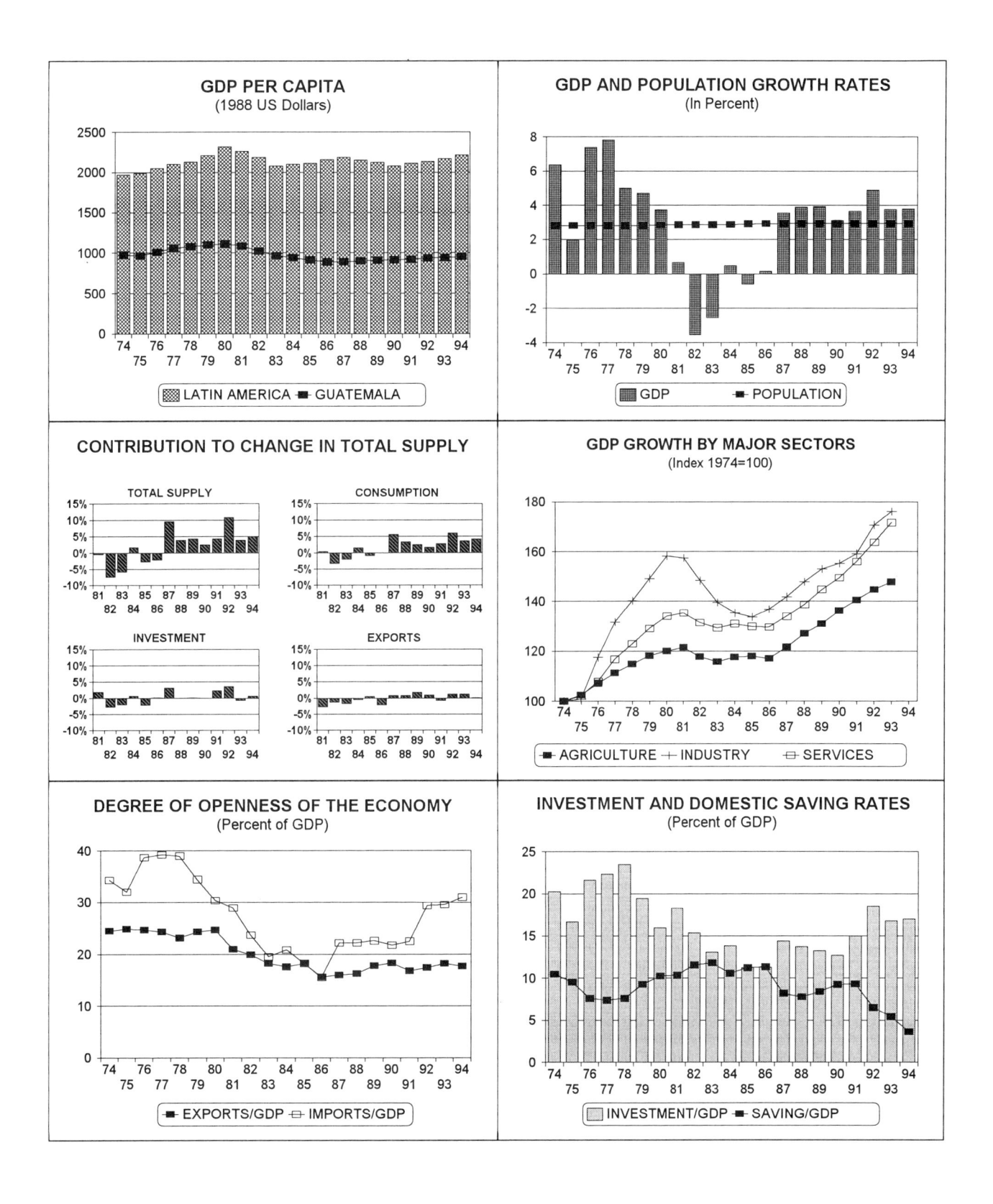

GUATEMALA
National Accounts in 1988 US Dollars

Statistics and Quantitative Analysis/IDB

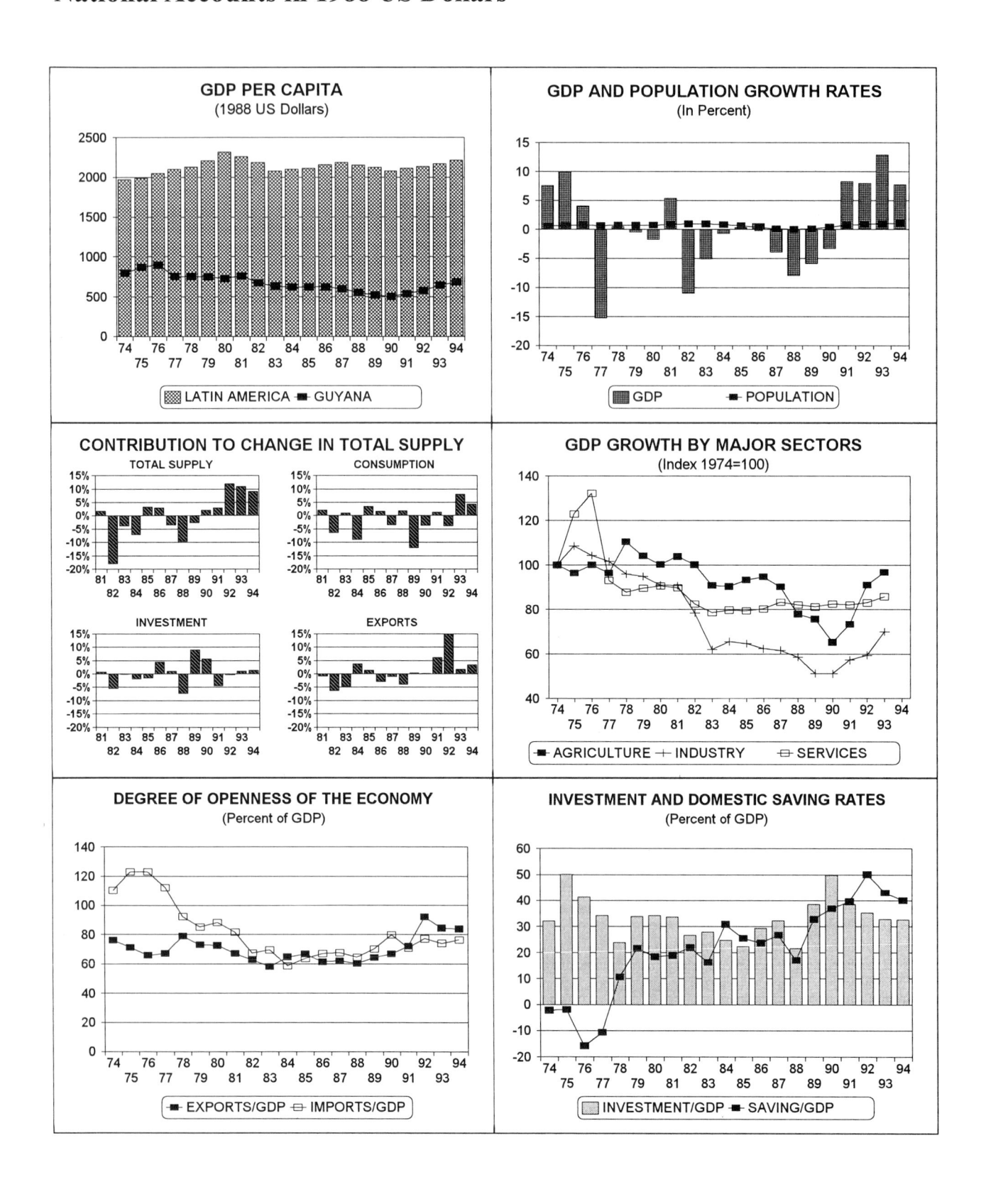

GUYANA
National Accounts in 1988 US Dollars

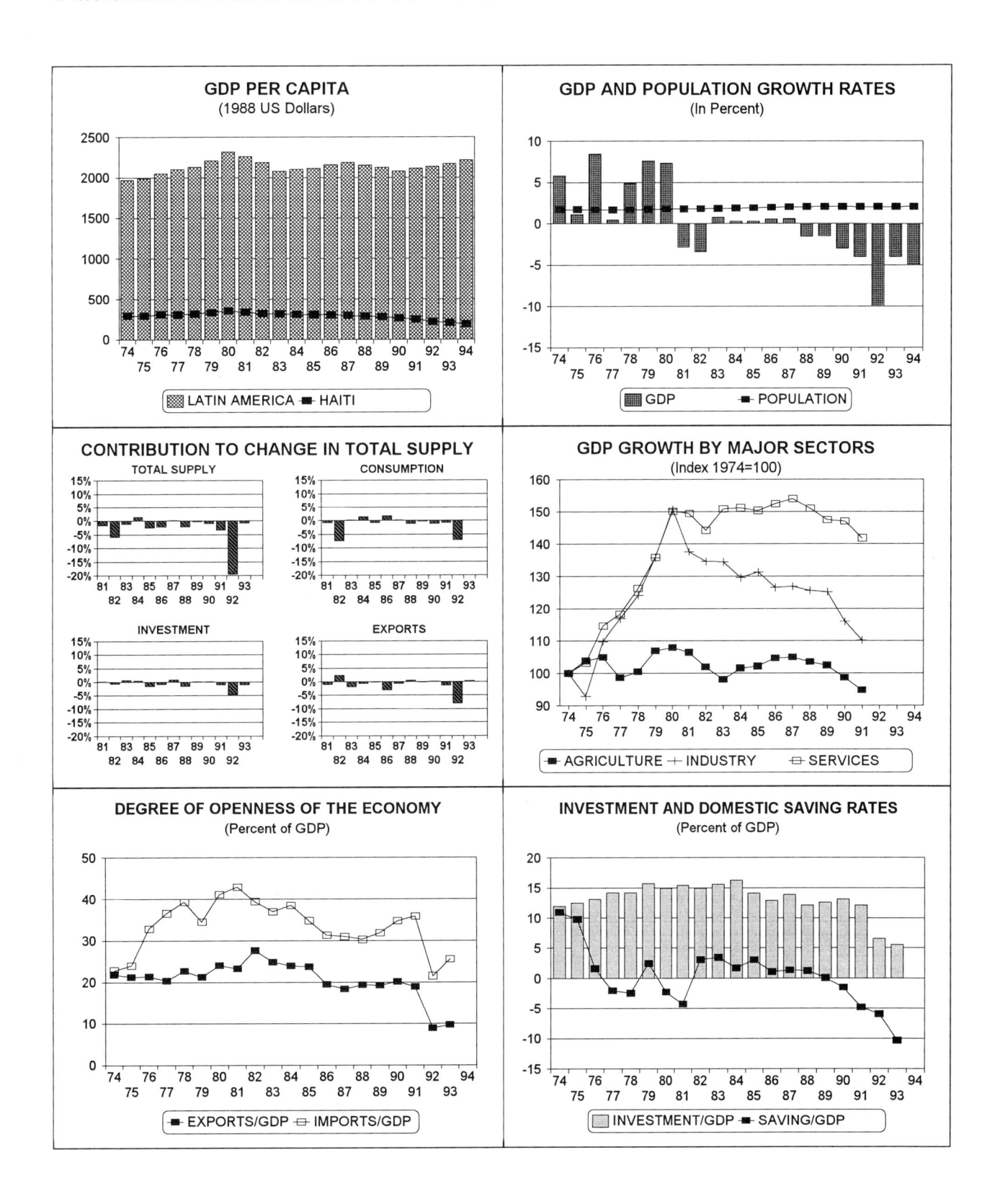

HAITI
National Accounts in 1988 US Dollars

GDP PER CAPITA
(1988 US Dollars)

LATIN AMERICA / HAITI

GDP AND POPULATION GROWTH RATES
(In Percent)

GDP / POPULATION

CONTRIBUTION TO CHANGE IN TOTAL SUPPLY

TOTAL SUPPLY

CONSUMPTION

INVESTMENT

EXPORTS

GDP GROWTH BY MAJOR SECTORS
(Index 1974=100)

AGRICULTURE / INDUSTRY / SERVICES

DEGREE OF OPENNESS OF THE ECONOMY
(Percent of GDP)

EXPORTS/GDP / IMPORTS/GDP

INVESTMENT AND DOMESTIC SAVING RATES
(Percent of GDP)

INVESTMENT/GDP / SAVING/GDP

Statistics and Quantitative Analysis/IDB

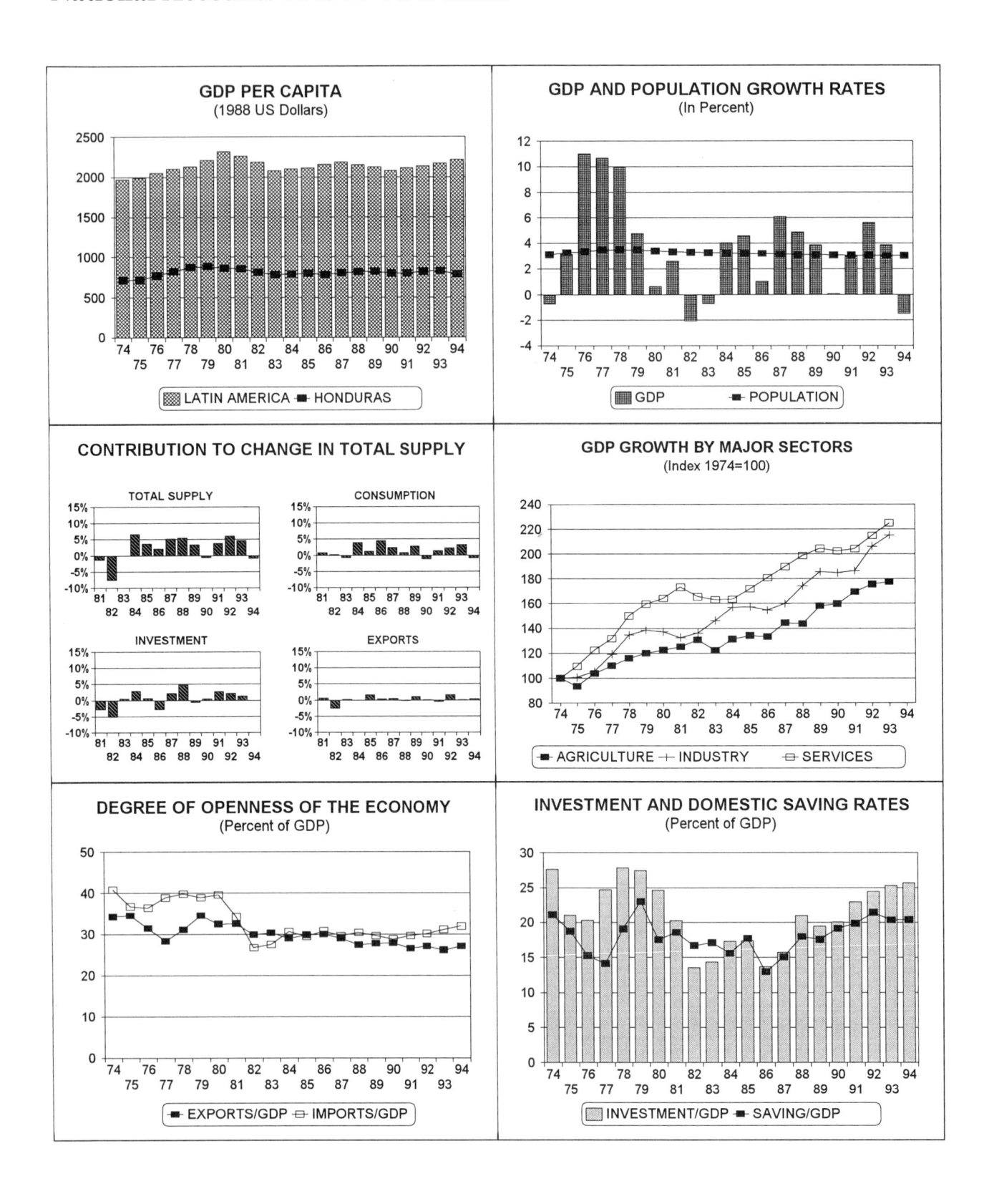

HONDURAS
National Accounts in 1988 US Dollars

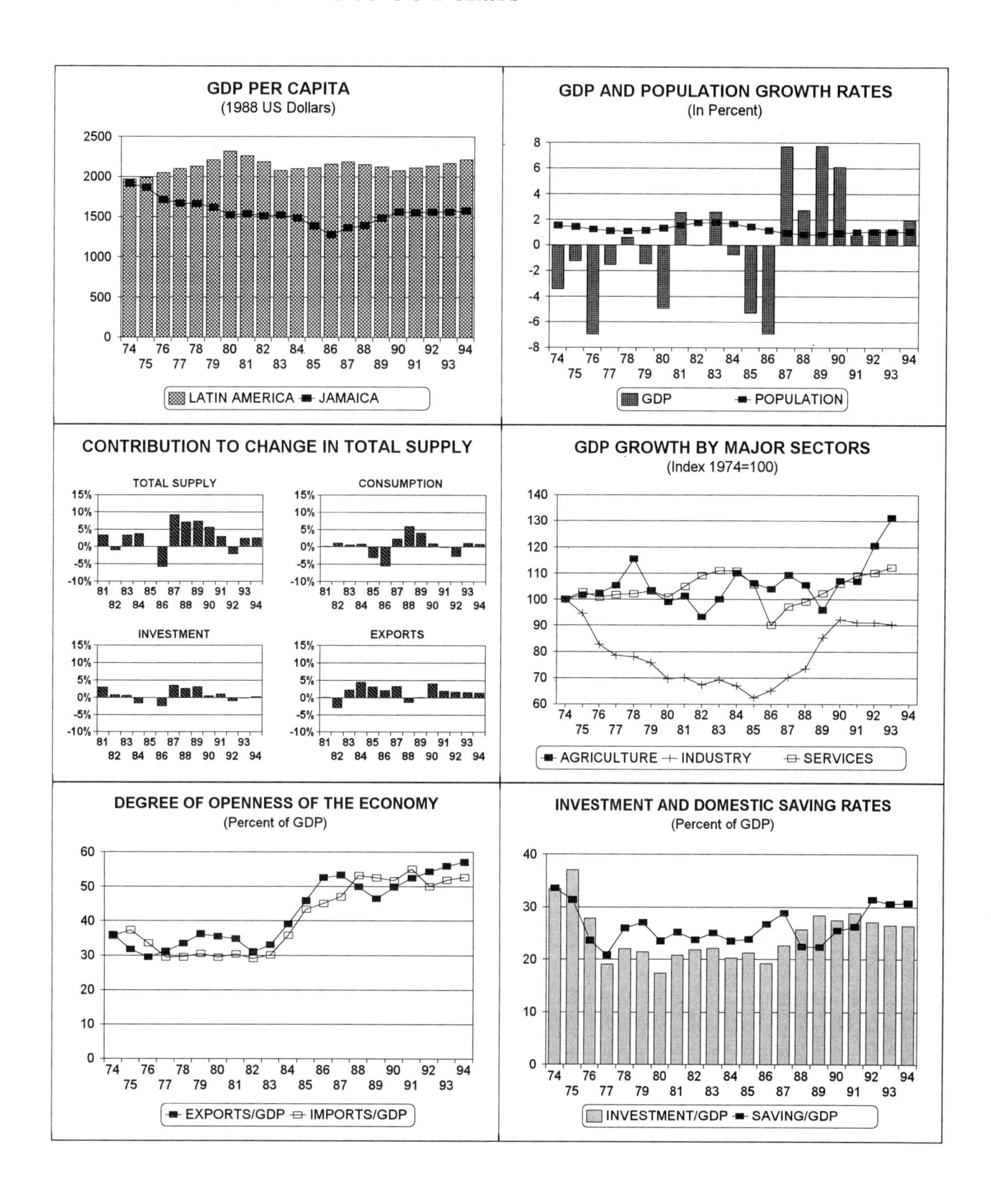

JAMAICA
National Accounts in 1988 US Dollars

Statistics and Quantitative Analysis/IDB

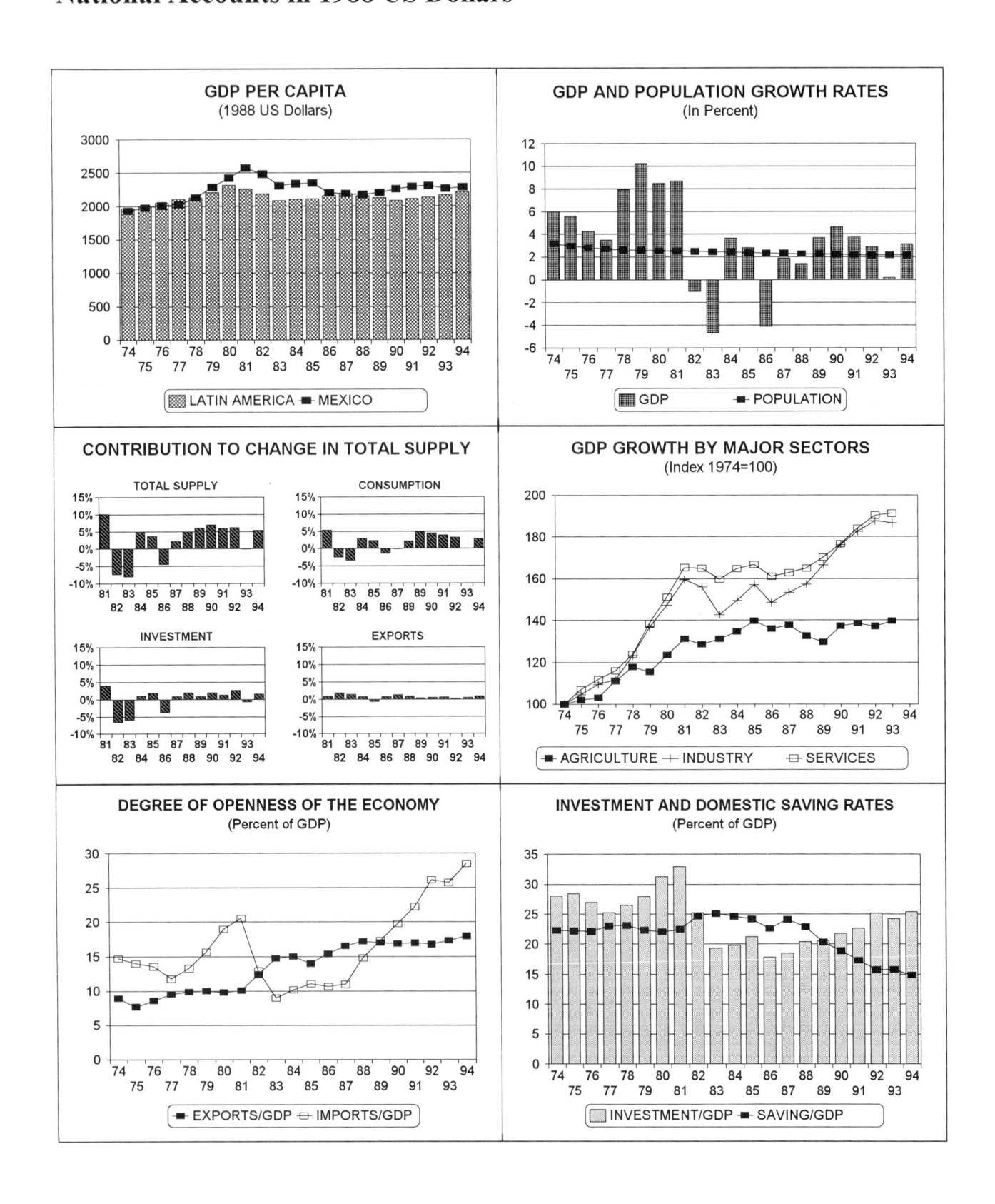

MEXICO
National Accounts in 1988 US Dollars

Statistics and Quantitative Analysis/IDB

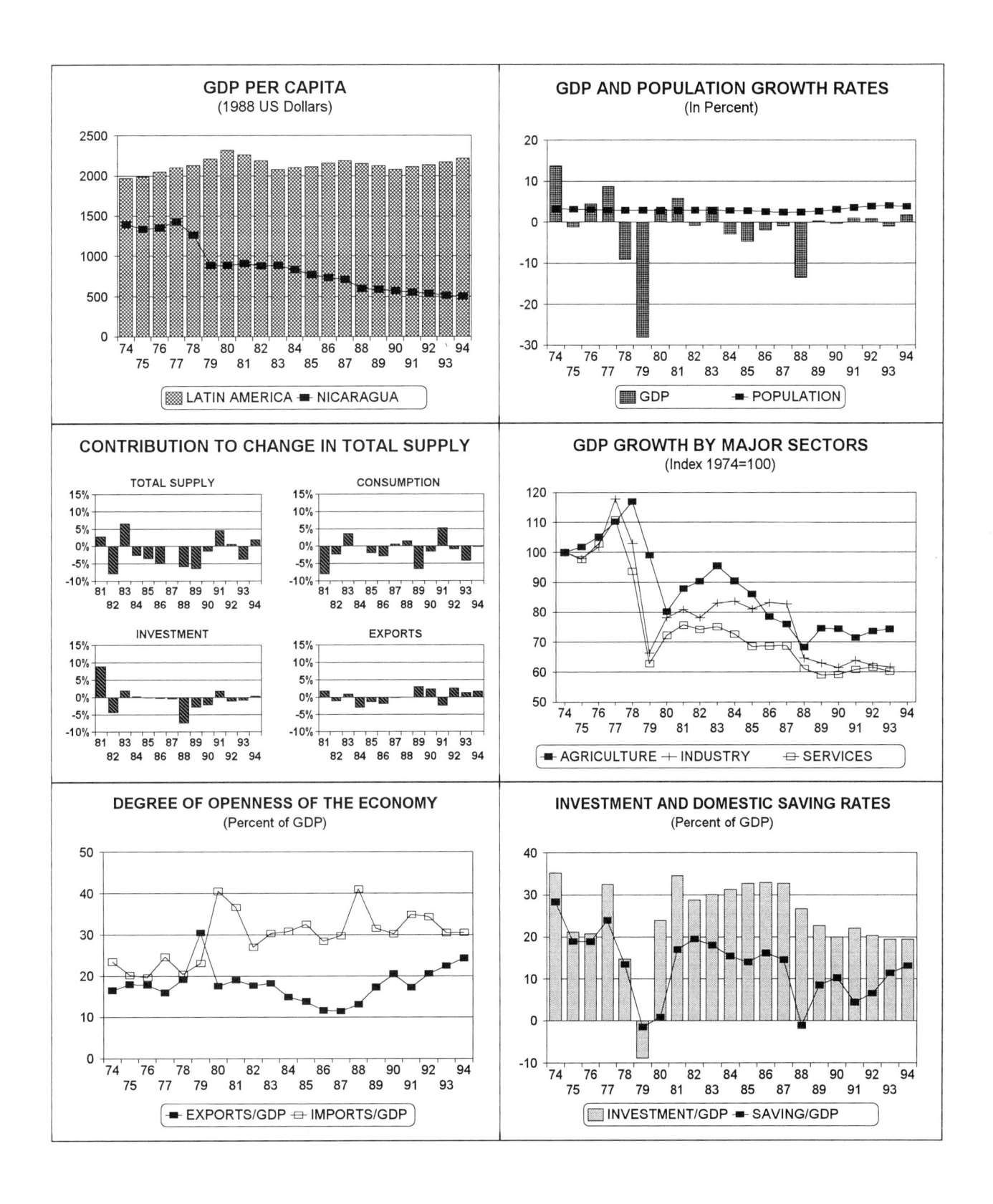

NICARAGUA
National Accounts in 1988 US Dollars

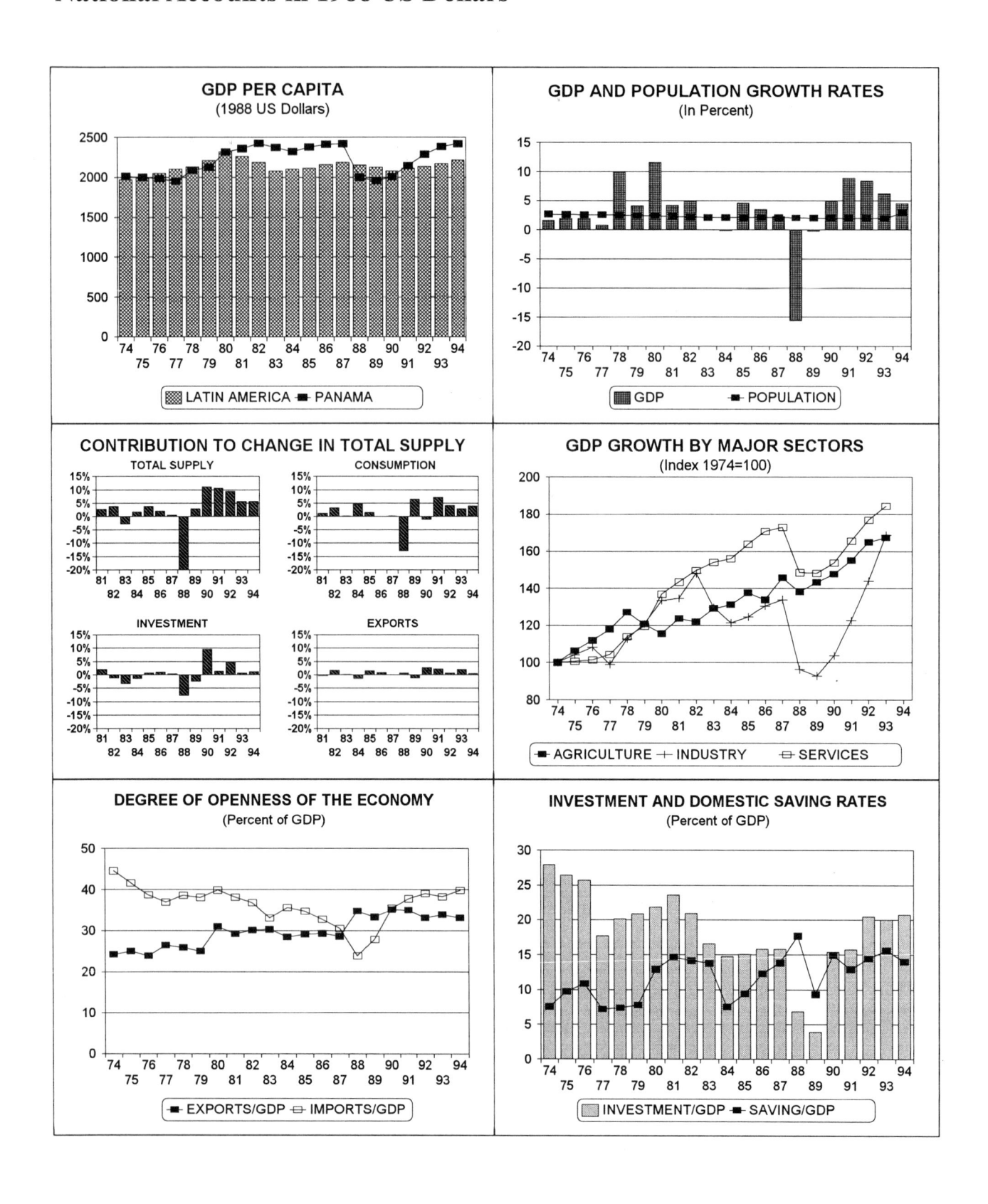

PANAMA
National Accounts in 1988 US Dollars

Statistics and Quantitative Analysis/IDB

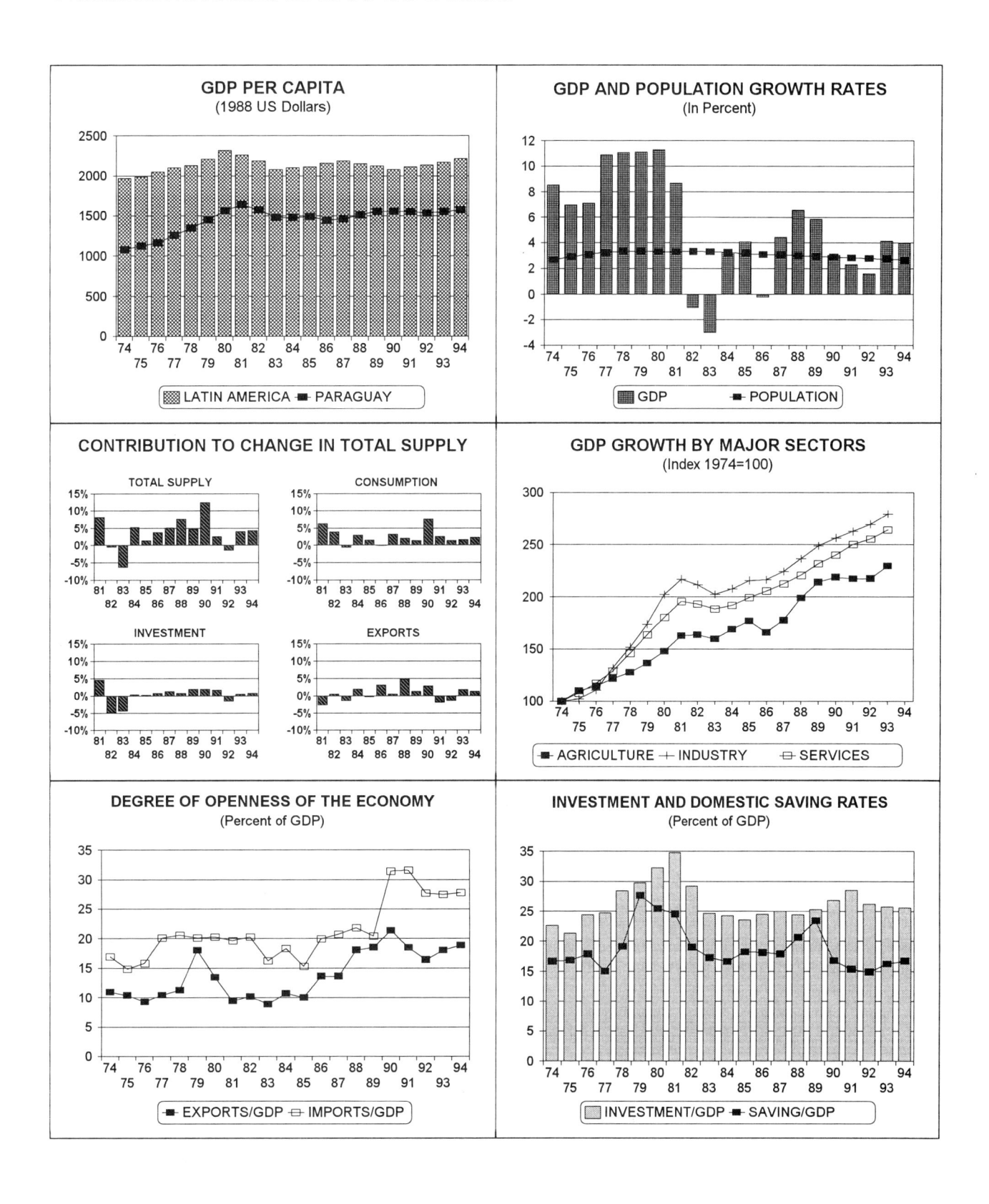

PARAGUAY
National Accounts in 1988 US Dollars

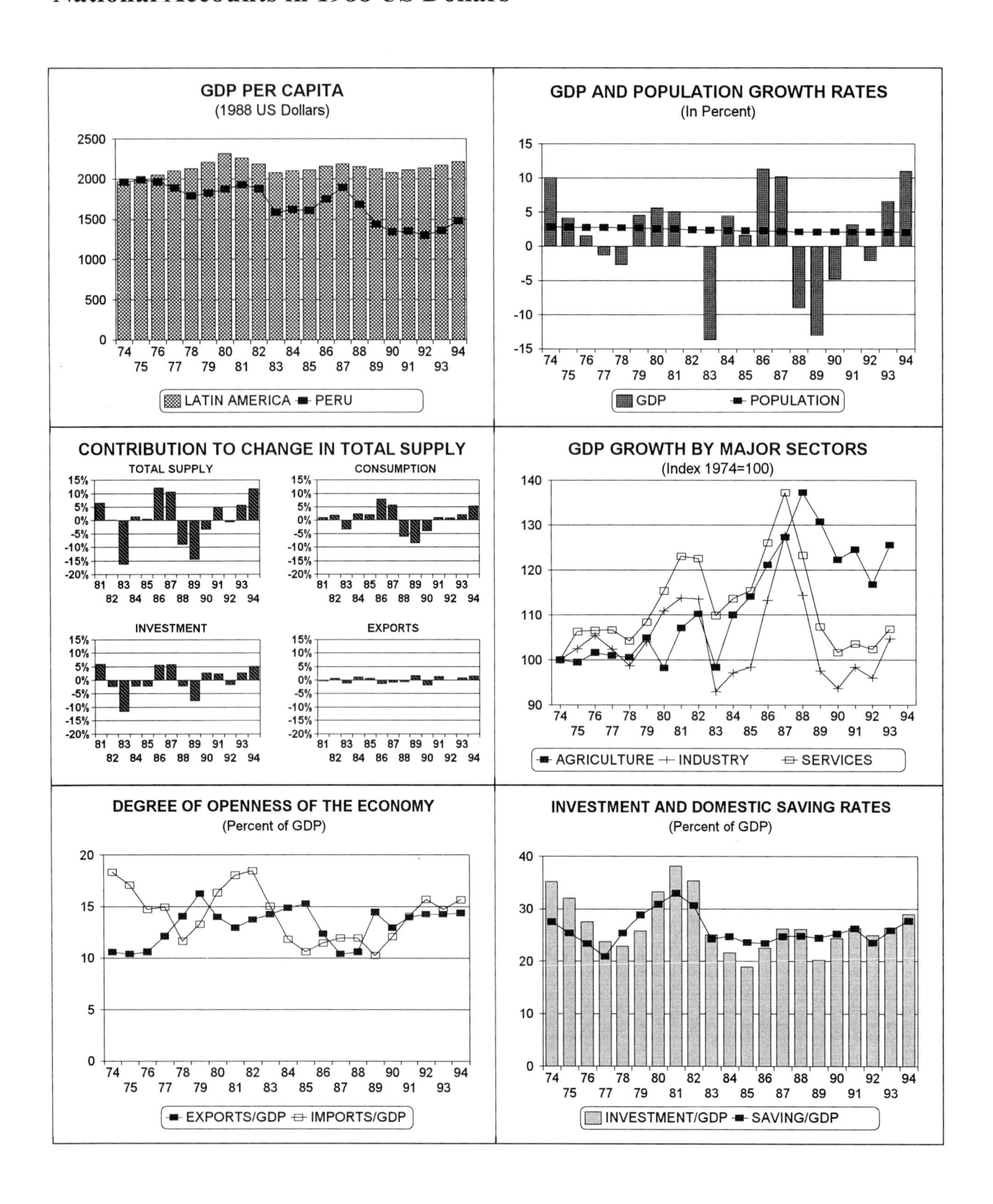

PERU
National Accounts in 1988 US Dollars

Statistics and Quantitative Analysis/IDB

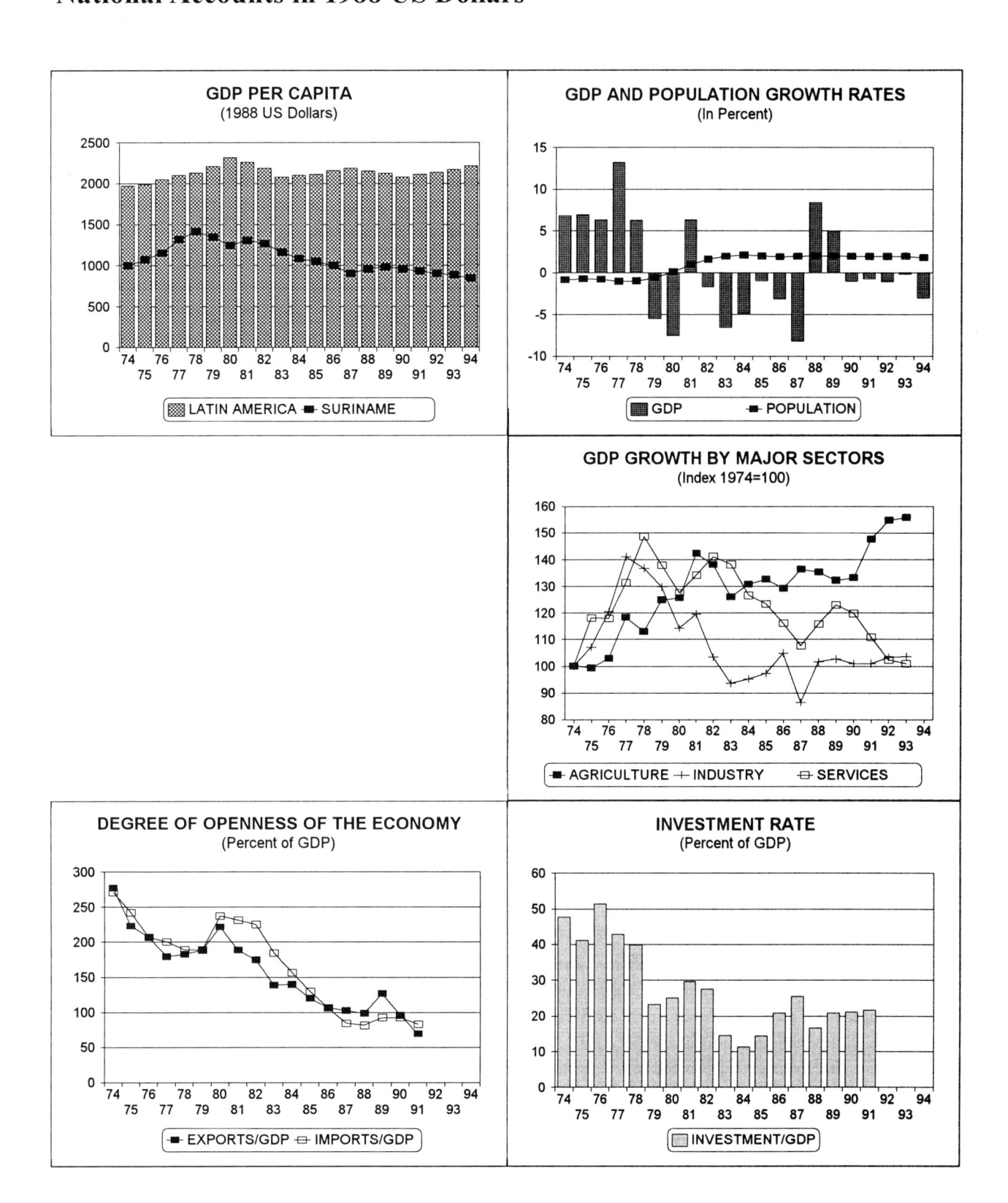

SURINAME
National Accounts in 1988 US Dollars

GDP PER CAPITA
(1988 US Dollars)

LATIN AMERICA — SURINAME

GDP AND POPULATION GROWTH RATES
(In Percent)

GDP — POPULATION

GDP GROWTH BY MAJOR SECTORS
(Index 1974=100)

AGRICULTURE — INDUSTRY — SERVICES

DEGREE OF OPENNESS OF THE ECONOMY
(Percent of GDP)

EXPORTS/GDP — IMPORTS/GDP

INVESTMENT RATE
(Percent of GDP)

INVESTMENT/GDP

Statistics and Quantitative Analysis/IDB

TRINIDAD AND TOBAGO
National Accounts in 1988 US Dollars

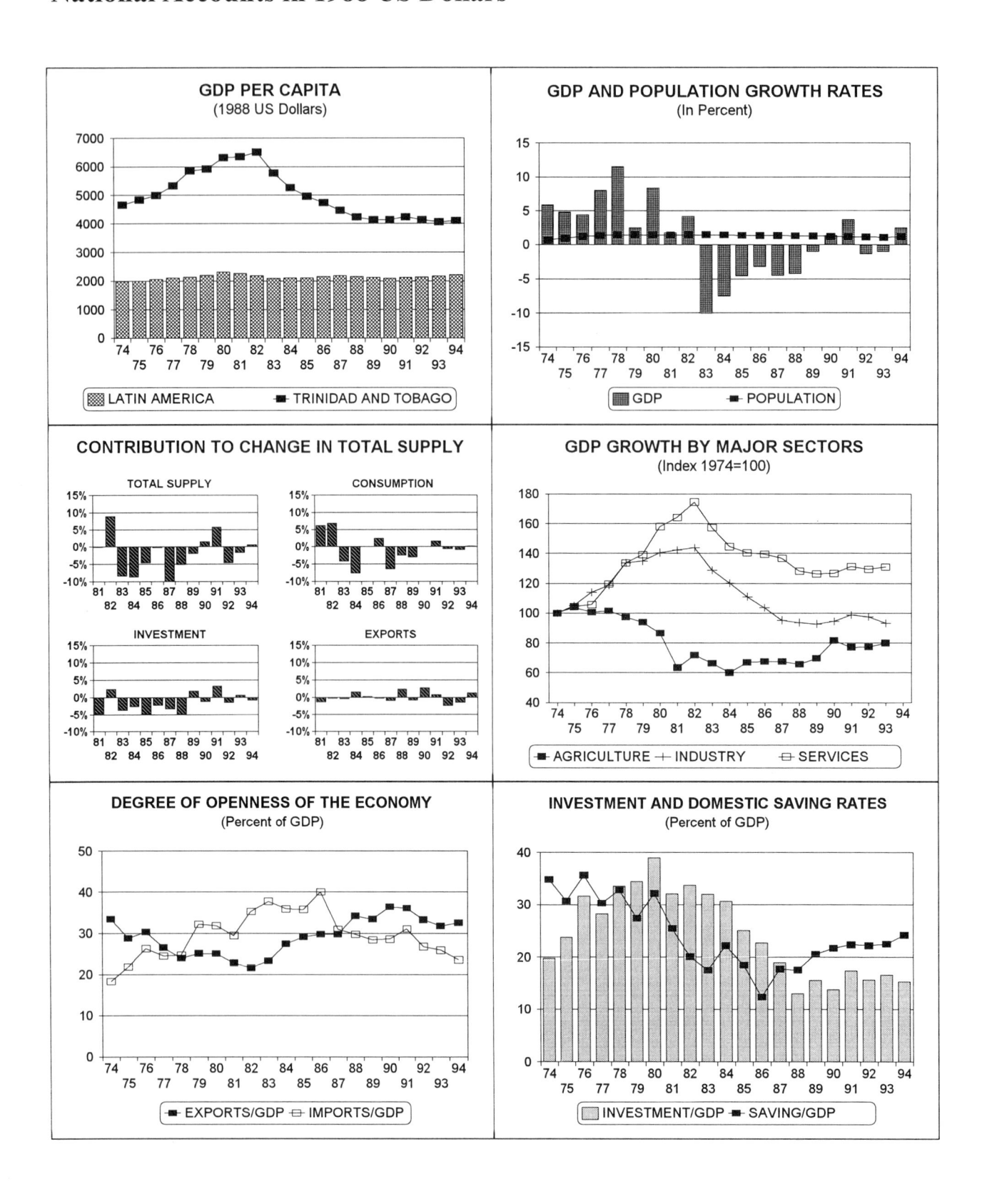

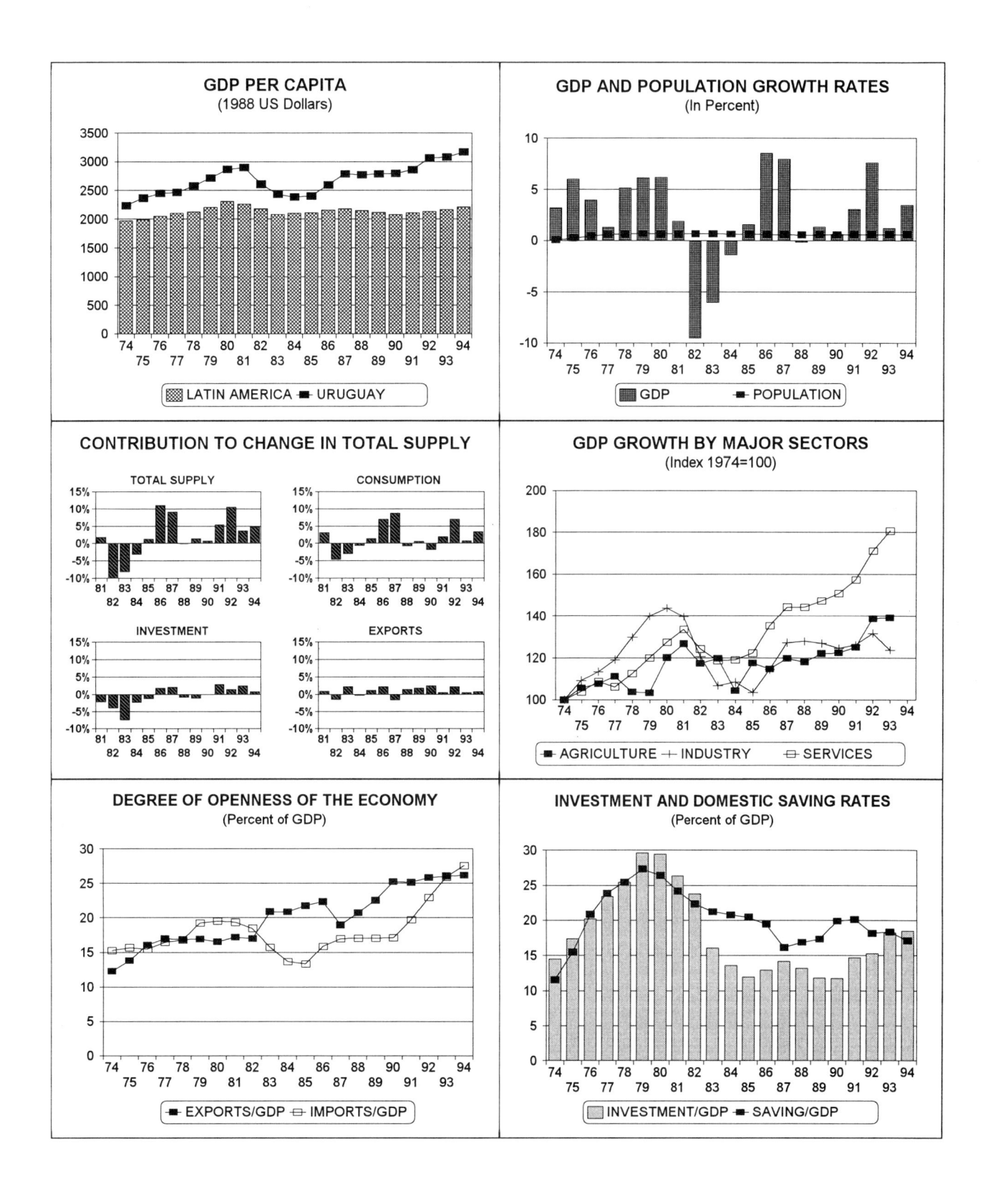

URUGUAY
National Accounts in 1988 US Dollars

GDP PER CAPITA
(1988 US Dollars)

LATIN AMERICA — URUGUAY

GDP AND POPULATION GROWTH RATES
(In Percent)

GDP — POPULATION

CONTRIBUTION TO CHANGE IN TOTAL SUPPLY

TOTAL SUPPLY

CONSUMPTION

INVESTMENT

EXPORTS

GDP GROWTH BY MAJOR SECTORS
(Index 1974=100)

AGRICULTURE — INDUSTRY — SERVICES

DEGREE OF OPENNESS OF THE ECONOMY
(Percent of GDP)

EXPORTS/GDP — IMPORTS/GDP

INVESTMENT AND DOMESTIC SAVING RATES
(Percent of GDP)

INVESTMENT/GDP — SAVING/GDP

Statistics and Quantitative Analysis/IDB

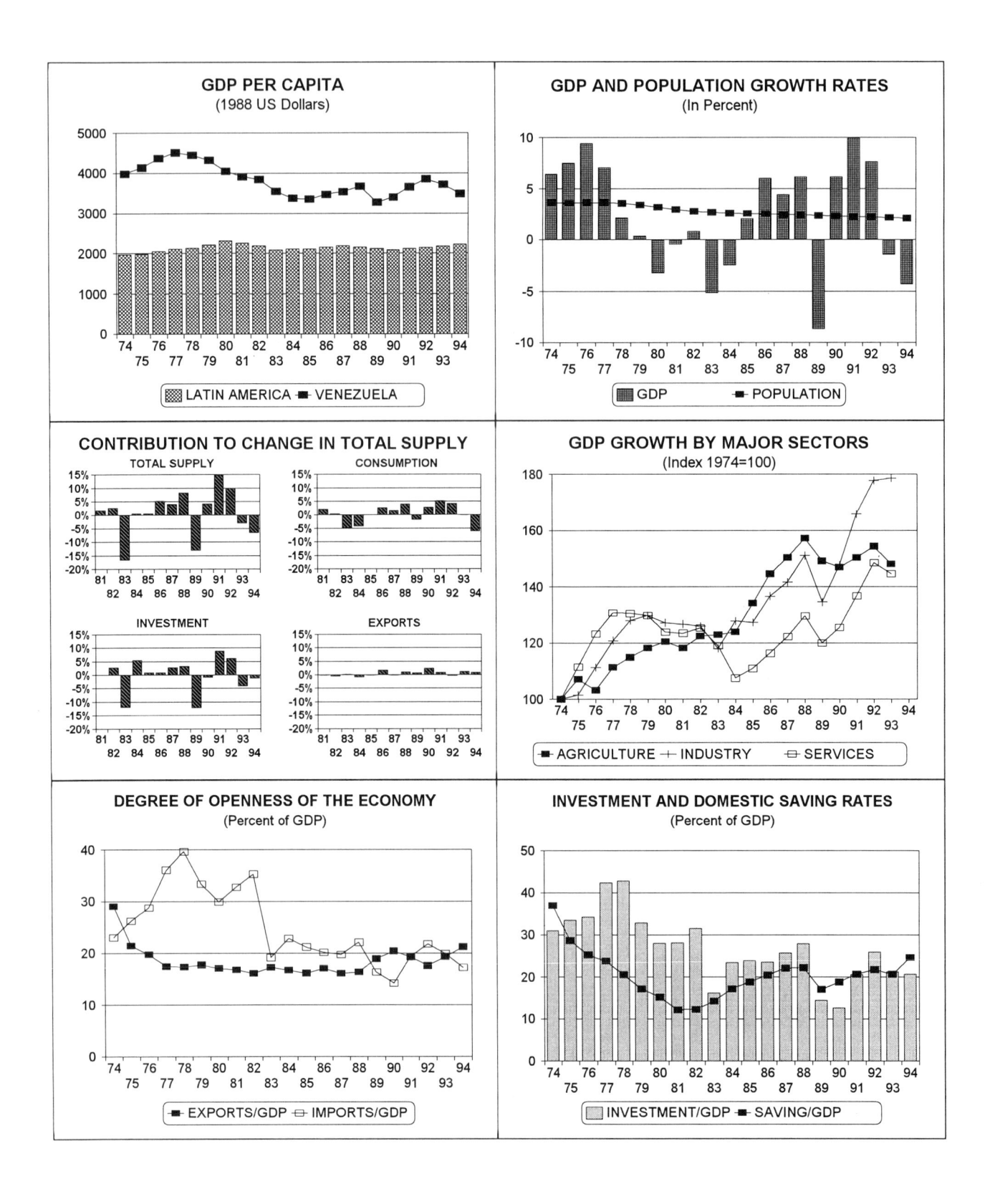

VENEZUELA
National Accounts in 1988 US Dollars

BALANCE OF PAYMENTS

Geographisches Institut
der Universität Kiel

BALANCE OF PAYMENTS

Data are from the International Monetary Fund (IMF) Balance of Payments tapes and IDB estimates for terminal years. Descriptions of the graphs follow:

1. CURRENT ACCOUNT BALANCE AS A PERCENT OF GDP

GDP in current dollars is calculated by using IDB estimated conversion factors. Expressed as a percentage of GDP, a Current Account deficit indicates the degree of external financing requirements. Unrequited Transfers from abroad (mainly workers remittances and official grants) are not considered as external financing since they are part of the Current Account Balance. As an example, in the case of Haiti, where grants are important, the degree of external financing appears low in some years compared to other countries.

2. CURRENT ACCOUNT COMPONENTS AS A PERCENT OF GDP

The graph shows a breakdown of the Current Account Balance between the balance of Goods, Non-Financial Services (NFS) and Transfers on the one hand and Net Investment Income on the other. Net Investment Income includes interest (on an accrued basis), dividends on shares and profits of enterprises. It almost always appears negative, reflecting the burden of external debt. The progressive drop in international interest rates since 1982 together with the reduction of external debt as a percent of GDP in the last few years, explains the decrease in interest payments in many countries.

3. EXPORTS AND IMPORTS OF GOODS, FOB

The graph shows for each country the level of total Exports (fob) and Imports (fob) of goods vis-a-vis the world as well as whithin Latin America. In the case of the four economic regions or Latin America, the graph indicates the level of total exports and imports vis-a-vis the world, on the left scale, and the percentage of intraregional trade, on the right scale.

4. PRIVATE AND GOVERNMENT CAPITAL FLOWS

Private capital flows are inflows net of outflows from the Non-Monetary Private Sector of the country. The Private Sector is the part of the economy most likely to be affected by market forces. It can be described as the Enterprise Sector (and therefore includes Government-owned Enterprises). Government capital flows are inflows net of outflows from the the government and the Central Monetary Institutions.

5. INVESTMENT IN THE PRIVATE SECTOR AS A PERCENT OF GDP

The graph shows the net flows, as a percent of GDP, of Direct and Private Portfolio Investment from abroad. Net Foreign Direct Investment includes re-invested earnings. Participation of foreign capital in national companies is considered as Direct Investment when their purchase of shares gives them a controlling voice in the enterprise, like in various recent privatizations operations.

Portfolio Investment includes essentially, transactions in equity securities and debt securities (mainly international bonds and treasury bills). Debt securities may be issued in local currency but must be held by non-residents. Of all the capital flows considered here, only bonds are debt-creating financial flows.

6. STOCK OF INTERNATIONAL RESERVES IN MONTHS OF IMPORTS OF GOODS

The end-year Stock of International Reserves (Total Reserves minus Gold as published by the IMF) is calculated in months of imports of goods.

Country Notes

Argentina
After 1989, the Current Account includes an estimate of interest receipts on forign assets held abroad by residents. It also includes transfers of retirement payments to residents from abroad. Because of this methodological change, data after and before 1989 are not strictly comparable.

Belize
Data are available only from 1983.

LATIN AMERICA
Balance of Payments in US Dollars

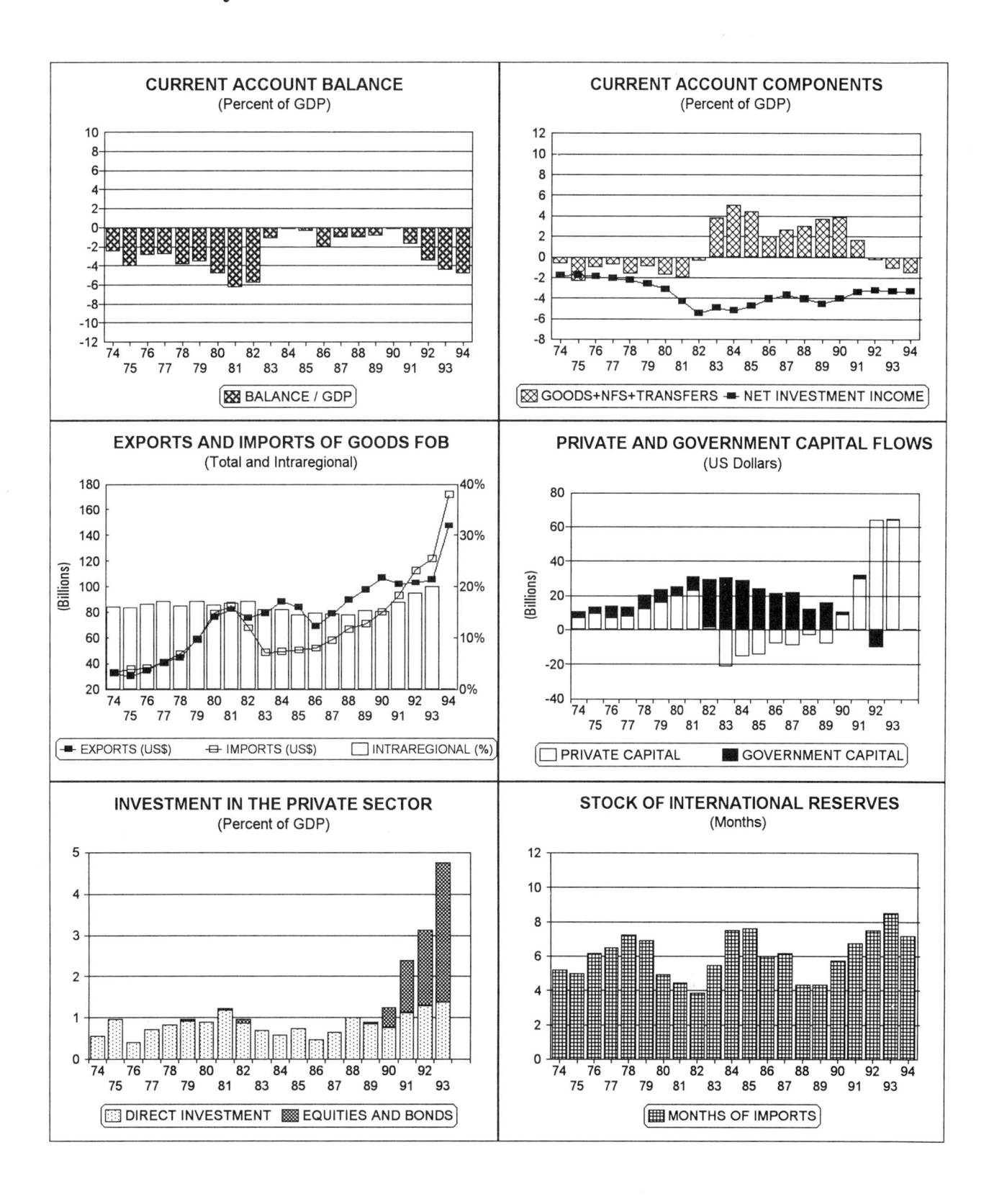

ANDEAN GROUP
Balance of Payments in US Dollars

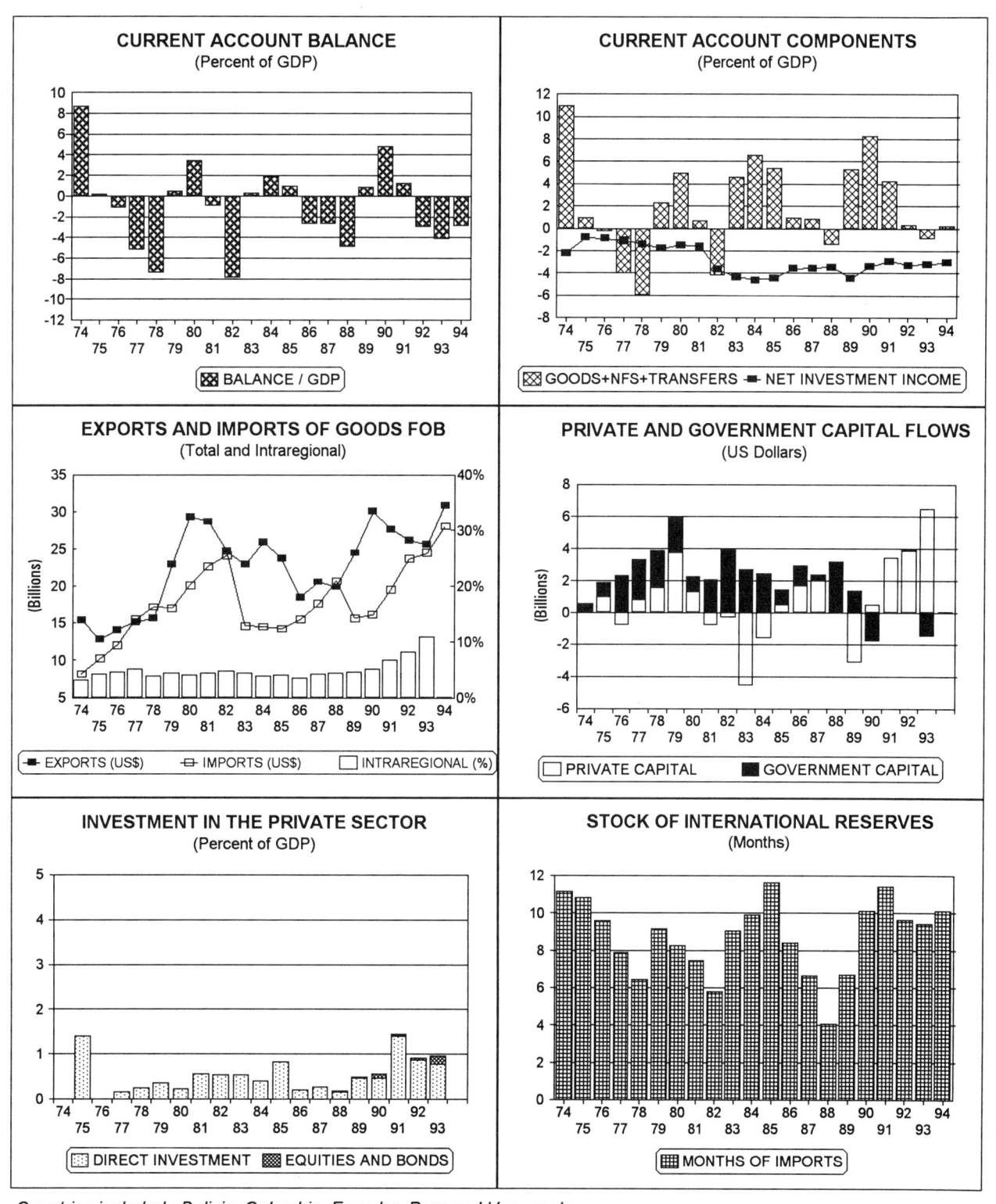

CURRENT ACCOUNT BALANCE
(Percent of GDP)

CURRENT ACCOUNT COMPONENTS
(Percent of GDP)

EXPORTS AND IMPORTS OF GOODS FOB
(Total and Intraregional)

PRIVATE AND GOVERNMENT CAPITAL FLOWS
(US Dollars)

INVESTMENT IN THE PRIVATE SECTOR
(Percent of GDP)

STOCK OF INTERNATIONAL RESERVES
(Months)

Countries included: Bolivia, Colombia, Ecuador, Peru and Venezuela.

Statistics and Quantitative Analysis/IDB

CACM
Balance of Payments in US Dollars

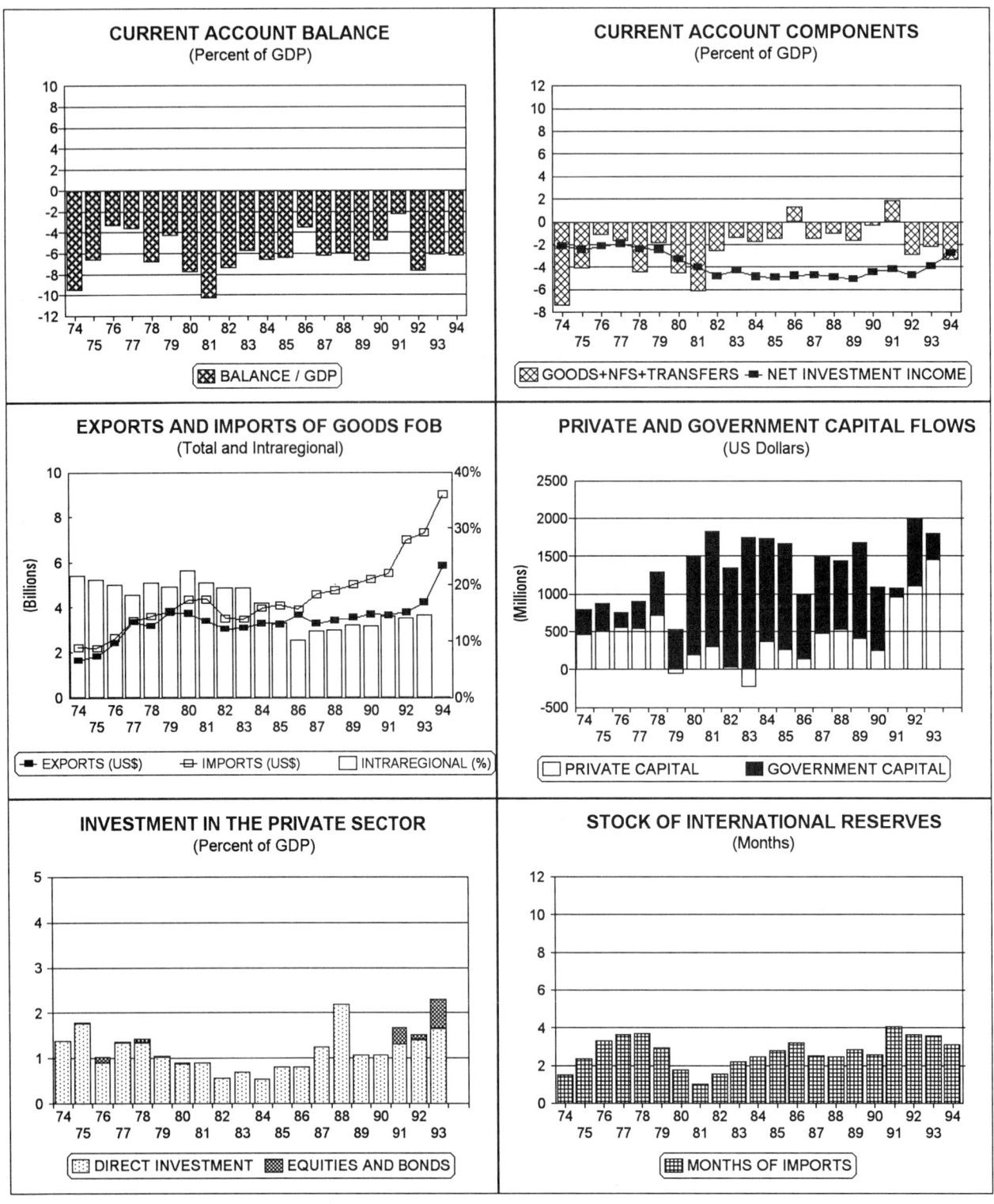

CURRENT ACCOUNT BALANCE
(Percent of GDP)

CURRENT ACCOUNT COMPONENTS
(Percent of GDP)

EXPORTS AND IMPORTS OF GOODS FOB
(Total and Intraregional)

PRIVATE AND GOVERNMENT CAPITAL FLOWS
(US Dollars)

INVESTMENT IN THE PRIVATE SECTOR
(Percent of GDP)

STOCK OF INTERNATIONAL RESERVES
(Months)

Countries included : Costa Rica, El Salvador, Guatemala, Honduras and Nicaragua.

CARICOM
Balance of Payments in US Dollars

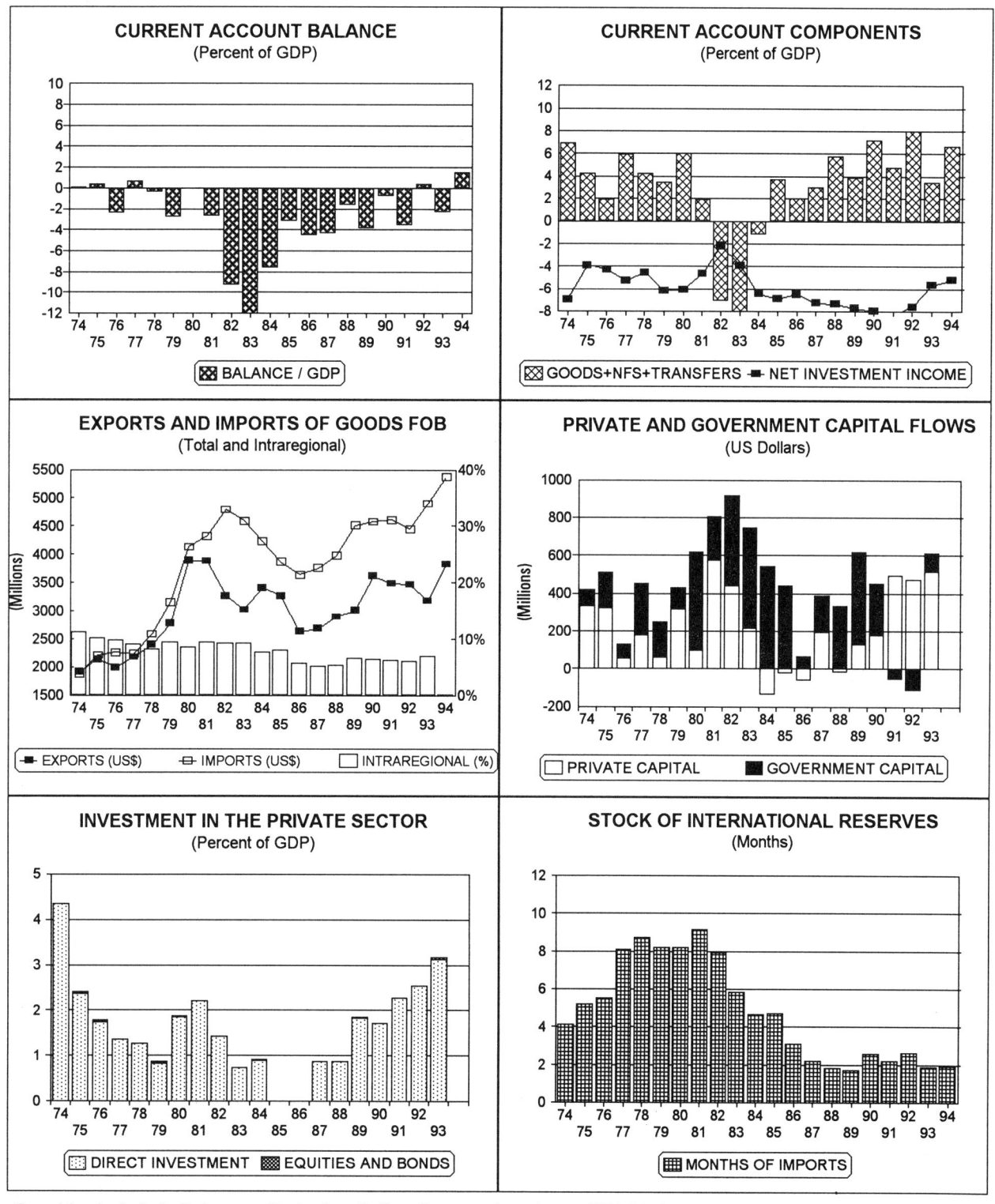

Countries included: Bahamas, Barbados, Belize, Guyana, Jamaica and Trinidad and Tobago.

Statistics and Quantitative Analysis/IDB

MERCOSUR
Balance of Payments in US Dollars

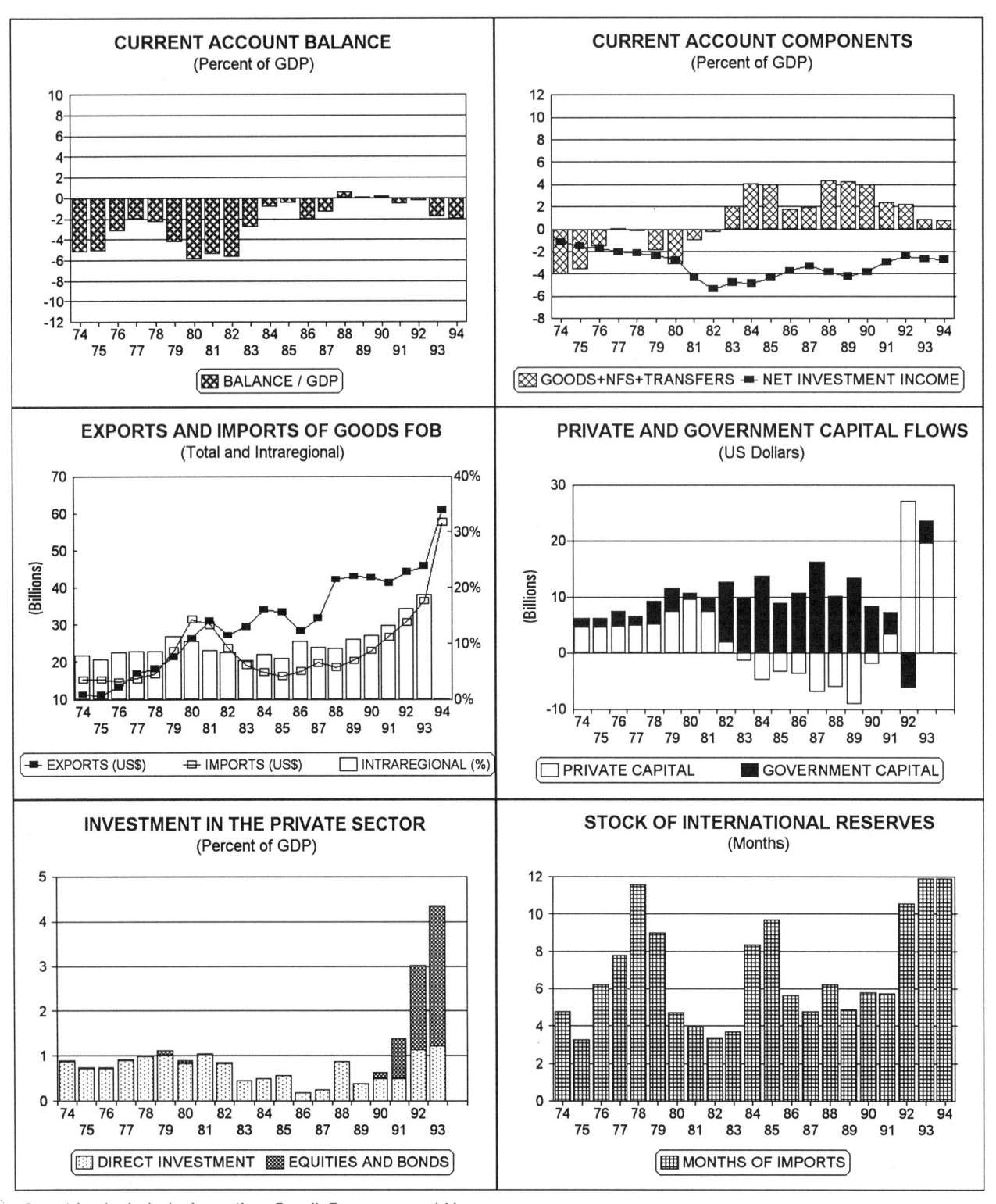

CURRENT ACCOUNT BALANCE
(Percent of GDP)

CURRENT ACCOUNT COMPONENTS
(Percent of GDP)

EXPORTS AND IMPORTS OF GOODS FOB
(Total and Intraregional)

PRIVATE AND GOVERNMENT CAPITAL FLOWS
(US Dollars)

INVESTMENT IN THE PRIVATE SECTOR
(Percent of GDP)

STOCK OF INTERNATIONAL RESERVES
(Months)

Countries included: Argentina, Brazil, Paraguay and Uruguay.

106   Statistics and Quantitative Analysis/IDB

ARGENTINA
Balance of Payments in US Dollars

Statistics and Quantitative Analysis/IDB

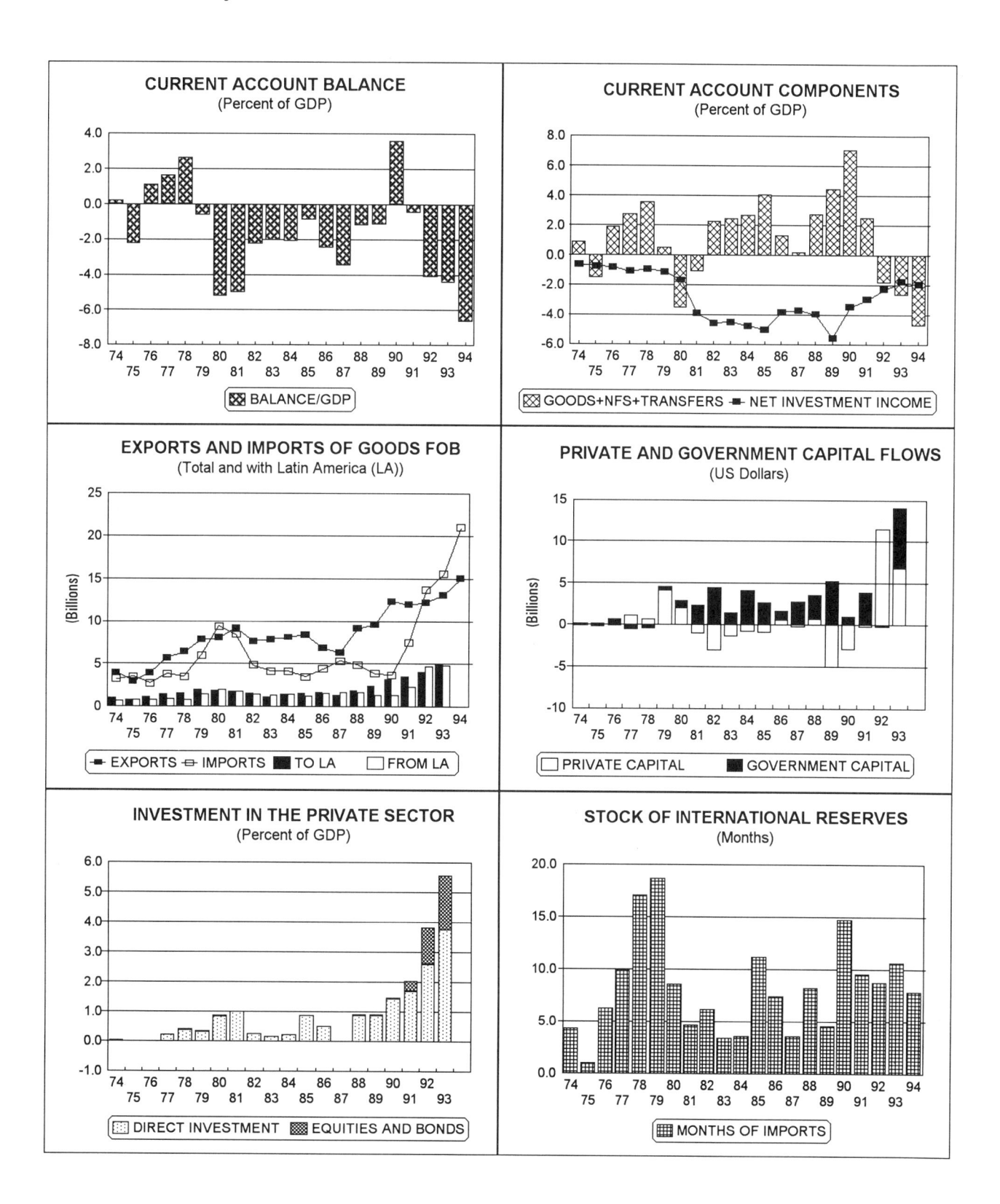

107

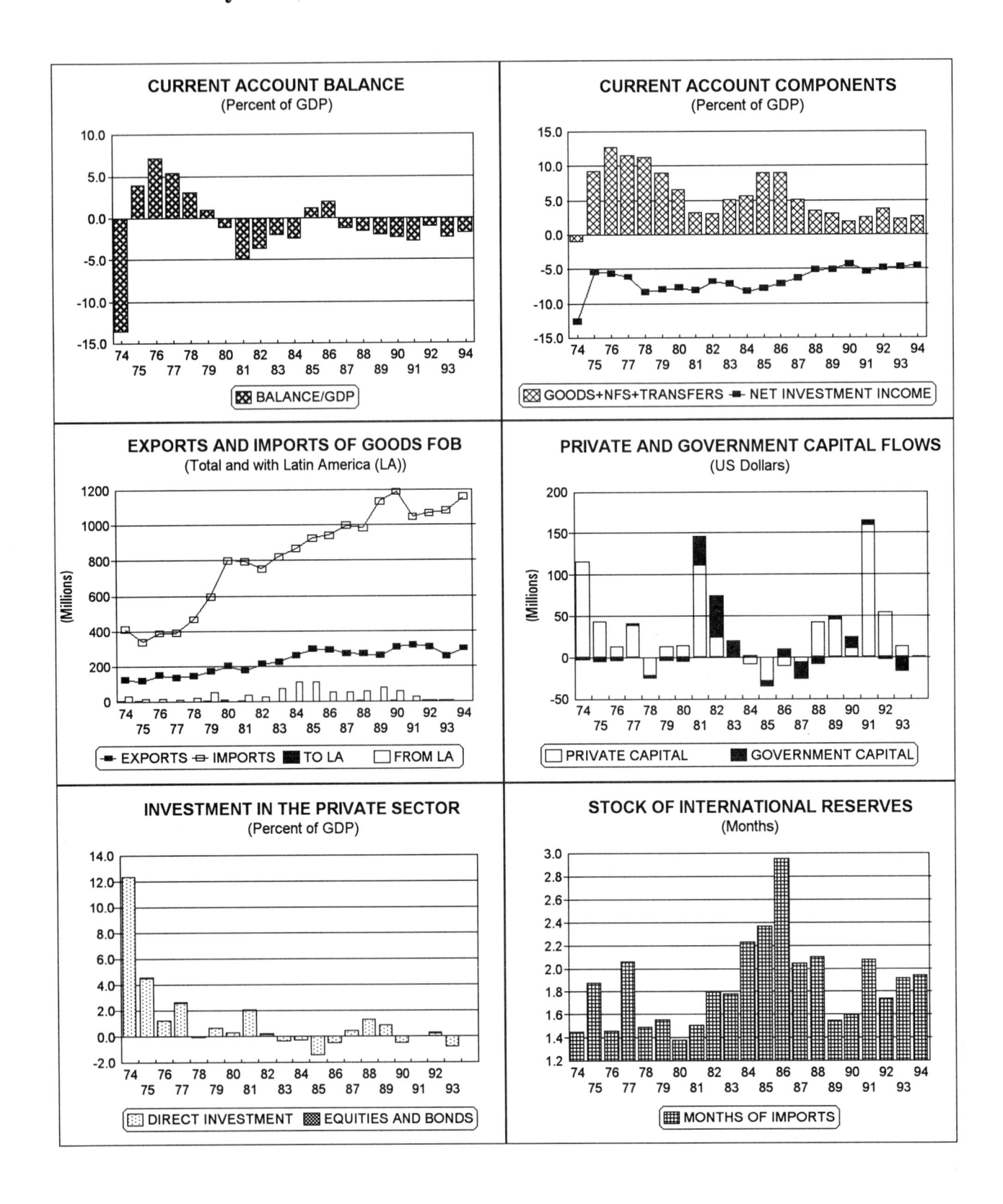

BAHAMAS
Balance of Payments in US Dollars

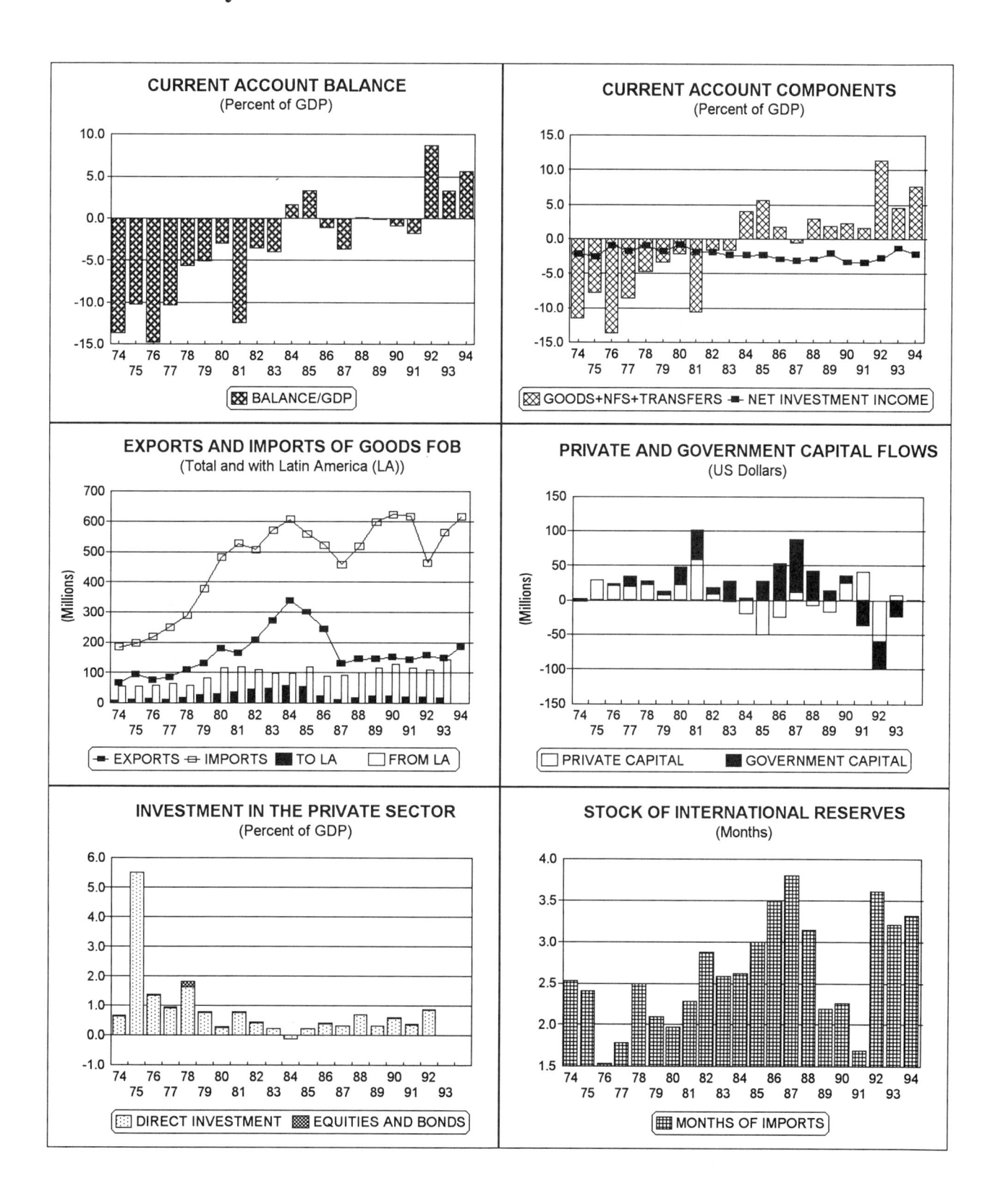

BARBADOS
Balance of Payments in US Dollars

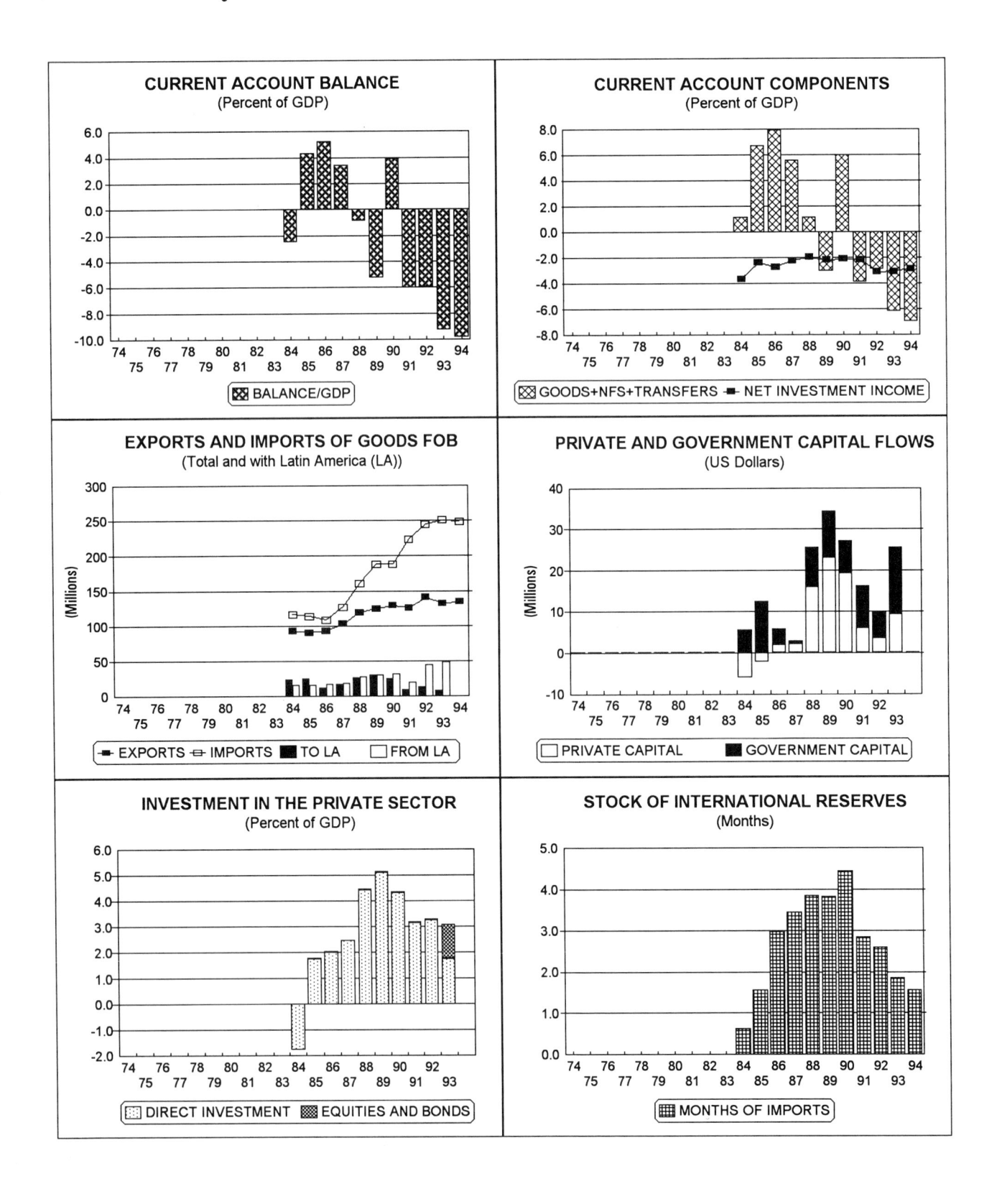

BELIZE
Balance of Payments in US Dollars

CURRENT ACCOUNT BALANCE
(Percent of GDP)

CURRENT ACCOUNT COMPONENTS
(Percent of GDP)

EXPORTS AND IMPORTS OF GOODS FOB
(Total and with Latin America (LA))

PRIVATE AND GOVERNMENT CAPITAL FLOWS
(US Dollars)

INVESTMENT IN THE PRIVATE SECTOR
(Percent of GDP)

STOCK OF INTERNATIONAL RESERVES
(Months)

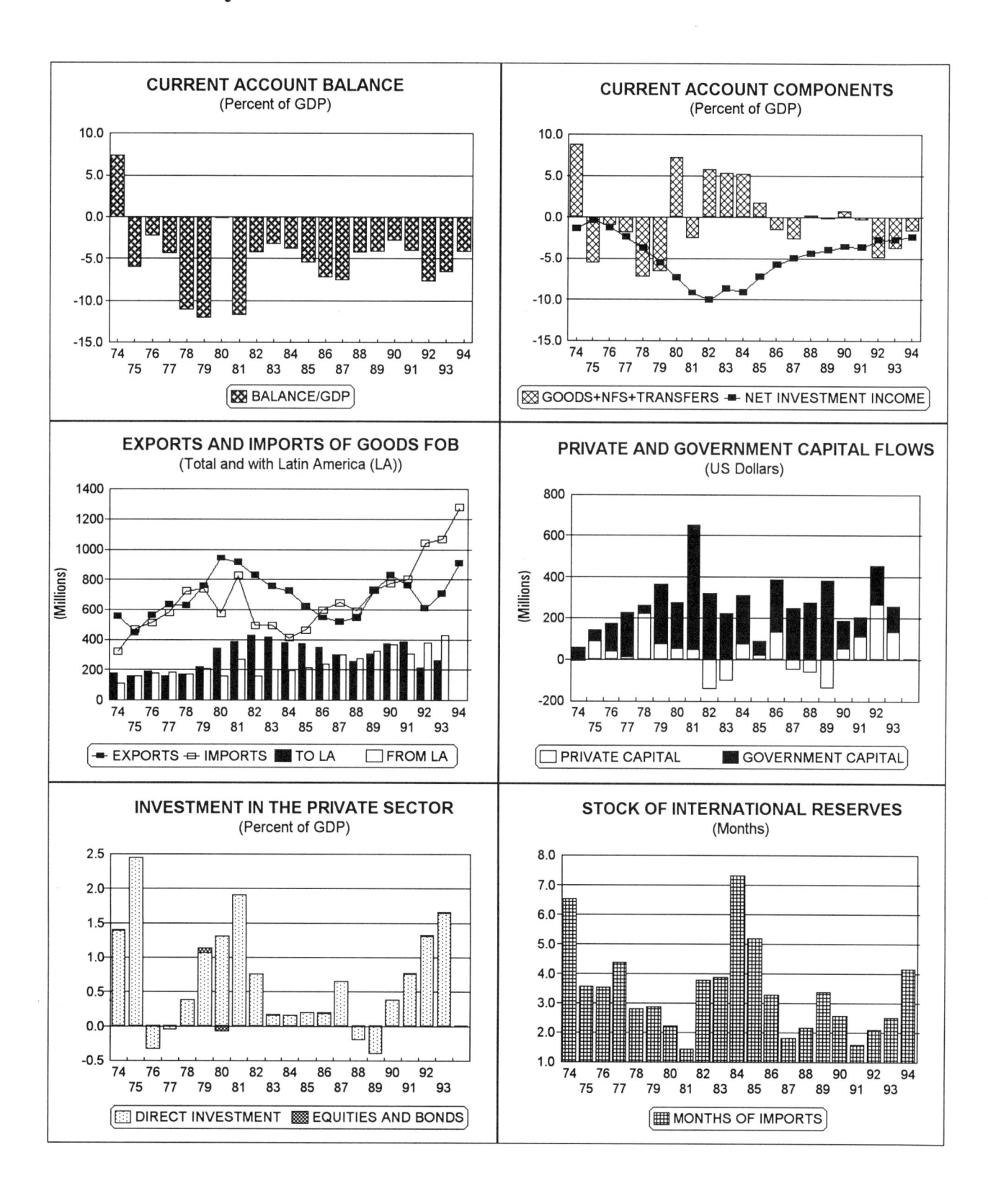

BOLIVIA
Balance of Payments in US Dollars

Statistics and Quantitative Analysis/IDB

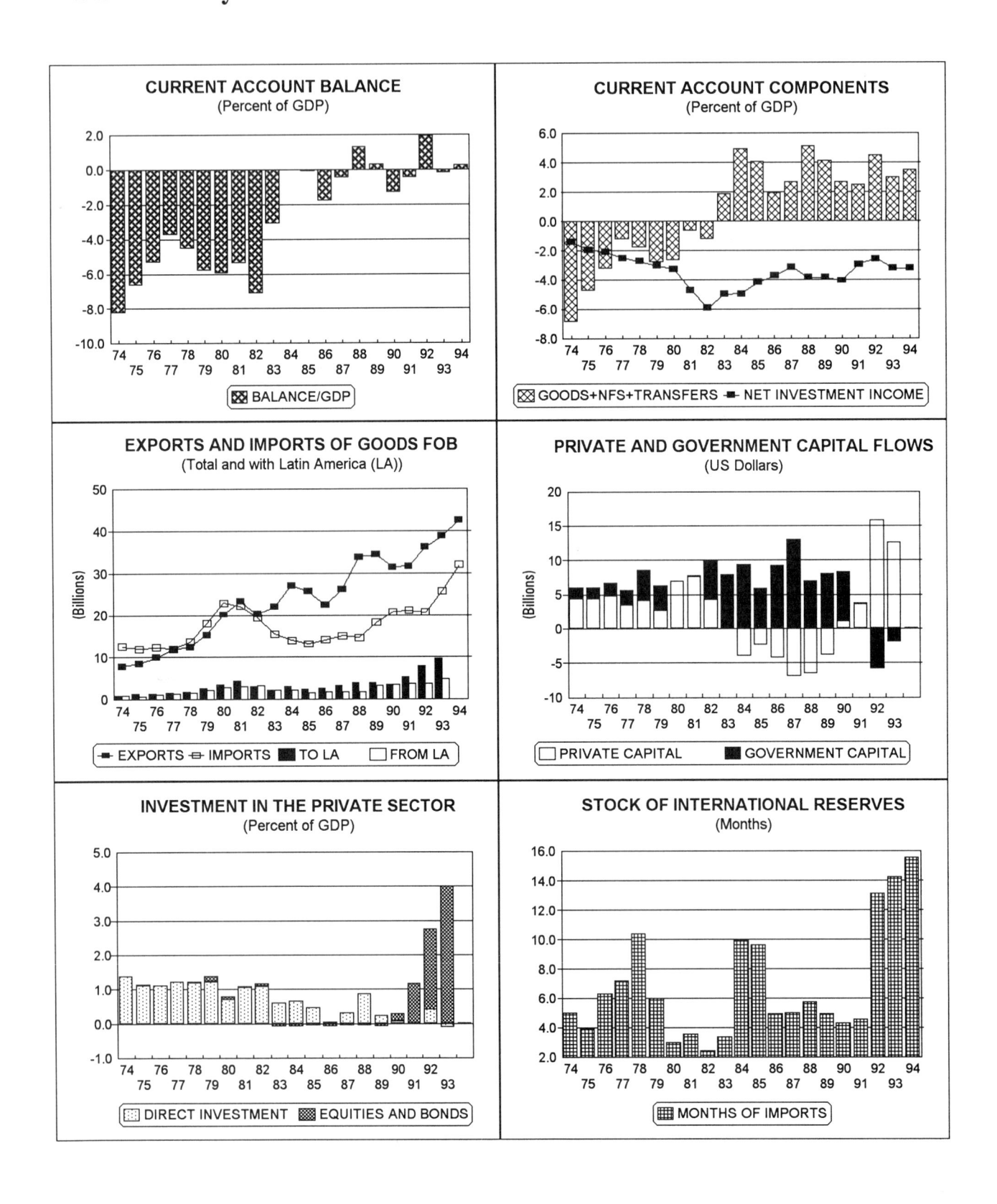

BRAZIL
Balance of Payments in US Dollars

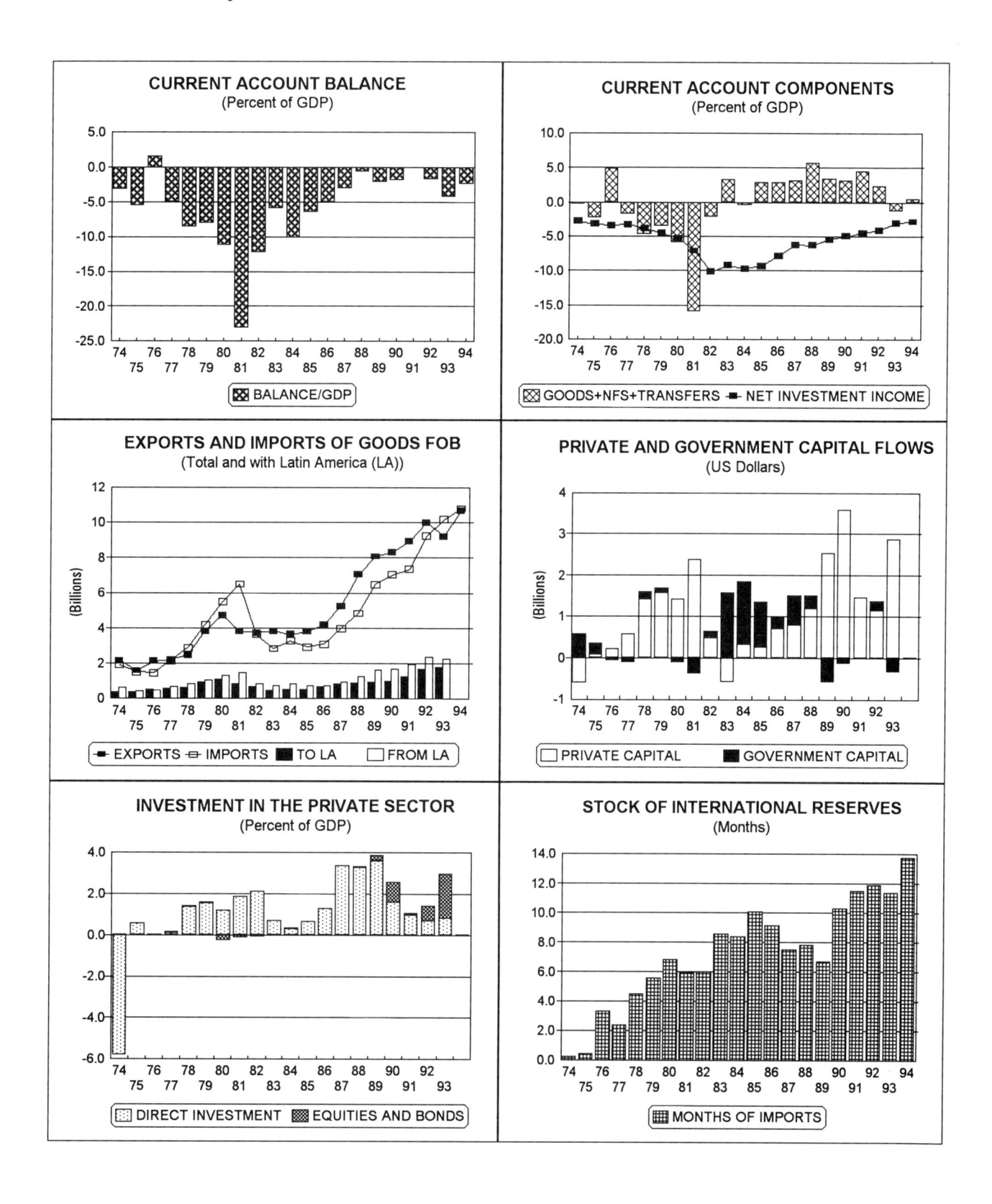

CHILE
Balance of Payments in US Dollars

Statistics and Quantitative Analysis/IDB

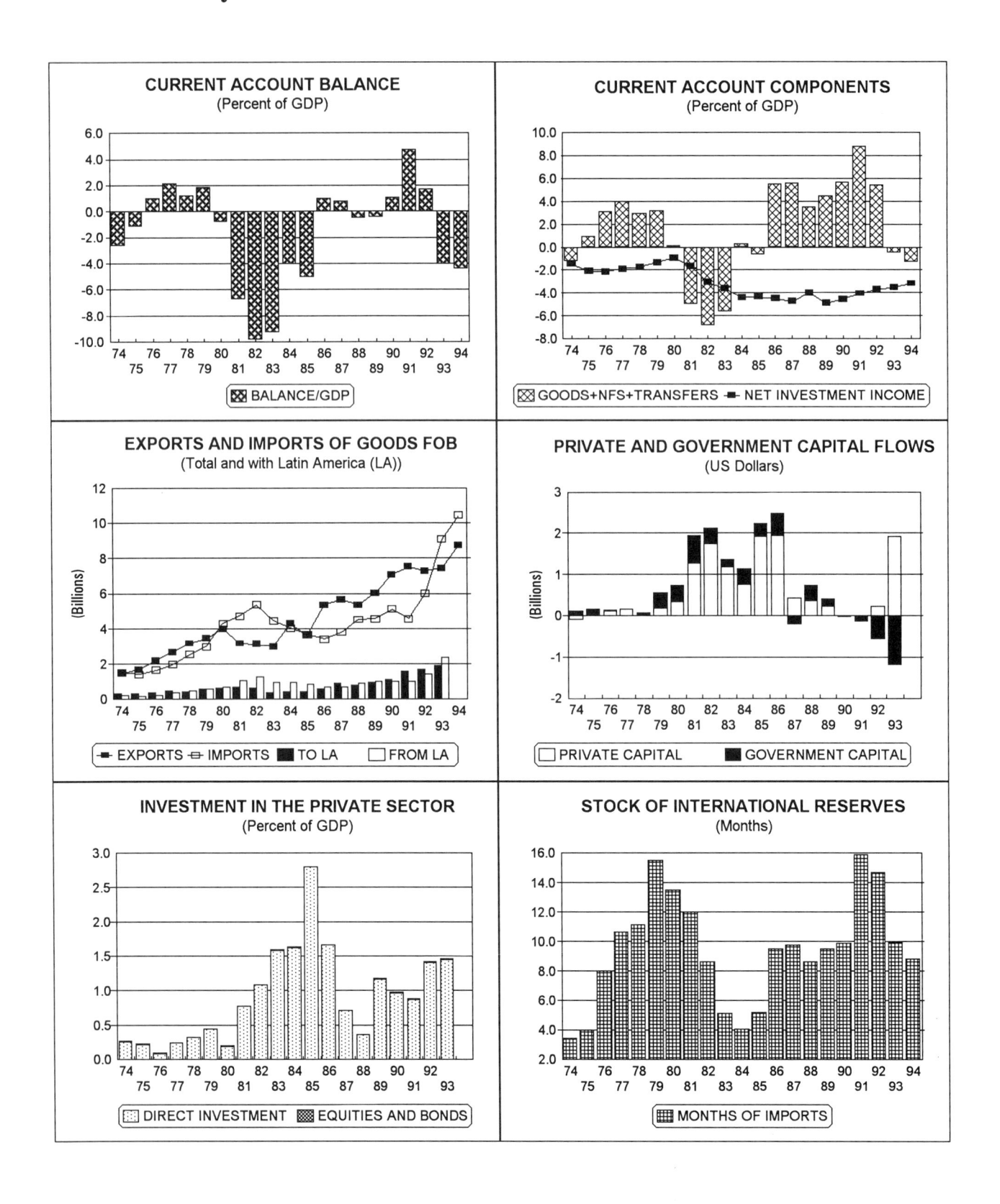

COLOMBIA
Balance of Payments in US Dollars

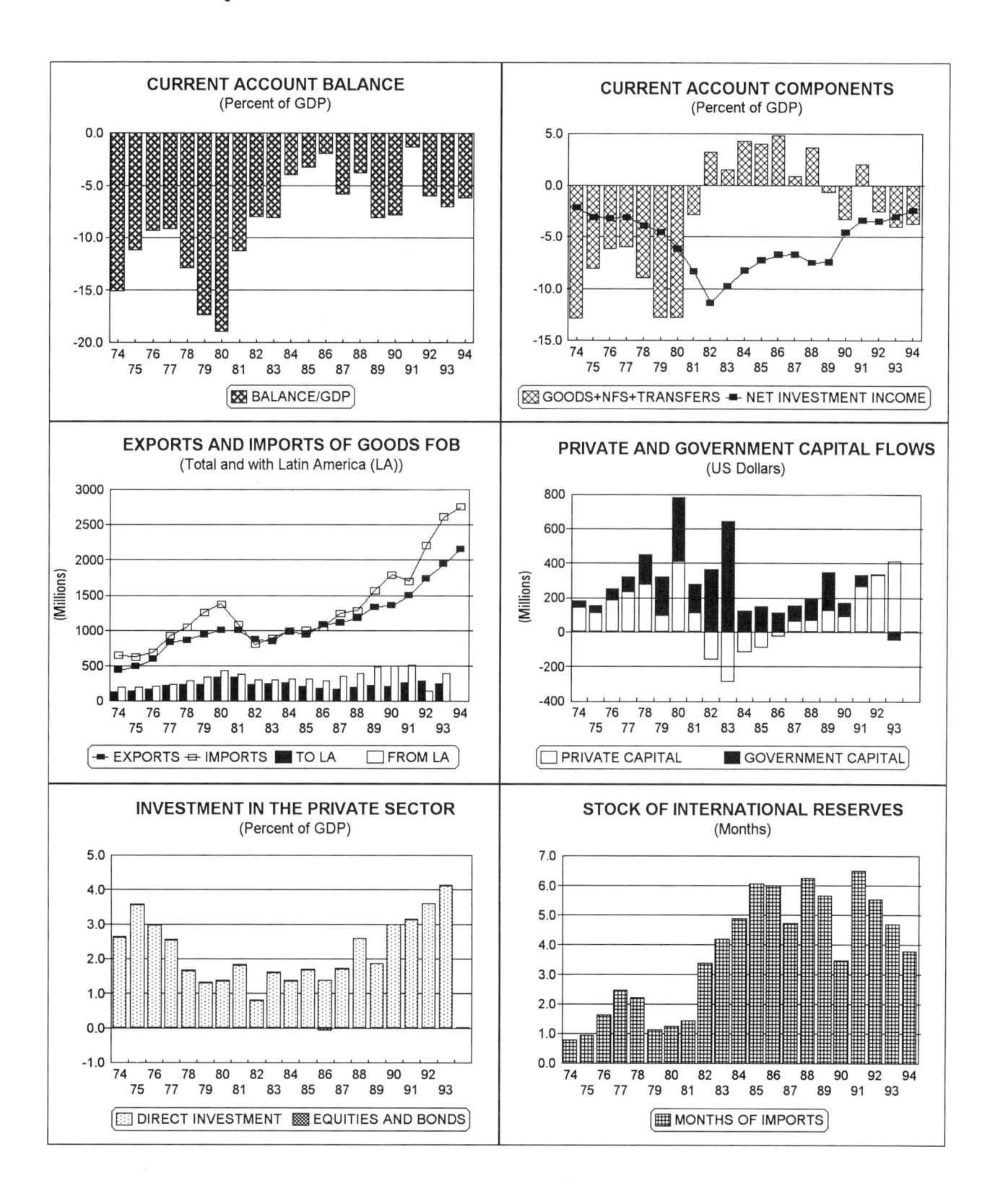

COSTA RICA
Balance of Payments in US Dollars

DOMINICAN REPUBLIC
Balance of Payments in US Dollars

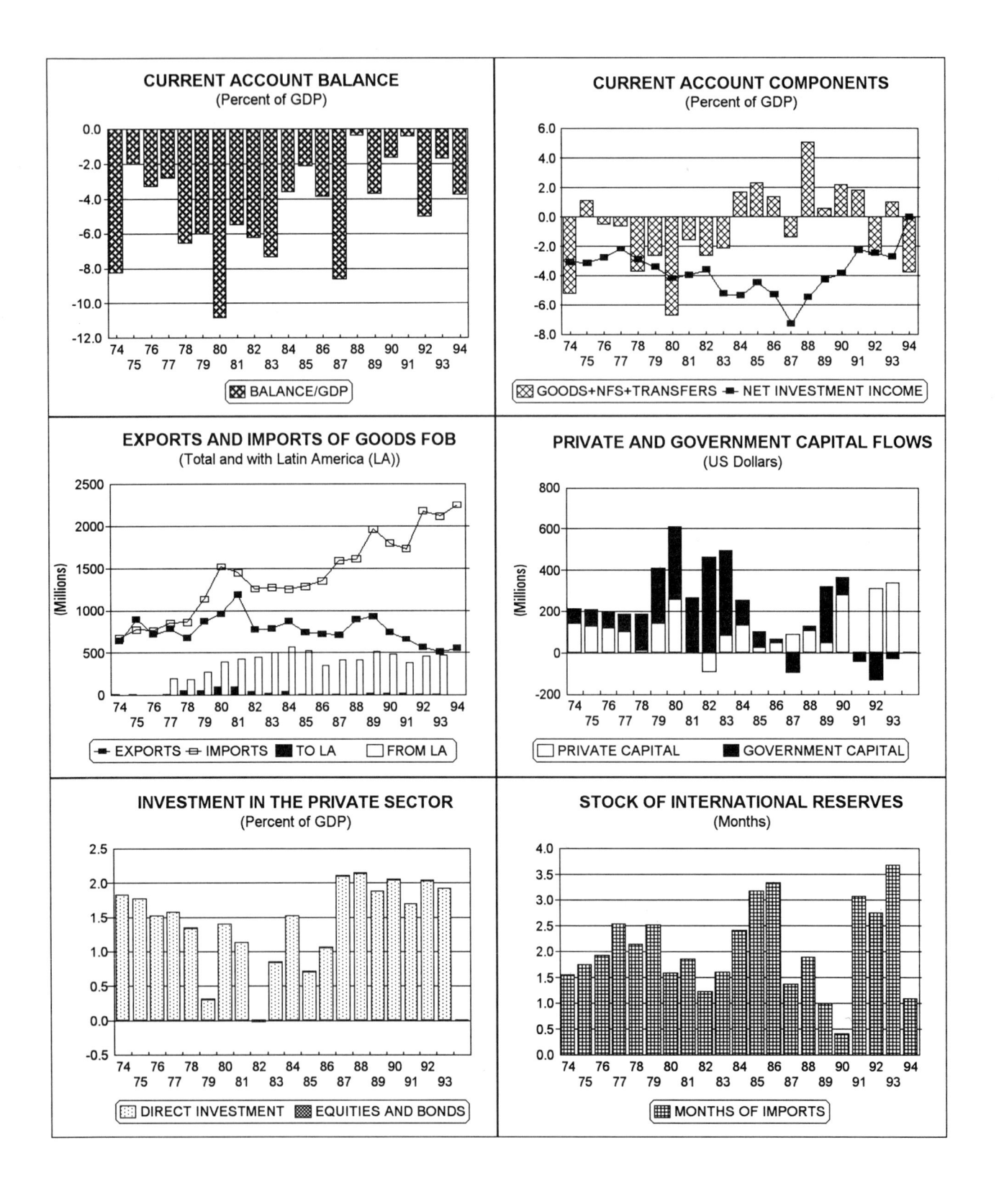

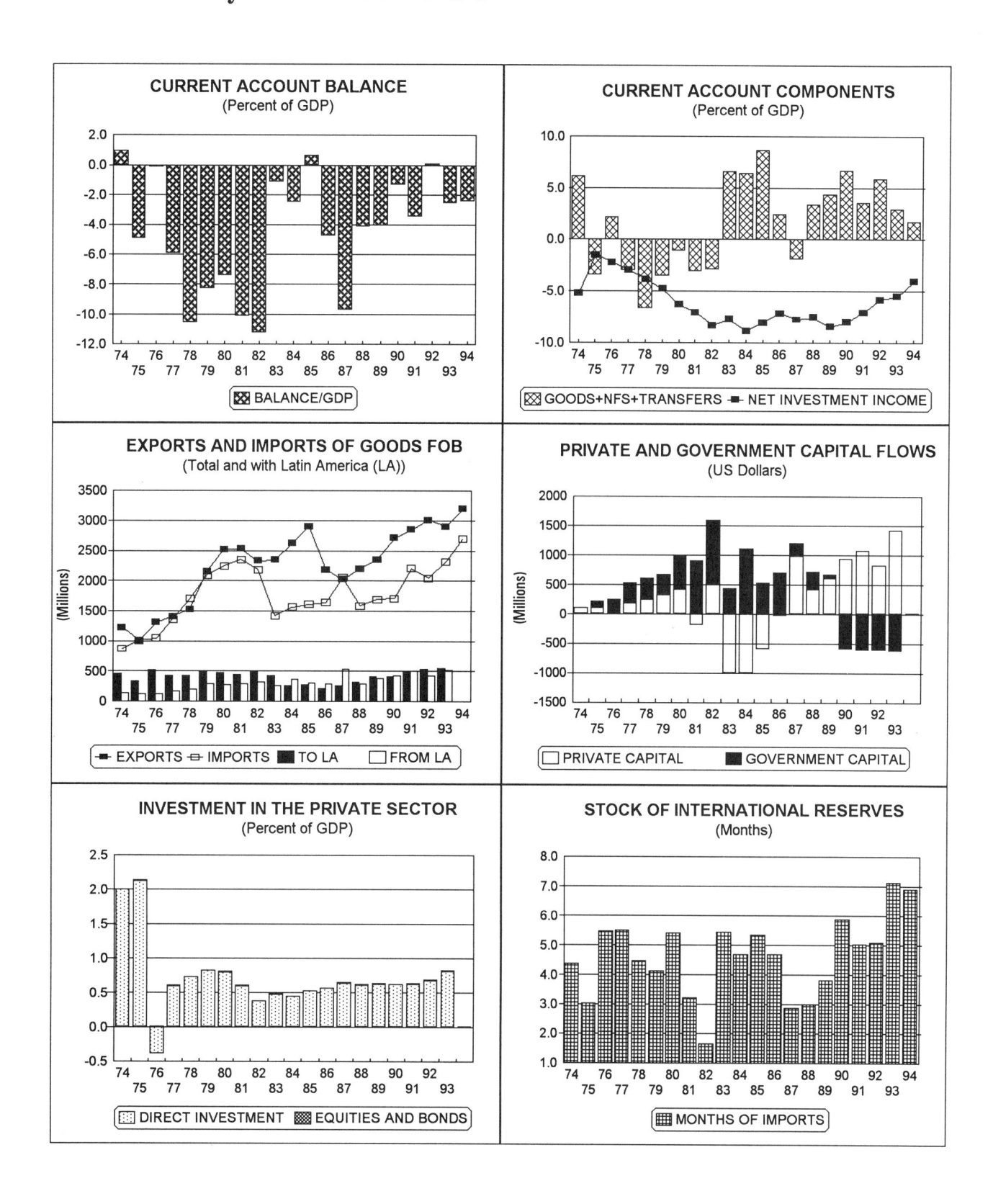

ECUADOR
Balance of Payments in US Dollars

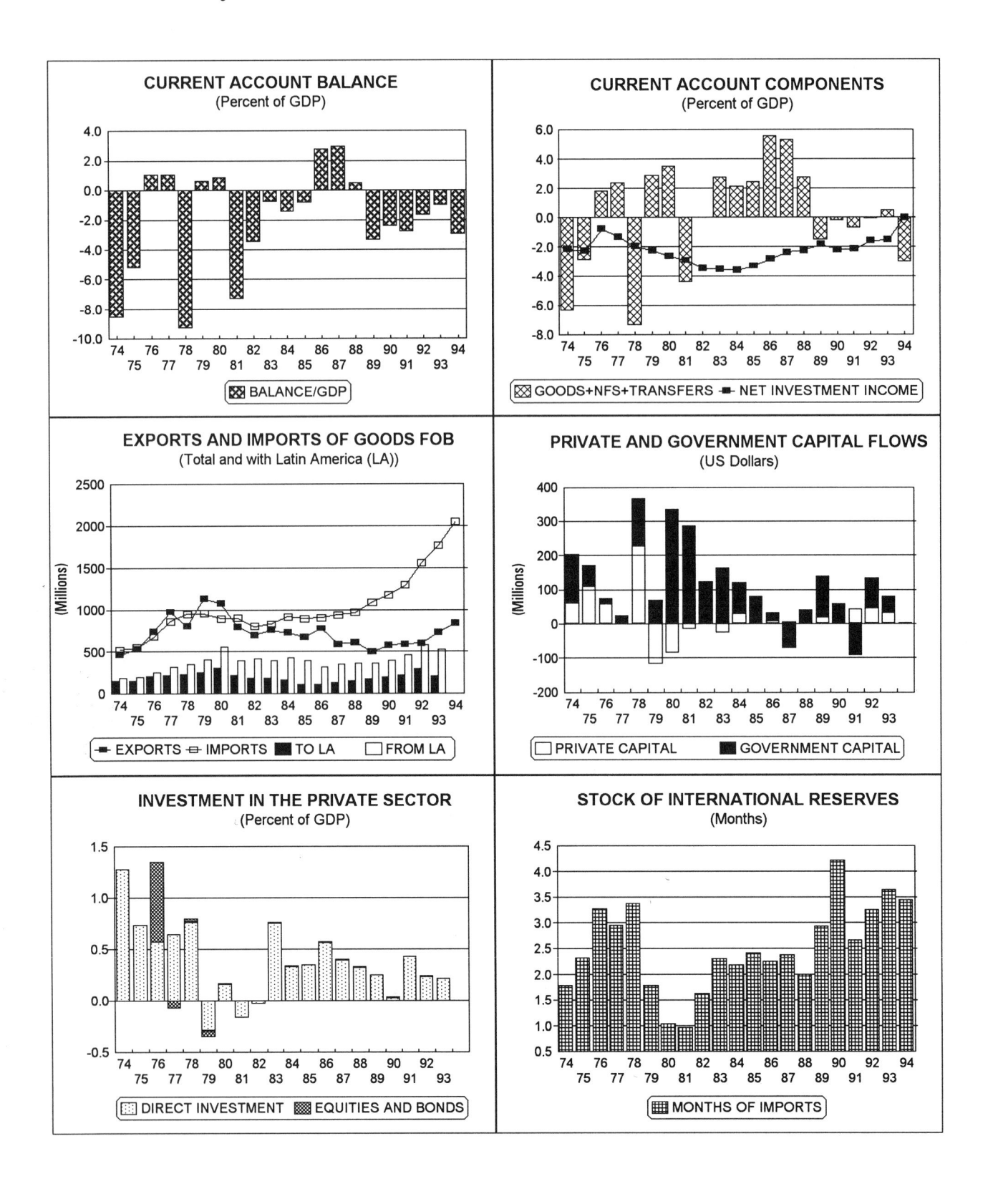

EL SALVADOR
Balance of Payments in US Dollars

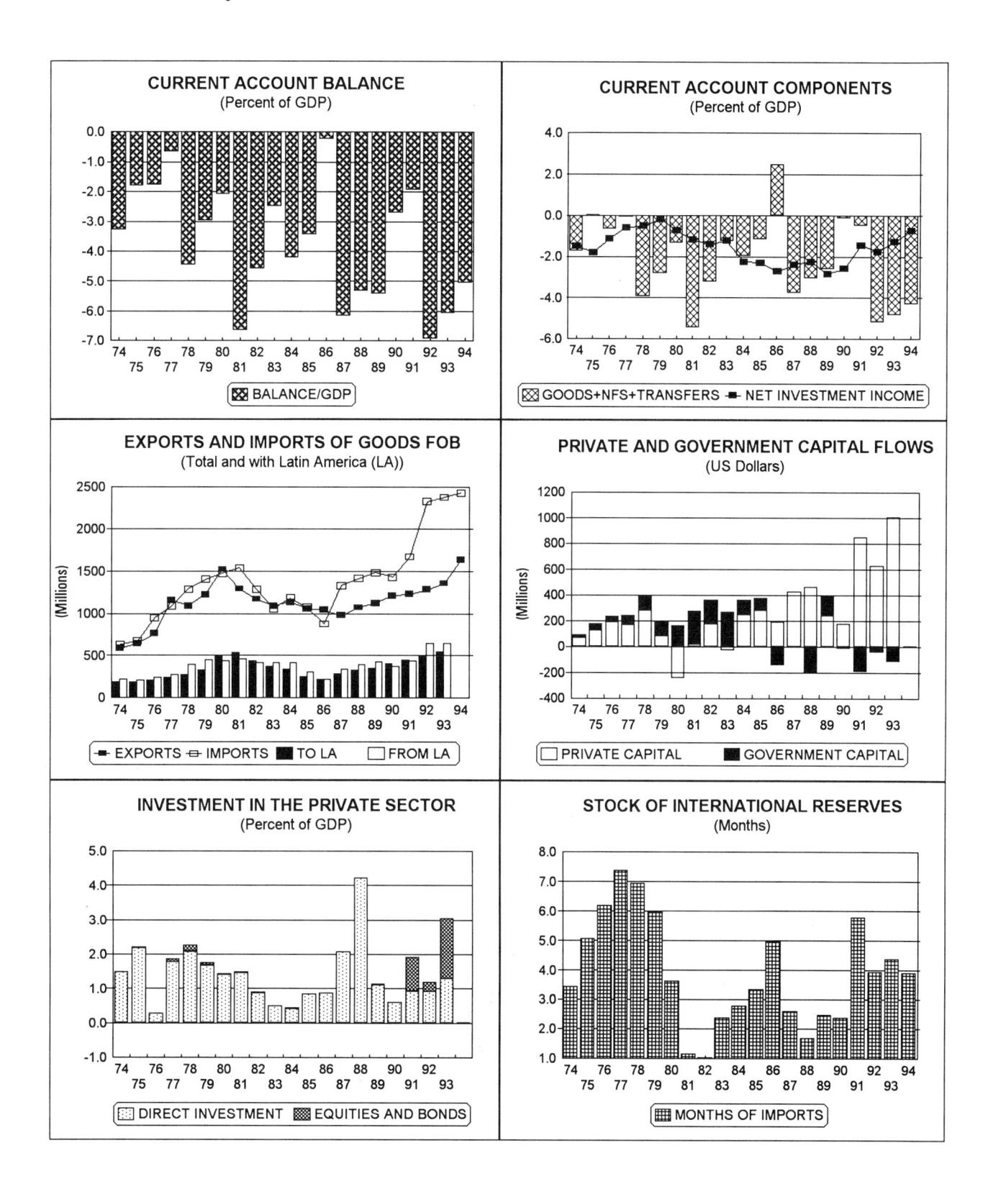

GUATEMALA
Balance of Payments in US Dollars

CURRENT ACCOUNT BALANCE
(Percent of GDP)

CURRENT ACCOUNT COMPONENTS
(Percent of GDP)

EXPORTS AND IMPORTS OF GOODS FOB
(Total and with Latin America (LA))

PRIVATE AND GOVERNMENT CAPITAL FLOWS
(US Dollars)

INVESTMENT IN THE PRIVATE SECTOR
(Percent of GDP)

STOCK OF INTERNATIONAL RESERVES
(Months)

Statistics and Quantitative Analysis/IDB   119

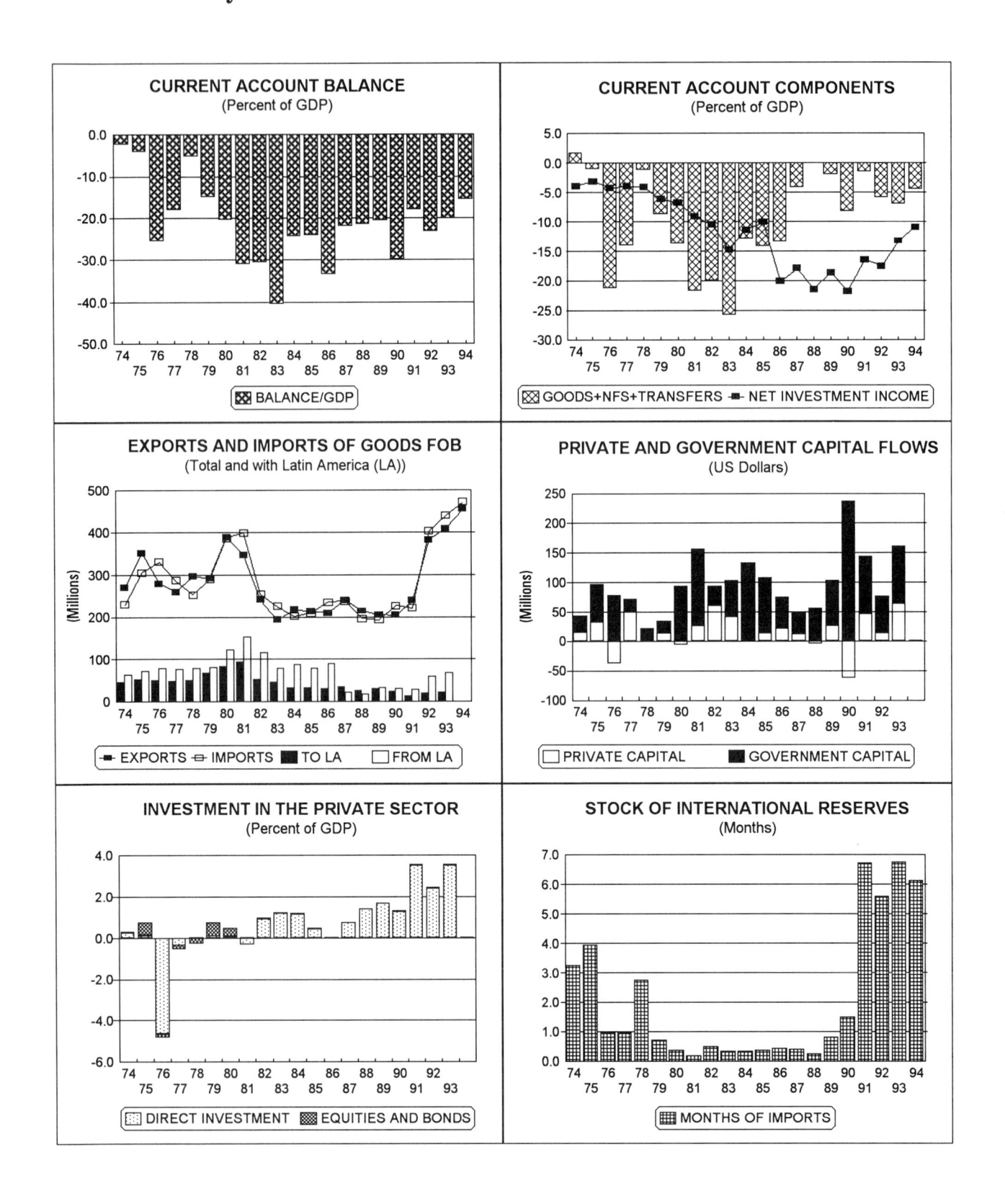

GUYANA
Balance of Payments in US Dollars

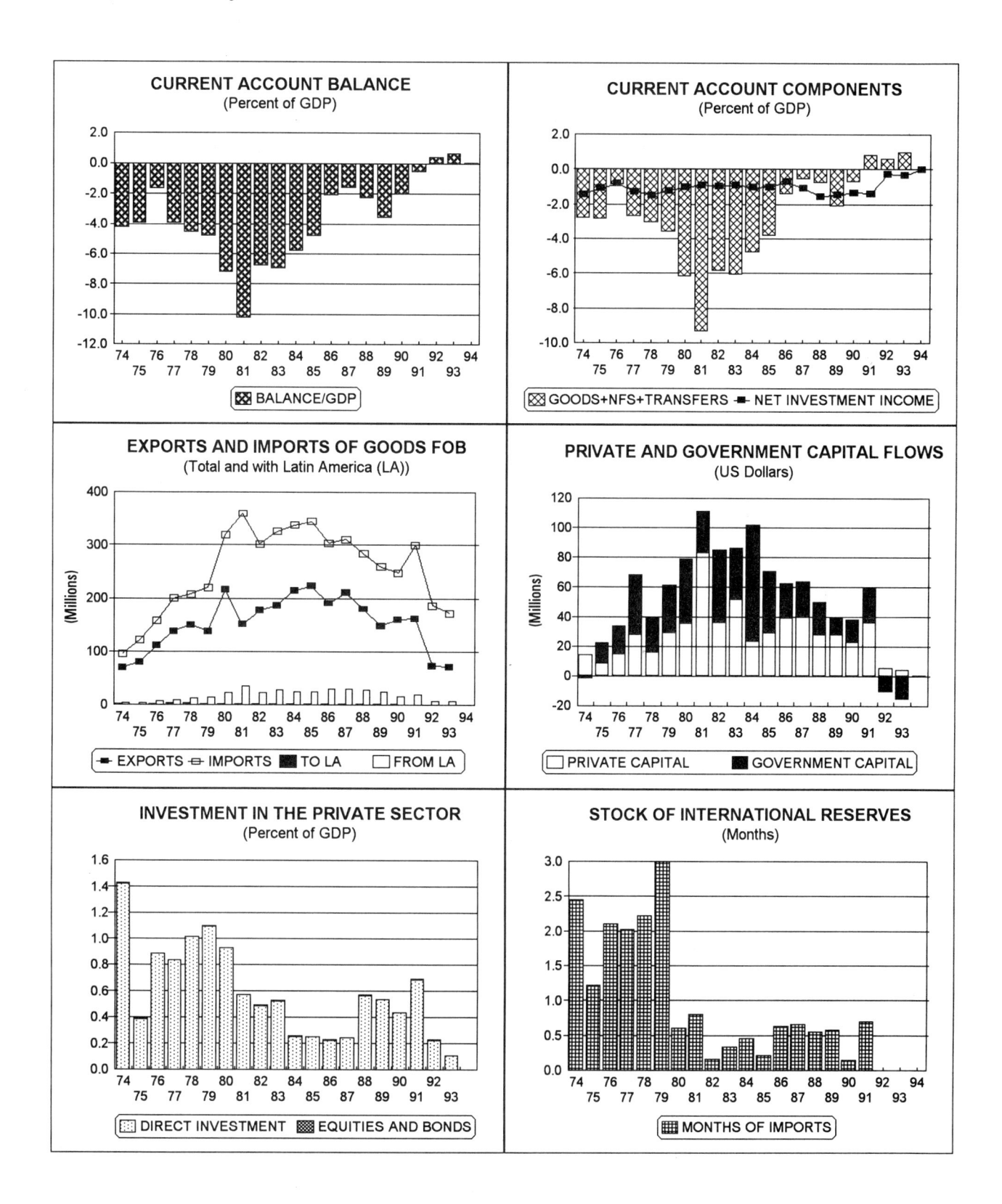

HAITI
Balance of Payments in US Dollars

Statistics and Quantitative Analysis/IDB

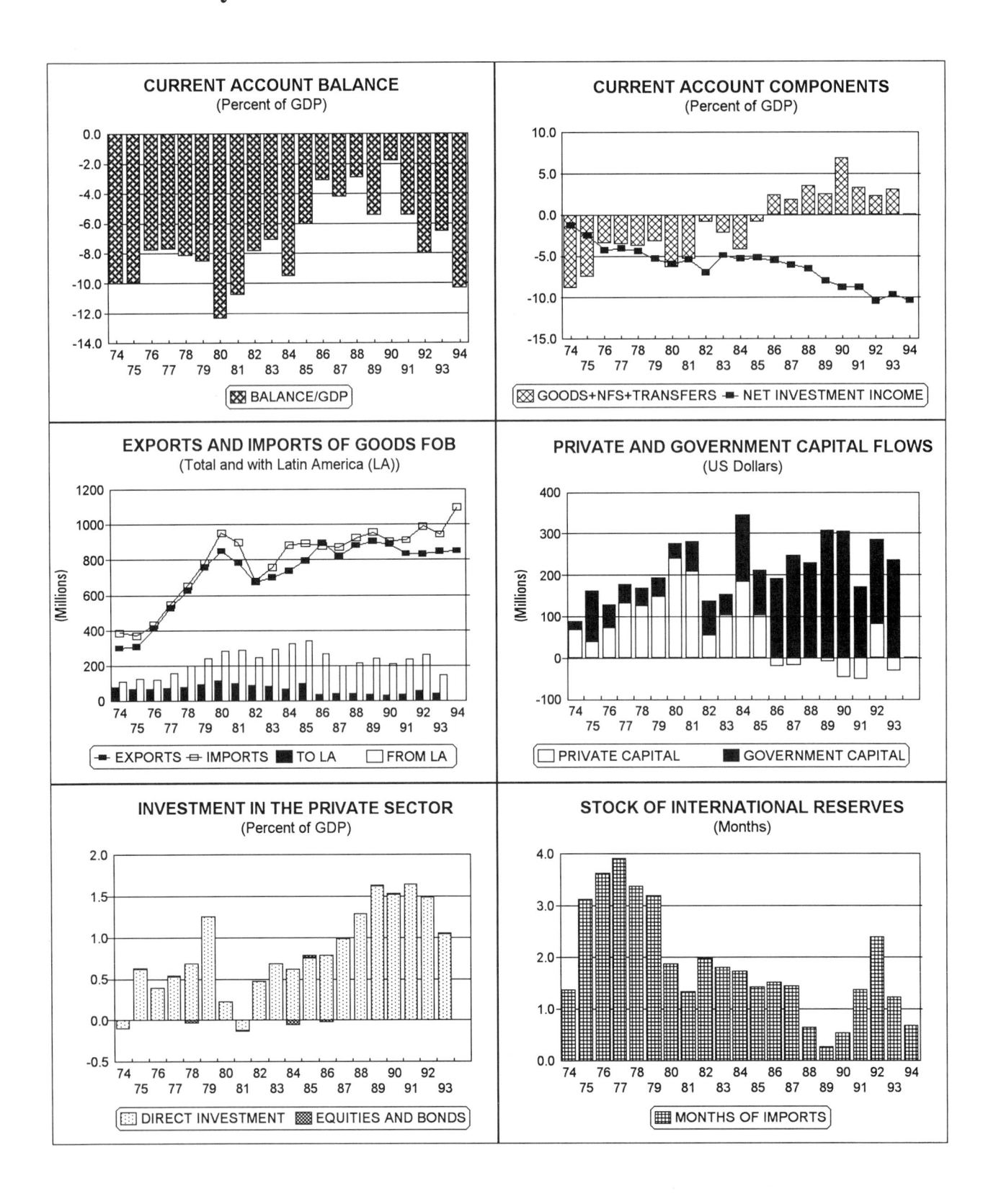

HONDURAS
Balance of Payments in US Dollars

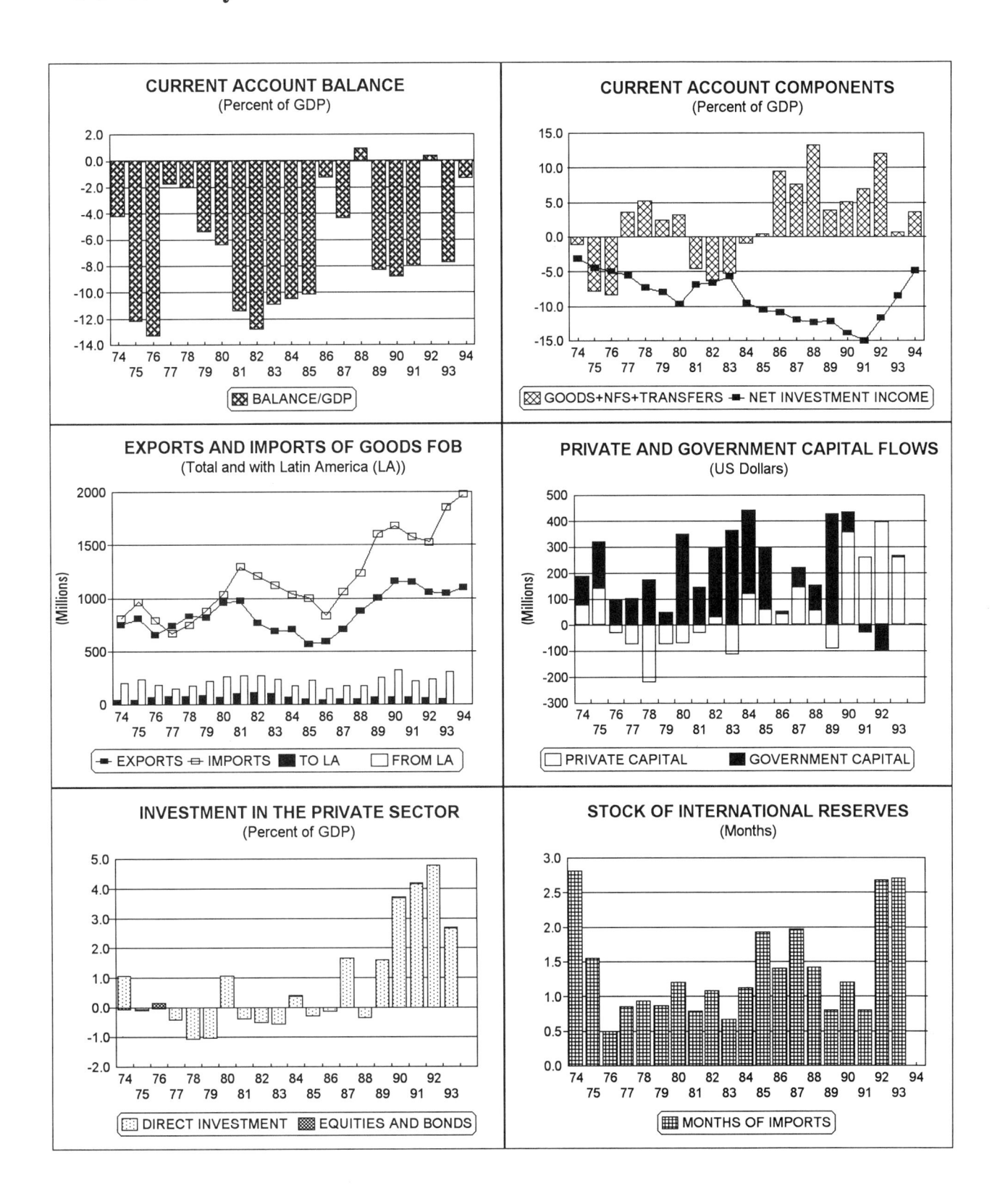

JAMAICA
Balance of Payments in US Dollars

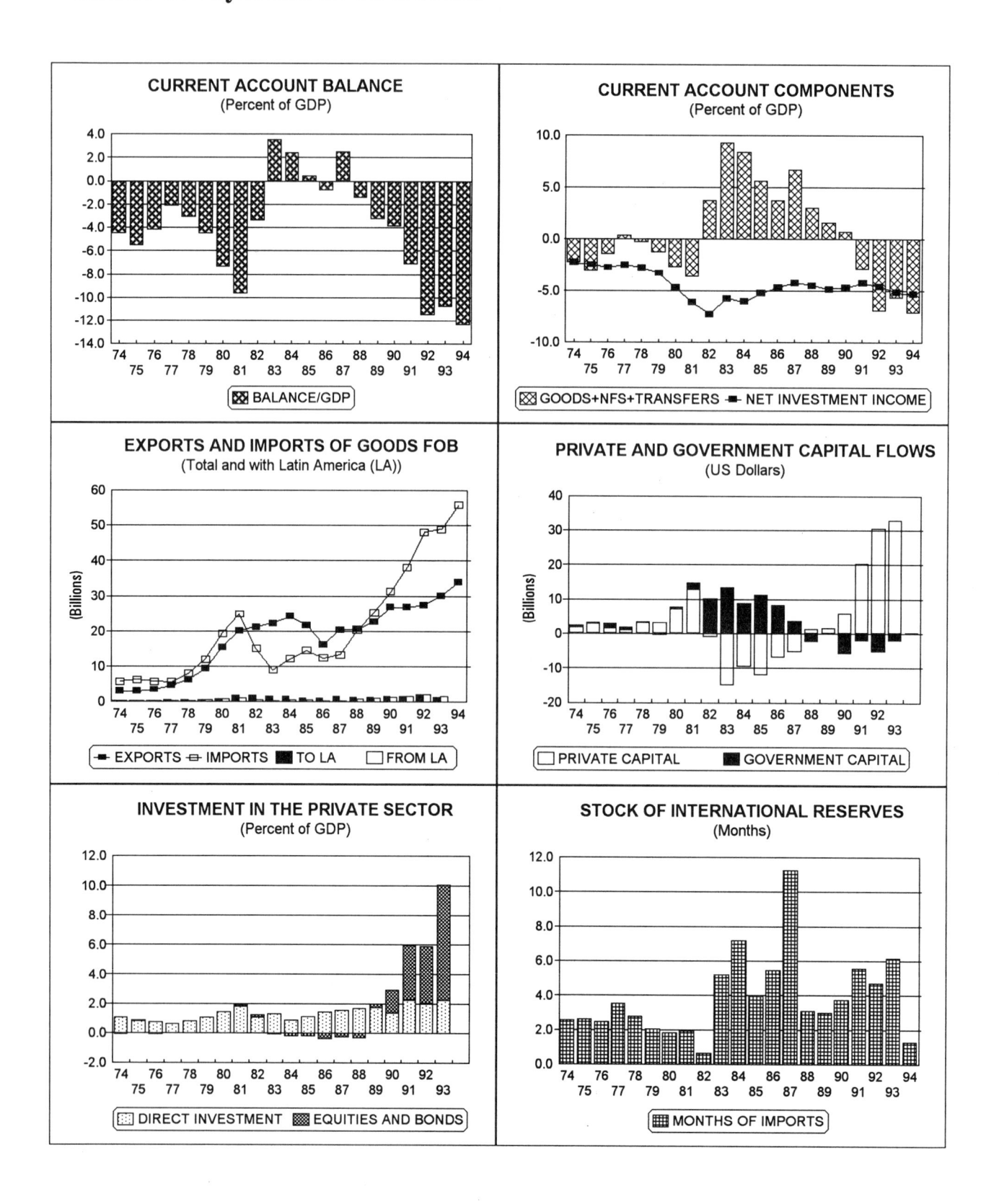

MEXICO
Balance of Payments in US Dollars

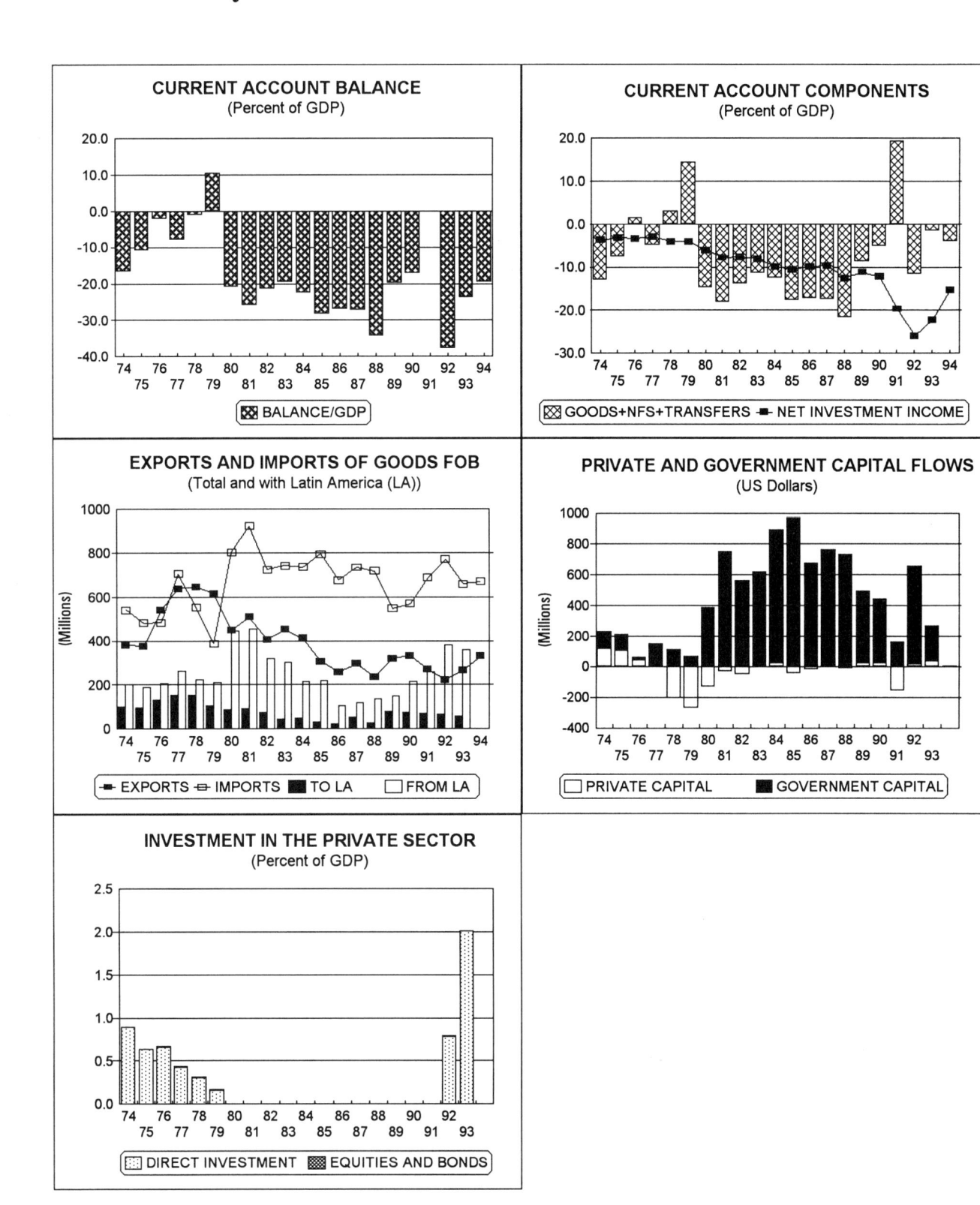

NICARAGUA
Balance of Payments in US Dollars

CURRENT ACCOUNT BALANCE
(Percent of GDP)

CURRENT ACCOUNT COMPONENTS
(Percent of GDP)

EXPORTS AND IMPORTS OF GOODS FOB
(Total and with Latin America (LA))

PRIVATE AND GOVERNMENT CAPITAL FLOWS
(US Dollars)

INVESTMENT IN THE PRIVATE SECTOR
(Percent of GDP)

Statistics and Quantitative Analysis/IDB

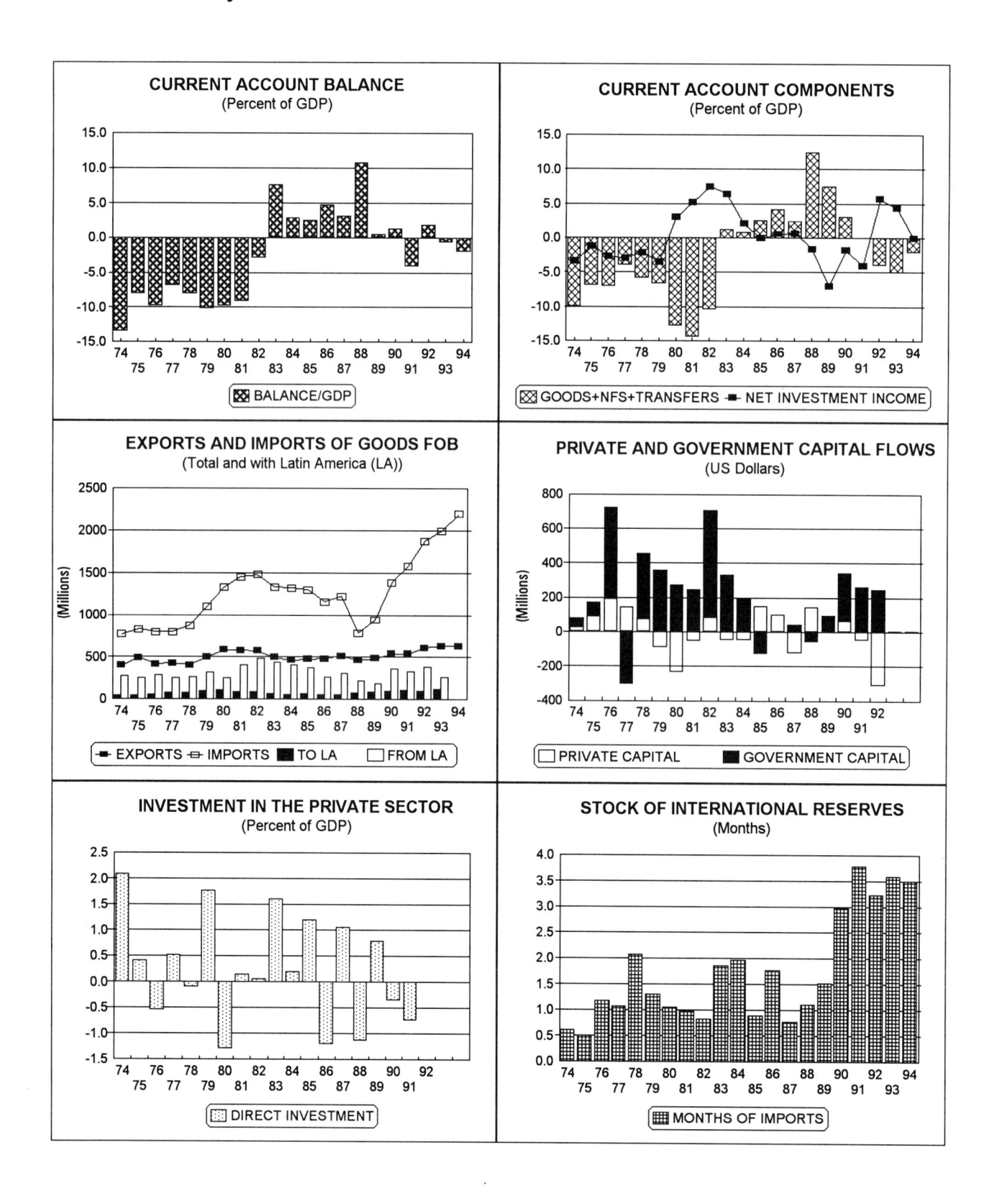

PANAMA
Balance of Payments in US Dollars

CURRENT ACCOUNT BALANCE
(Percent of GDP)

CURRENT ACCOUNT COMPONENTS
(Percent of GDP)

EXPORTS AND IMPORTS OF GOODS FOB
(Total and with Latin America (LA))

PRIVATE AND GOVERNMENT CAPITAL FLOWS
(US Dollars)

INVESTMENT IN THE PRIVATE SECTOR
(Percent of GDP)

STOCK OF INTERNATIONAL RESERVES
(Months)

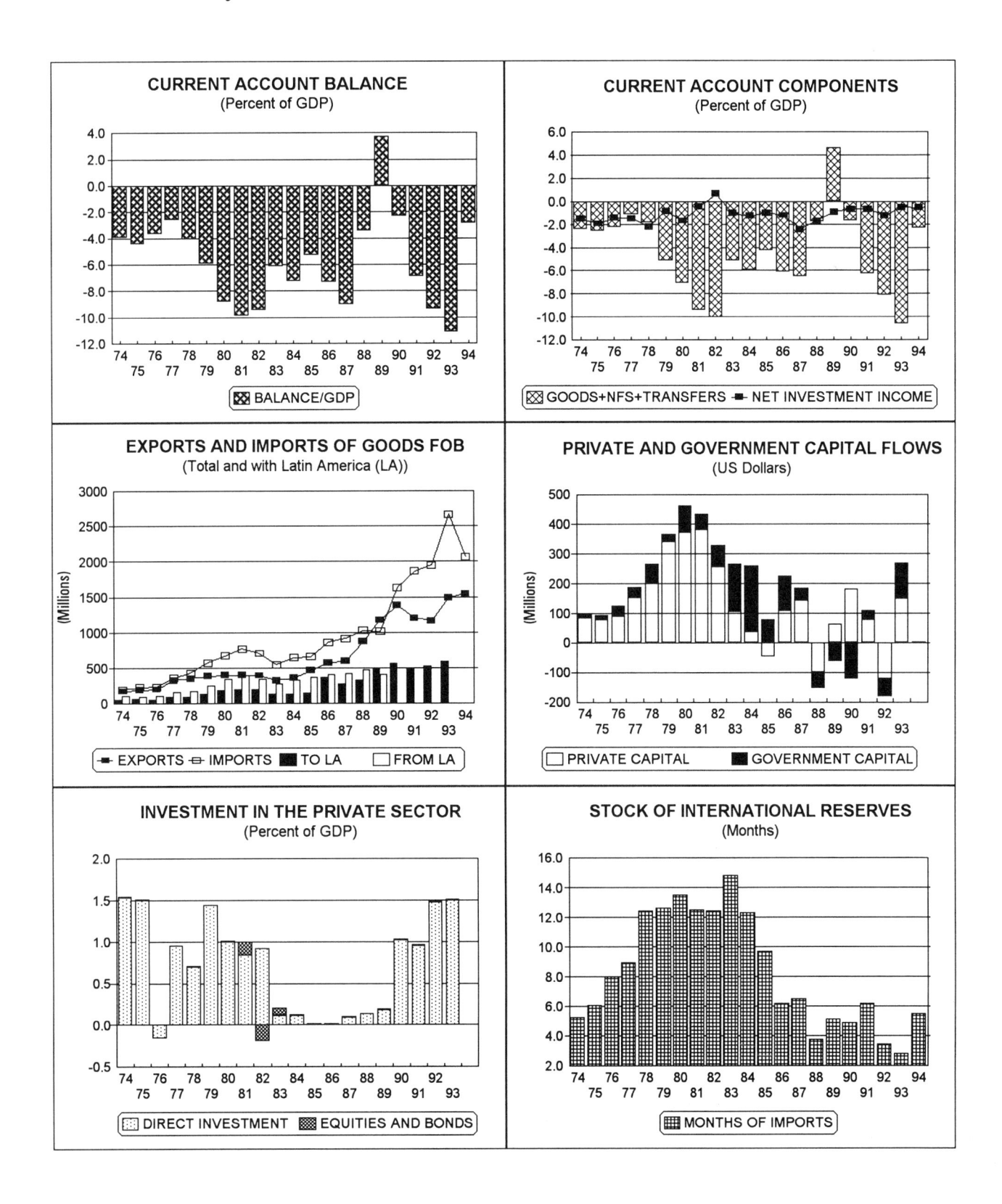

PARAGUAY
Balance of Payments in US Dollars

Statistics and Quantitative Analysis/IDB

127

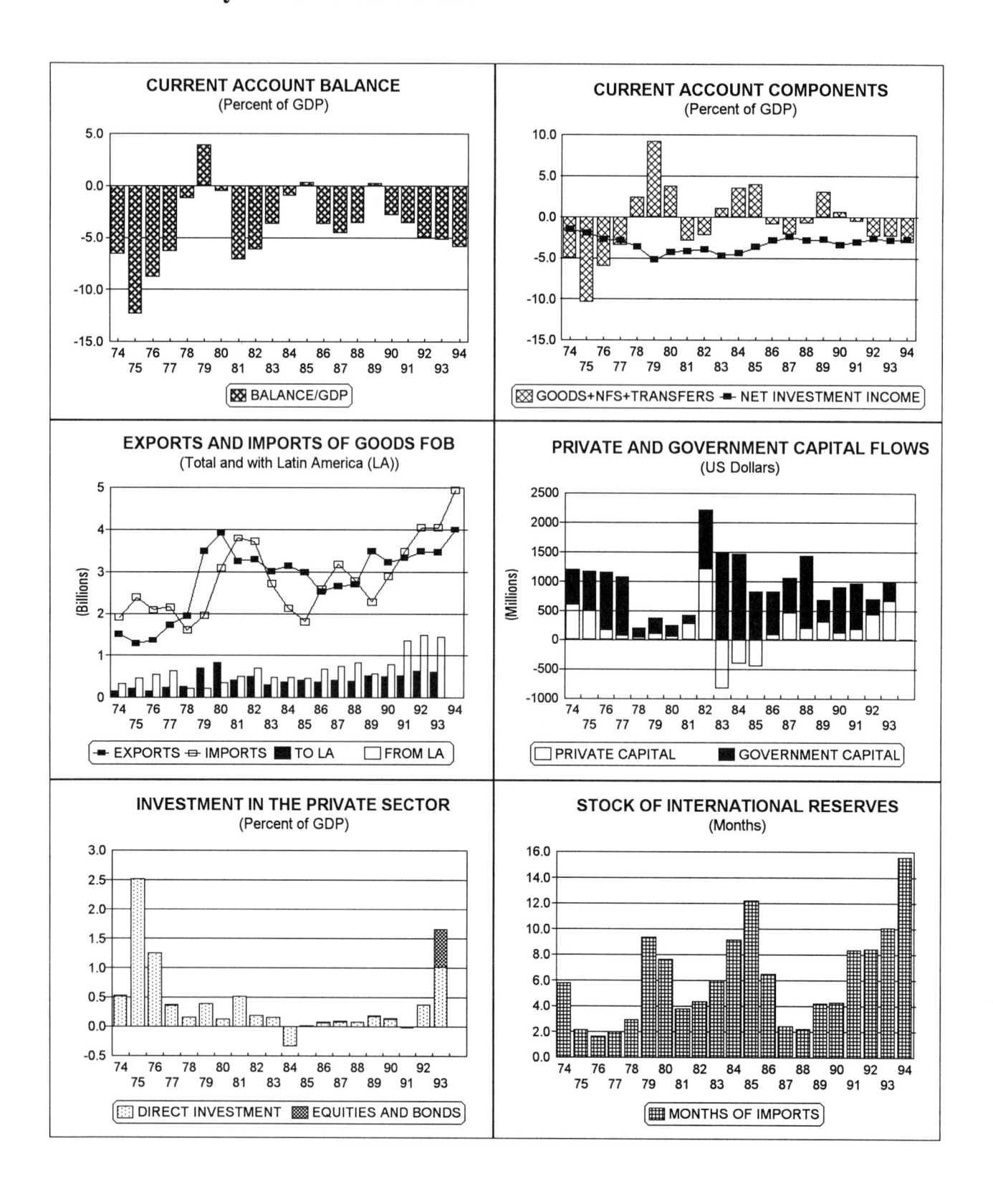

PERU
Balance of Payments in US Dollars

CURRENT ACCOUNT BALANCE
(Percent of GDP)

CURRENT ACCOUNT COMPONENTS
(Percent of GDP)

EXPORTS AND IMPORTS OF GOODS FOB
(Total and with Latin America (LA))

PRIVATE AND GOVERNMENT CAPITAL FLOWS
(US Dollars)

INVESTMENT IN THE PRIVATE SECTOR
(Percent of GDP)

STOCK OF INTERNATIONAL RESERVES
(Months)

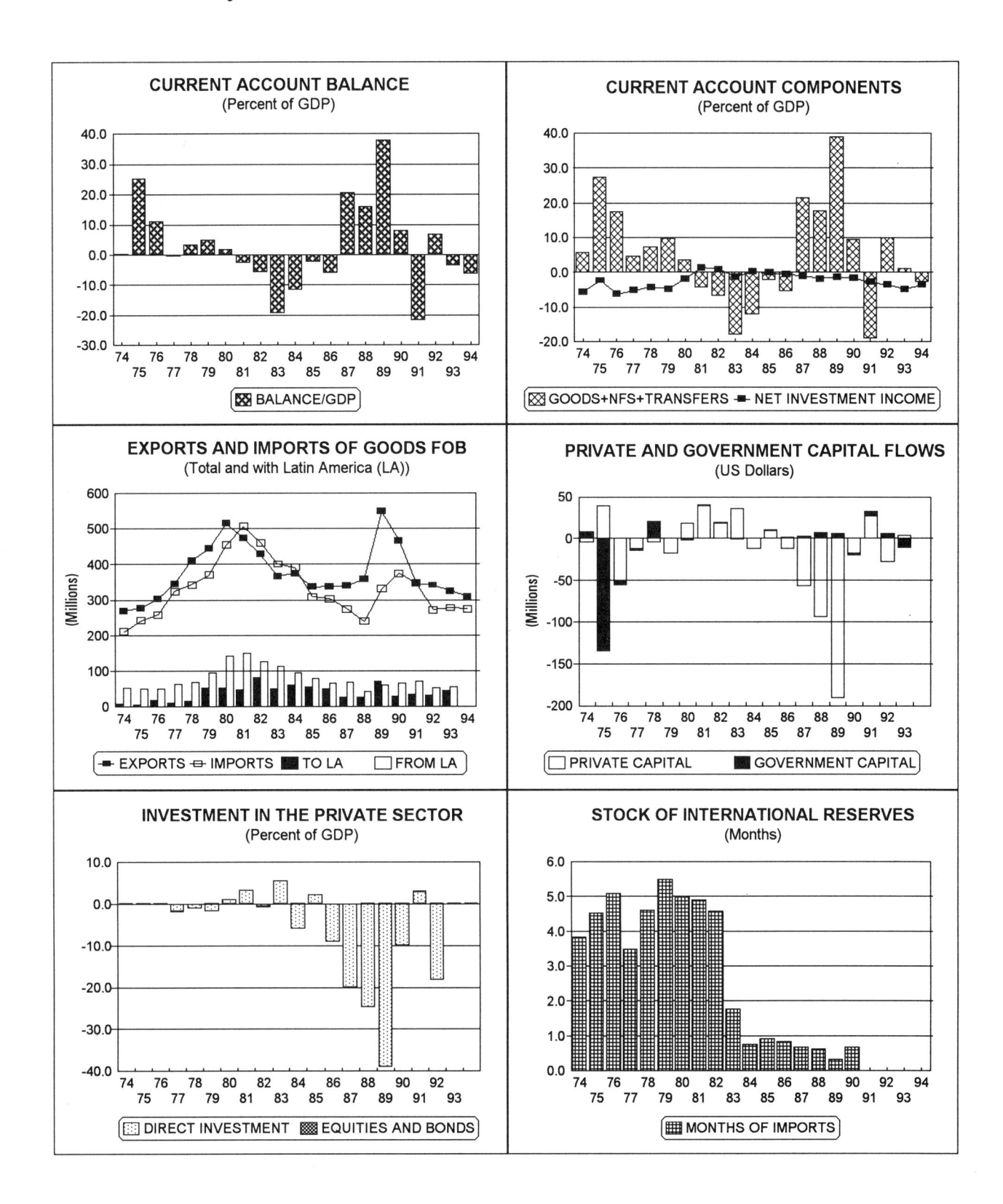

SURINAME
Balance of Payments in US Dollars

TRINIDAD AND TOBAGO
Balance of Payments in US Dollars

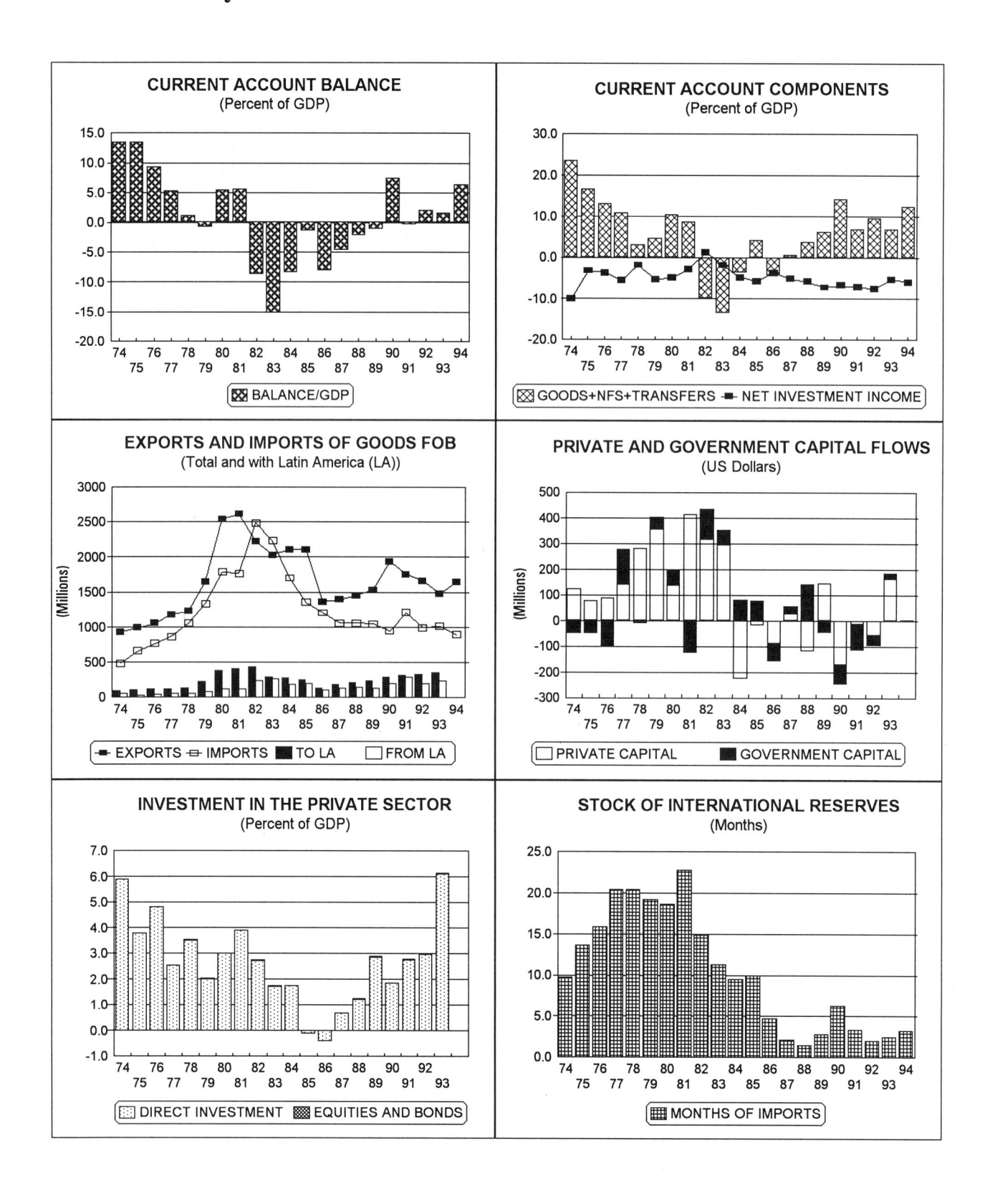

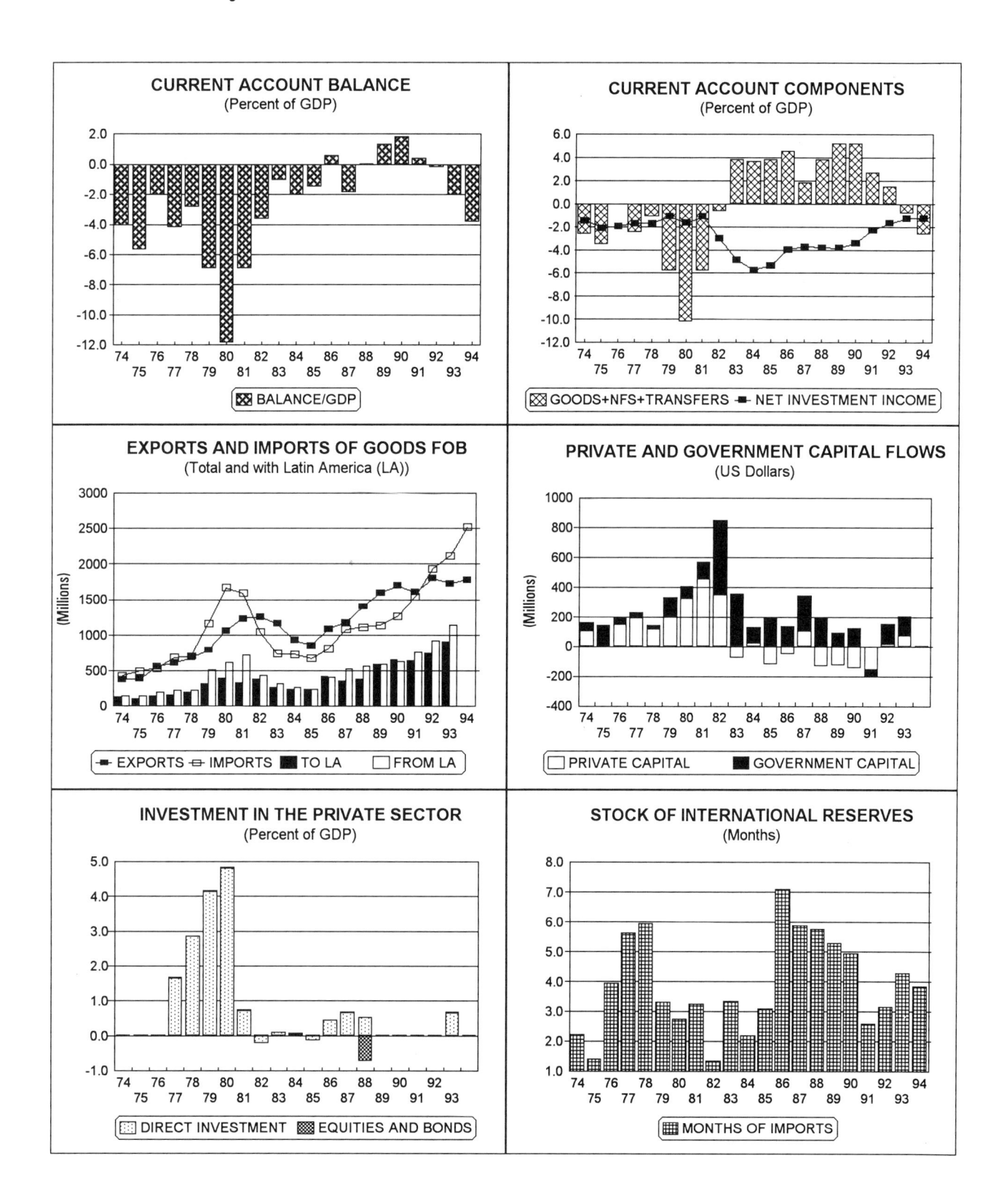

URUGUAY
Balance of Payments in US Dollars

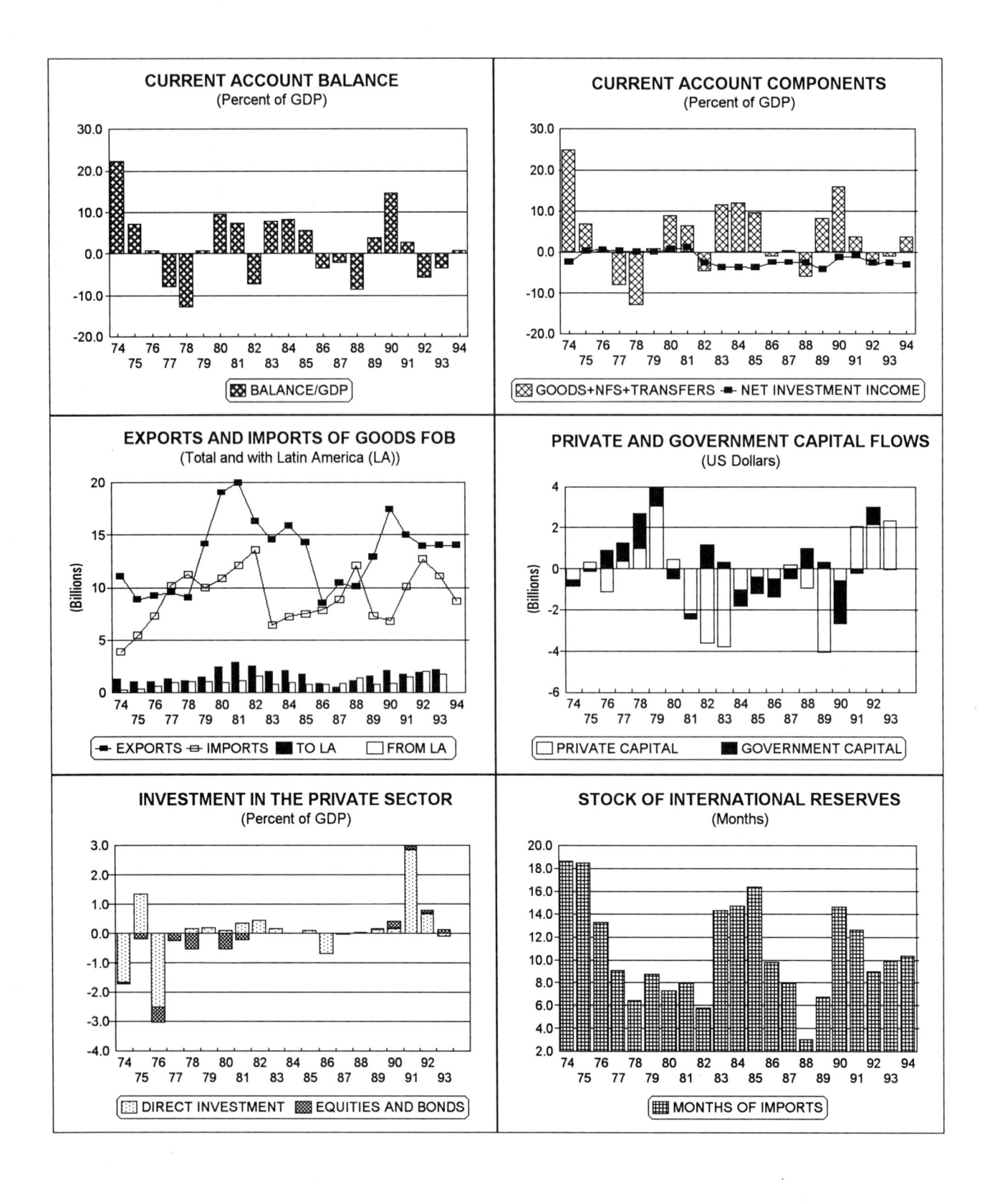

VENEZUELA
Balance of Payments in US Dollars

ENERGY

ENERGY

Data on Energy are from the United Nations Statistical Division. All data are in volume expressed in Metric Tons of Oil Equivalent (MTOE). The reader may refer to the technical note on page 3 for definitions of energy concepts. Description on the graphs follow:

1. PRODUCTION AND CONSUMPTION OF ENERGY (COMMERCIAL ONLY, IN MTOE)

The production of commercial primary energy is compared with commercial energy consumption. If there is a gap, it must be filled by imports. In the case of a positive difference, there is an exportable surplus. In some cases, a sharp increase in production also provokes a substantial upwards swing in consumption.

2. PRODUCTION OF PRIMARY ENERGY (STRUCTURE IN VOLUME)

The structure of primary energy production by major fuel except biomass is shown in oil equivalent from 1973 to 1992. *Petroleum* includes Crude Oil and Natural Gas Liquids. *Gas* includes Natural Gas. *Electricity* includes Geothermal, Hydro, Nuclear, Solar, Tide, Wind and Wave. *Coal* includes Coal, Lignite, Peat and Oil Shale.

3. GDP AND ENERGY CONSUMPTION. (INDEX 1973 = 100)

The evolution of energy consumption (final consumption + losses) is compared to GDP growth. Structural shifts towards urbanization and changes in production structures may mean a higher growth in energy consumption than in GDP for some developing countries. An economic analysis should refer to the changing pattern of relative prices and to energy policies to better measure the change of energy consumption per unit of GDP.

4. ENERGY SURPLUS (NET EXPORTS AS % OF CONSUMPTION)

The energy gap shown in the first graph is expressed here as a percent of total consumption. When positive, it represents an exportable surplus. When negative, it shows an energy deficit, i.e. an import dependency.

5. SUPPLY OF PRIMARY ENERGY BY MAJOR FUEL (1992 STRUCTURE IN VOLUME)

The graph shows the percentage breakdown of the total supply of primary energy in 1992 between primary production and net imports for each major category of fuels, including biomass. Negative net imports means that the country is exporting more of the fuel than it imports. In such cases, the supply of that fuel will be production minus net exports.

6. ENERGY REQUIREMENT PER CAPITA, 1992 (INDEX EUROPEAN UNION = 100)

The total energy requirement per capita is compared with the median for Latin America and the median for the European Union (and with the USA in the case of the graph on Latin America). Differences essentially reflect relative levels of development. They also derive from disparities in structures of production and in consumption patterns. They are finaly explained by differences in efficiency in the production process as well as at the consumption level (mainly due to pricing policies). The total energy requirement is satisfied by the use of commercial energy or biomass. The graph visualizes the proportion of biomass use. It is still important in countries with relatively low commercial production and external constraints, particularly in Central America.

Country Notes

Panama

Data are available only from 1980.

LATIN AMERICA
Energy

Statistics and Quantitative Analysis/IDB

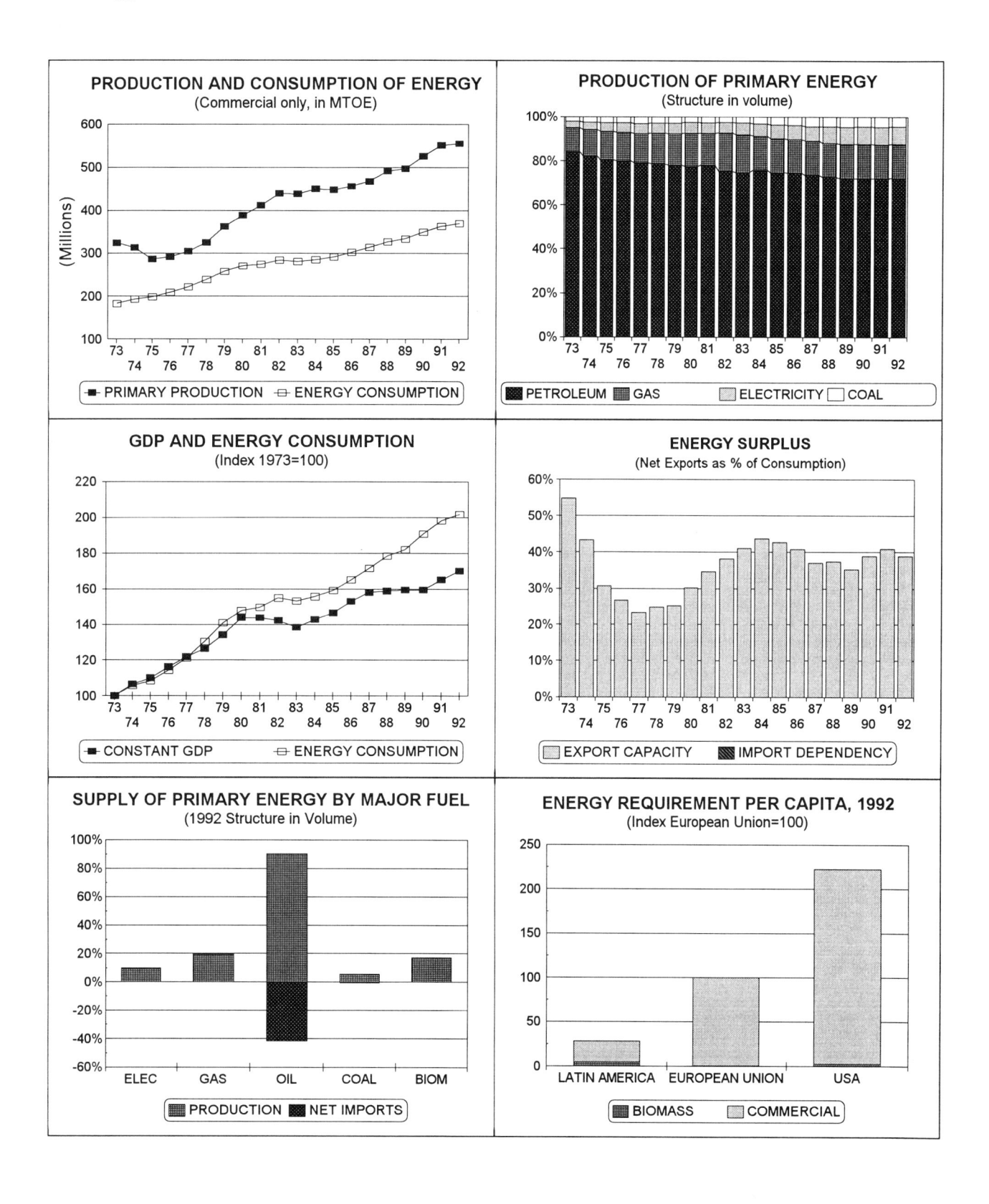

135

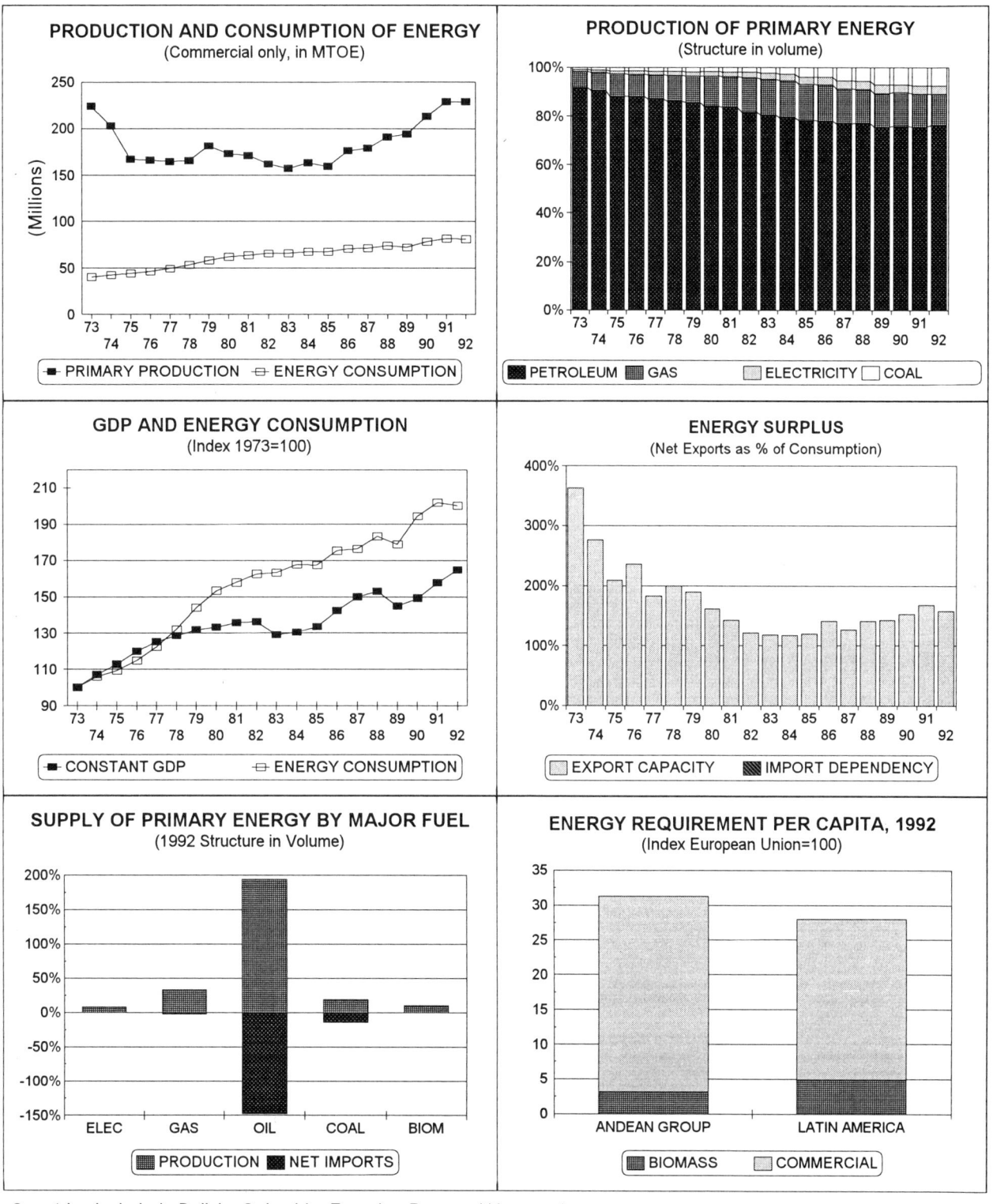

ANDEAN GROUP
Energy

PRODUCTION AND CONSUMPTION OF ENERGY
(Commercial only, in MTOE)

- PRIMARY PRODUCTION
- ENERGY CONSUMPTION

PRODUCTION OF PRIMARY ENERGY
(Structure in volume)

PETROLEUM | GAS | ELECTRICITY | COAL

GDP AND ENERGY CONSUMPTION
(Index 1973=100)

- CONSTANT GDP
- ENERGY CONSUMPTION

ENERGY SURPLUS
(Net Exports as % of Consumption)

EXPORT CAPACITY | IMPORT DEPENDENCY

SUPPLY OF PRIMARY ENERGY BY MAJOR FUEL
(1992 Structure in Volume)

ELEC | GAS | OIL | COAL | BIOM

PRODUCTION | NET IMPORTS

ENERGY REQUIREMENT PER CAPITA, 1992
(Index European Union=100)

ANDEAN GROUP | LATIN AMERICA

BIOMASS | COMMERCIAL

Countries included: Bolivia, Colombia, Ecuador, Peru and Venezuela.

Statistics and Quantitative Analysis/IDB

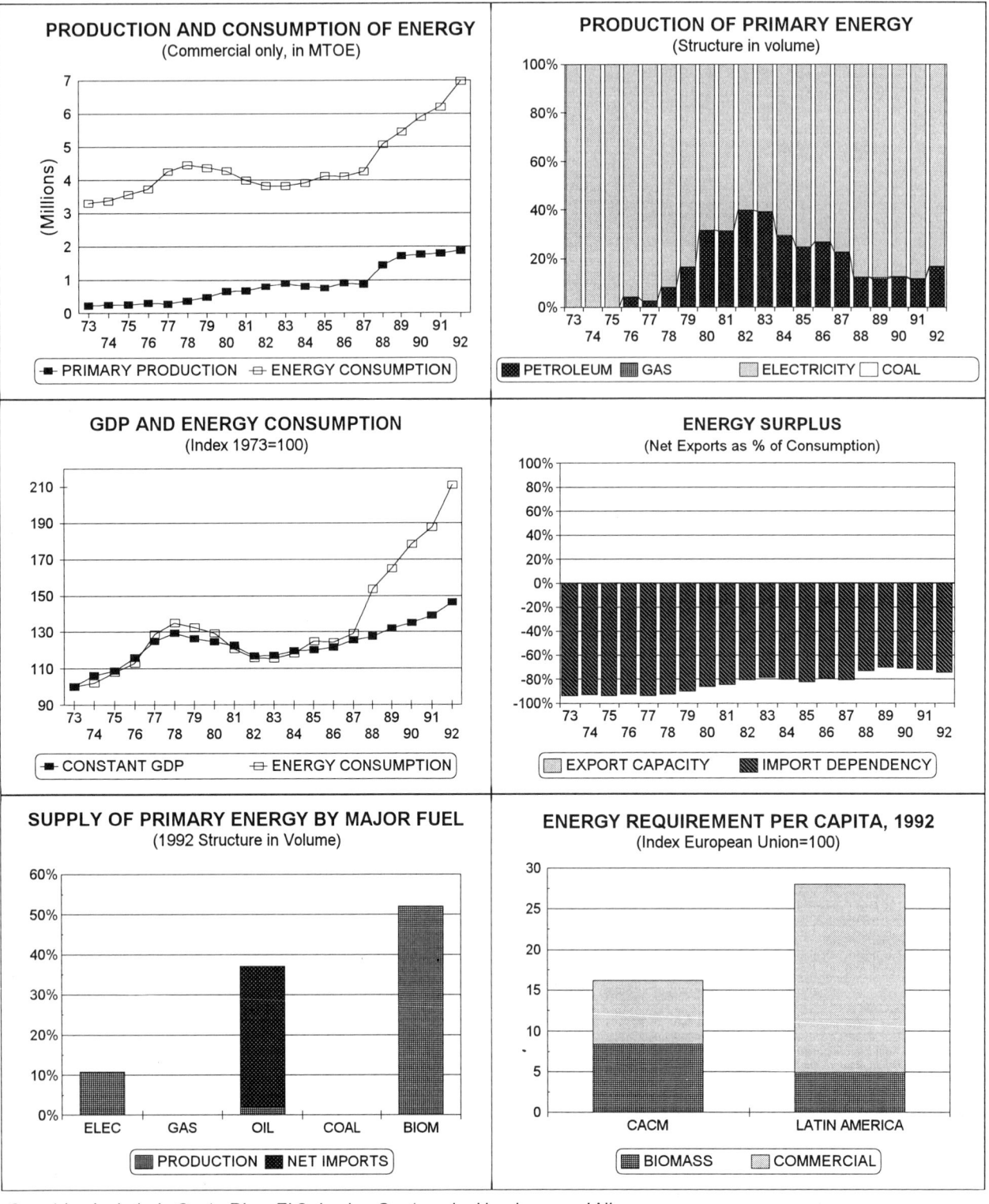

CACM
Energy

PRODUCTION AND CONSUMPTION OF ENERGY
(Commercial only, in MTOE)

PRODUCTION OF PRIMARY ENERGY
(Structure in volume)

■ PETROLEUM ■ GAS ▨ ELECTRICITY □ COAL

GDP AND ENERGY CONSUMPTION
(Index 1973=100)

ENERGY SURPLUS
(Net Exports as % of Consumption)

▨ EXPORT CAPACITY ■ IMPORT DEPENDENCY

SUPPLY OF PRIMARY ENERGY BY MAJOR FUEL
(1992 Structure in Volume)

ENERGY REQUIREMENT PER CAPITA, 1992
(Index European Union=100)

Countries included : Costa Rica, El Salvador, Guatemala, Honduras and Nicaragua.

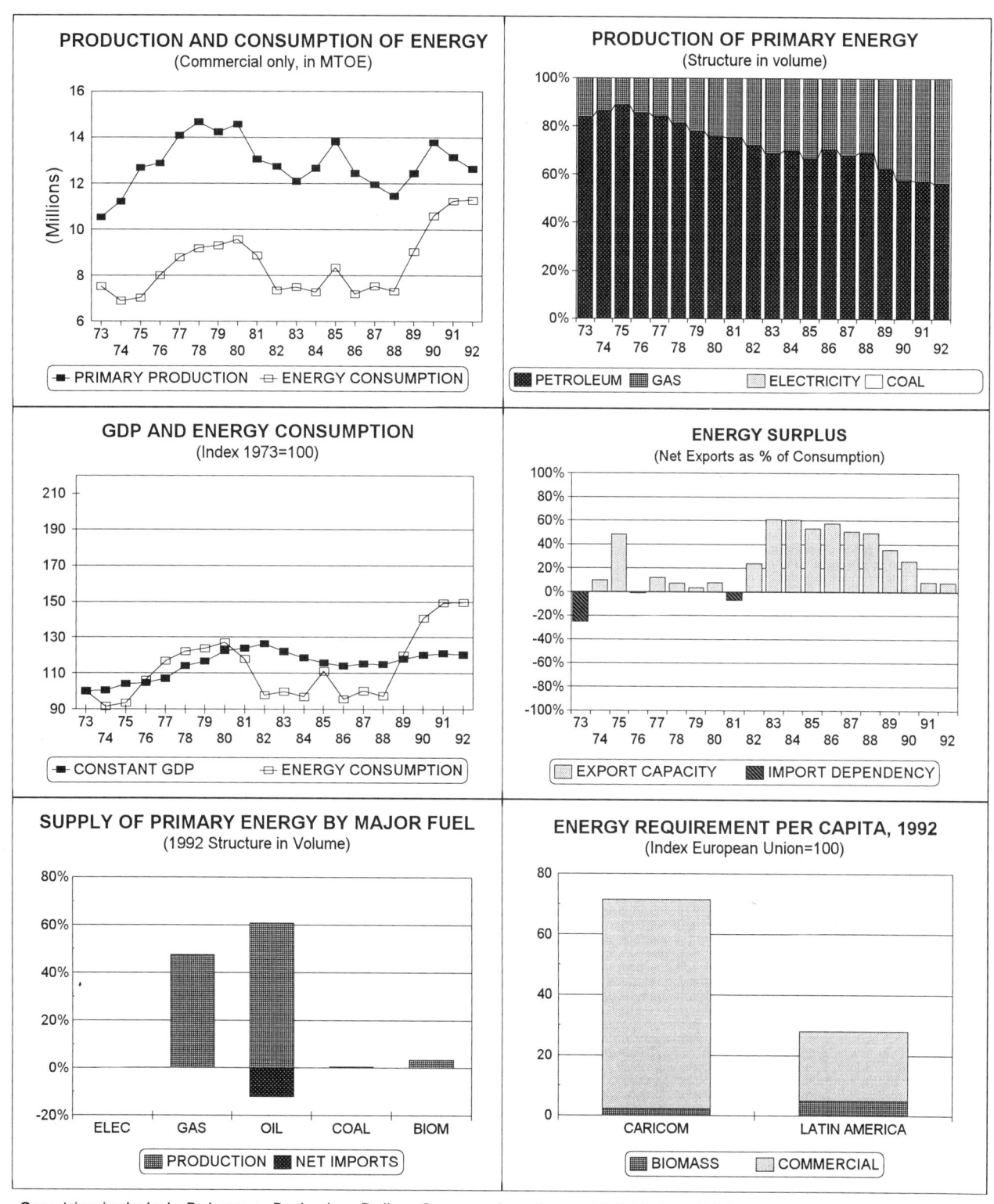

CARICOM
Energy

PRODUCTION AND CONSUMPTION OF ENERGY
(Commercial only, in MTOE)

- PRIMARY PRODUCTION
- ENERGY CONSUMPTION

PRODUCTION OF PRIMARY ENERGY
(Structure in volume)

- PETROLEUM
- GAS
- ELECTRICITY
- COAL

GDP AND ENERGY CONSUMPTION
(Index 1973=100)

- CONSTANT GDP
- ENERGY CONSUMPTION

ENERGY SURPLUS
(Net Exports as % of Consumption)

- EXPORT CAPACITY
- IMPORT DEPENDENCY

SUPPLY OF PRIMARY ENERGY BY MAJOR FUEL
(1992 Structure in Volume)

- PRODUCTION
- NET IMPORTS

ENERGY REQUIREMENT PER CAPITA, 1992
(Index European Union=100)

- BIOMASS
- COMMERCIAL

Countries included : Bahamas, Barbados, Belize, Guyana, Jamaica and Trinidad and Tobago.

Statistics and Quantitative Analysis/IDB

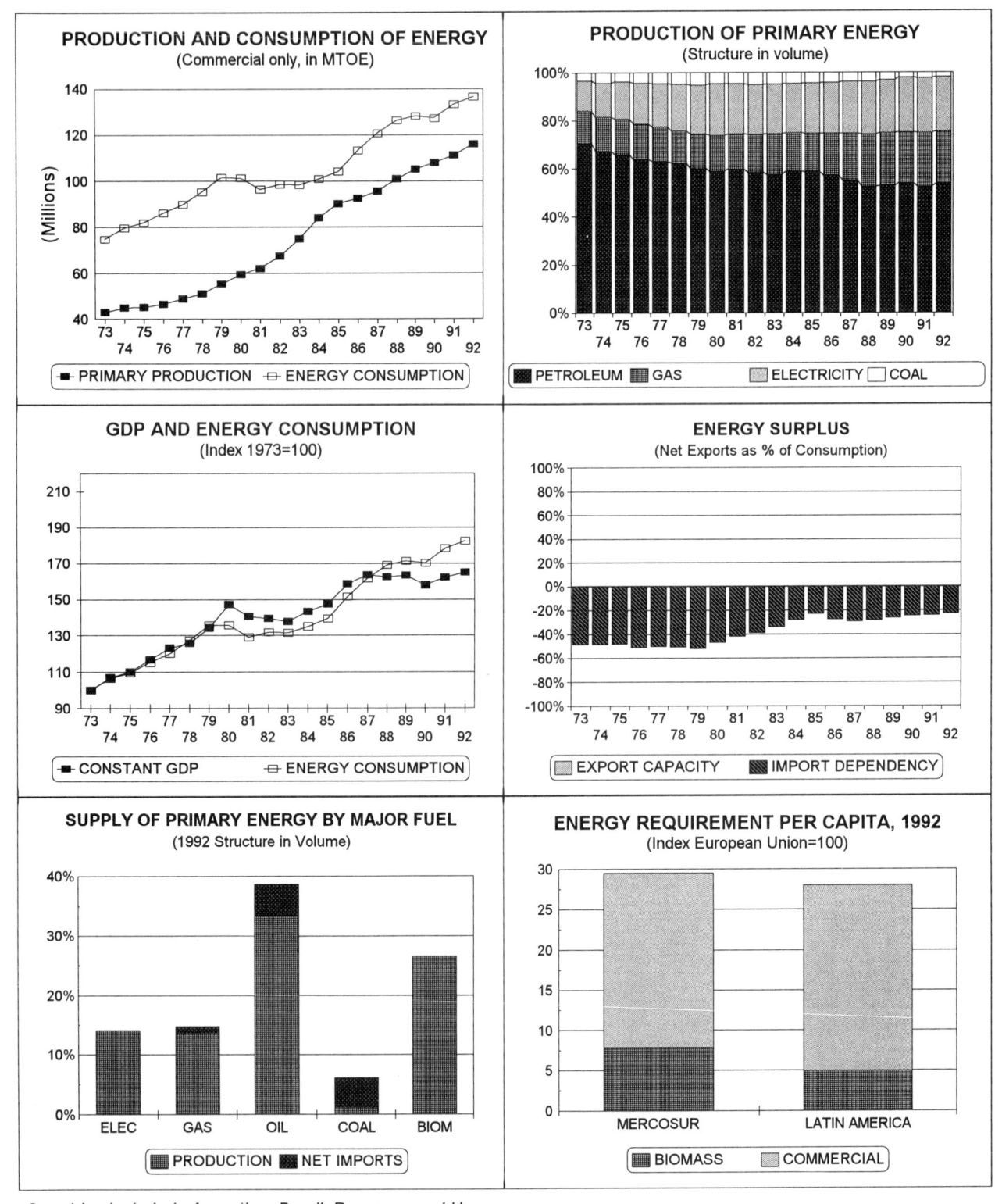

MERCOSUR
Energy

PRODUCTION AND CONSUMPTION OF ENERGY
(Commercial only, in MTOE)

- PRIMARY PRODUCTION
- ENERGY CONSUMPTION

PRODUCTION OF PRIMARY ENERGY
(Structure in volume)

- PETROLEUM
- GAS
- ELECTRICITY
- COAL

GDP AND ENERGY CONSUMPTION
(Index 1973=100)

- CONSTANT GDP
- ENERGY CONSUMPTION

ENERGY SURPLUS
(Net Exports as % of Consumption)

- EXPORT CAPACITY
- IMPORT DEPENDENCY

SUPPLY OF PRIMARY ENERGY BY MAJOR FUEL
(1992 Structure in Volume)

ELEC, GAS, OIL, COAL, BIOM

- PRODUCTION
- NET IMPORTS

ENERGY REQUIREMENT PER CAPITA, 1992
(Index European Union=100)

MERCOSUR, LATIN AMERICA

- BIOMASS
- COMMERCIAL

Countries included : Argentina, Brazil, Paraguay and Uruguay.

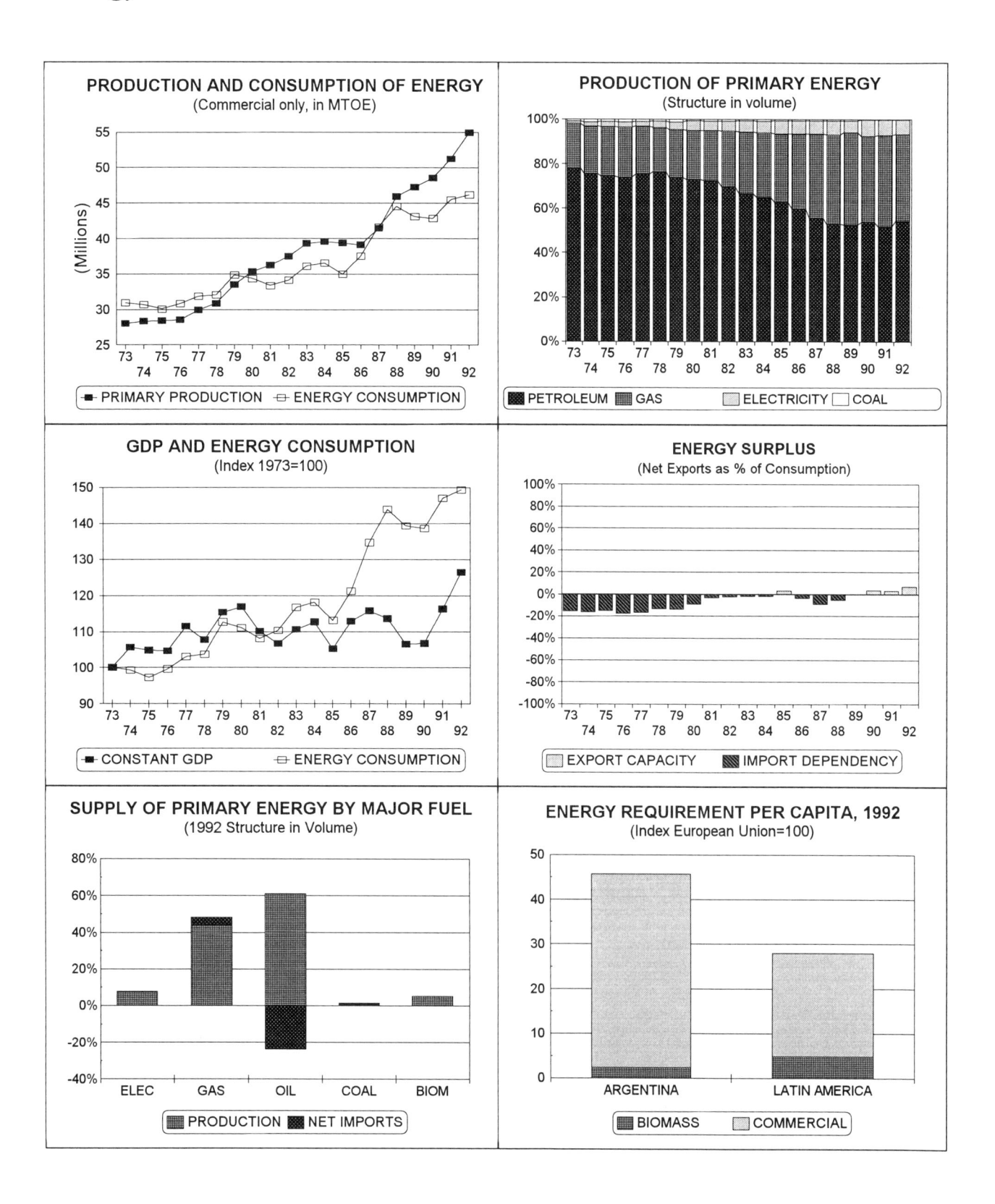

ARGENTINA
Energy

PRODUCTION AND CONSUMPTION OF ENERGY
(Commercial only, in MTOE)

PRODUCTION OF PRIMARY ENERGY
(Structure in volume)

GDP AND ENERGY CONSUMPTION
(Index 1973=100)

ENERGY SURPLUS
(Net Exports as % of Consumption)

SUPPLY OF PRIMARY ENERGY BY MAJOR FUEL
(1992 Structure in Volume)

ENERGY REQUIREMENT PER CAPITA, 1992
(Index European Union=100)

Statistics and Quantitative Analysis/IDB

BAHAMAS
Energy

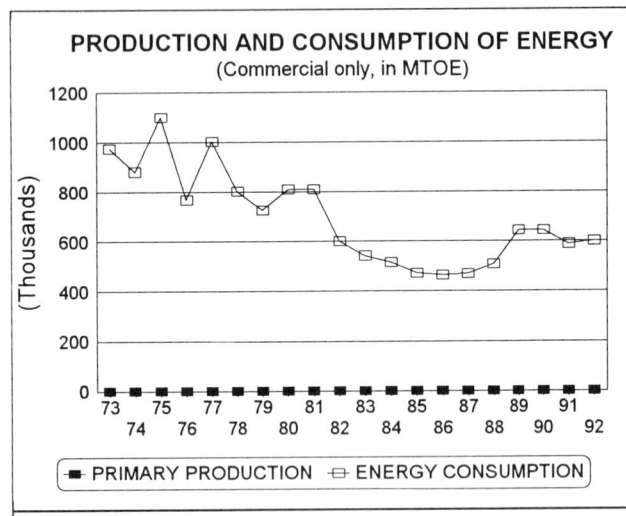

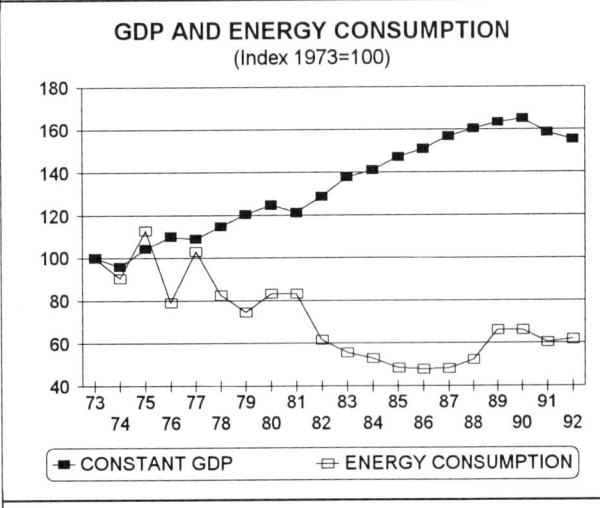

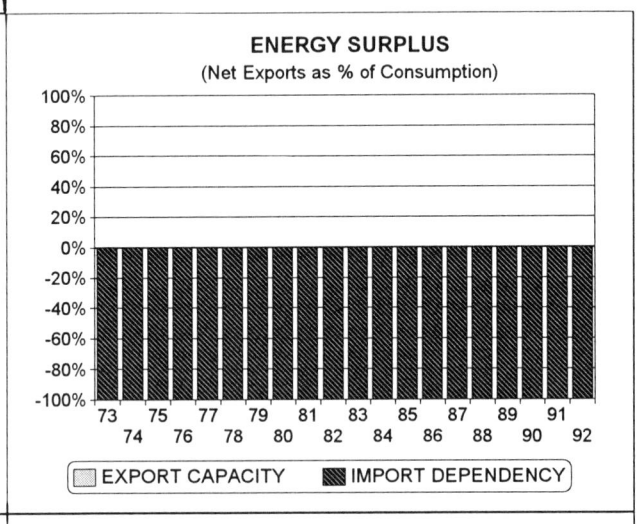

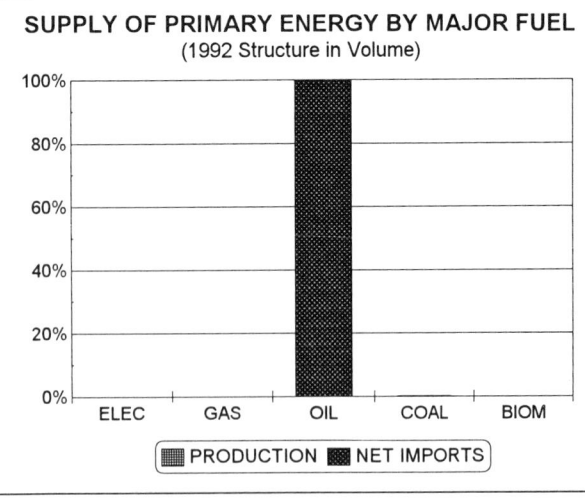

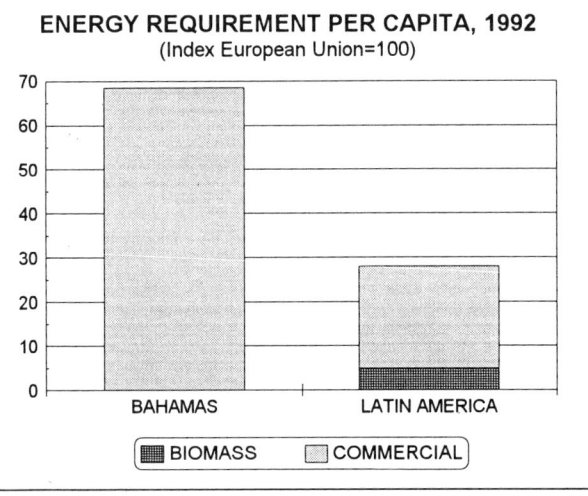

PRODUCTION AND CONSUMPTION OF ENERGY
(Commercial only, in MTOE)

GDP AND ENERGY CONSUMPTION
(Index 1973=100)

ENERGY SURPLUS
(Net Exports as % of Consumption)

SUPPLY OF PRIMARY ENERGY BY MAJOR FUEL
(1992 Structure in Volume)

ENERGY REQUIREMENT PER CAPITA, 1992
(Index European Union=100)

BARBADOS
Energy

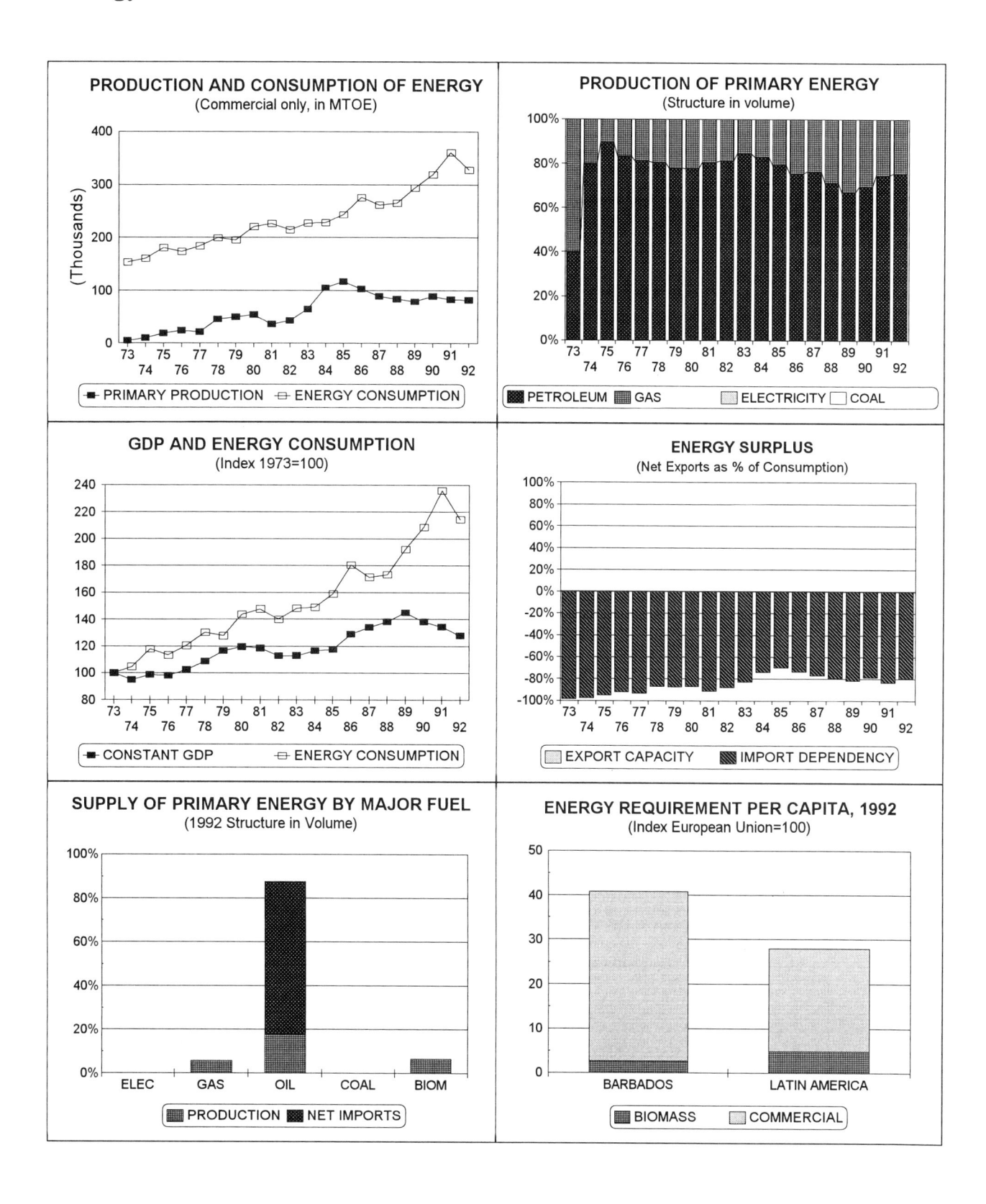

PRODUCTION AND CONSUMPTION OF ENERGY
(Commercial only, in MTOE)

PRODUCTION OF PRIMARY ENERGY
(Structure in volume)

GDP AND ENERGY CONSUMPTION
(Index 1973=100)

ENERGY SURPLUS
(Net Exports as % of Consumption)

SUPPLY OF PRIMARY ENERGY BY MAJOR FUEL
(1992 Structure in Volume)

ENERGY REQUIREMENT PER CAPITA, 1992
(Index European Union=100)

Statistics and Quantitative Analysis/IDB

BELIZE
Energy

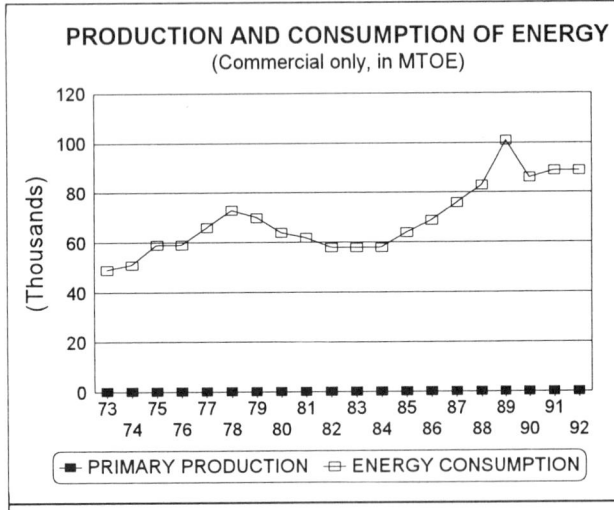

PRODUCTION AND CONSUMPTION OF ENERGY
(Commercial only, in MTOE)

- PRIMARY PRODUCTION
- ENERGY CONSUMPTION

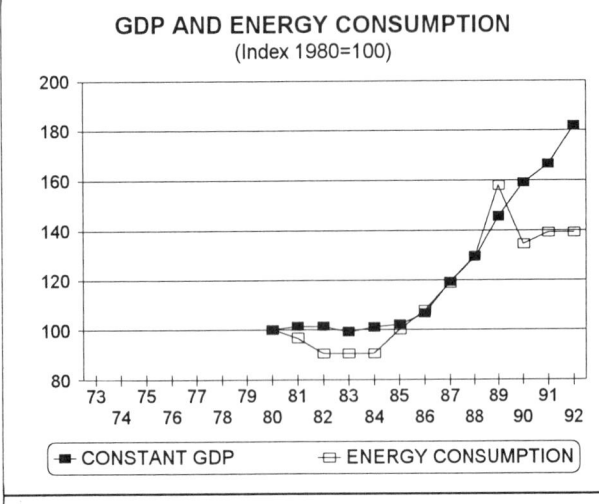

GDP AND ENERGY CONSUMPTION
(Index 1980=100)

- CONSTANT GDP
- ENERGY CONSUMPTION

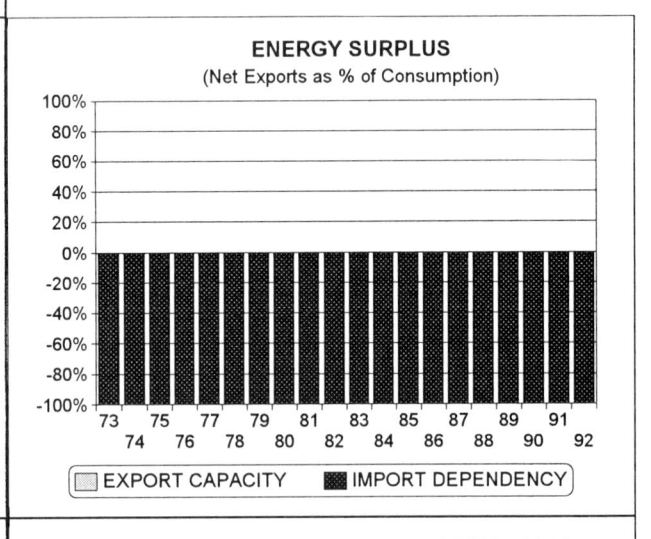

ENERGY SURPLUS
(Net Exports as % of Consumption)

- EXPORT CAPACITY
- IMPORT DEPENDENCY

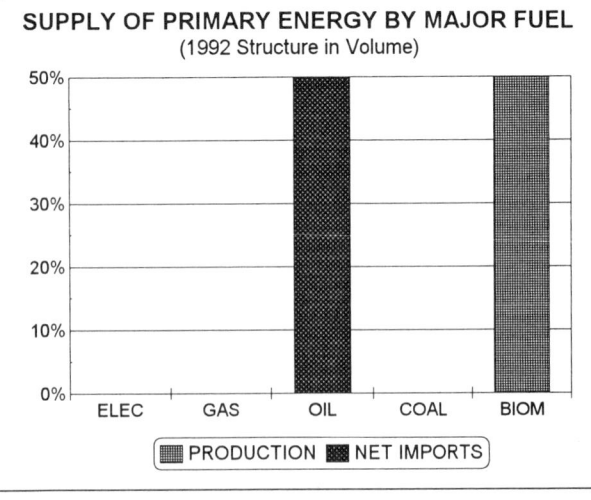

SUPPLY OF PRIMARY ENERGY BY MAJOR FUEL
(1992 Structure in Volume)

- PRODUCTION
- NET IMPORTS

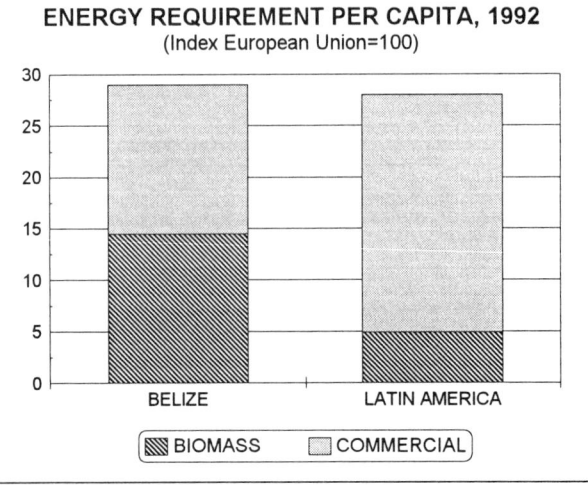

ENERGY REQUIREMENT PER CAPITA, 1992
(Index European Union=100)

- BIOMASS
- COMMERCIAL

Statistics and Quantitative Analysis/IDB

BOLIVIA
Energy

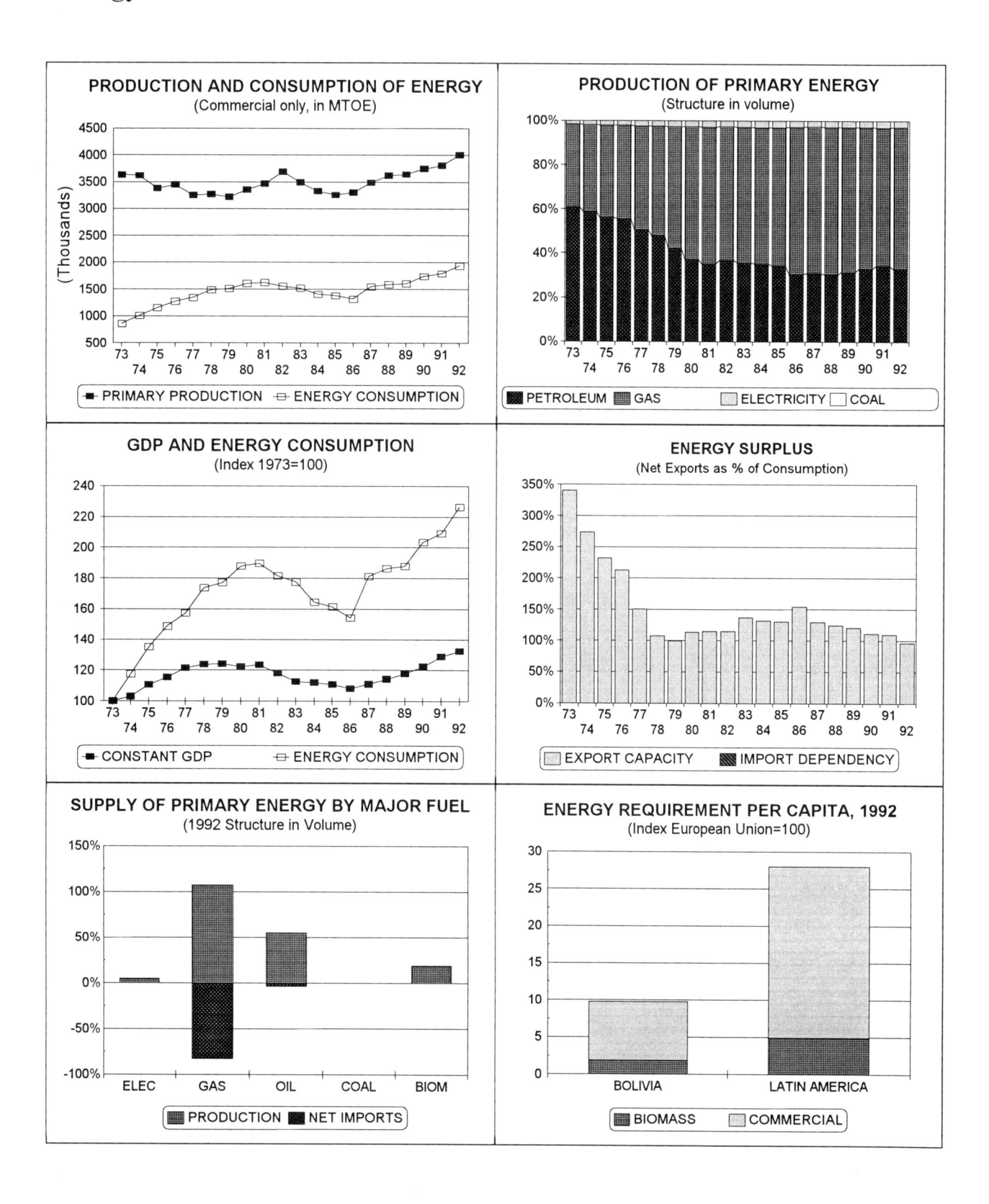

PRODUCTION AND CONSUMPTION OF ENERGY
(Commercial only, in MTOE)

PRODUCTION OF PRIMARY ENERGY
(Structure in volume)

GDP AND ENERGY CONSUMPTION
(Index 1973=100)

ENERGY SURPLUS
(Net Exports as % of Consumption)

SUPPLY OF PRIMARY ENERGY BY MAJOR FUEL
(1992 Structure in Volume)

ENERGY REQUIREMENT PER CAPITA, 1992
(Index European Union=100)

Statistics and Quantitative Analysis/IDB

BRAZIL
Energy

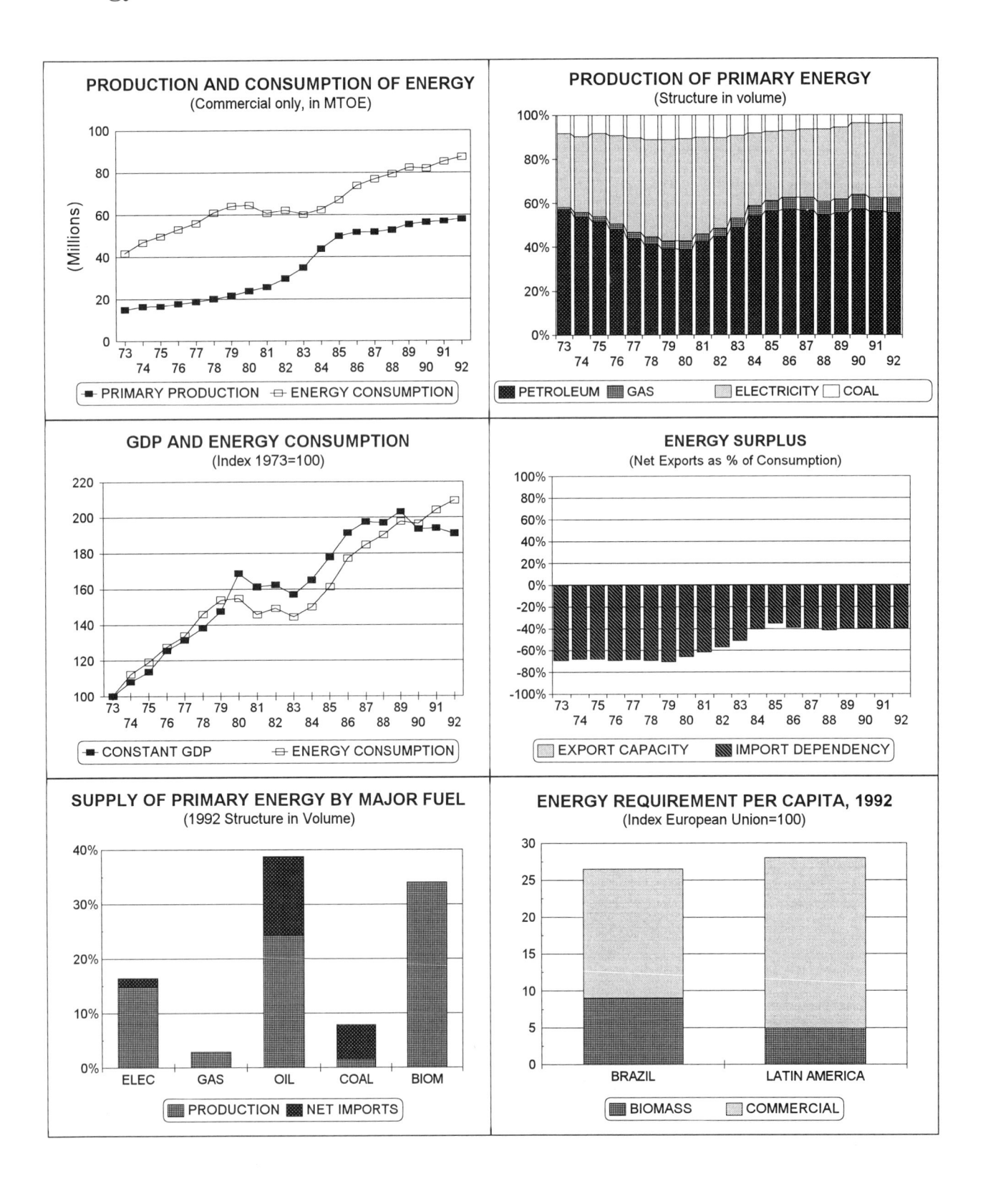

PRODUCTION AND CONSUMPTION OF ENERGY
(Commercial only, in MTOE)
- PRIMARY PRODUCTION
- ENERGY CONSUMPTION

PRODUCTION OF PRIMARY ENERGY
(Structure in volume)
- PETROLEUM
- GAS
- ELECTRICITY
- COAL

GDP AND ENERGY CONSUMPTION
(Index 1973=100)
- CONSTANT GDP
- ENERGY CONSUMPTION

ENERGY SURPLUS
(Net Exports as % of Consumption)
- EXPORT CAPACITY
- IMPORT DEPENDENCY

SUPPLY OF PRIMARY ENERGY BY MAJOR FUEL
(1992 Structure in Volume)
- ELEC, GAS, OIL, COAL, BIOM
- PRODUCTION
- NET IMPORTS

ENERGY REQUIREMENT PER CAPITA, 1992
(Index European Union=100)
- BRAZIL
- LATIN AMERICA
- BIOMASS
- COMMERCIAL

CHILE
Energy

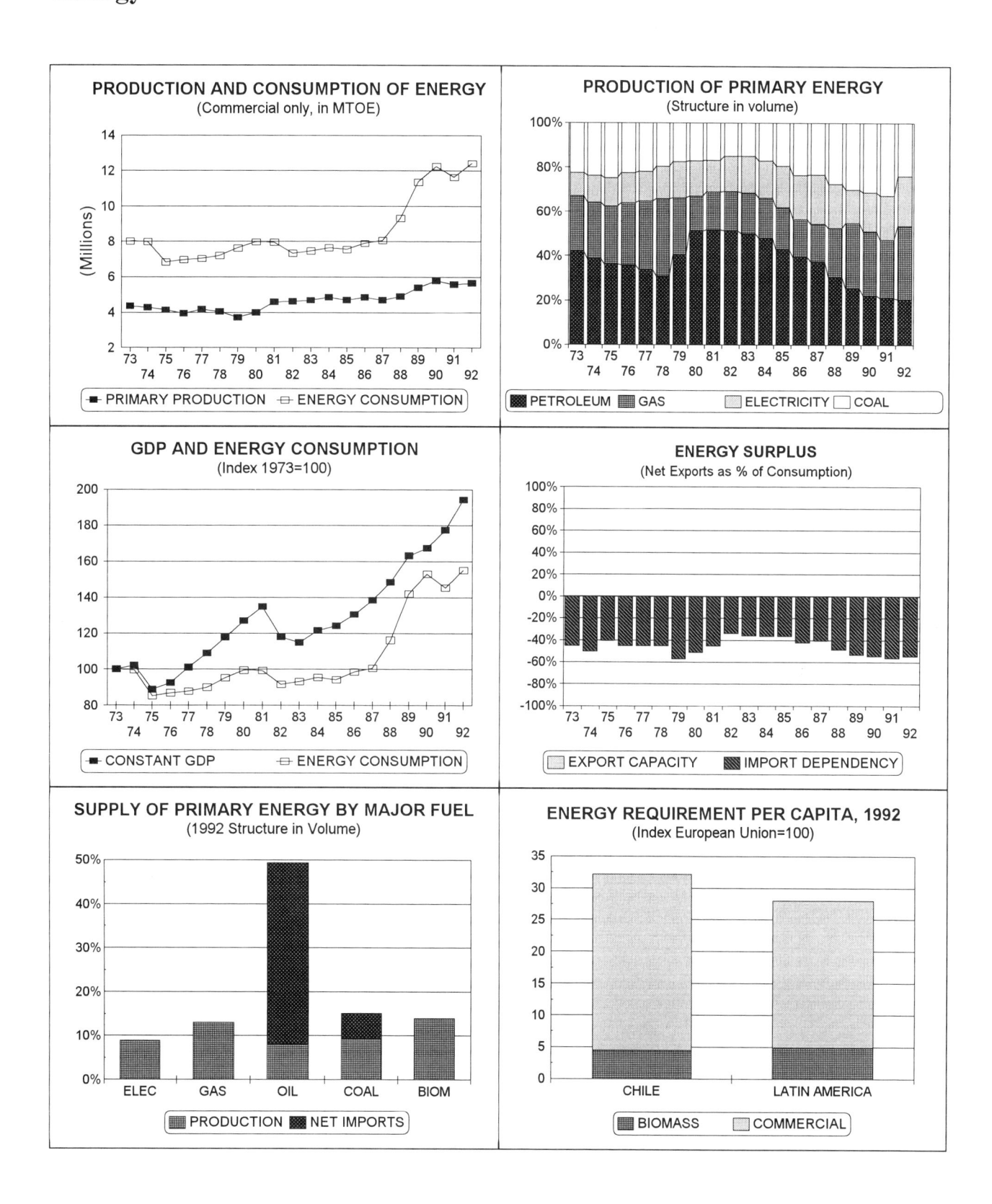

PRODUCTION AND CONSUMPTION OF ENERGY
(Commercial only, in MTOE)

■ PRIMARY PRODUCTION □ ENERGY CONSUMPTION

PRODUCTION OF PRIMARY ENERGY
(Structure in volume)

■ PETROLEUM ■ GAS ▨ ELECTRICITY □ COAL

GDP AND ENERGY CONSUMPTION
(Index 1973=100)

■ CONSTANT GDP □ ENERGY CONSUMPTION

ENERGY SURPLUS
(Net Exports as % of Consumption)

▨ EXPORT CAPACITY ■ IMPORT DEPENDENCY

SUPPLY OF PRIMARY ENERGY BY MAJOR FUEL
(1992 Structure in Volume)

ELEC GAS OIL COAL BIOM

■ PRODUCTION ■ NET IMPORTS

ENERGY REQUIREMENT PER CAPITA, 1992
(Index European Union=100)

CHILE LATIN AMERICA

■ BIOMASS ▨ COMMERCIAL

Statistics and Quantitative Analysis/IDB

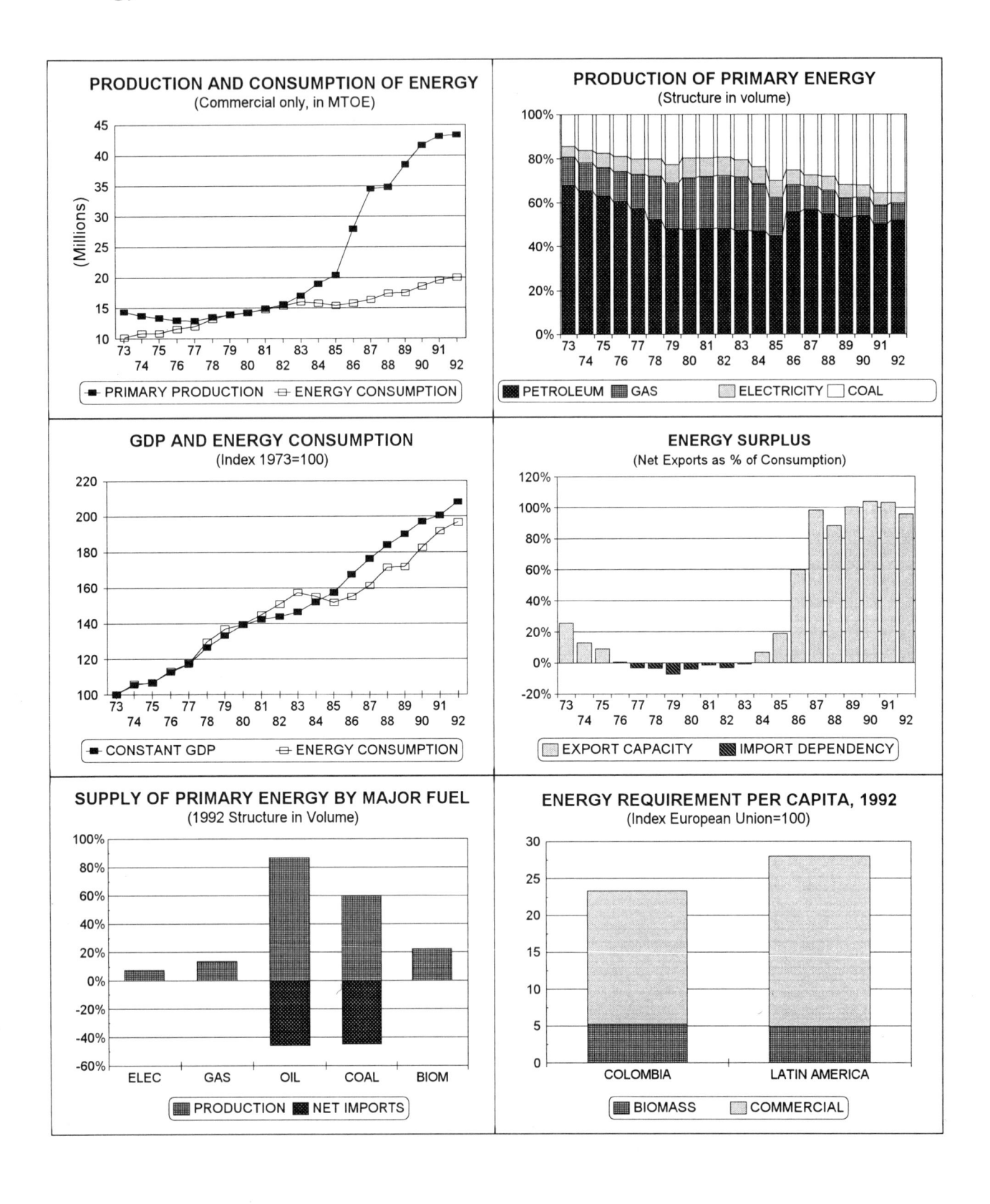

COLOMBIA
Energy

PRODUCTION AND CONSUMPTION OF ENERGY
(Commercial only, in MTOE)

PRODUCTION OF PRIMARY ENERGY
(Structure in volume)

GDP AND ENERGY CONSUMPTION
(Index 1973=100)

ENERGY SURPLUS
(Net Exports as % of Consumption)

SUPPLY OF PRIMARY ENERGY BY MAJOR FUEL
(1992 Structure in Volume)

ENERGY REQUIREMENT PER CAPITA, 1992
(Index European Union=100)

Statistics and Quantitative Analysis/IDB

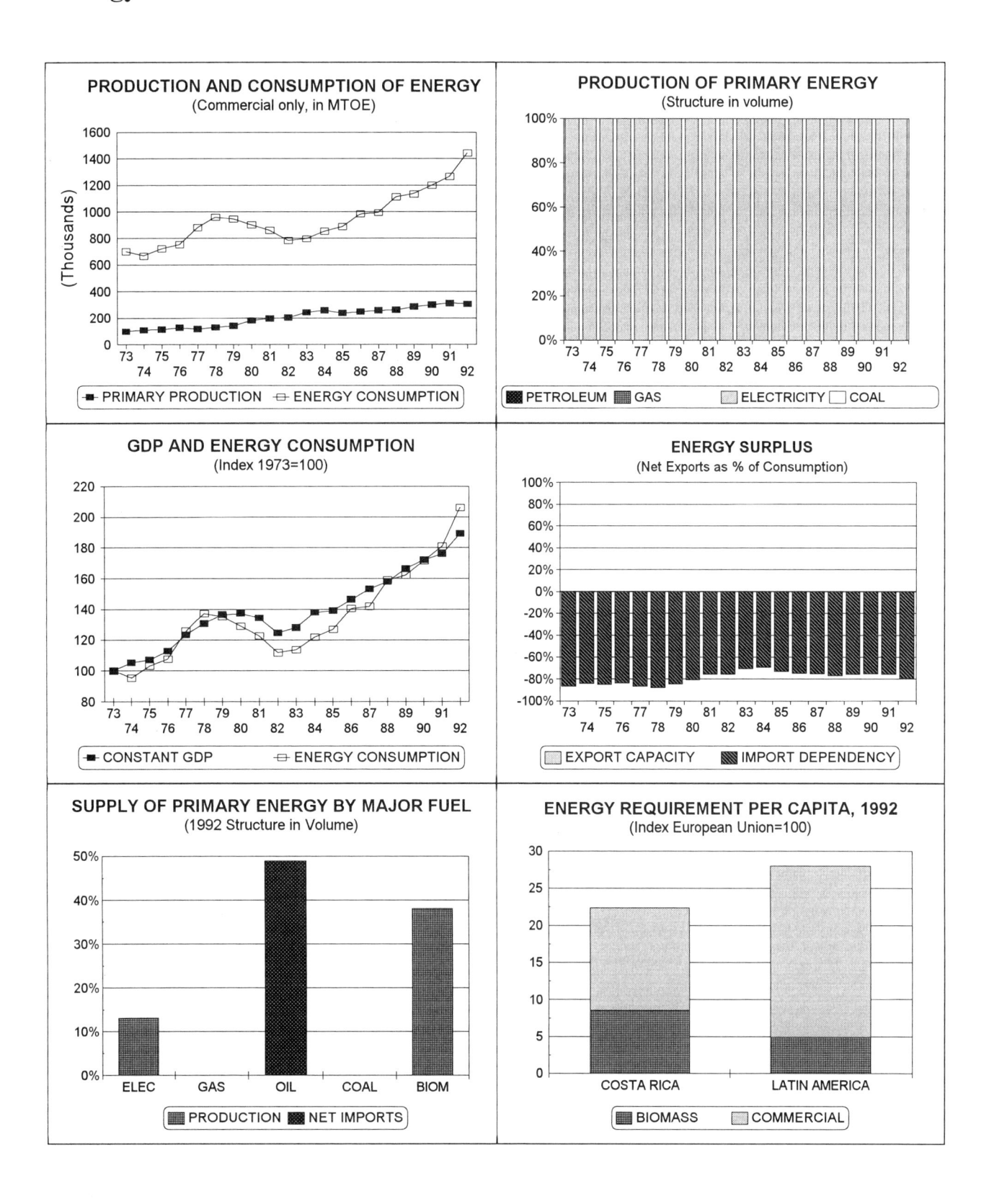

COSTA RICA
Energy

PRODUCTION AND CONSUMPTION OF ENERGY
(Commercial only, in MTOE)

PRODUCTION OF PRIMARY ENERGY
(Structure in volume)

GDP AND ENERGY CONSUMPTION
(Index 1973=100)

ENERGY SURPLUS
(Net Exports as % of Consumption)

SUPPLY OF PRIMARY ENERGY BY MAJOR FUEL
(1992 Structure in Volume)

ENERGY REQUIREMENT PER CAPITA, 1992
(Index European Union=100)

Statistics and Quantitative Analysis/IDB

DOMINICAN REPUBLIC
Energy

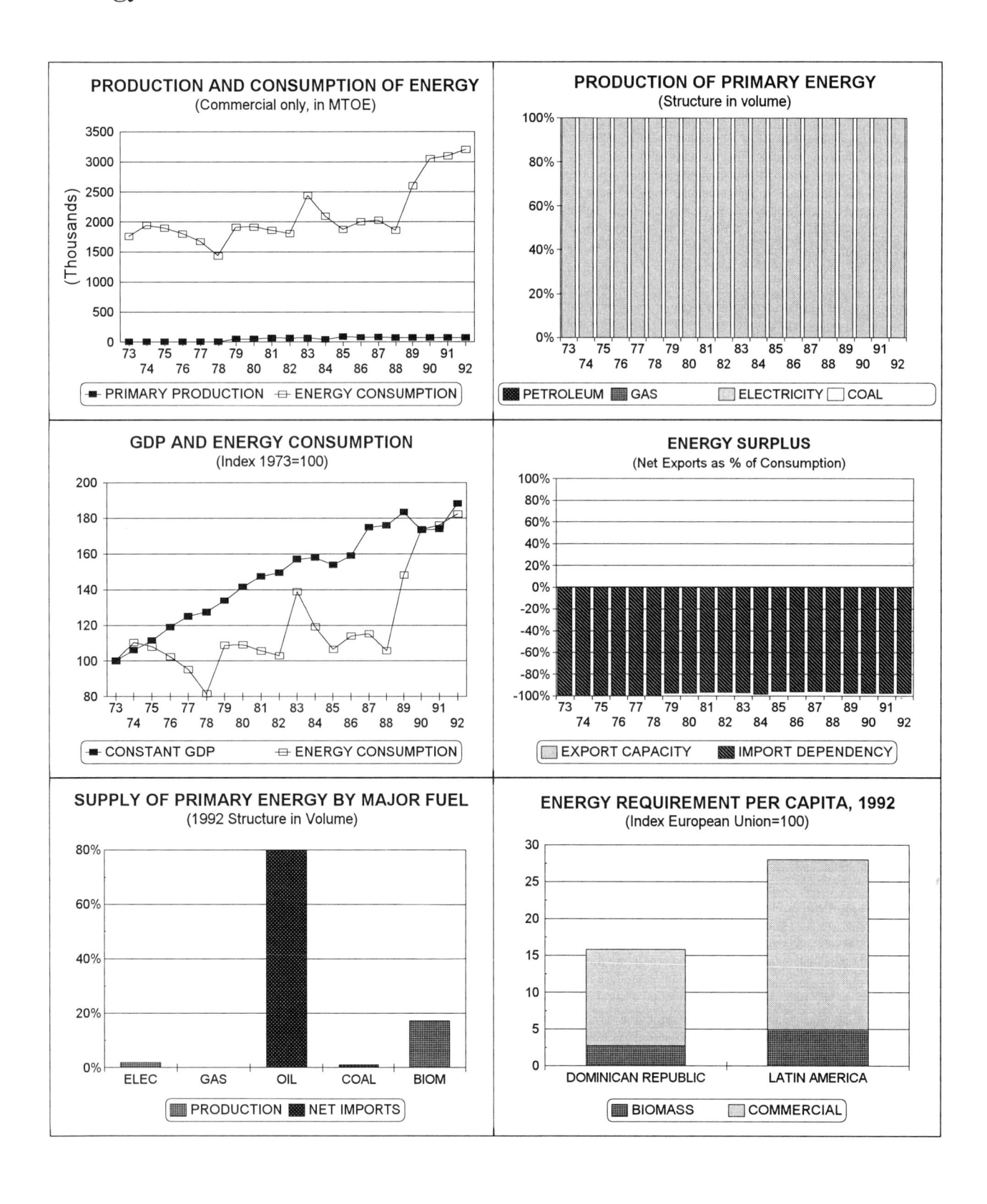

PRODUCTION AND CONSUMPTION OF ENERGY
(Commercial only, in MTOE)

PRODUCTION OF PRIMARY ENERGY
(Structure in volume)

GDP AND ENERGY CONSUMPTION
(Index 1973=100)

ENERGY SURPLUS
(Net Exports as % of Consumption)

SUPPLY OF PRIMARY ENERGY BY MAJOR FUEL
(1992 Structure in Volume)

ENERGY REQUIREMENT PER CAPITA, 1992
(Index European Union=100)

Statistics and Quantitative Analysis/IDB

ECUADOR
Energy

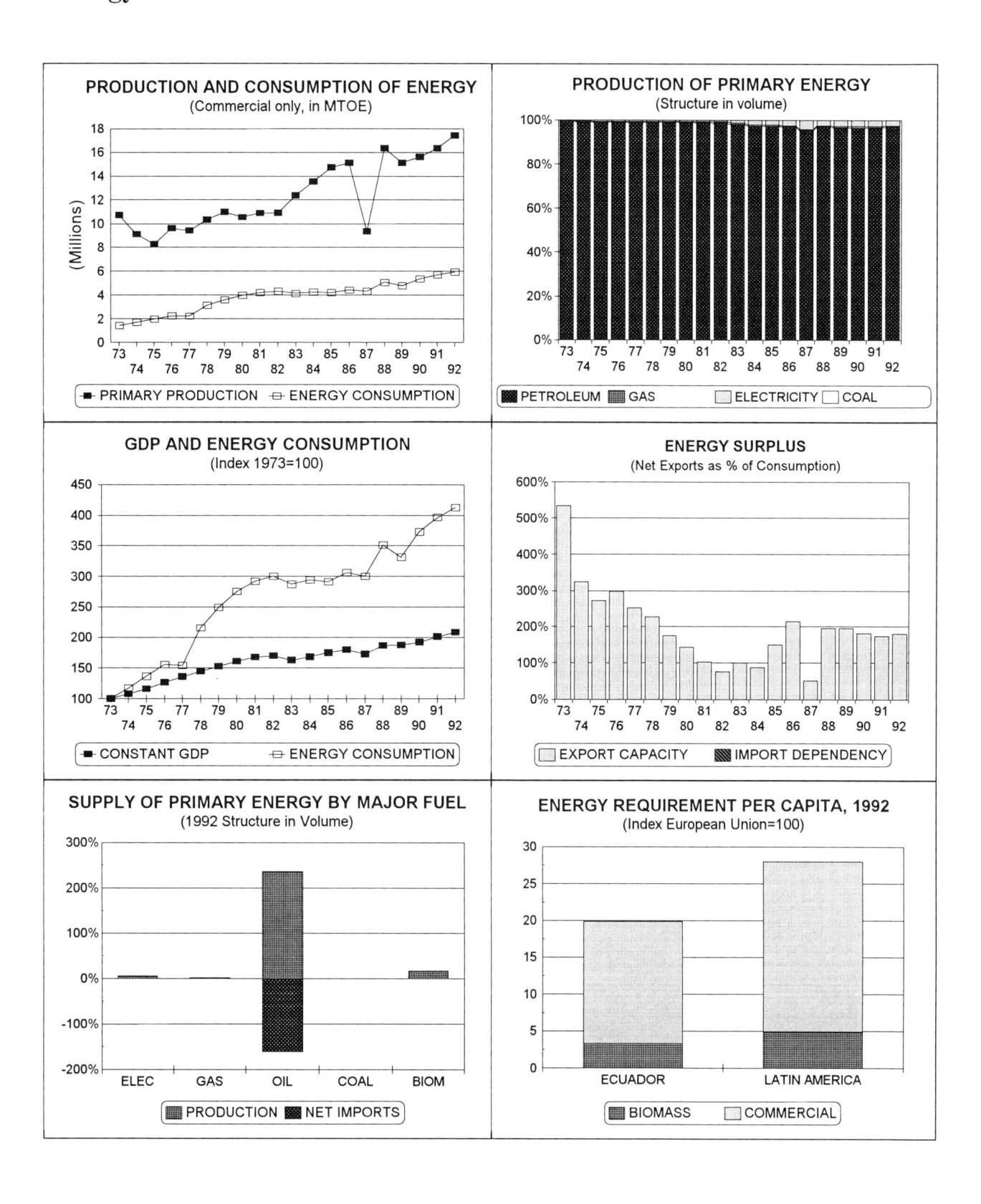

PRODUCTION AND CONSUMPTION OF ENERGY
(Commercial only, in MTOE)

— PRIMARY PRODUCTION   — ENERGY CONSUMPTION

PRODUCTION OF PRIMARY ENERGY
(Structure in volume)

PETROLEUM   GAS   ELECTRICITY   COAL

GDP AND ENERGY CONSUMPTION
(Index 1973=100)

— CONSTANT GDP   — ENERGY CONSUMPTION

ENERGY SURPLUS
(Net Exports as % of Consumption)

EXPORT CAPACITY   IMPORT DEPENDENCY

SUPPLY OF PRIMARY ENERGY BY MAJOR FUEL
(1992 Structure in Volume)

PRODUCTION   NET IMPORTS

ENERGY REQUIREMENT PER CAPITA, 1992
(Index European Union=100)

BIOMASS   COMMERCIAL

Statistics and Quantitative Analysis/IDB

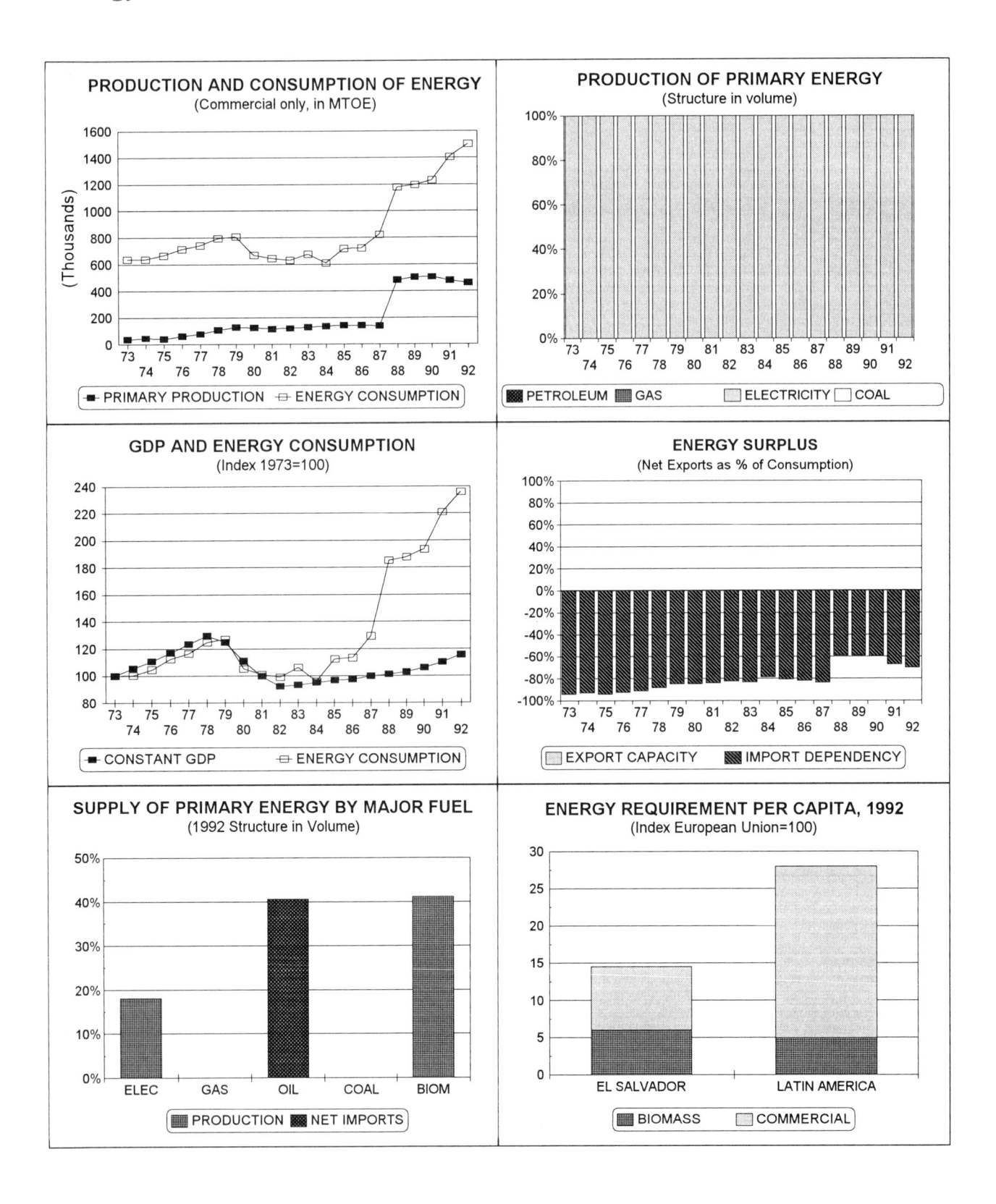

EL SALVADOR
Energy

PRODUCTION AND CONSUMPTION OF ENERGY
(Commercial only, in MTOE)

PRODUCTION OF PRIMARY ENERGY
(Structure in volume)

GDP AND ENERGY CONSUMPTION
(Index 1973=100)

ENERGY SURPLUS
(Net Exports as % of Consumption)

SUPPLY OF PRIMARY ENERGY BY MAJOR FUEL
(1992 Structure in Volume)

ENERGY REQUIREMENT PER CAPITA, 1992
(Index European Union=100)

Statistics and Quantitative Analysis/IDB

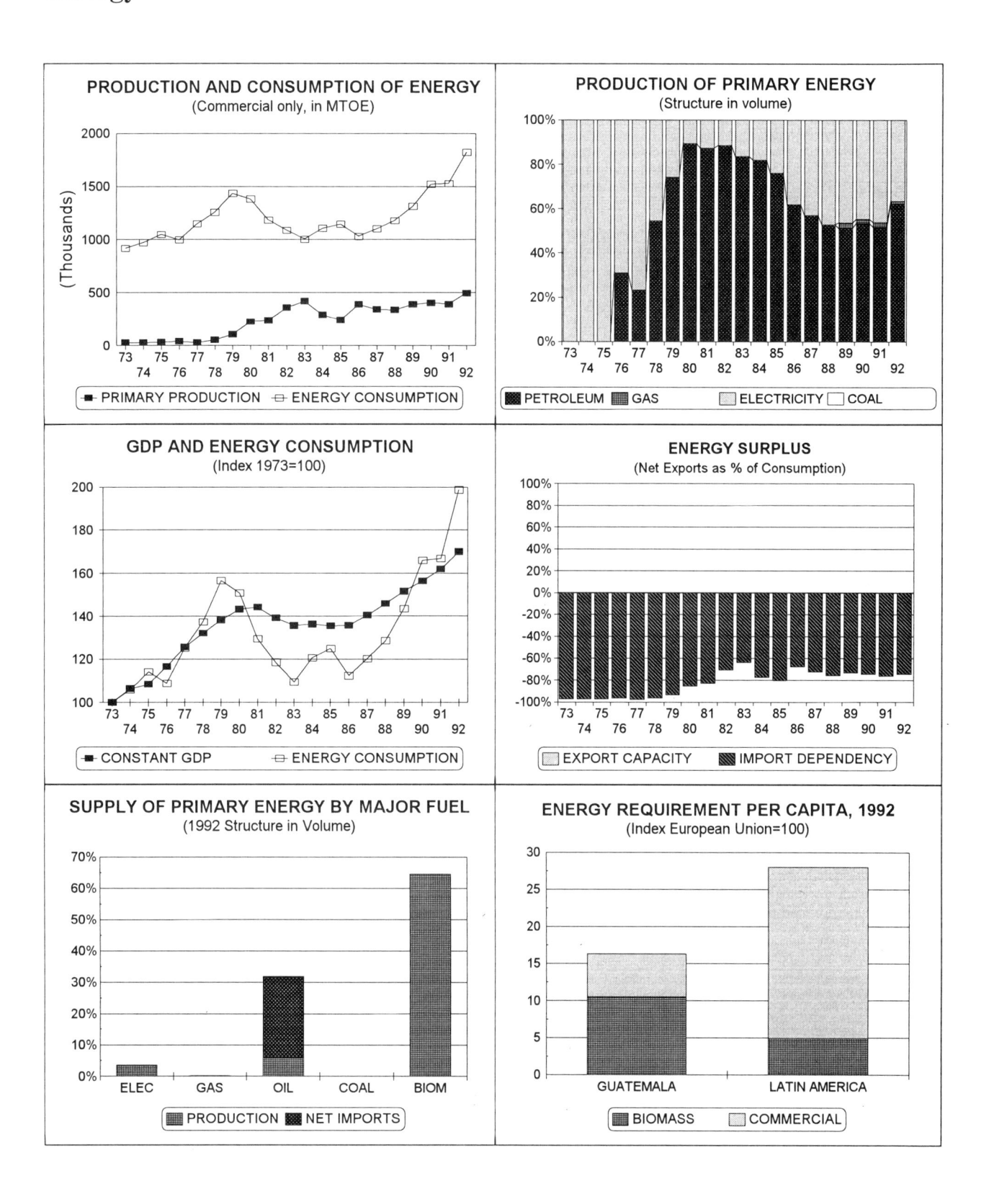

GUATEMALA
Energy

PRODUCTION AND CONSUMPTION OF ENERGY
(Commercial only, in MTOE)

PRODUCTION OF PRIMARY ENERGY
(Structure in volume)

GDP AND ENERGY CONSUMPTION
(Index 1973=100)

ENERGY SURPLUS
(Net Exports as % of Consumption)

SUPPLY OF PRIMARY ENERGY BY MAJOR FUEL
(1992 Structure in Volume)

ENERGY REQUIREMENT PER CAPITA, 1992
(Index European Union=100)

Statistics and Quantitative Analysis/IDB

GUYANA
Energy

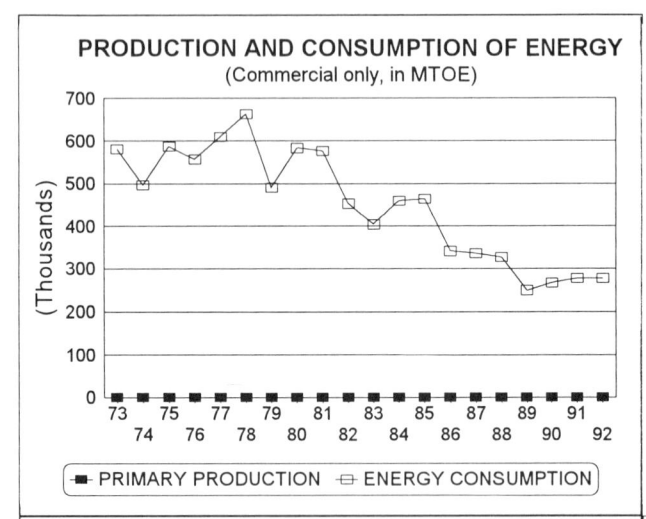

PRODUCTION AND CONSUMPTION OF ENERGY
(Commercial only, in MTOE)

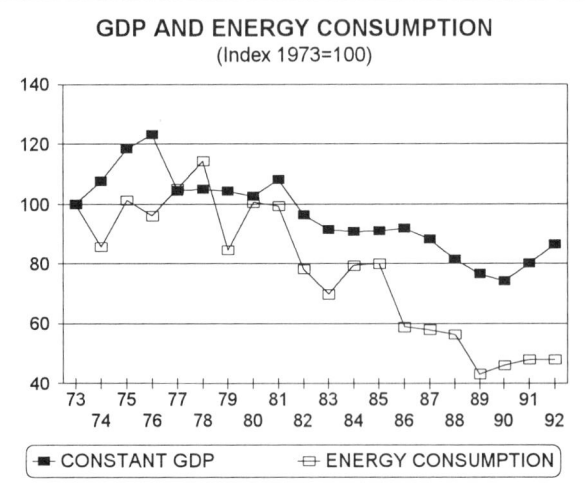

- PRIMARY PRODUCTION
- ENERGY CONSUMPTION

GDP AND ENERGY CONSUMPTION
(Index 1973=100)

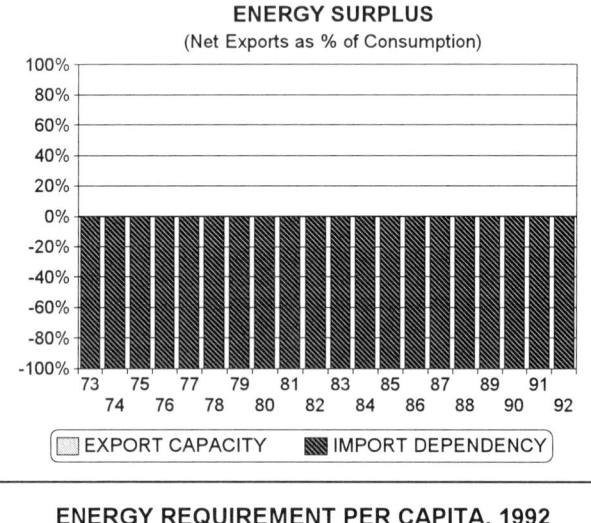

- CONSTANT GDP
- ENERGY CONSUMPTION

ENERGY SURPLUS
(Net Exports as % of Consumption)

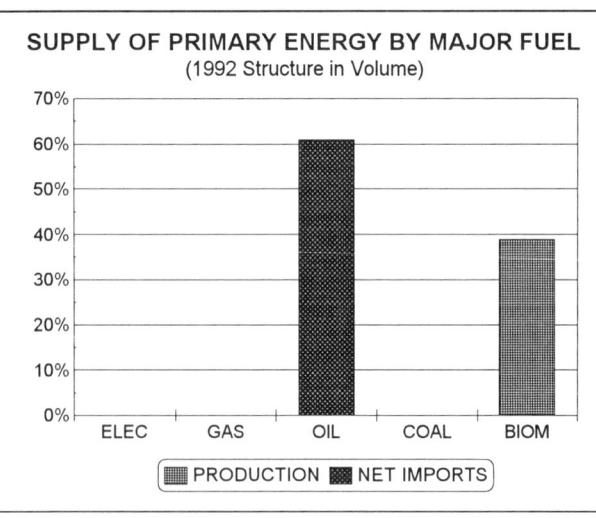

- EXPORT CAPACITY
- IMPORT DEPENDENCY

SUPPLY OF PRIMARY ENERGY BY MAJOR FUEL
(1992 Structure in Volume)

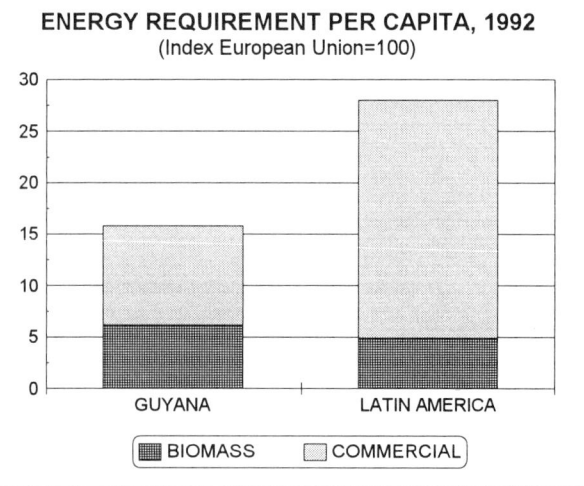

ELEC, GAS, OIL, COAL, BIOM

- PRODUCTION
- NET IMPORTS

ENERGY REQUIREMENT PER CAPITA, 1992
(Index European Union=100)

GUYANA, LATIN AMERICA

- BIOMASS
- COMMERCIAL

Statistics and Quantitative Analysis/IDB

HAITI
Energy

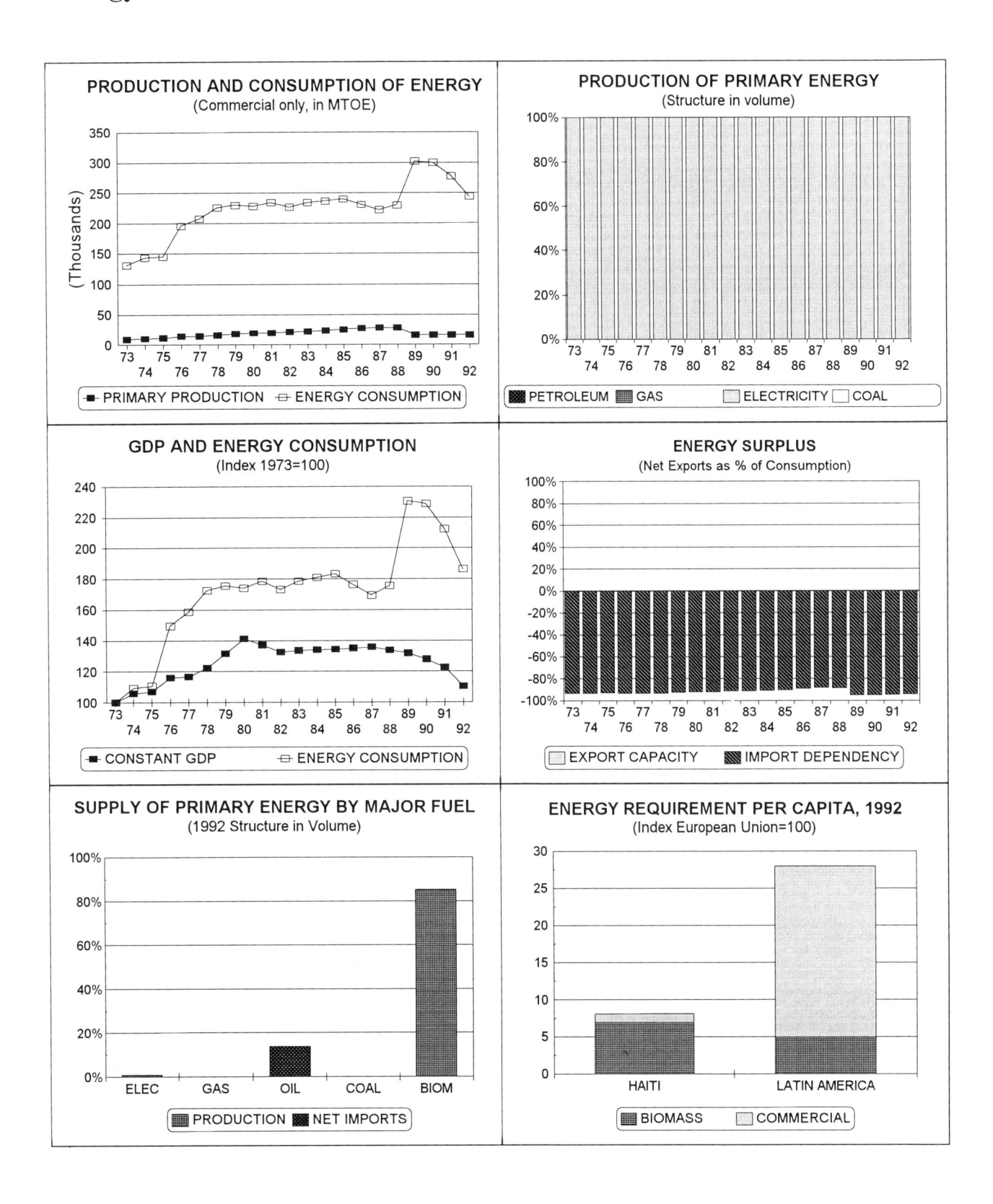

PRODUCTION AND CONSUMPTION OF ENERGY
(Commercial only, in MTOE)

- PRIMARY PRODUCTION
- ENERGY CONSUMPTION

PRODUCTION OF PRIMARY ENERGY
(Structure in volume)

- PETROLEUM
- GAS
- ELECTRICITY
- COAL

GDP AND ENERGY CONSUMPTION
(Index 1973=100)

- CONSTANT GDP
- ENERGY CONSUMPTION

ENERGY SURPLUS
(Net Exports as % of Consumption)

- EXPORT CAPACITY
- IMPORT DEPENDENCY

SUPPLY OF PRIMARY ENERGY BY MAJOR FUEL
(1992 Structure in Volume)

- PRODUCTION
- NET IMPORTS

ENERGY REQUIREMENT PER CAPITA, 1992
(Index European Union=100)

- BIOMASS
- COMMERCIAL

Statistics and Quantitative Analysis/IDB

HONDURAS
Energy

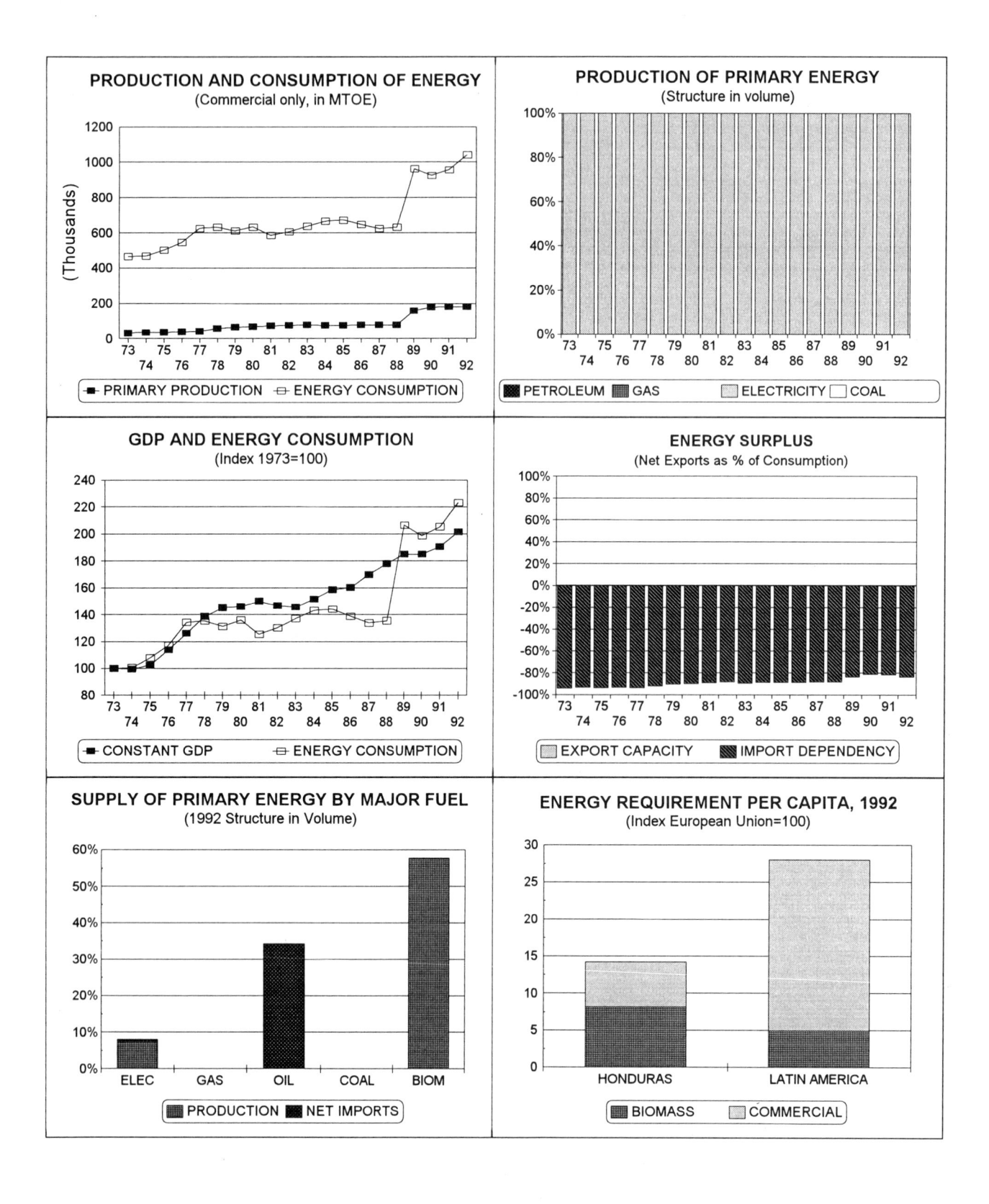

PRODUCTION AND CONSUMPTION OF ENERGY
(Commercial only, in MTOE)

PRODUCTION OF PRIMARY ENERGY
(Structure in volume)

GDP AND ENERGY CONSUMPTION
(Index 1973=100)

ENERGY SURPLUS
(Net Exports as % of Consumption)

SUPPLY OF PRIMARY ENERGY BY MAJOR FUEL
(1992 Structure in Volume)

ENERGY REQUIREMENT PER CAPITA, 1992
(Index European Union=100)

Statistics and Quantitative Analysis/IDB

JAMAICA
Energy

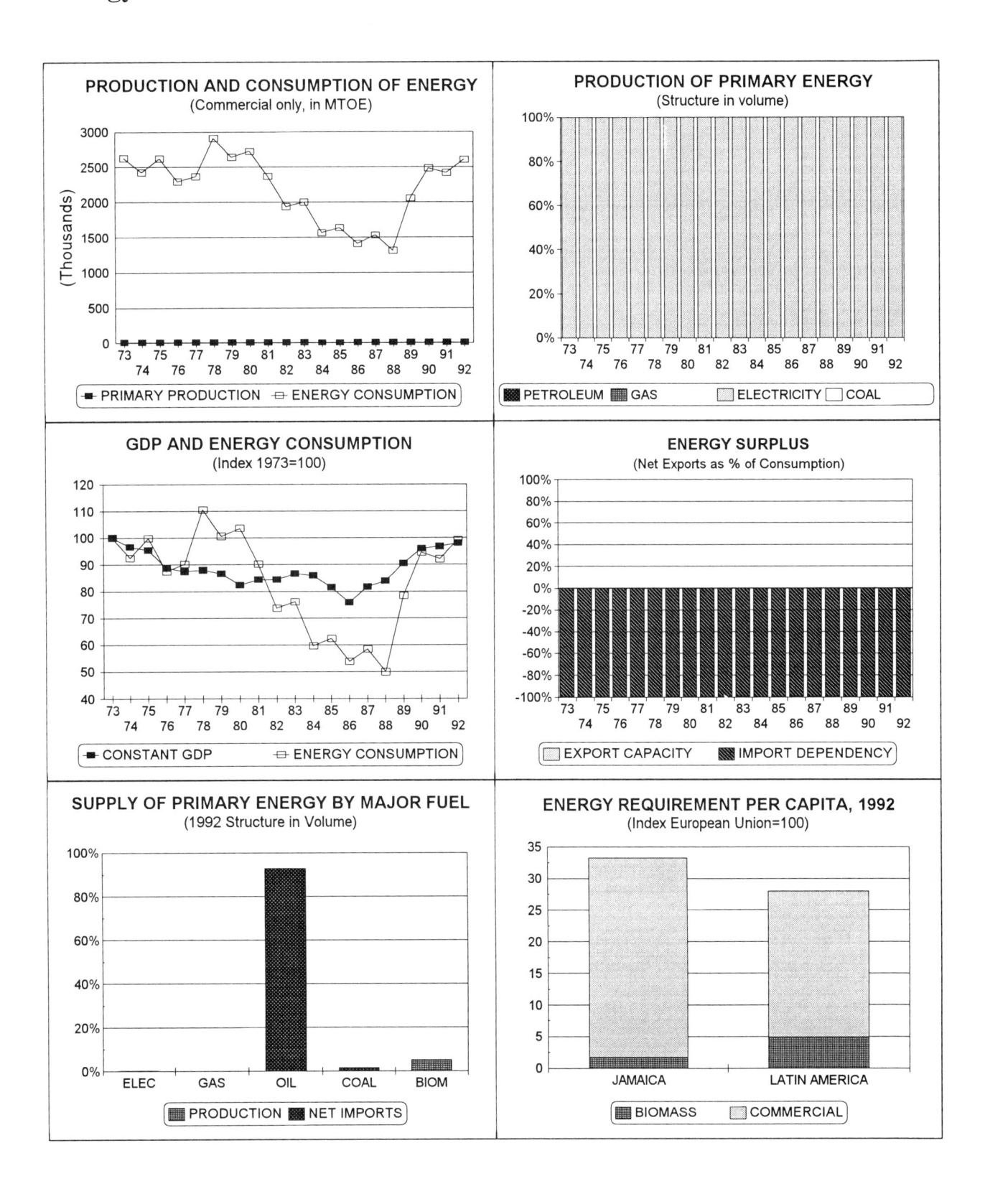

PRODUCTION AND CONSUMPTION OF ENERGY
(Commercial only, in MTOE)

- PRIMARY PRODUCTION
- ENERGY CONSUMPTION

PRODUCTION OF PRIMARY ENERGY
(Structure in volume)

- PETROLEUM
- GAS
- ELECTRICITY
- COAL

GDP AND ENERGY CONSUMPTION
(Index 1973=100)

- CONSTANT GDP
- ENERGY CONSUMPTION

ENERGY SURPLUS
(Net Exports as % of Consumption)

- EXPORT CAPACITY
- IMPORT DEPENDENCY

SUPPLY OF PRIMARY ENERGY BY MAJOR FUEL
(1992 Structure in Volume)

ELEC, GAS, OIL, COAL, BIOM

- PRODUCTION
- NET IMPORTS

ENERGY REQUIREMENT PER CAPITA, 1992
(Index European Union=100)

JAMAICA, LATIN AMERICA

- BIOMASS
- COMMERCIAL

Statistics and Quantitative Analysis/IDB

MEXICO
Energy

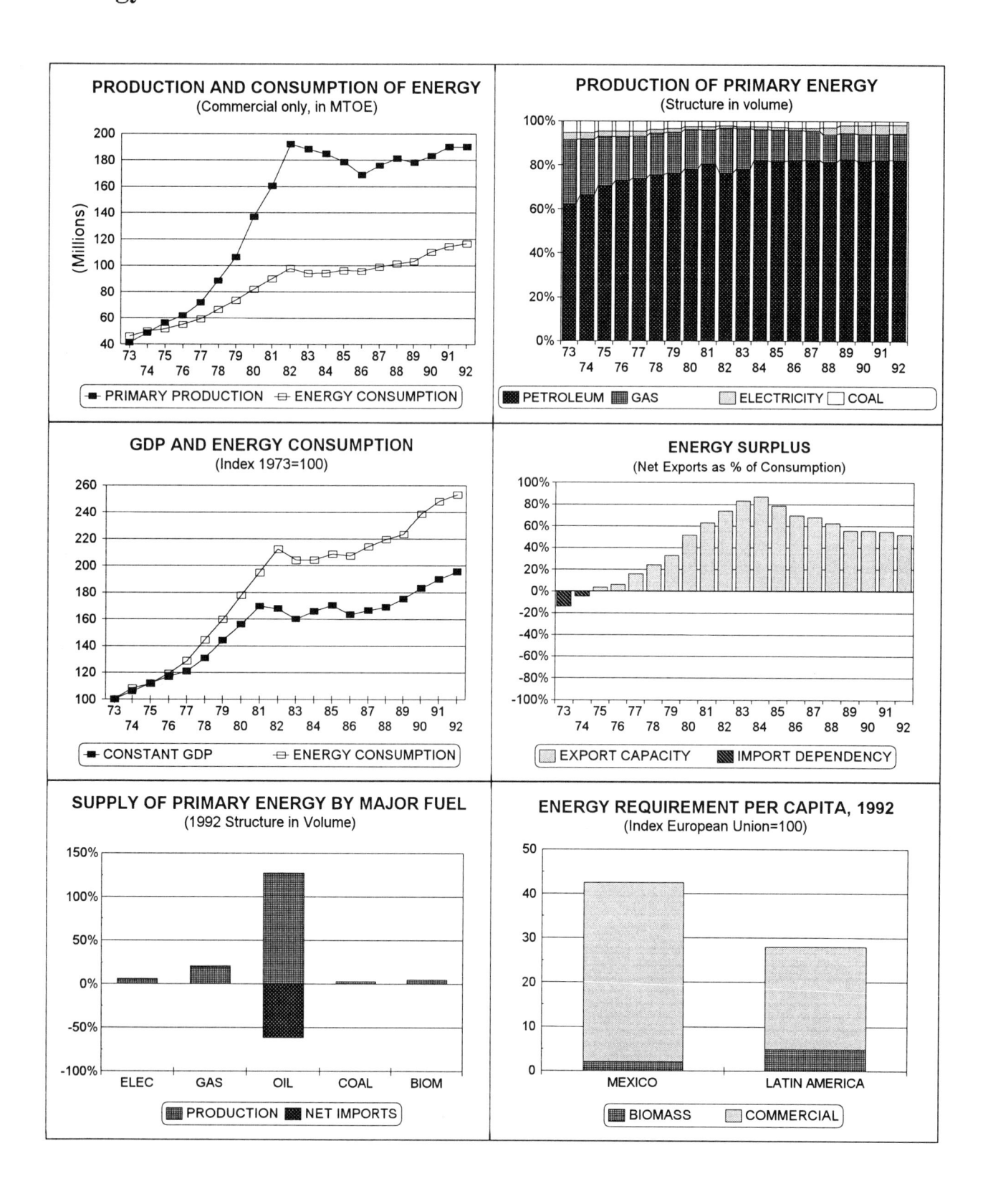

PRODUCTION AND CONSUMPTION OF ENERGY
(Commercial only, in MTOE)

PRODUCTION OF PRIMARY ENERGY
(Structure in volume)

GDP AND ENERGY CONSUMPTION
(Index 1973=100)

ENERGY SURPLUS
(Net Exports as % of Consumption)

SUPPLY OF PRIMARY ENERGY BY MAJOR FUEL
(1992 Structure in Volume)

ENERGY REQUIREMENT PER CAPITA, 1992
(Index European Union=100)

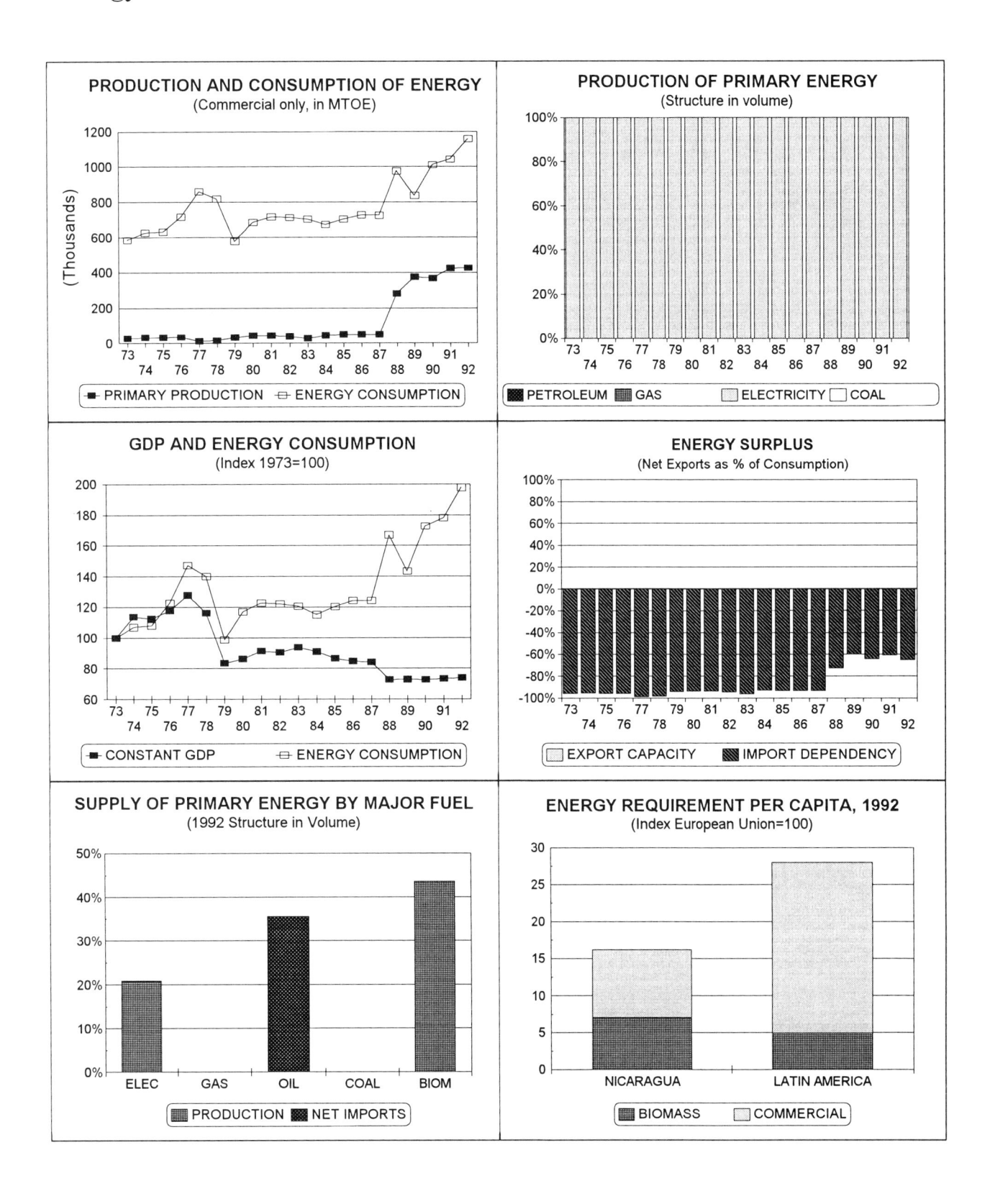

NICARAGUA
Energy

PRODUCTION AND CONSUMPTION OF ENERGY
(Commercial only, in MTOE)

PRODUCTION OF PRIMARY ENERGY
(Structure in volume)

GDP AND ENERGY CONSUMPTION
(Index 1973=100)

ENERGY SURPLUS
(Net Exports as % of Consumption)

SUPPLY OF PRIMARY ENERGY BY MAJOR FUEL
(1992 Structure in Volume)

ENERGY REQUIREMENT PER CAPITA, 1992
(Index European Union=100)

Statistics and Quantitative Analysis/IDB

PANAMA
Energy

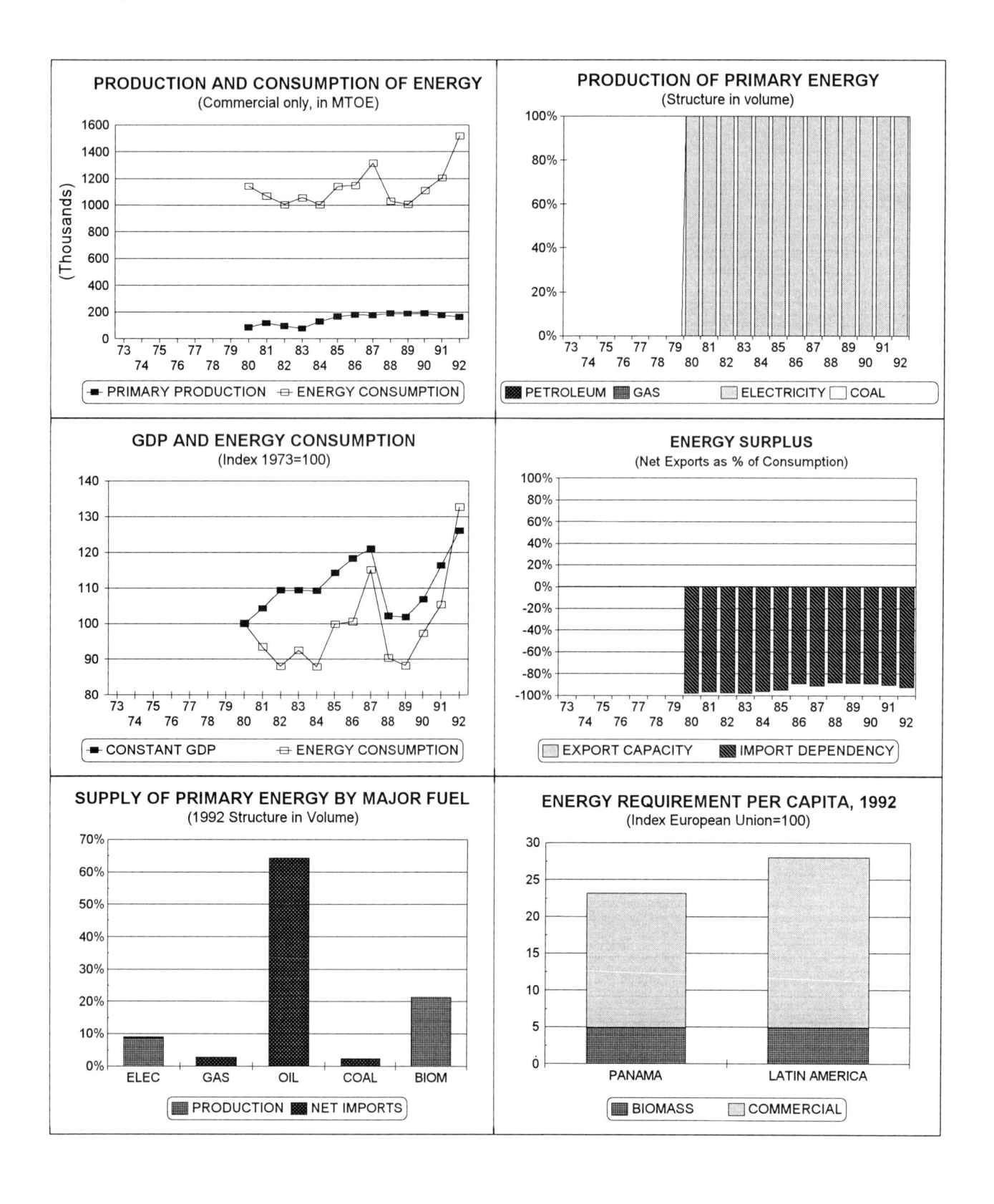

PRODUCTION AND CONSUMPTION OF ENERGY
(Commercial only, in MTOE)

- PRIMARY PRODUCTION
- ENERGY CONSUMPTION

PRODUCTION OF PRIMARY ENERGY
(Structure in volume)

PETROLEUM | GAS | ELECTRICITY | COAL

GDP AND ENERGY CONSUMPTION
(Index 1973=100)

- CONSTANT GDP
- ENERGY CONSUMPTION

ENERGY SURPLUS
(Net Exports as % of Consumption)

EXPORT CAPACITY | IMPORT DEPENDENCY

SUPPLY OF PRIMARY ENERGY BY MAJOR FUEL
(1992 Structure in Volume)

ELEC | GAS | OIL | COAL | BIOM

PRODUCTION | NET IMPORTS

ENERGY REQUIREMENT PER CAPITA, 1992
(Index European Union=100)

PANAMA | LATIN AMERICA

BIOMASS | COMMERCIAL

Statistics and Quantitative Analysis/IDB

PARAGUAY
Energy

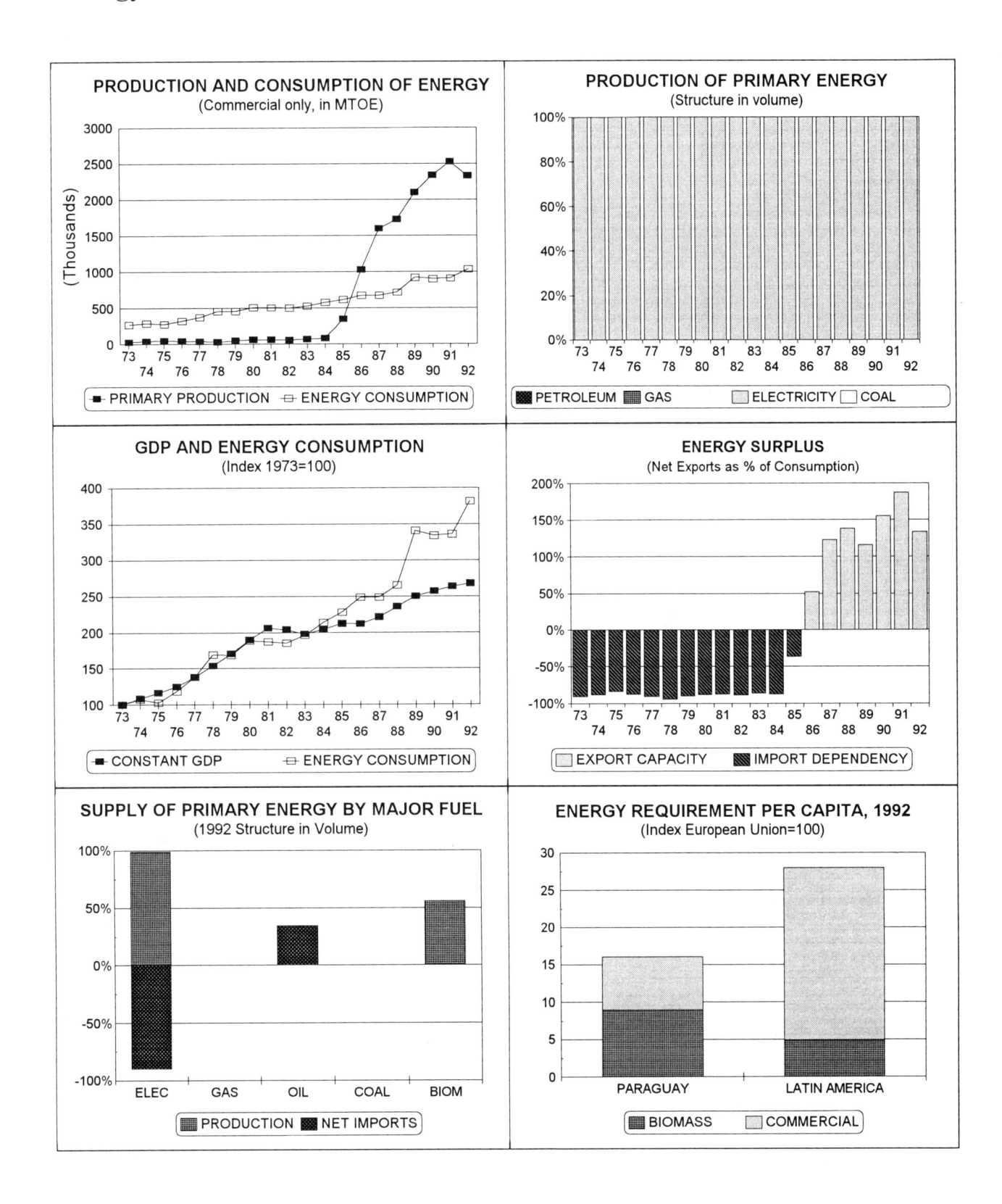

PRODUCTION AND CONSUMPTION OF ENERGY
(Commercial only, in MTOE)

PRODUCTION OF PRIMARY ENERGY
(Structure in volume)

GDP AND ENERGY CONSUMPTION
(Index 1973=100)

ENERGY SURPLUS
(Net Exports as % of Consumption)

SUPPLY OF PRIMARY ENERGY BY MAJOR FUEL
(1992 Structure in Volume)

ENERGY REQUIREMENT PER CAPITA, 1992
(Index European Union=100)

Statistics and Quantitative Analysis/IDB

PERU
Energy

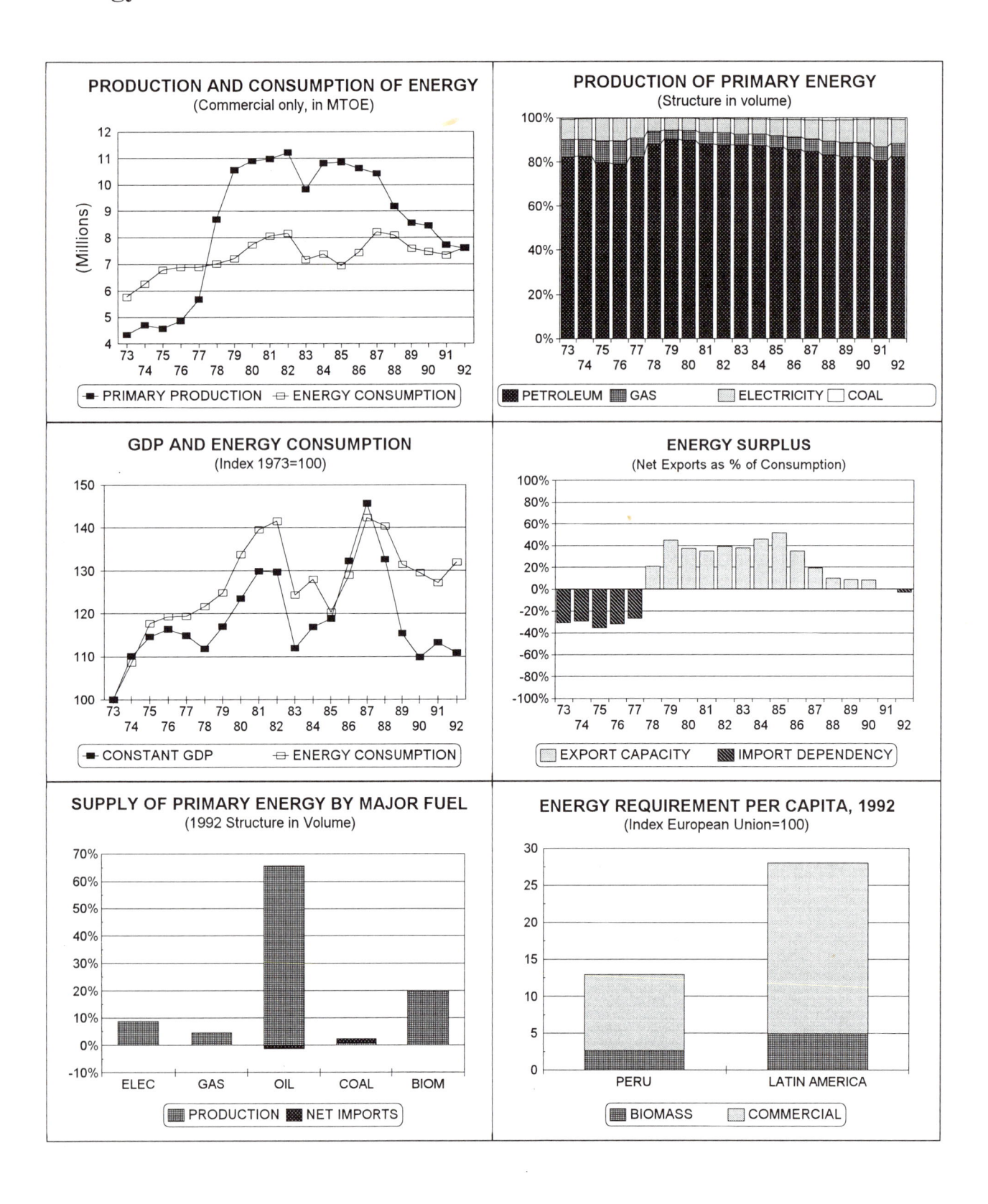

PRODUCTION AND CONSUMPTION OF ENERGY
(Commercial only, in MTOE)

- PRIMARY PRODUCTION
- ENERGY CONSUMPTION

PRODUCTION OF PRIMARY ENERGY
(Structure in volume)

- PETROLEUM
- GAS
- ELECTRICITY
- COAL

GDP AND ENERGY CONSUMPTION
(Index 1973=100)

- CONSTANT GDP
- ENERGY CONSUMPTION

ENERGY SURPLUS
(Net Exports as % of Consumption)

- EXPORT CAPACITY
- IMPORT DEPENDENCY

SUPPLY OF PRIMARY ENERGY BY MAJOR FUEL
(1992 Structure in Volume)

ELEC, GAS, OIL, COAL, BIOM

- PRODUCTION
- NET IMPORTS

ENERGY REQUIREMENT PER CAPITA, 1992
(Index European Union=100)

PERU, LATIN AMERICA

- BIOMASS
- COMMERCIAL

Statistics and Quantitative Analysis/IDB

SURINAME
Energy

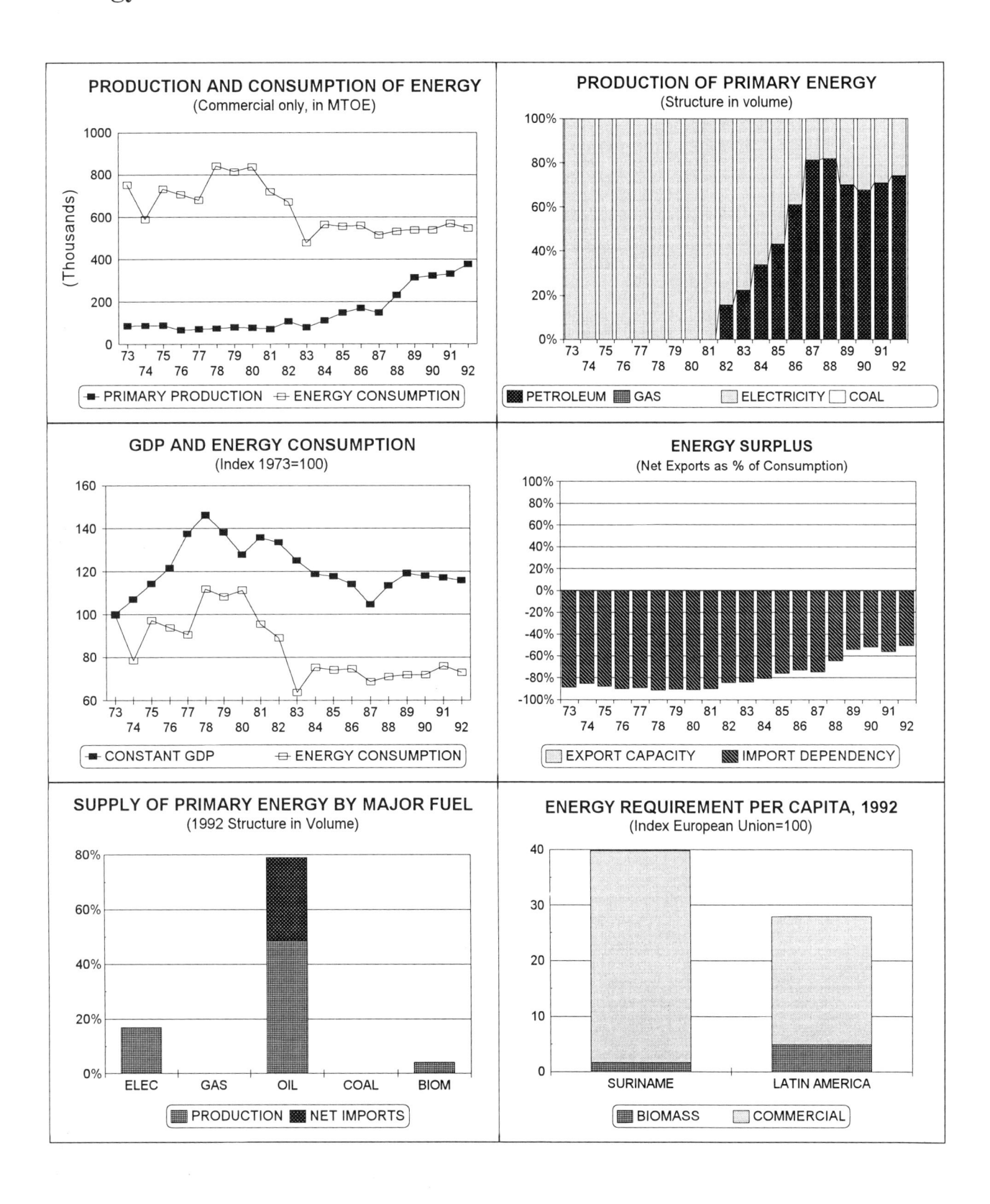

PRODUCTION AND CONSUMPTION OF ENERGY
(Commercial only, in MTOE)

PRODUCTION OF PRIMARY ENERGY
(Structure in volume)

GDP AND ENERGY CONSUMPTION
(Index 1973=100)

ENERGY SURPLUS
(Net Exports as % of Consumption)

SUPPLY OF PRIMARY ENERGY BY MAJOR FUEL
(1992 Structure in Volume)

ENERGY REQUIREMENT PER CAPITA, 1992
(Index European Union=100)

Statistics and Quantitative Analysis/IDB

TRINIDAD AND TOBAGO
Energy

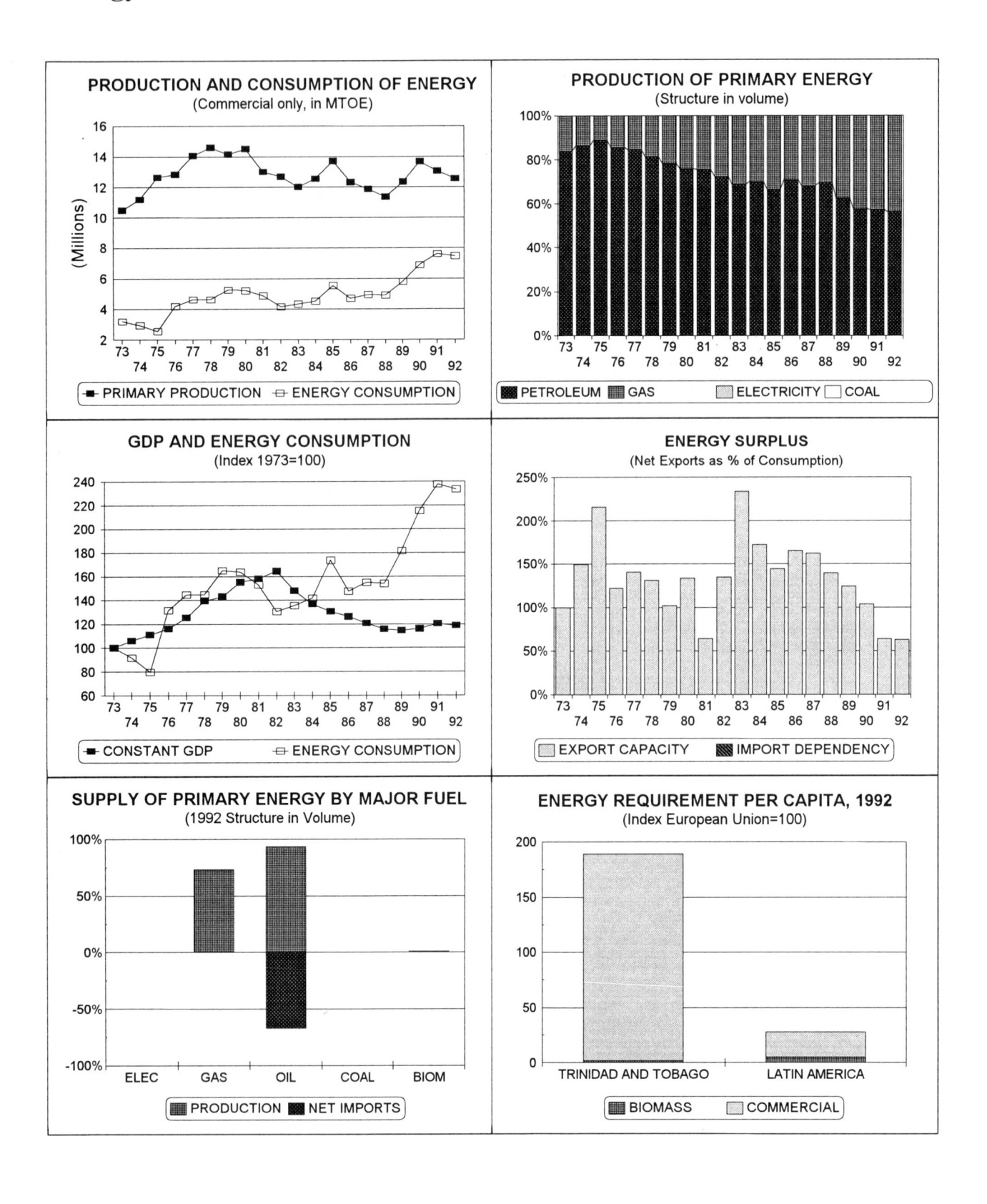

PRODUCTION AND CONSUMPTION OF ENERGY
(Commercial only, in MTOE)

PRODUCTION OF PRIMARY ENERGY
(Structure in volume)

GDP AND ENERGY CONSUMPTION
(Index 1973=100)

ENERGY SURPLUS
(Net Exports as % of Consumption)

SUPPLY OF PRIMARY ENERGY BY MAJOR FUEL
(1992 Structure in Volume)

ENERGY REQUIREMENT PER CAPITA, 1992
(Index European Union=100)

URUGUAY
Energy

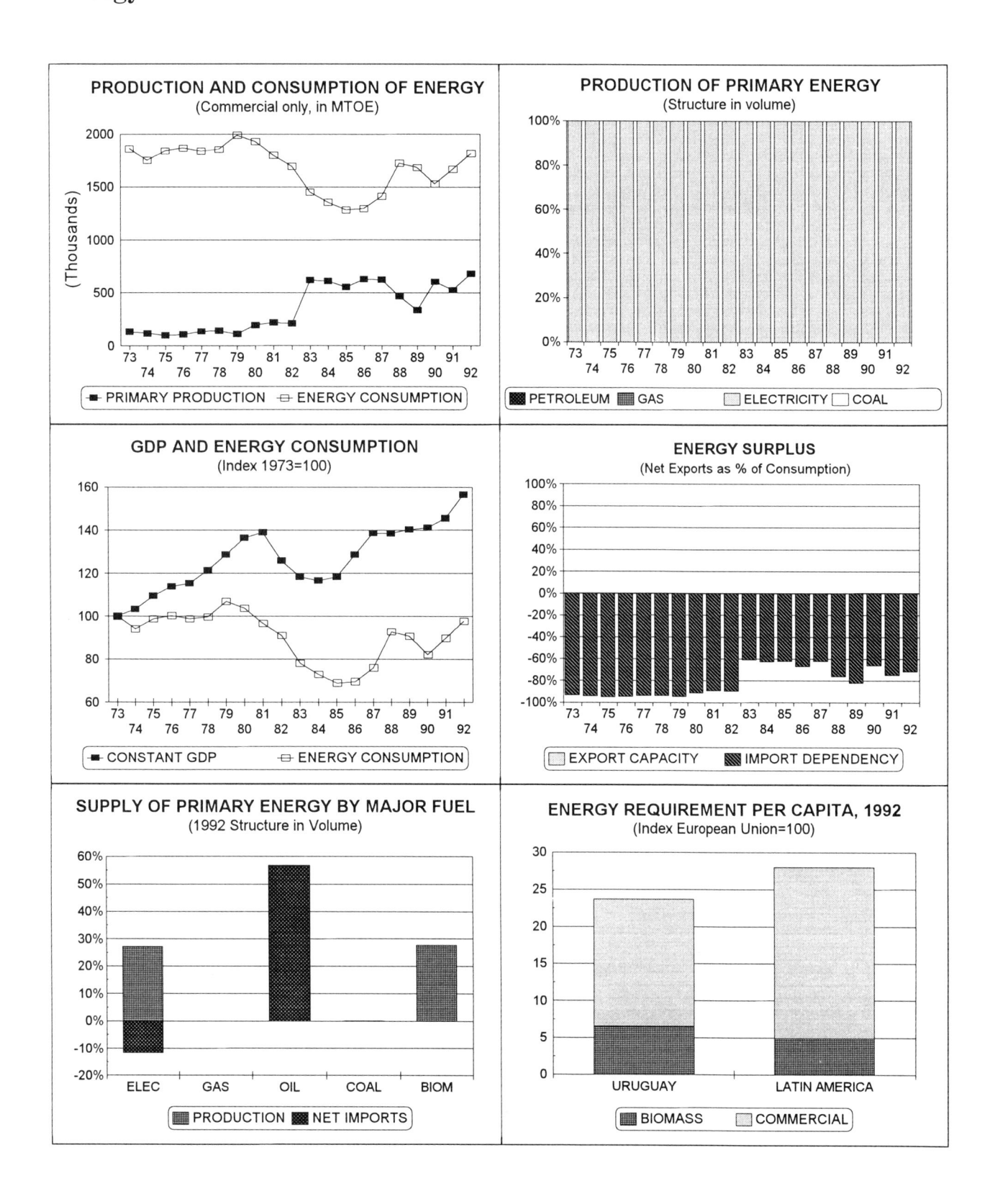

PRODUCTION AND CONSUMPTION OF ENERGY
(Commercial only, in MTOE)

PRODUCTION OF PRIMARY ENERGY
(Structure in volume)

GDP AND ENERGY CONSUMPTION
(Index 1973=100)

ENERGY SURPLUS
(Net Exports as % of Consumption)

SUPPLY OF PRIMARY ENERGY BY MAJOR FUEL
(1992 Structure in Volume)

ENERGY REQUIREMENT PER CAPITA, 1992
(Index European Union=100)

Statistics and Quantitative Analysis/IDB

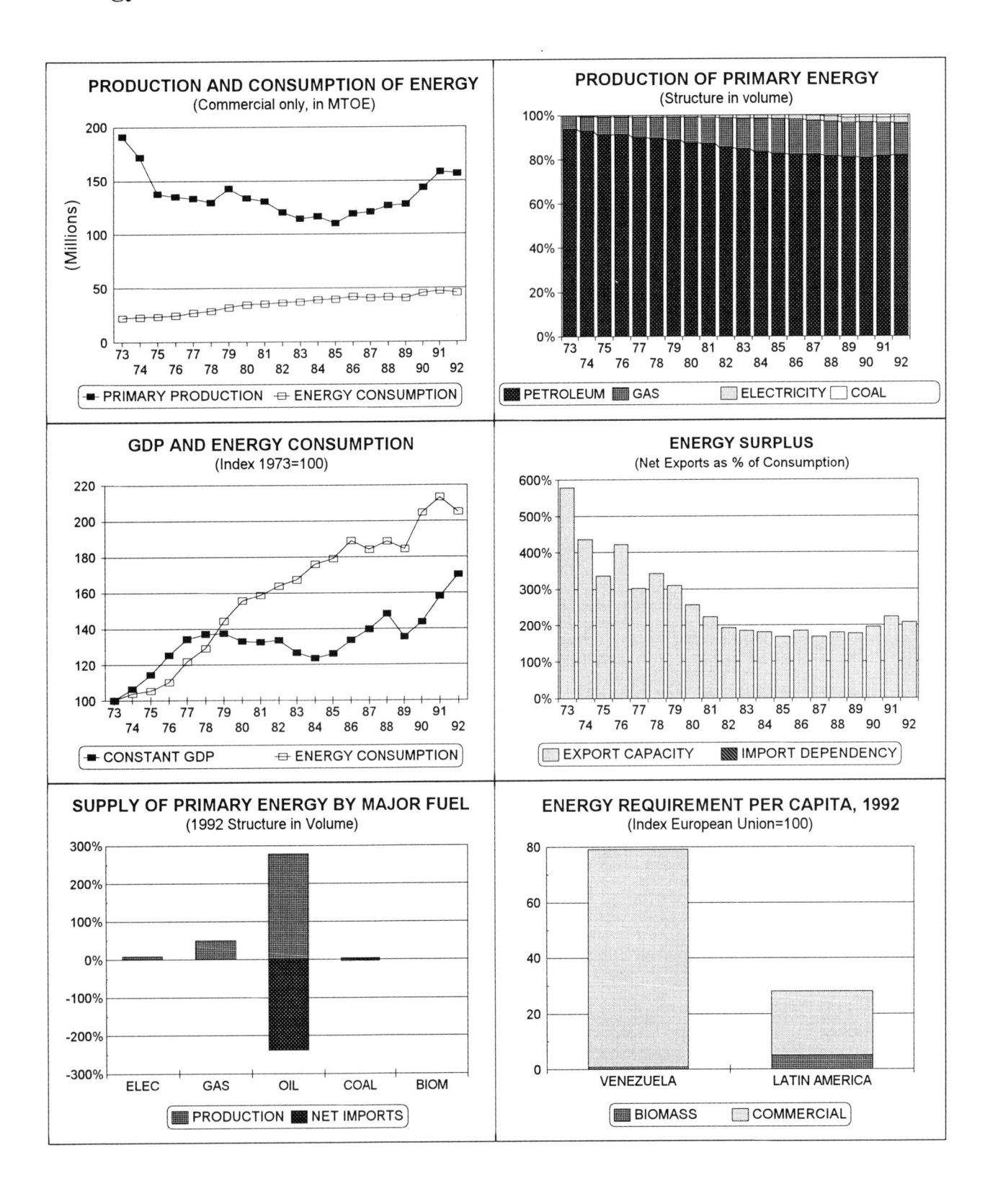

VENEZUELA
Energy

PRODUCTION AND CONSUMPTION OF ENERGY
(Commercial only, in MTOE)

PRODUCTION OF PRIMARY ENERGY
(Structure in volume)

GDP AND ENERGY CONSUMPTION
(Index 1973=100)

ENERGY SURPLUS
(Net Exports as % of Consumption)

SUPPLY OF PRIMARY ENERGY BY MAJOR FUEL
(1992 Structure in Volume)

ENERGY REQUIREMENT PER CAPITA, 1992
(Index European Union=100)

Statistics and Quantitative Analysis/IDB

EXTERNAL DEBT

EXTERNAL DEBT

Data on Debt are from the World Bank, World Debt Tables tapes and World Bank estimates. The External Debt excludes here, according to the World Bank methodology, the External Debt issued in local currency. Descriptions of the graphs follow.

1. NET EXTERNAL DEBT PER CAPITA

Net External Debt is Total External Debt disbursed net of the Stock of Reserves of the country. The per capita estimate is compared to the Latin American average.

2. EXTERNAL DEBT AS A PERCENT OF GDP

The graph shows the evolution of the structure of Total External Debt disbursed as a percent of GDP in current Dollars at year's end. *Long-Term Debt* has an original or extended maturity of more than one year. *Short-Term Debt* includes the stock of Interest in Arrears on Long-Term Debt. The *Use of IMF Credit* includes purchases outstanding under the Credit Tranche, Special Facilities (e.g., the Oil Facility), Trust Fund loans and the Structural Adjustment loans.

Data on *Short-Term Debt* are not available before 1977 and have been estimated for previous years by applying the ratio of *Short-Term Debt* to *Long-Term Debt* in 1977.

3. STRUCTURE OF EXTERNAL DEBT BY TYPE OF CREDITOR

The graph shows the evolution of the structure of Total External Debt disbursed by type of creditor. *Multilateral Debt* includes debt from Multilateral Institutions as well as the *Use of IMF Credit*. *Bilateral Debt* mainly includes loans from Governments and their agencies (including official export credit agencies). *Private Debt* includes *Private Long-Term Non-guaranteed Debt*, *Public Long-Term Guaranteed Debt* other than Bilateral or Multilateral and *Short-Term Debt*.

4. INTEREST PAYMENTS AS A PERCENT OF EXPORTS

This ratio shows the proportion of earnings from Exports of Goods and Non-factor Services that has to be dedicated to interest payments that are due (accrued basis) according to balance-of-payments figures. It also shows the proportion which was actually dedicated to interest payments (actually paid), as recorded by the World Bank. The World Bank does not record interest payments on local currency debt to non-residents.

5. IMPLICIT INTEREST RATE VERSUS LIBOR

The implicit interest rate is the ratio of accrued interest payments over the debt stock at mid-year (estimated as the simple average of start and end year stocks of Total External Debt disbursed). The three-month LIBOR (London InterBank Offered Rate) is taken as an indicator of the international level of interest rates. The gap depends on the respective proportion of concessional and variable interest rates in Total External Debt disbursed, as well as the average grace period and the spread.

6. DEBT AND ACCUMULATED CURRENT DEFICITS

The graph shows the interrelationship between the external position of the country and the cumulative balance of payments flows. External Debt should match the accumulation of Current Account deficits in the case where net external borrowings are the unique source of financing.

The accumulated deficits series is the simple accumulation of Current Account Deficits added to the initial level of debt at the end of 1973. Nevertheless, this series generally does not match the Net External Debt for various reasons. First because part of the deficit may be financed by non-debt creating flows such as Net Direct Investment and Portofolio Equity Investment. Second because of capital flight. Third because the value of the External Debt may change due to exchange rate variations or debt reductions. The debt reduction, contrary to the debt forgiveness, is not reflected in the current account of the country because it is considered as a valuation adjustment of the international position of the country.

For some countries, the main explanation for the increasing gap in the early 1980's was the existence of large amounts of capital flight. Since 1987-88, the gap has been reduced dramatically by debt reductions packages (like the Brady Plan), the partial return of capital flight and an increase of Net Direct and Equity Portfolio Investment.

Country Notes

Mexico: In 1991, 92 and 93, Government bonds in local currency were purchased by non-residents for 3.4, 8.1 and 6.5 billion US$. The graphs shown here, do not include this debt.

LATIN AMERICA
External Debt in US Dollars

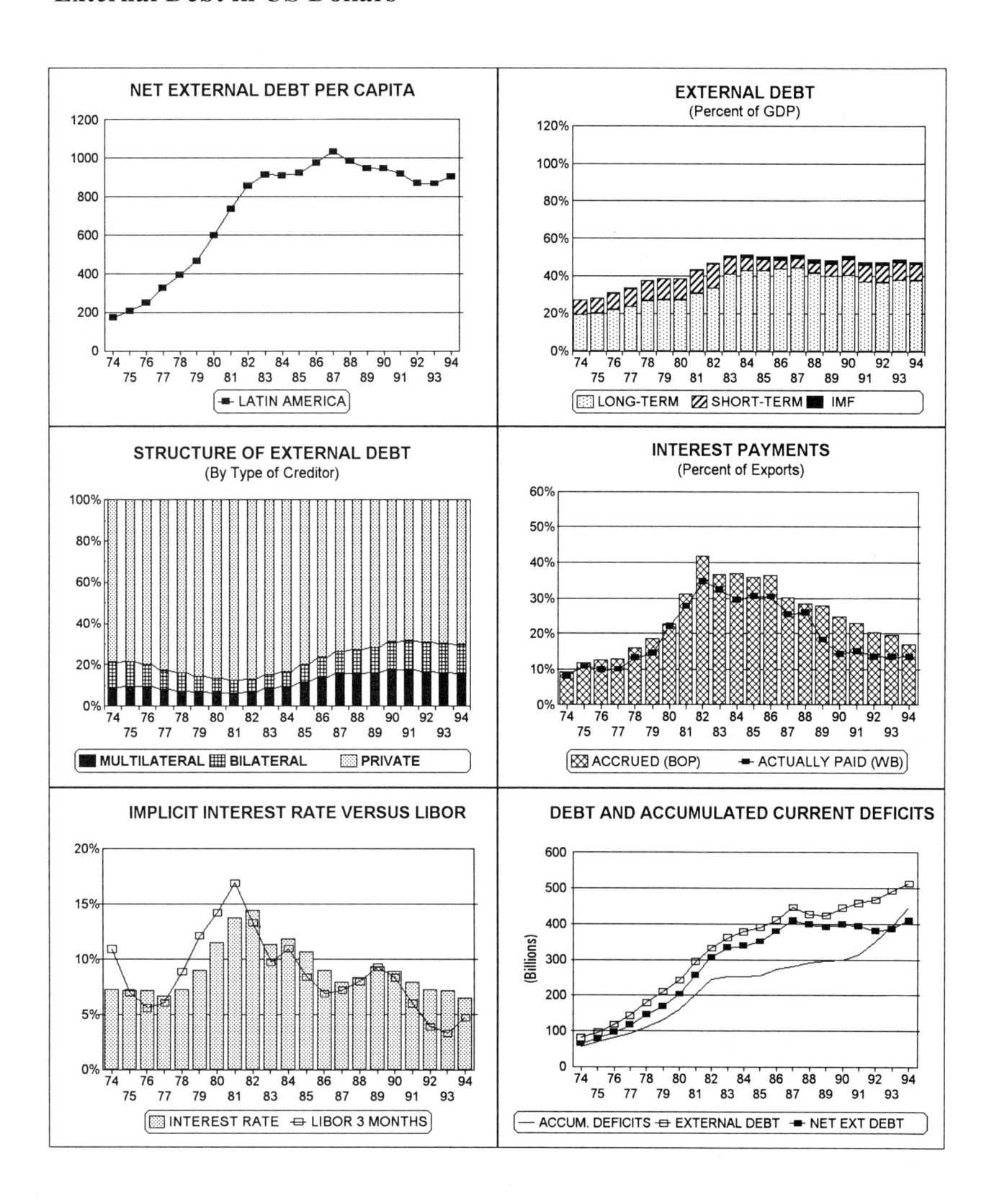

NET EXTERNAL DEBT PER CAPITA

EXTERNAL DEBT
(Percent of GDP)

LONG-TERM ◪ SHORT-TERM ■ IMF

STRUCTURE OF EXTERNAL DEBT
(By Type of Creditor)

■ MULTILATERAL ⊞ BILATERAL ▦ PRIVATE

INTEREST PAYMENTS
(Percent of Exports)

▩ ACCRUED (BOP) ■ ACTUALLY PAID (WB)

IMPLICIT INTEREST RATE VERSUS LIBOR

▦ INTEREST RATE ▫ LIBOR 3 MONTHS

DEBT AND ACCUMULATED CURRENT DEFICITS

(Billions)

— ACCUM. DEFICITS ▫ EXTERNAL DEBT ■ NET EXT DEBT

Statistics and Quantitative Analysis/IDB

ANDEAN GROUP
External Debt in US Dollars

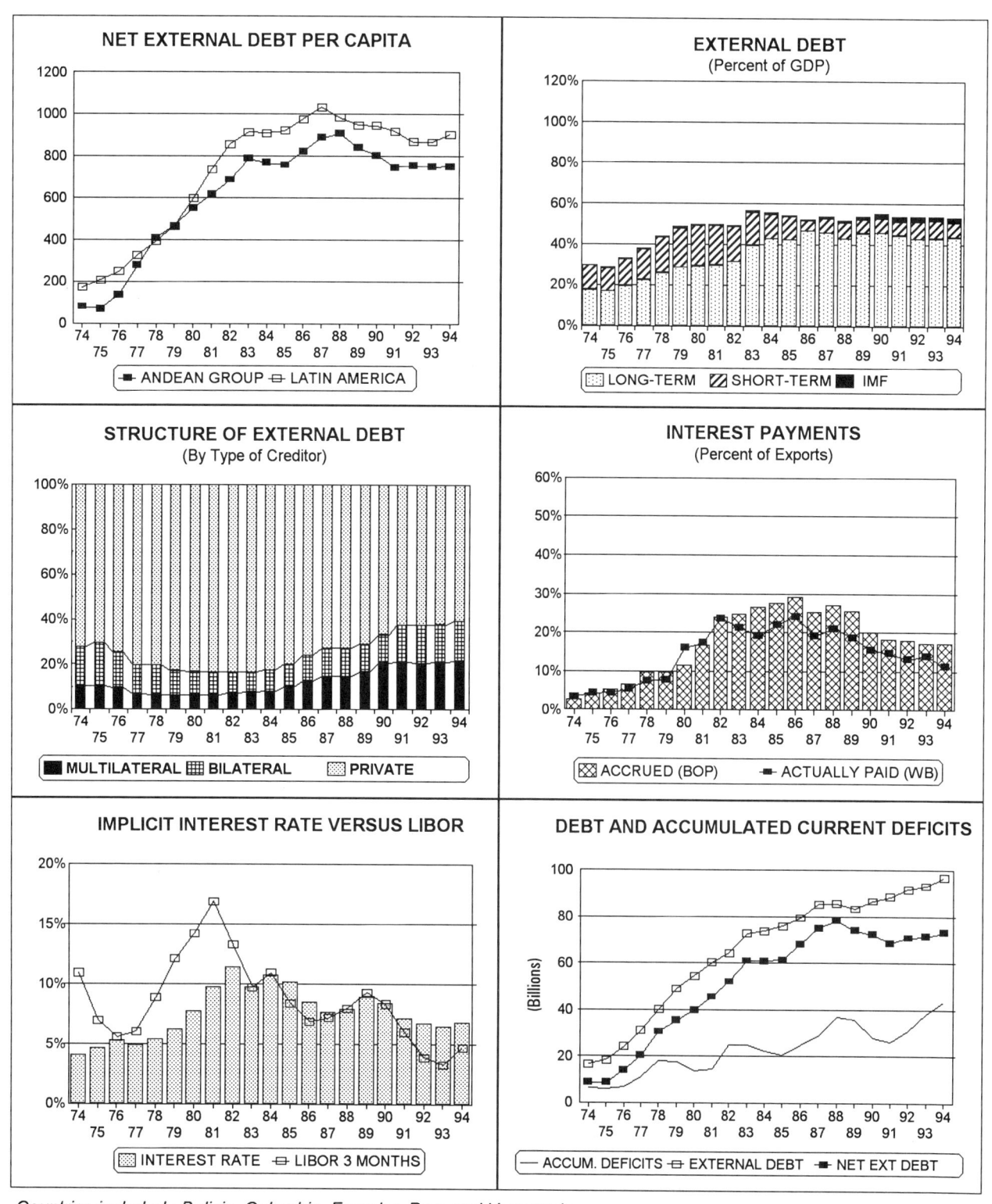

NET EXTERNAL DEBT PER CAPITA
(ANDEAN GROUP, LATIN AMERICA)

EXTERNAL DEBT
(Percent of GDP)
(LONG-TERM, SHORT-TERM, IMF)

STRUCTURE OF EXTERNAL DEBT
(By Type of Creditor)
(MULTILATERAL, BILATERAL, PRIVATE)

INTEREST PAYMENTS
(Percent of Exports)
(ACCRUED (BOP), ACTUALLY PAID (WB))

IMPLICIT INTEREST RATE VERSUS LIBOR
(INTEREST RATE, LIBOR 3 MONTHS)

DEBT AND ACCUMULATED CURRENT DEFICITS
(ACCUM. DEFICITS, EXTERNAL DEBT, NET EXT DEBT)

Countries included : Bolivia, Colombia, Ecuador, Peru and Venezuela.

Statistics and Quantitative Analysis/IDB

CACM
External Debt in US Dollars

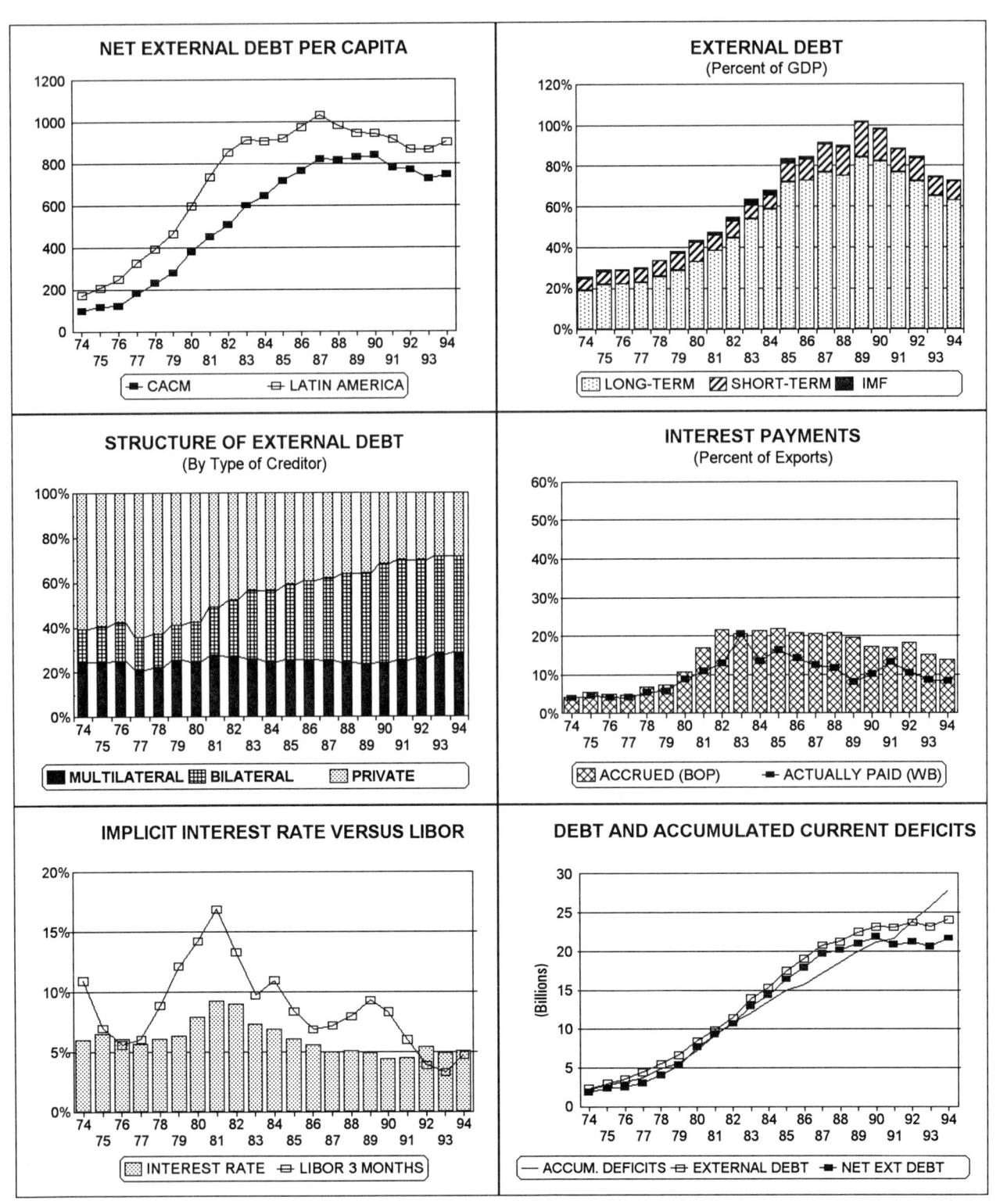

NET EXTERNAL DEBT PER CAPITA
- CACM
- LATIN AMERICA

EXTERNAL DEBT
(Percent of GDP)
- LONG-TERM
- SHORT-TERM
- IMF

STRUCTURE OF EXTERNAL DEBT
(By Type of Creditor)
- MULTILATERAL
- BILATERAL
- PRIVATE

INTEREST PAYMENTS
(Percent of Exports)
- ACCRUED (BOP)
- ACTUALLY PAID (WB)

IMPLICIT INTEREST RATE VERSUS LIBOR
- INTEREST RATE
- LIBOR 3 MONTHS

DEBT AND ACCUMULATED CURRENT DEFICITS
- ACCUM. DEFICITS
- EXTERNAL DEBT
- NET EXT DEBT

Countries included : Costa Rica, El Salvador, Guatemala, Honduras and Nicaragua.

Statistics and Quantitative Analysis/IDB

CARICOM
External Debt in US Dollars

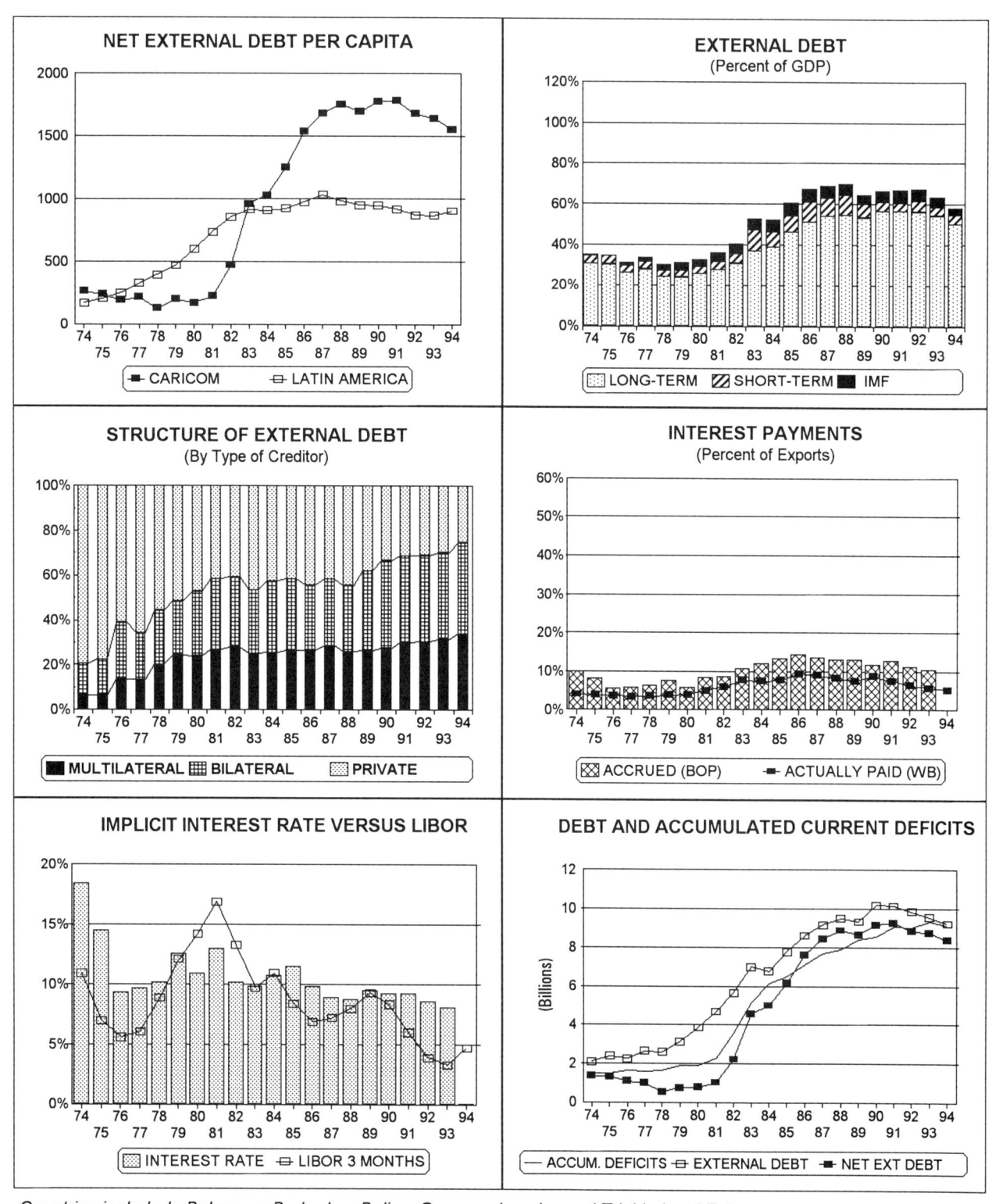

NET EXTERNAL DEBT PER CAPITA
- CARICOM
- LATIN AMERICA

EXTERNAL DEBT
(Percent of GDP)
- LONG-TERM
- SHORT-TERM
- IMF

STRUCTURE OF EXTERNAL DEBT
(By Type of Creditor)
- MULTILATERAL
- BILATERAL
- PRIVATE

INTEREST PAYMENTS
(Percent of Exports)
- ACCRUED (BOP)
- ACTUALLY PAID (WB)

IMPLICIT INTEREST RATE VERSUS LIBOR
- INTEREST RATE
- LIBOR 3 MONTHS

DEBT AND ACCUMULATED CURRENT DEFICITS
(Billions)
- ACCUM. DEFICITS
- EXTERNAL DEBT
- NET EXT DEBT

Countries included: Bahamas, Barbados, Belize, Guyana, Jamaica and Trinidad and Tobago.

Statistics and Quantitative Analysis/IDB

MERCOSUR
External Debt in US Dollars

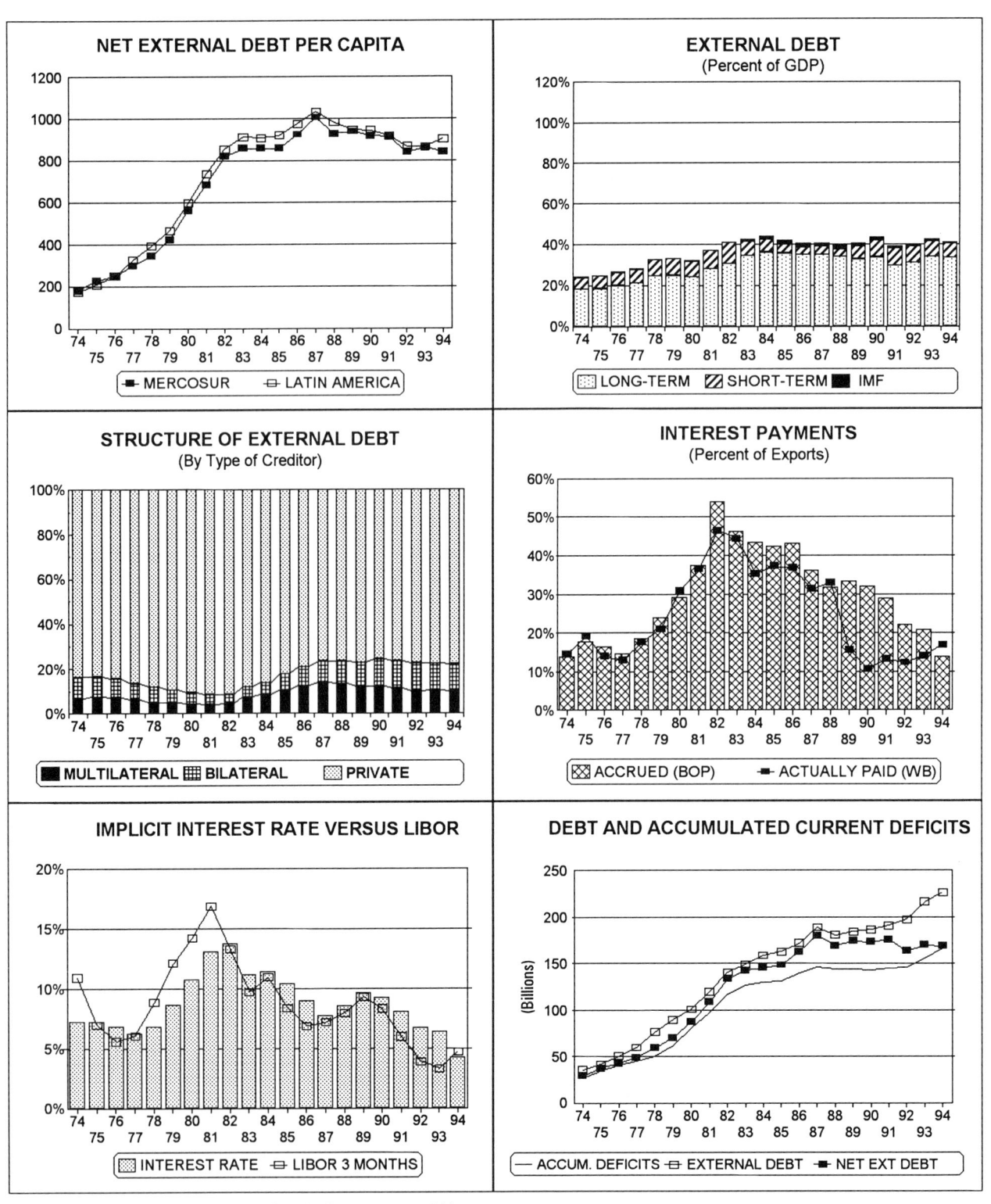

NET EXTERNAL DEBT PER CAPITA
■ MERCOSUR □ LATIN AMERICA

EXTERNAL DEBT
(Percent of GDP)
LONG-TERM SHORT-TERM IMF

STRUCTURE OF EXTERNAL DEBT
(By Type of Creditor)
MULTILATERAL BILATERAL PRIVATE

INTEREST PAYMENTS
(Percent of Exports)
ACCRUED (BOP) ACTUALLY PAID (WB)

IMPLICIT INTEREST RATE VERSUS LIBOR
INTEREST RATE LIBOR 3 MONTHS

DEBT AND ACCUMULATED CURRENT DEFICITS
(Billions)
ACCUM. DEFICITS EXTERNAL DEBT NET EXT DEBT

Countries included: Argentina, Brazil, Paraguay and Uruguay.

ARGENTINA
External Debt in US Dollars

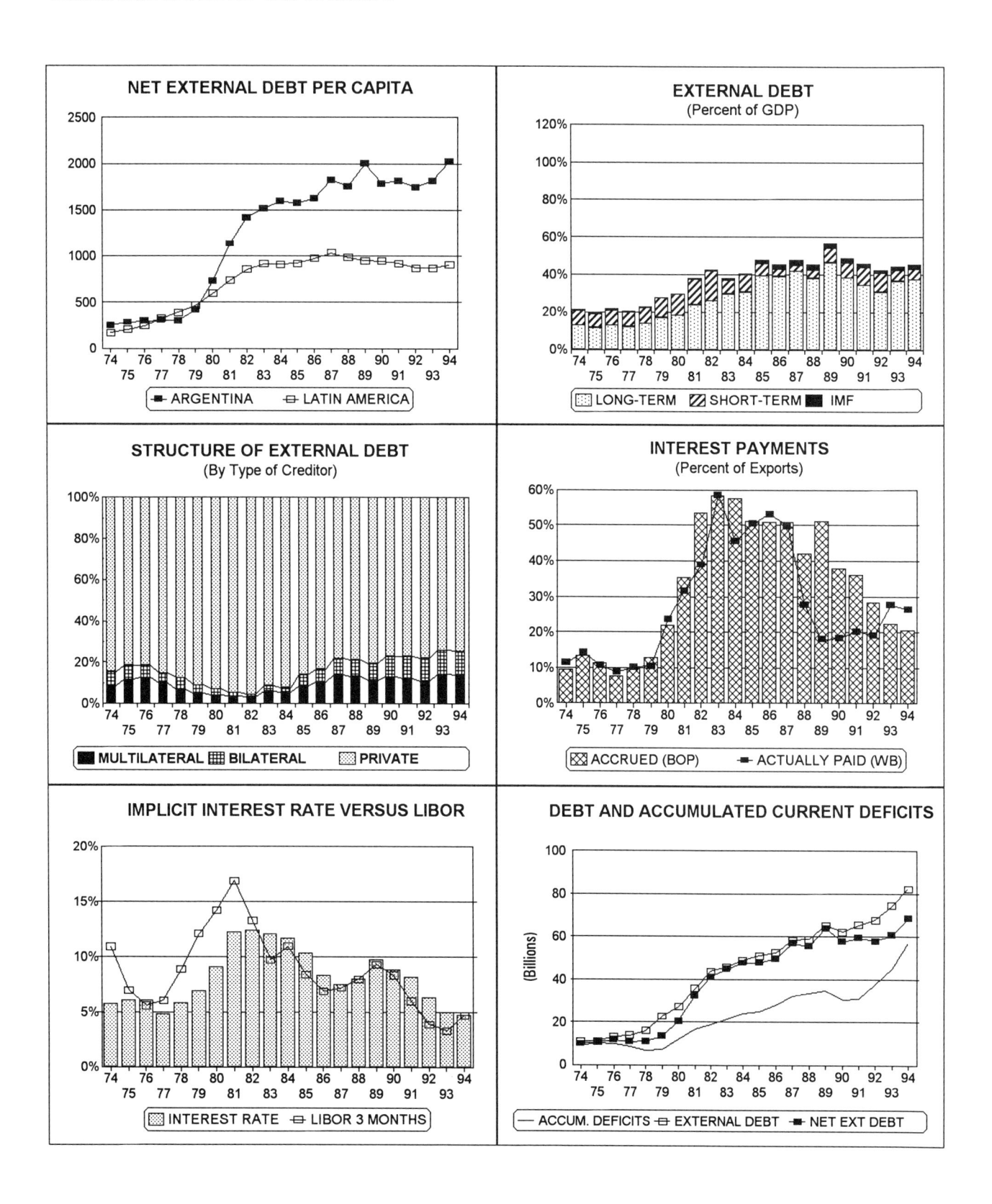

BAHAMAS
External Debt in US Dollars

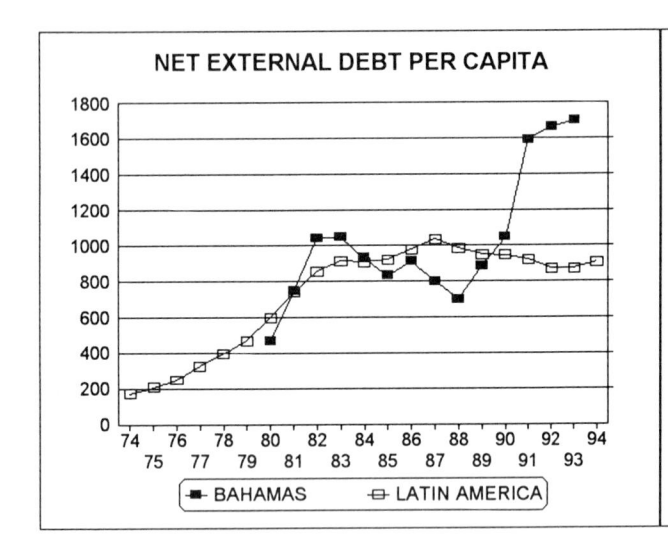

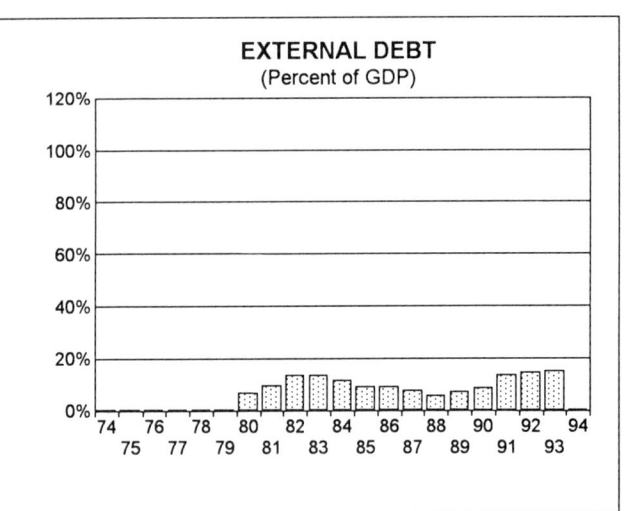

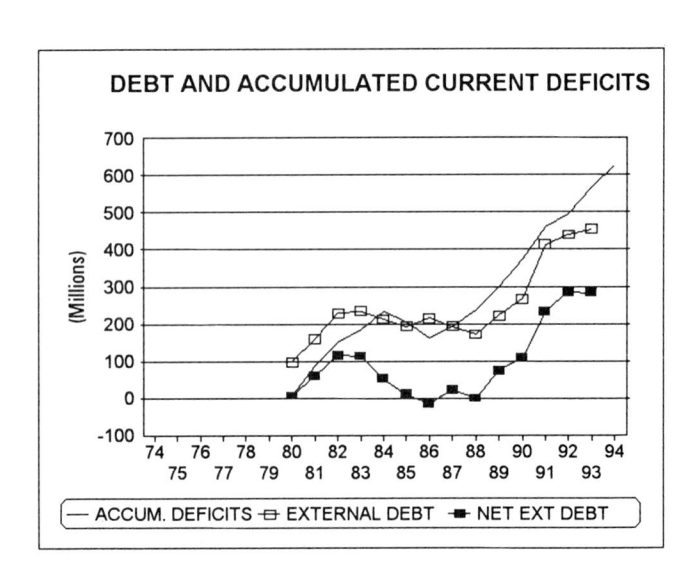

BARBADOS
External Debt in US Dollars

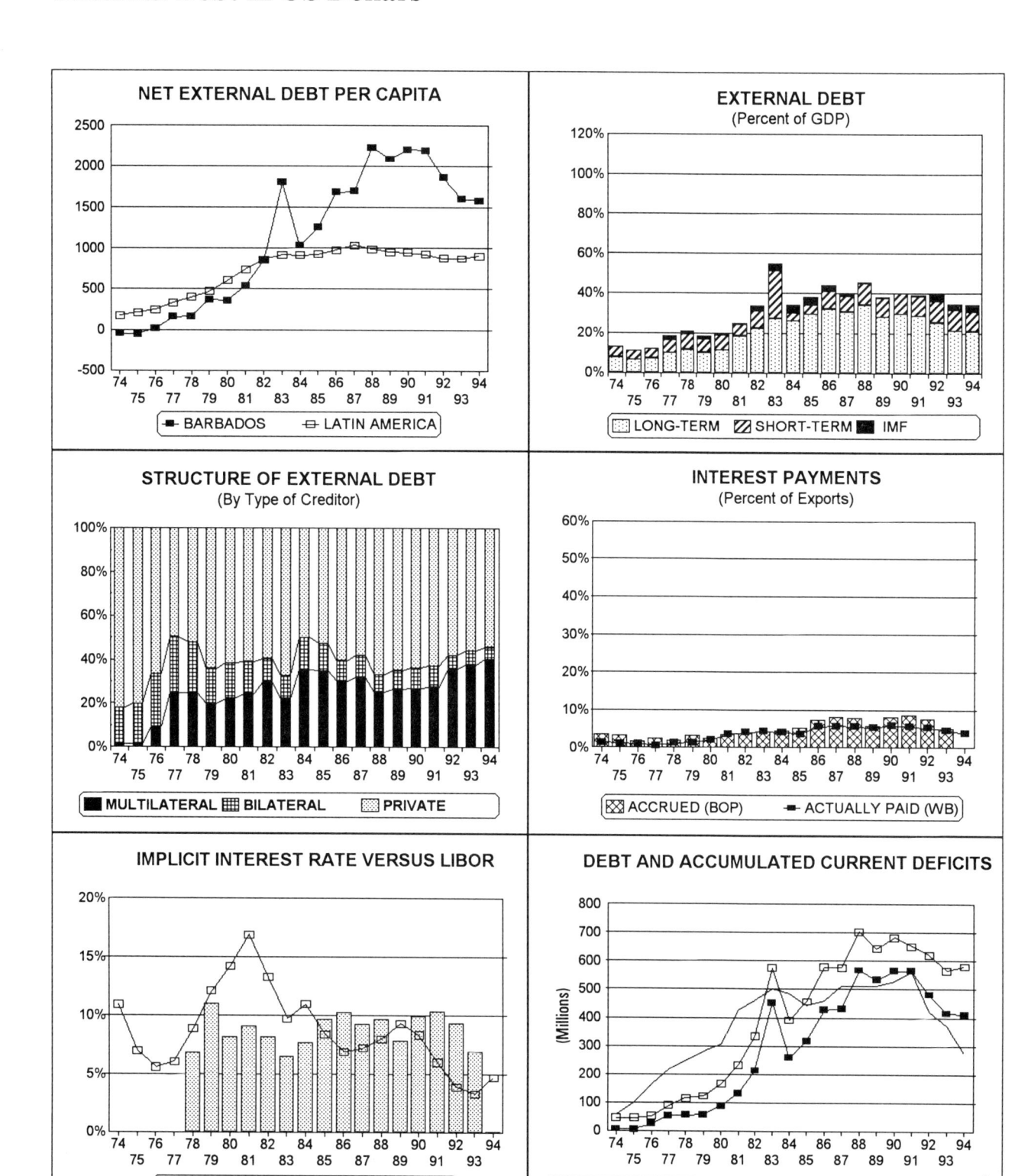

NET EXTERNAL DEBT PER CAPITA
- BARBADOS
- LATIN AMERICA

EXTERNAL DEBT
(Percent of GDP)
- LONG-TERM
- SHORT-TERM
- IMF

STRUCTURE OF EXTERNAL DEBT
(By Type of Creditor)
- MULTILATERAL
- BILATERAL
- PRIVATE

INTEREST PAYMENTS
(Percent of Exports)
- ACCRUED (BOP)
- ACTUALLY PAID (WB)

IMPLICIT INTEREST RATE VERSUS LIBOR
- INTEREST RATE
- LIBOR 3 MONTHS

DEBT AND ACCUMULATED CURRENT DEFICITS
(Millions)
- ACCUM. DEFICITS
- EXTERNAL DEBT
- NET EXT DEBT

Statistics and Quantitative Analysis/IDB

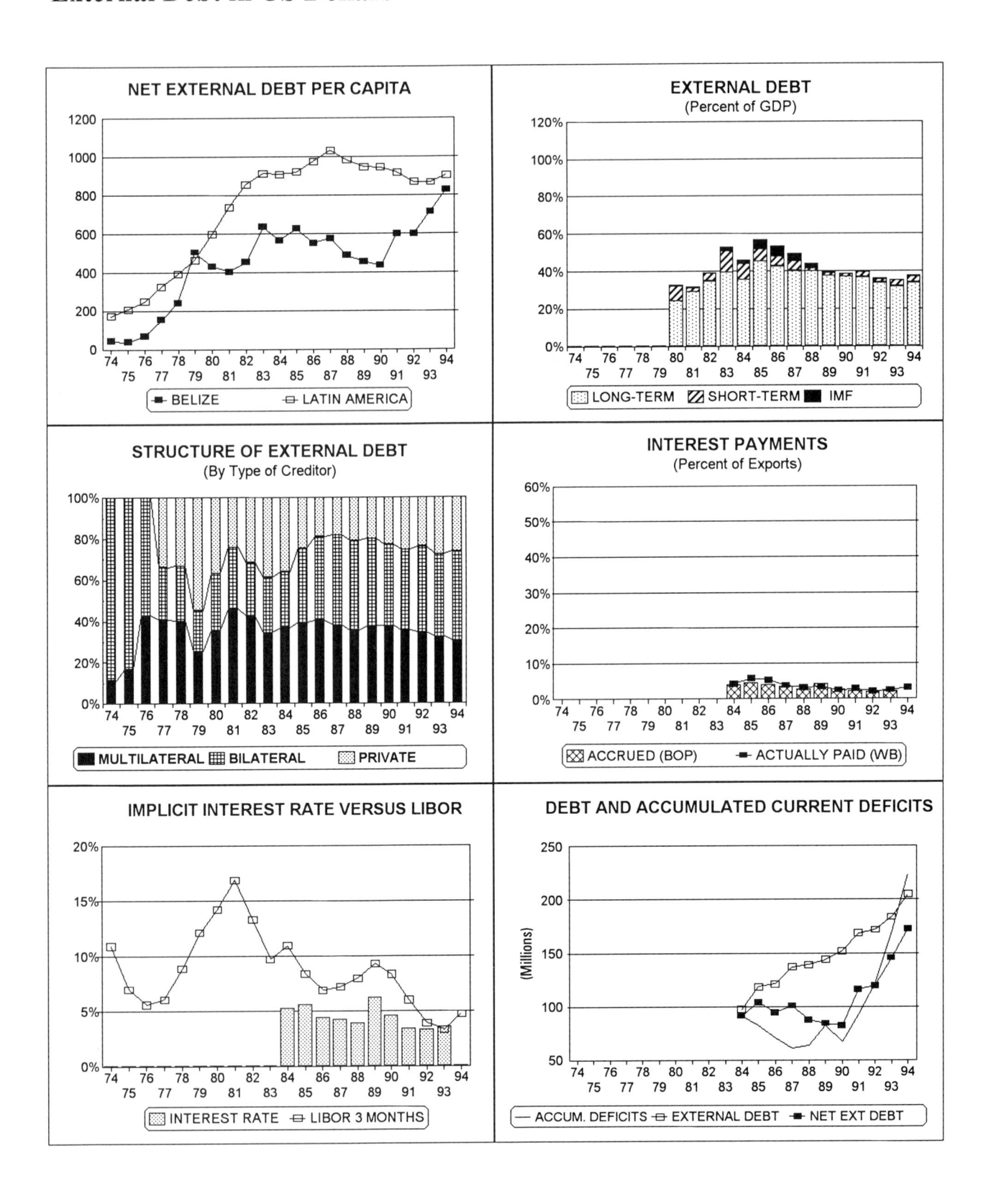

BELIZE
External Debt in US Dollars

178   Statistics and Quantitative Analysis/IDB

BOLIVIA
External Debt in US Dollars

NET EXTERNAL DEBT PER CAPITA
- BOLIVIA
- LATIN AMERICA

EXTERNAL DEBT
(Percent of GDP)
- LONG-TERM
- SHORT-TERM
- IMF

STRUCTURE OF EXTERNAL DEBT
(By Type of Creditor)
- MULTILATERAL
- BILATERAL
- PRIVATE

INTEREST PAYMENTS
(Percent of Exports)
- ACCRUED (BOP)
- ACTUALLY PAID (WB)

IMPLICIT INTEREST RATE VERSUS LIBOR
- INTEREST RATE
- LIBOR 3 MONTHS

DEBT AND ACCUMULATED CURRENT DEFICITS
- ACCUM. DEFICITS
- EXTERNAL DEBT
- NET EXT DEBT

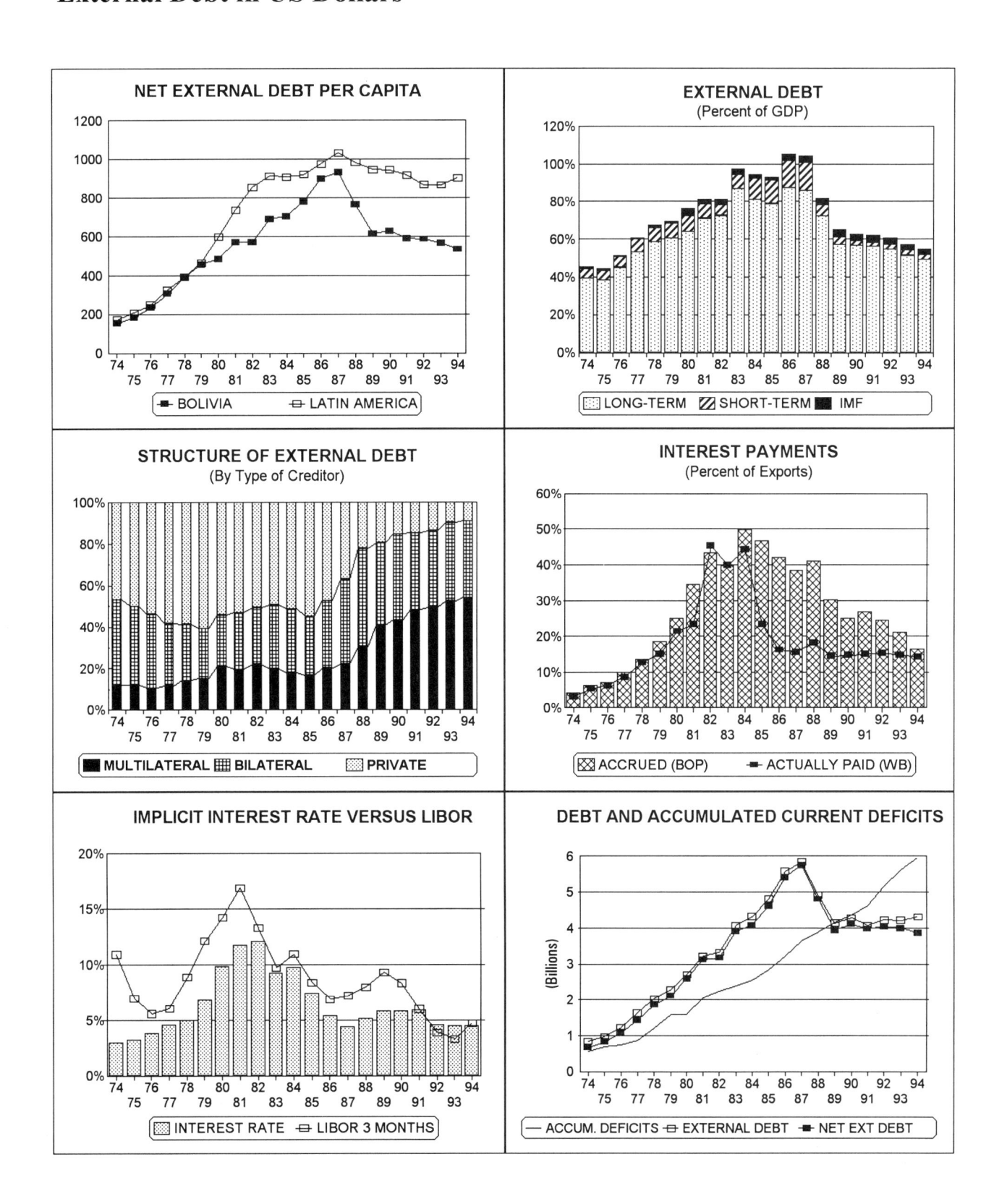

Statistics and Quantitative Analysis/IDB

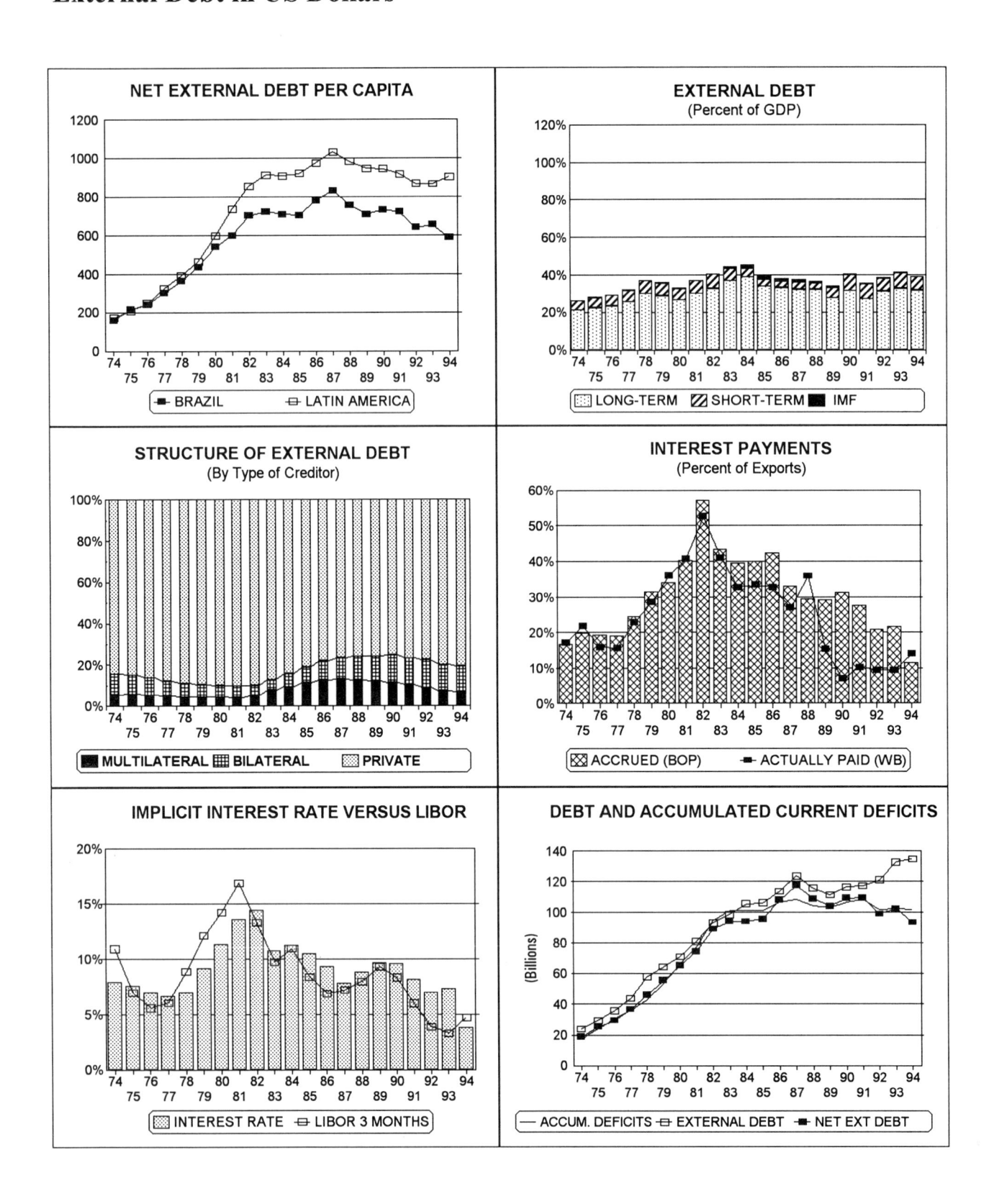

BRAZIL
External Debt in US Dollars

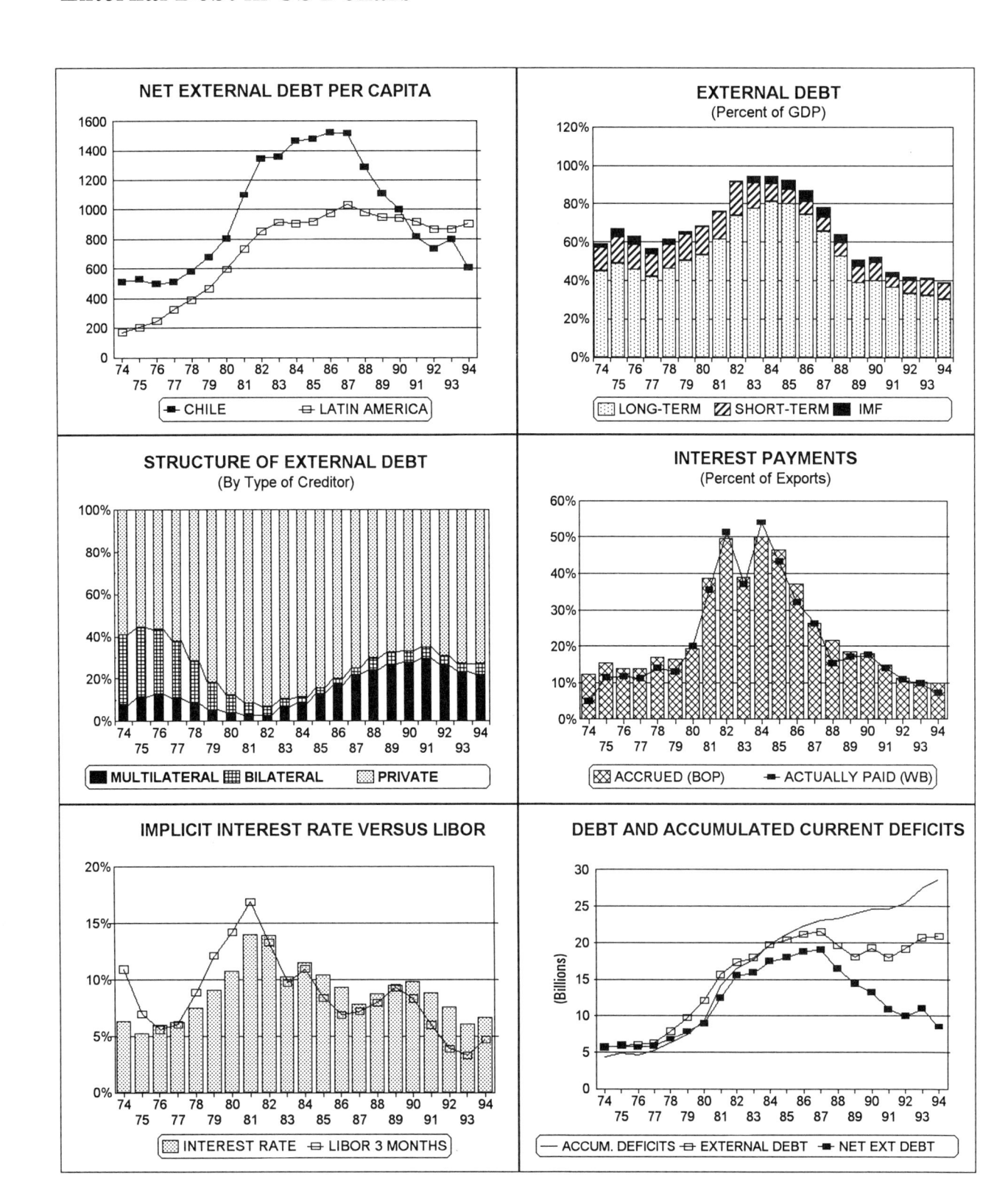

CHILE
External Debt in US Dollars

Statistics and Quantitative Analysis/IDB

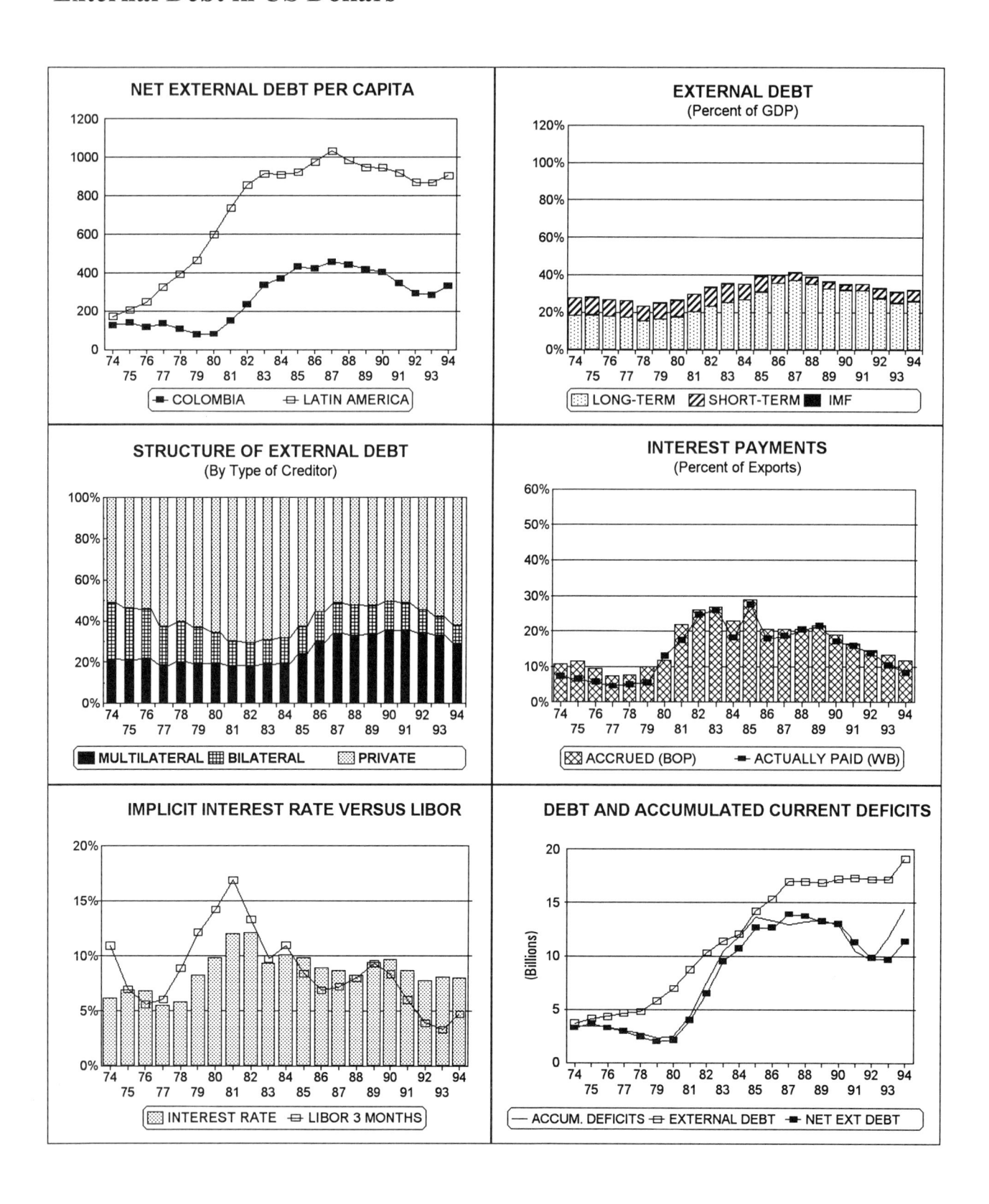

COLOMBIA
External Debt in US Dollars

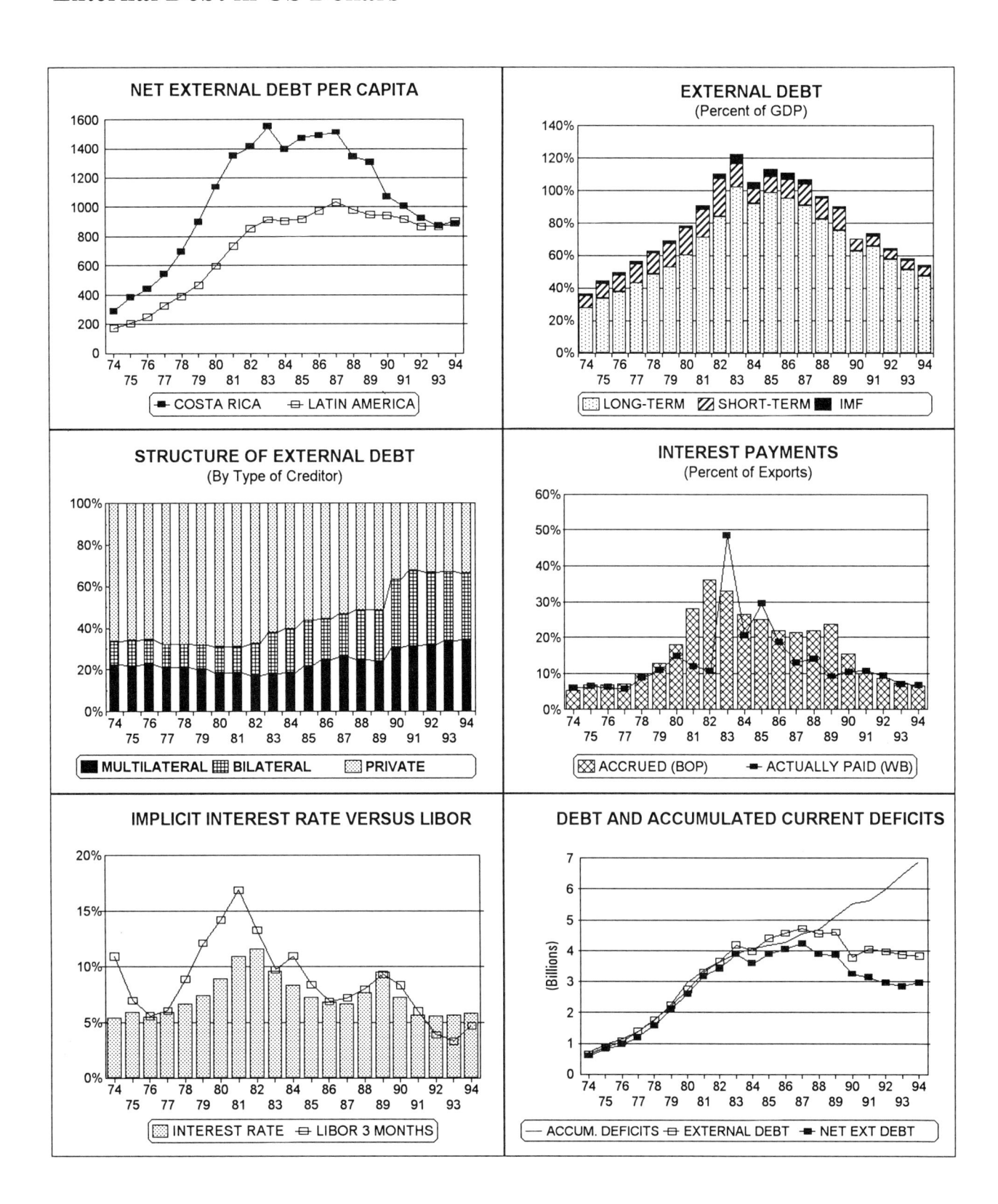

COSTA RICA
External Debt in US Dollars

NET EXTERNAL DEBT PER CAPITA
— COSTA RICA   — LATIN AMERICA

EXTERNAL DEBT
(Percent of GDP)
LONG-TERM   SHORT-TERM   IMF

STRUCTURE OF EXTERNAL DEBT
(By Type of Creditor)
MULTILATERAL   BILATERAL   PRIVATE

INTEREST PAYMENTS
(Percent of Exports)
ACCRUED (BOP)   ACTUALLY PAID (WB)

IMPLICIT INTEREST RATE VERSUS LIBOR
INTEREST RATE   LIBOR 3 MONTHS

DEBT AND ACCUMULATED CURRENT DEFICITS
(Billions)
ACCUM. DEFICITS   EXTERNAL DEBT   NET EXT DEBT

Statistics and Quantitative Analysis/IDB

DOMINICAN REPUBLIC
External Debt in US Dollars

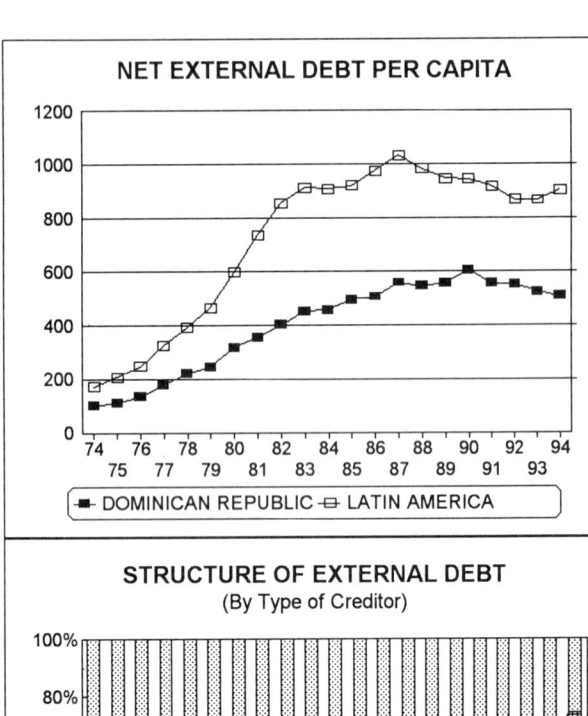

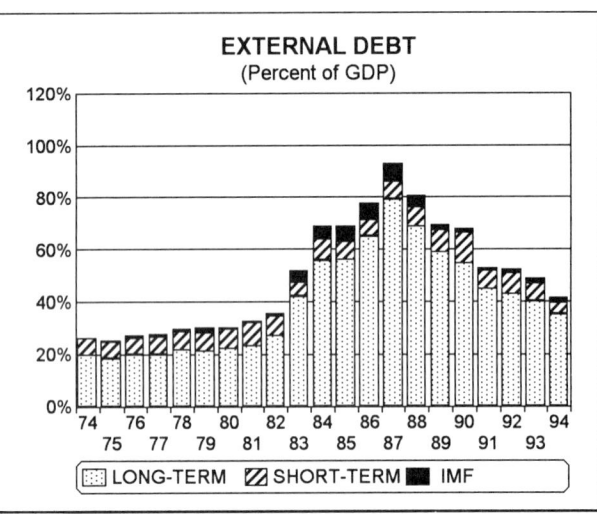

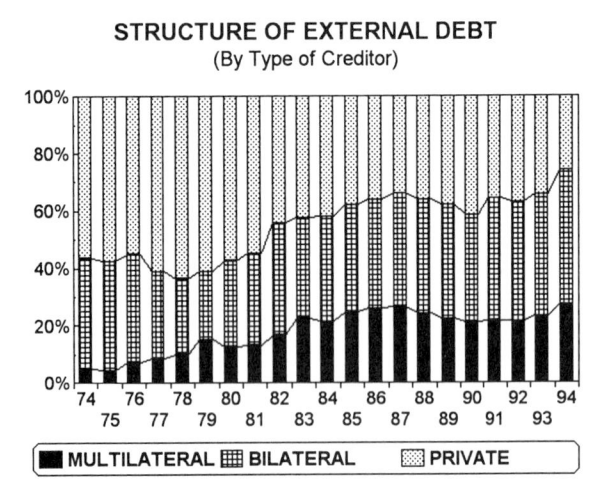

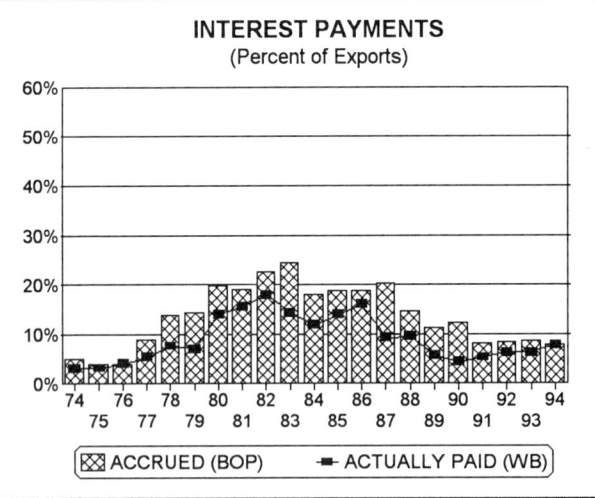

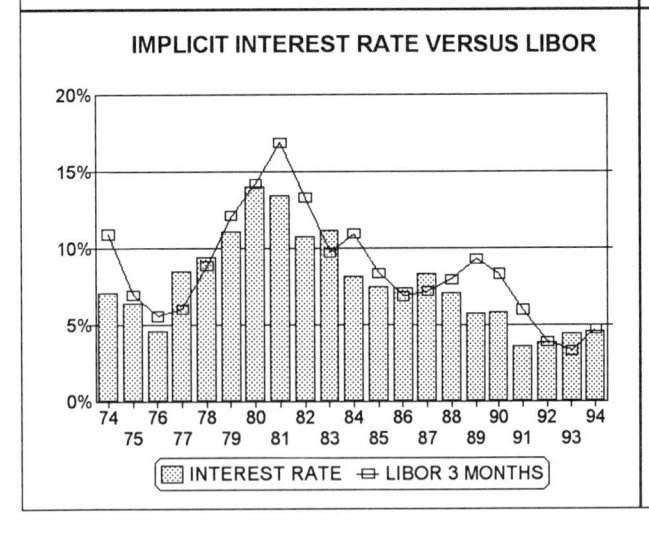

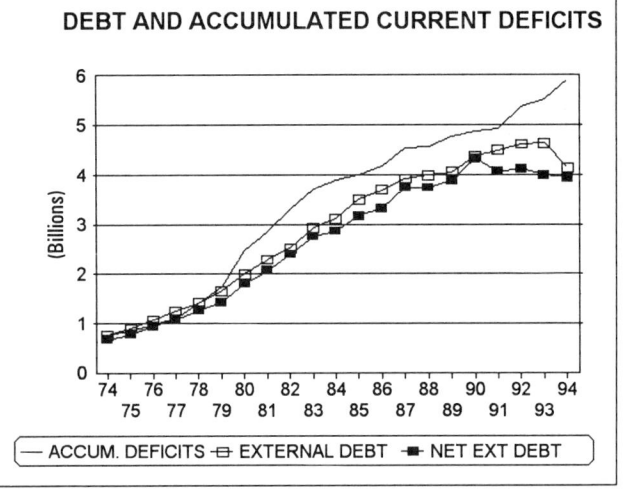

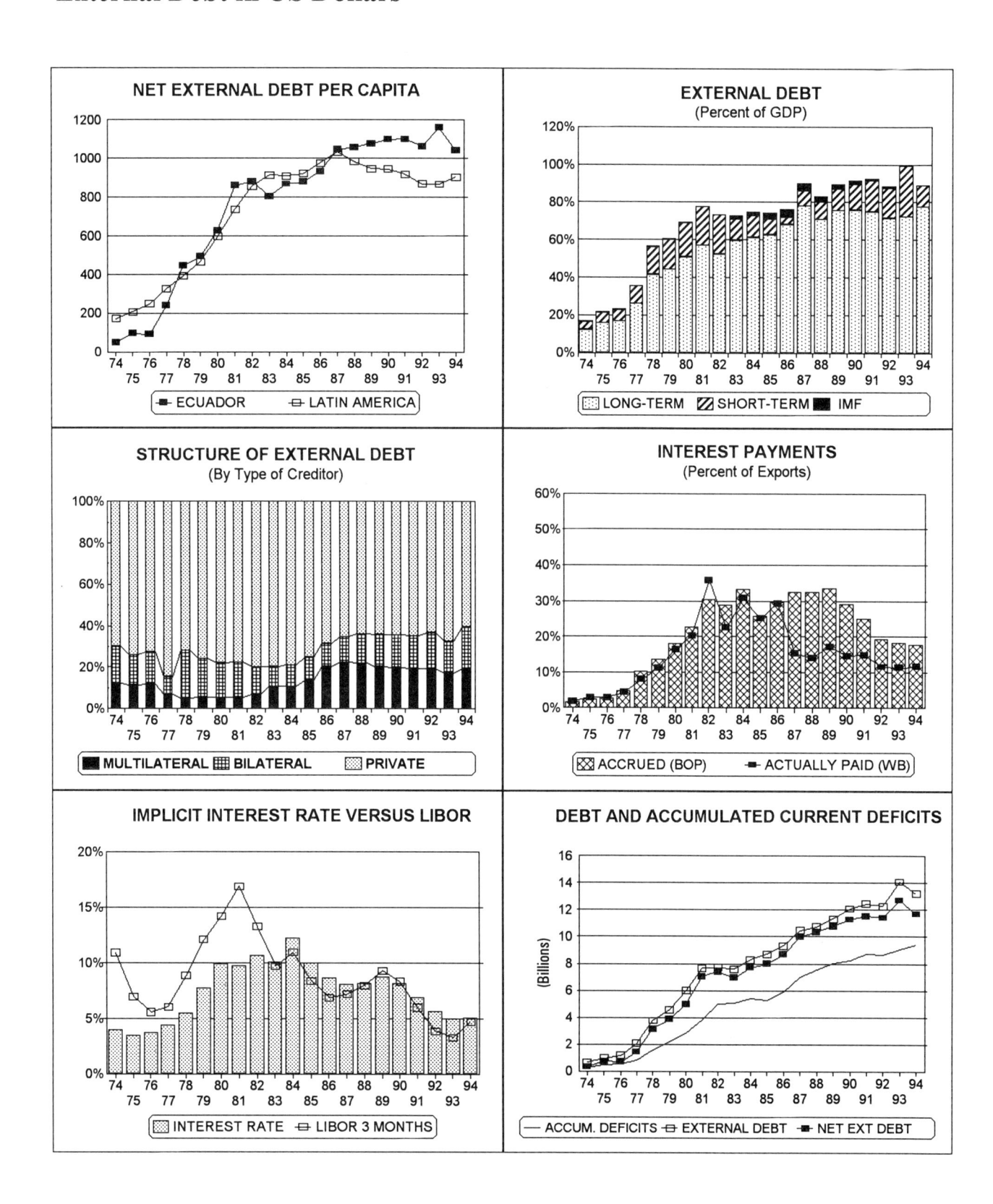

ECUADOR
External Debt in US Dollars

NET EXTERNAL DEBT PER CAPITA
ECUADOR — LATIN AMERICA

EXTERNAL DEBT
(Percent of GDP)
LONG-TERM / SHORT-TERM / IMF

STRUCTURE OF EXTERNAL DEBT
(By Type of Creditor)
MULTILATERAL / BILATERAL / PRIVATE

INTEREST PAYMENTS
(Percent of Exports)
ACCRUED (BOP) — ACTUALLY PAID (WB)

IMPLICIT INTEREST RATE VERSUS LIBOR
INTEREST RATE / LIBOR 3 MONTHS

DEBT AND ACCUMULATED CURRENT DEFICITS
(Billions)
ACCUM. DEFICITS / EXTERNAL DEBT / NET EXT DEBT

Statistics and Quantitative Analysis/IDB

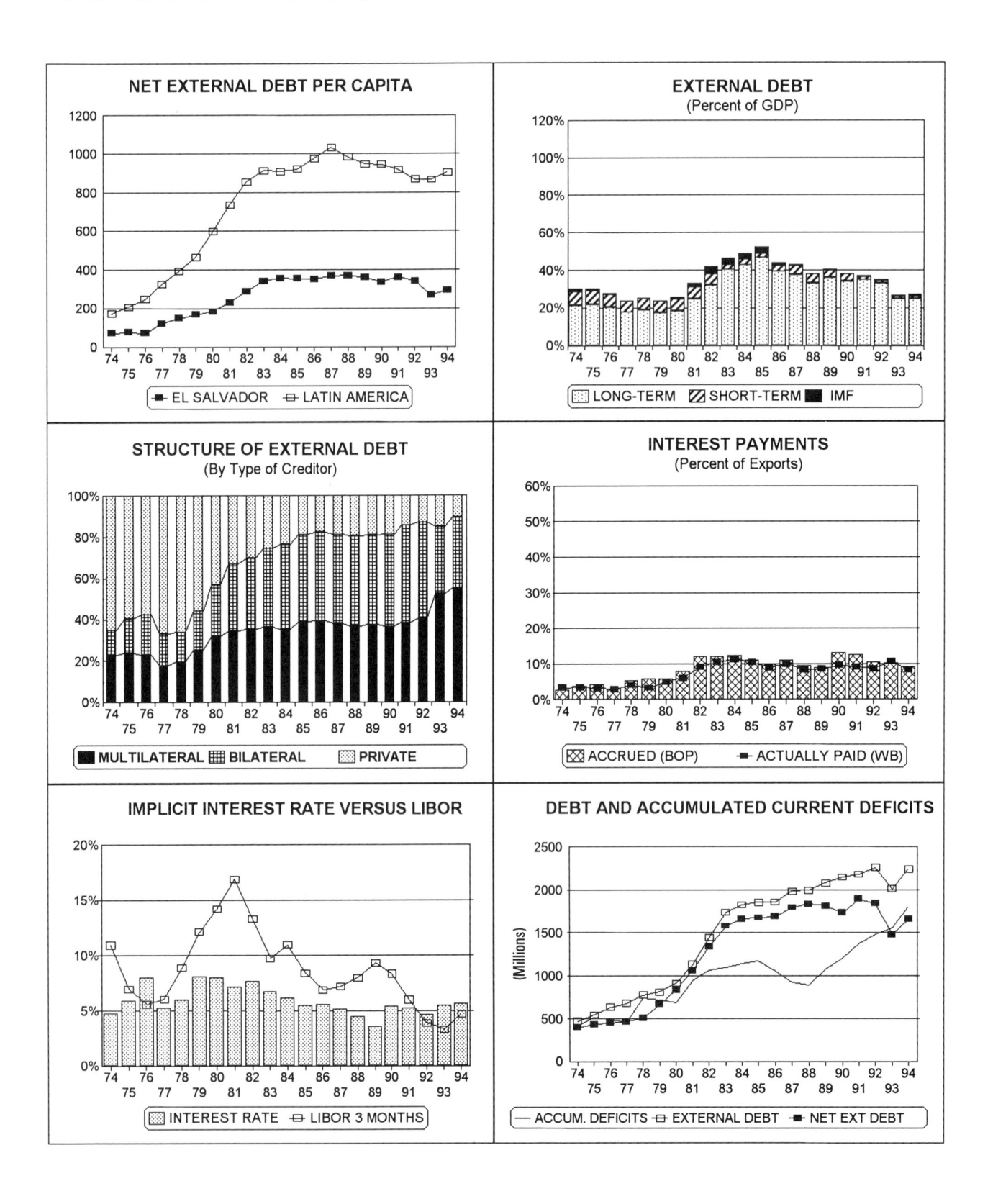

EL SALVADOR
External Debt in US Dollars

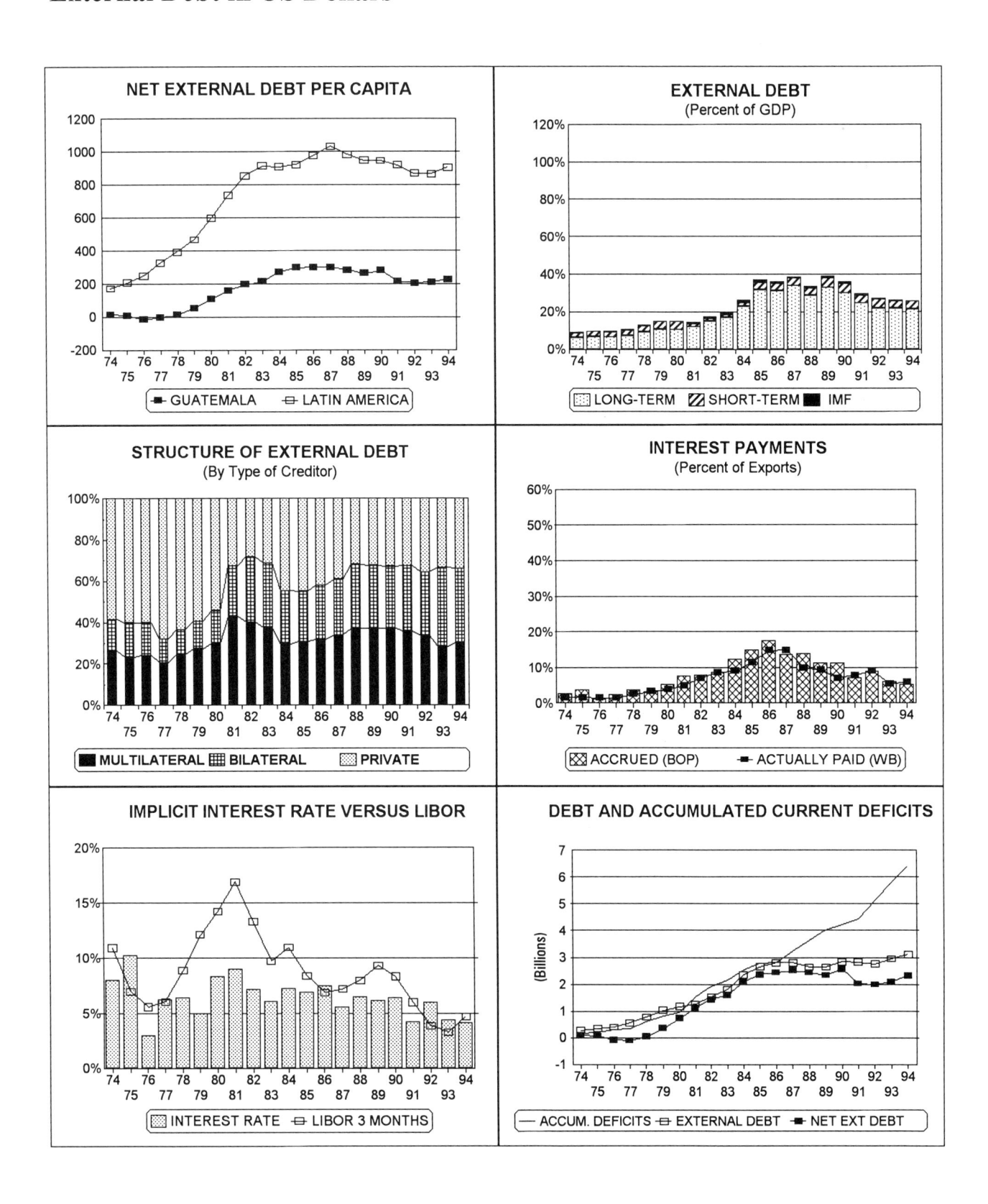

GUATEMALA
External Debt in US Dollars

Statistics and Quantitative Analysis/IDB

187

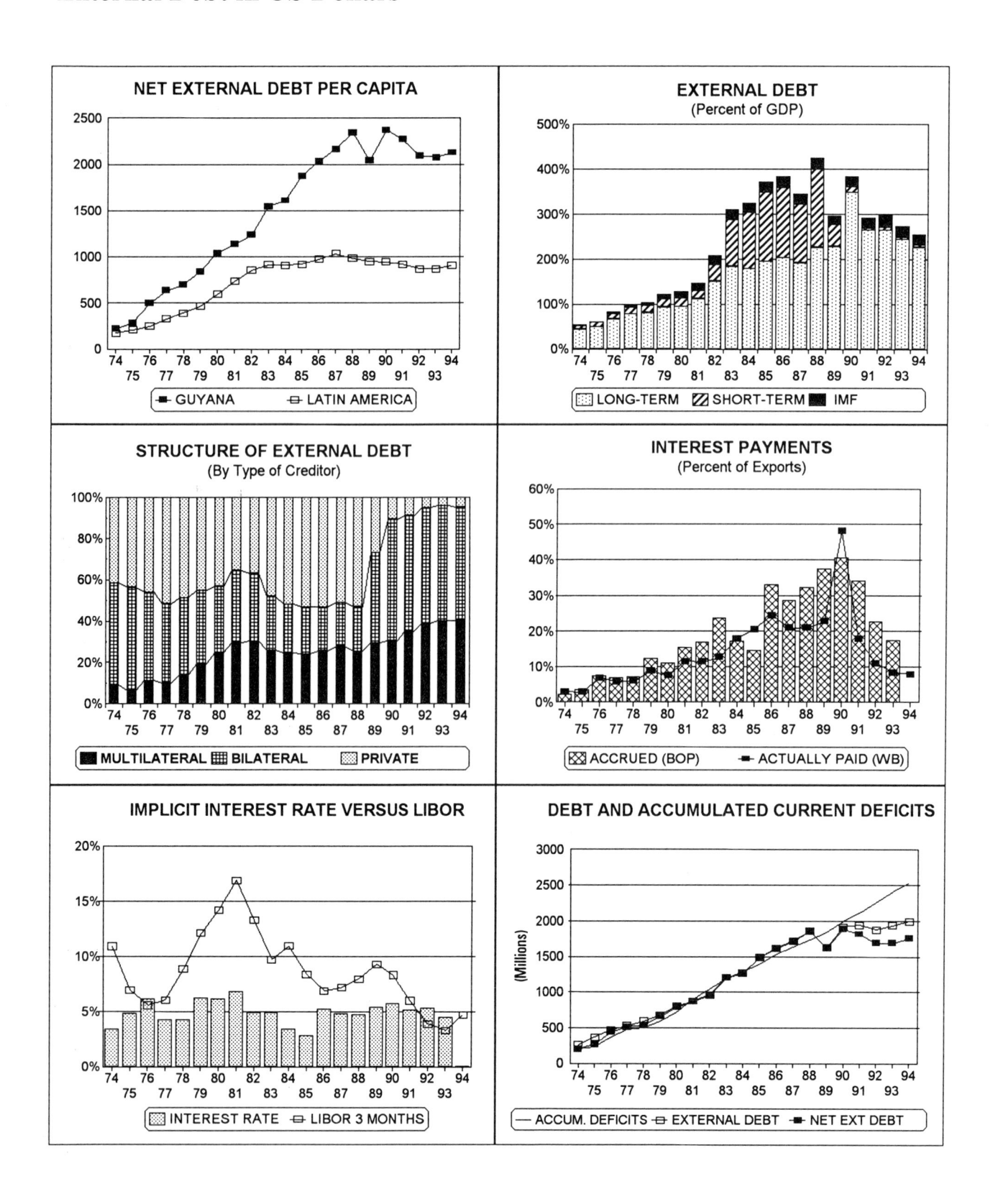

GUYANA
External Debt in US Dollars

NET EXTERNAL DEBT PER CAPITA
- GUYANA
- LATIN AMERICA

EXTERNAL DEBT
(Percent of GDP)
- LONG-TERM
- SHORT-TERM
- IMF

STRUCTURE OF EXTERNAL DEBT
(By Type of Creditor)
- MULTILATERAL
- BILATERAL
- PRIVATE

INTEREST PAYMENTS
(Percent of Exports)
- ACCRUED (BOP)
- ACTUALLY PAID (WB)

IMPLICIT INTEREST RATE VERSUS LIBOR
- INTEREST RATE
- LIBOR 3 MONTHS

DEBT AND ACCUMULATED CURRENT DEFICITS
- ACCUM. DEFICITS
- EXTERNAL DEBT
- NET EXT DEBT

Statistics and Quantitative Analysis/IDB

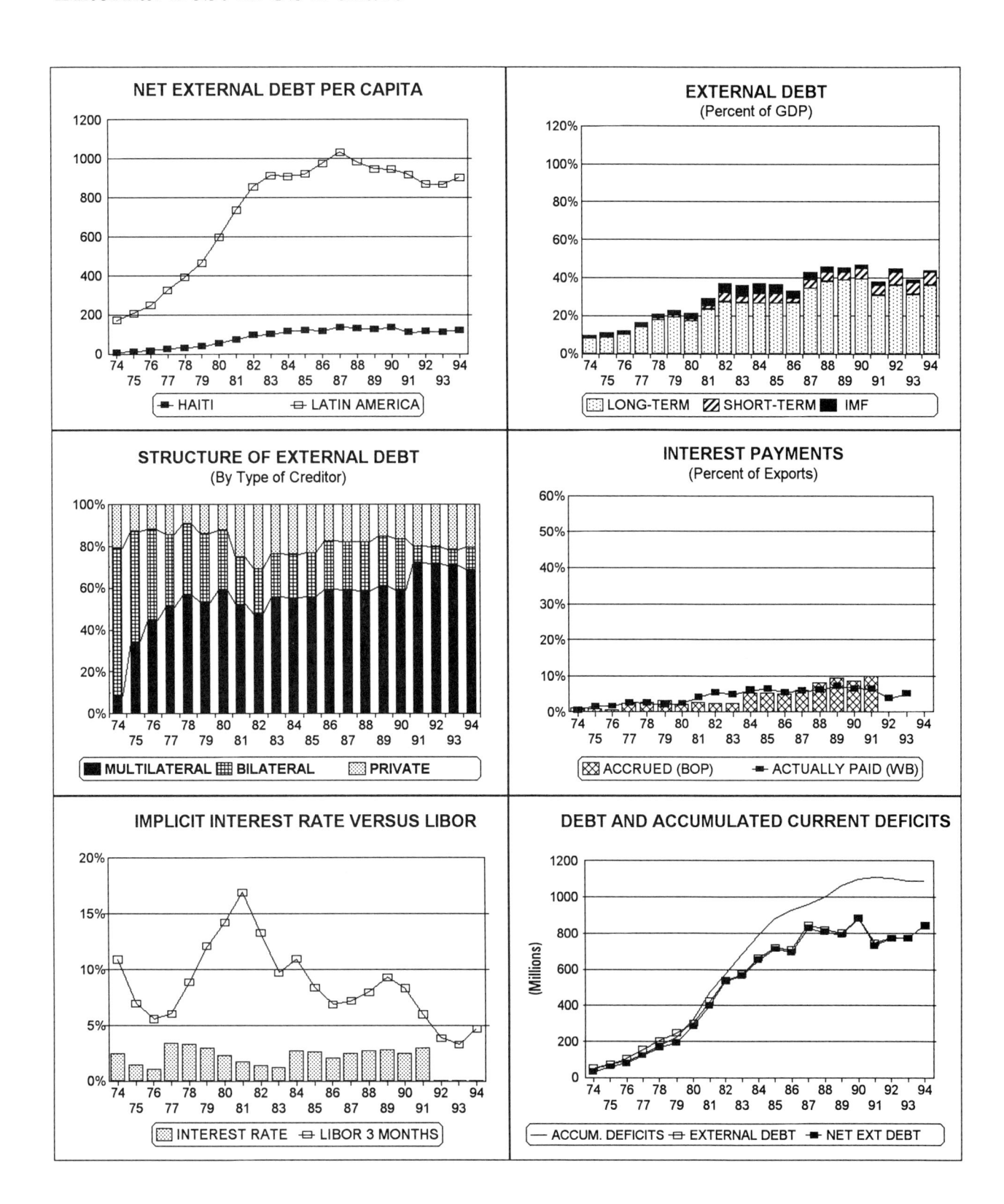

HAITI
External Debt in US Dollars

Statistics and Quantitative Analysis/IDB

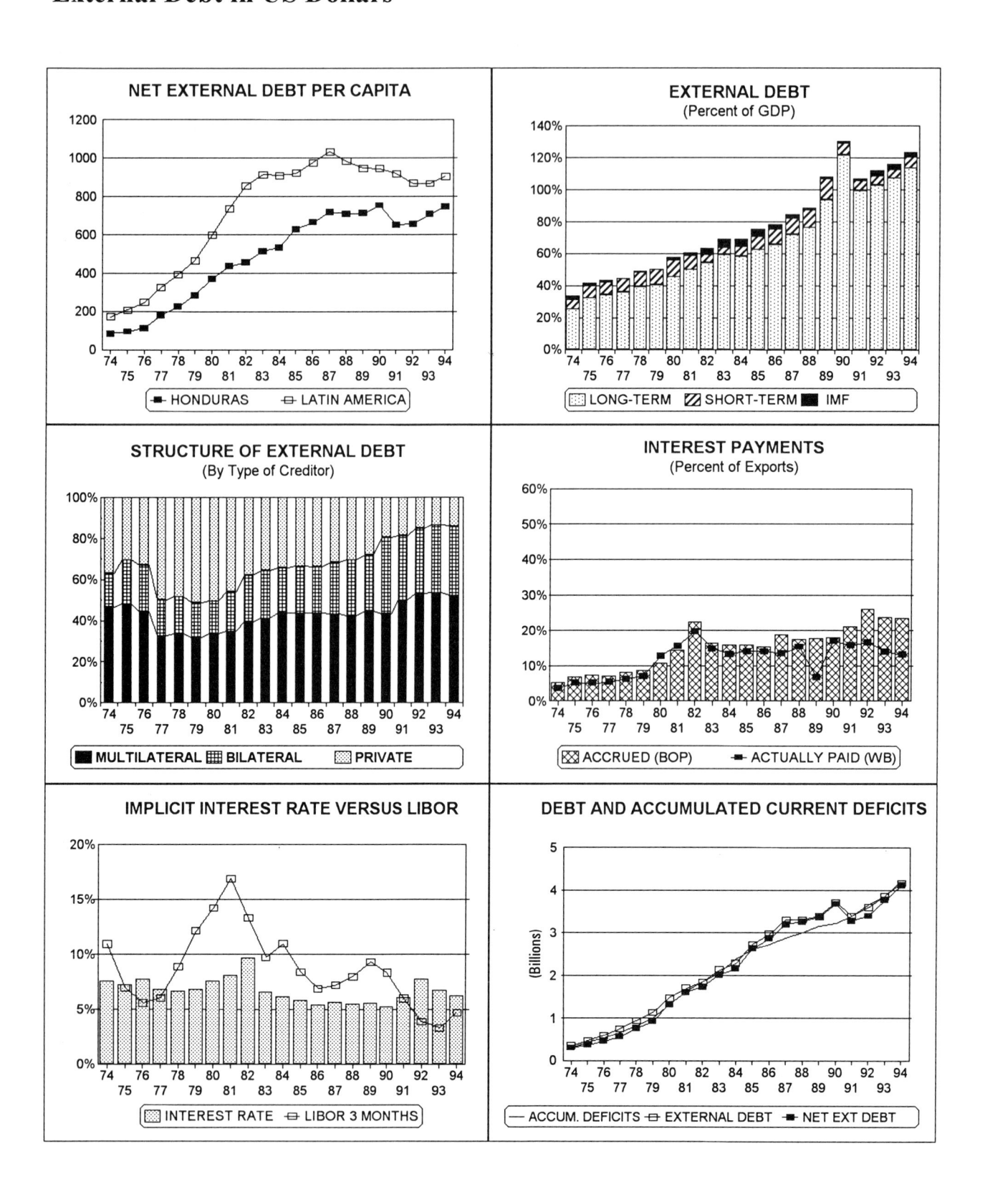

HONDURAS
External Debt in US Dollars

Statistics and Quantitative Analysis/IDB

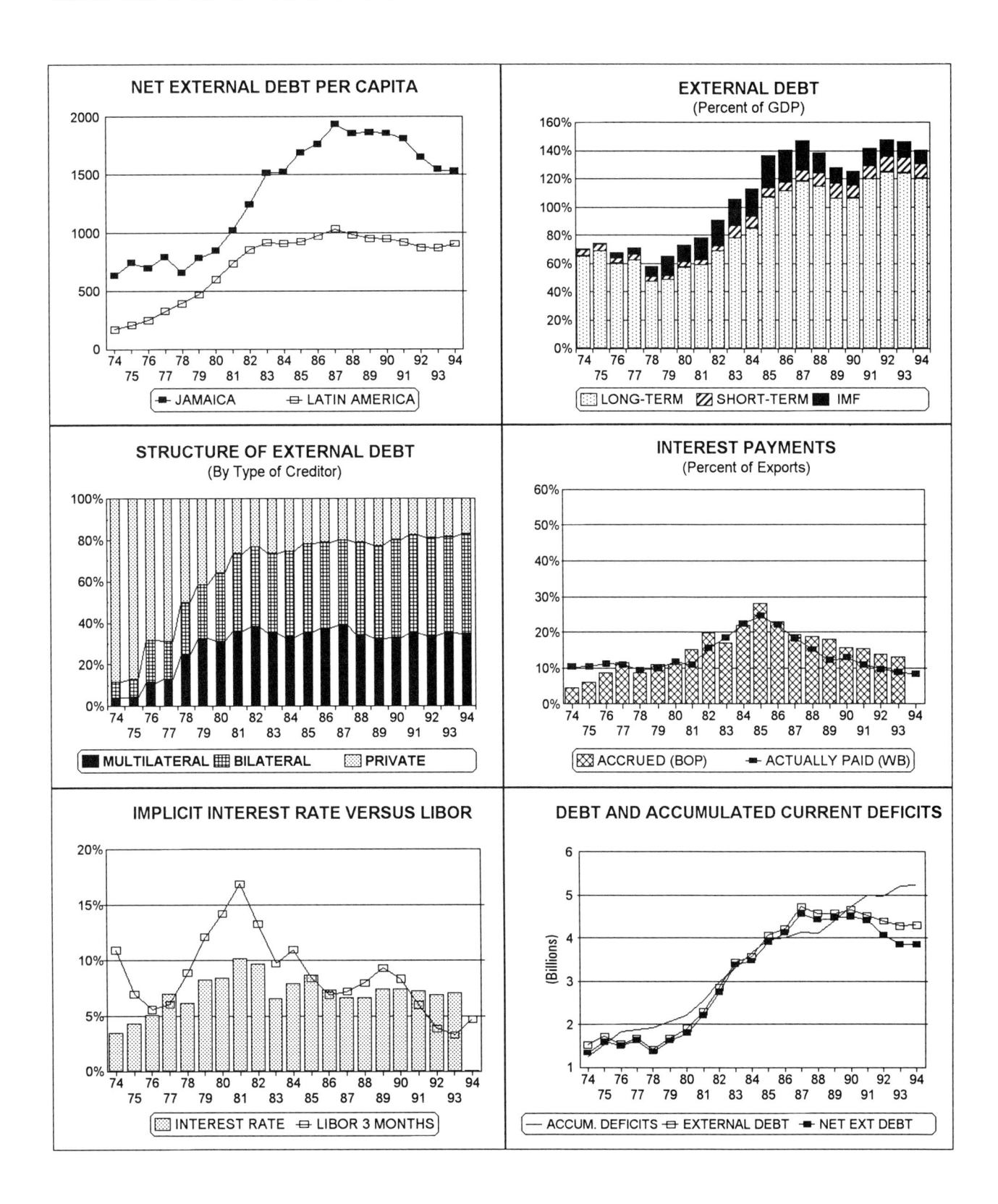

JAMAICA
External Debt in US Dollars

NET EXTERNAL DEBT PER CAPITA
JAMAICA — LATIN AMERICA

EXTERNAL DEBT
(Percent of GDP)
LONG-TERM — SHORT-TERM — IMF

STRUCTURE OF EXTERNAL DEBT
(By Type of Creditor)
MULTILATERAL — BILATERAL — PRIVATE

INTEREST PAYMENTS
(Percent of Exports)
ACCRUED (BOP) — ACTUALLY PAID (WB)

IMPLICIT INTEREST RATE VERSUS LIBOR
INTEREST RATE — LIBOR 3 MONTHS

DEBT AND ACCUMULATED CURRENT DEFICITS
(Billions)
ACCUM. DEFICITS — EXTERNAL DEBT — NET EXT DEBT

Statistics and Quantitative Analysis/IDB

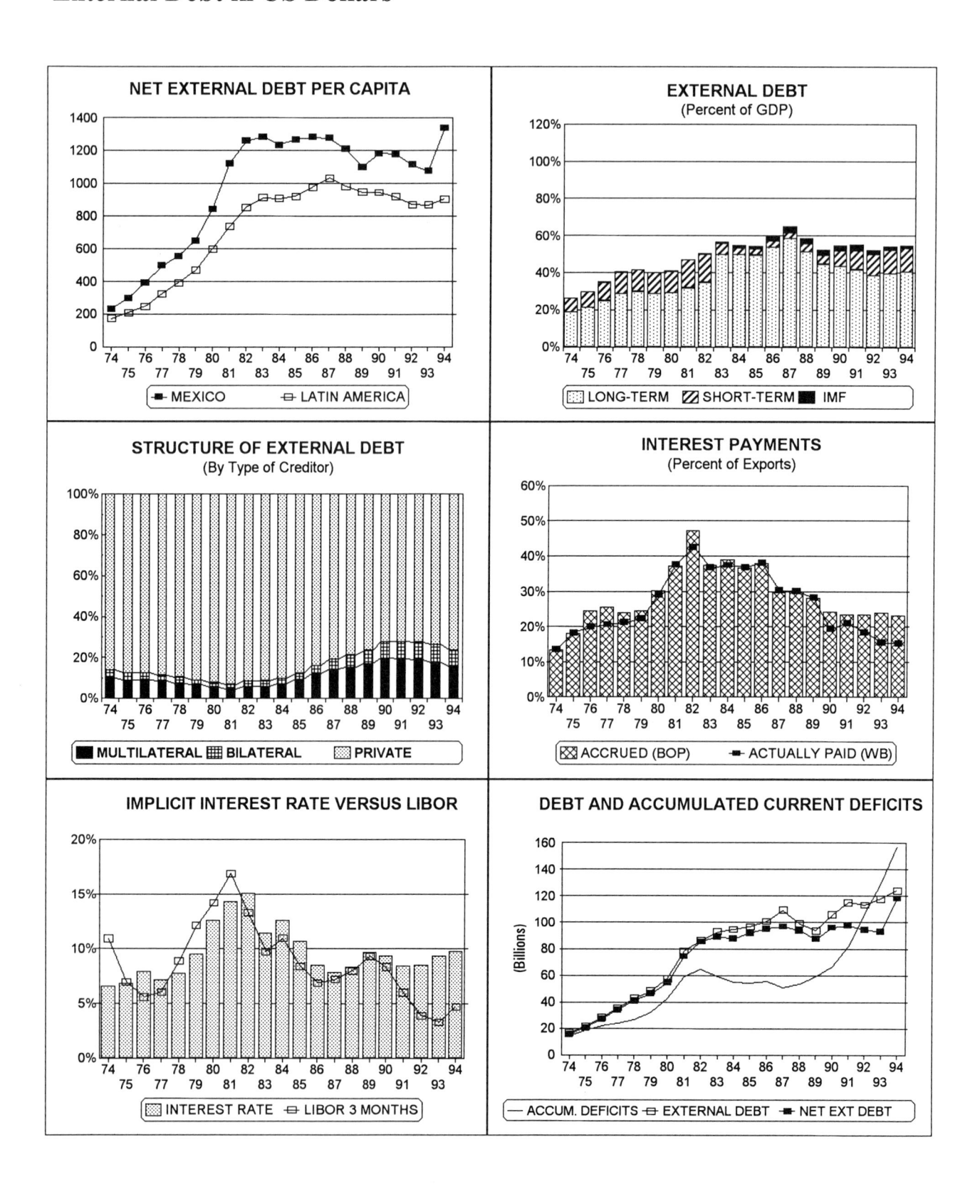

MEXICO
External Debt in US Dollars

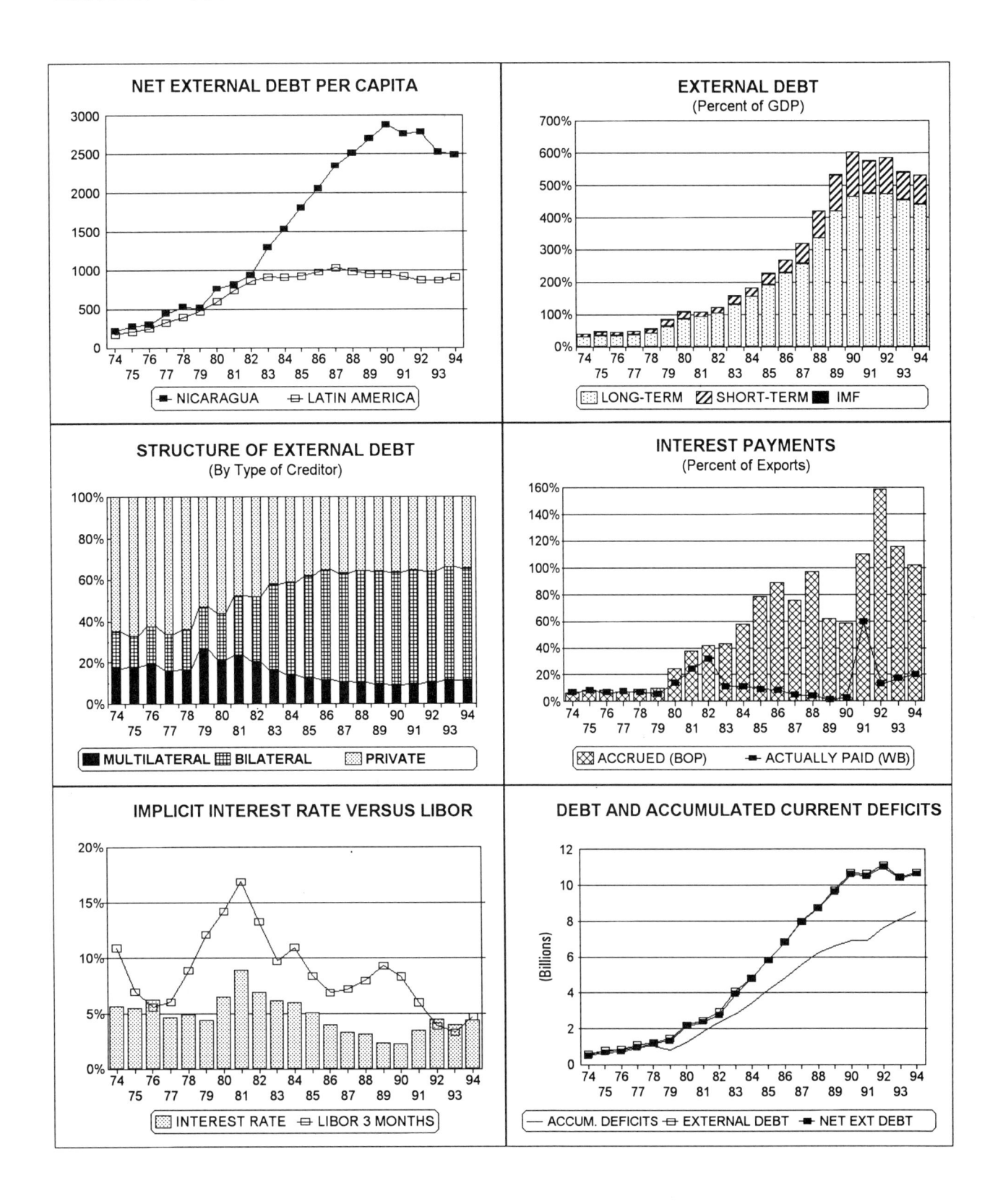

NICARAGUA
External Debt in US Dollars

NET EXTERNAL DEBT PER CAPITA
- NICARAGUA
- LATIN AMERICA

EXTERNAL DEBT
(Percent of GDP)
- LONG-TERM
- SHORT-TERM
- IMF

STRUCTURE OF EXTERNAL DEBT
(By Type of Creditor)
- MULTILATERAL
- BILATERAL
- PRIVATE

INTEREST PAYMENTS
(Percent of Exports)
- ACCRUED (BOP)
- ACTUALLY PAID (WB)

IMPLICIT INTEREST RATE VERSUS LIBOR
- INTEREST RATE
- LIBOR 3 MONTHS

DEBT AND ACCUMULATED CURRENT DEFICITS
- ACCUM. DEFICITS
- EXTERNAL DEBT
- NET EXT DEBT

Statistics and Quantitative Analysis/IDB

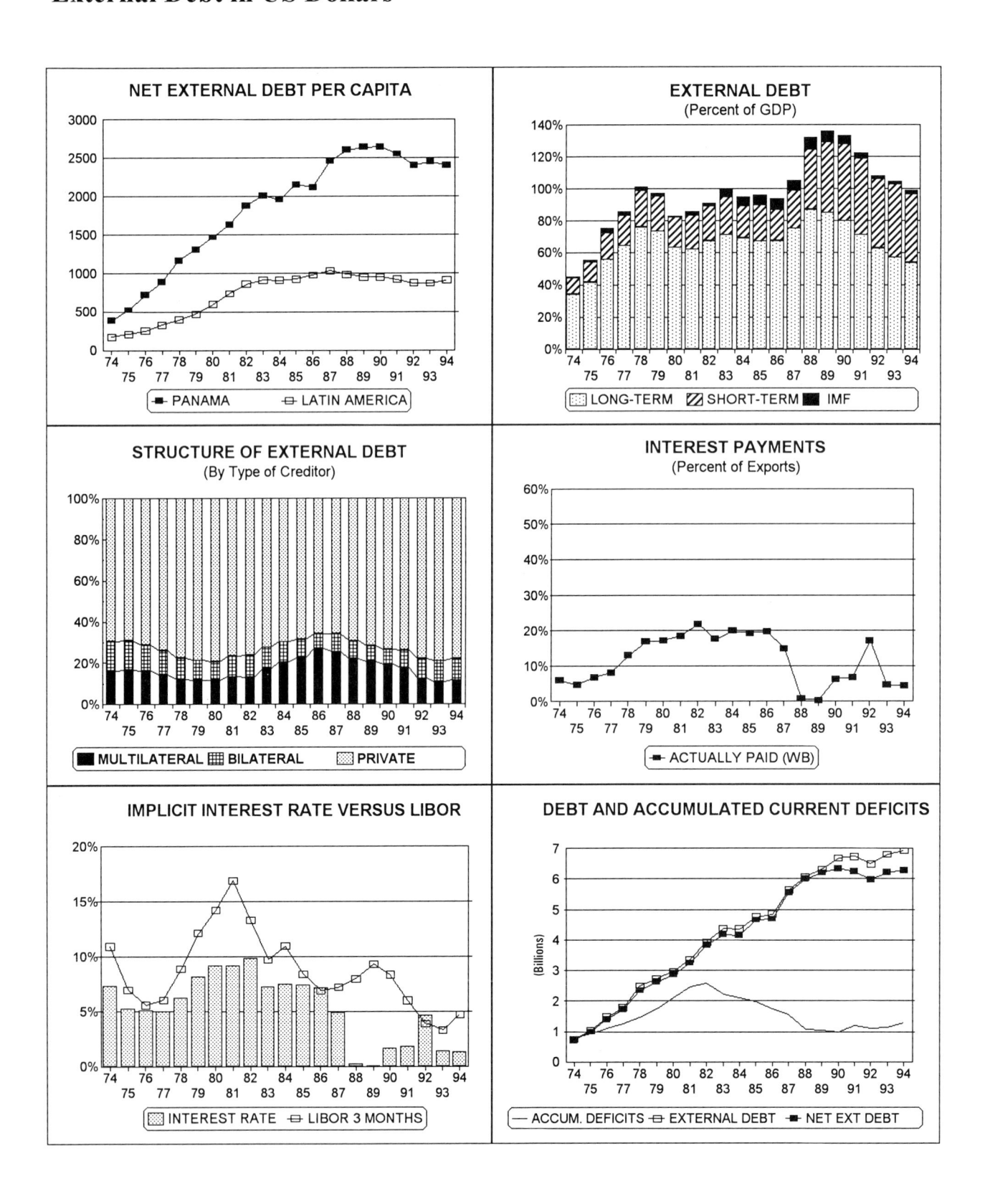

PANAMA
External Debt in US Dollars

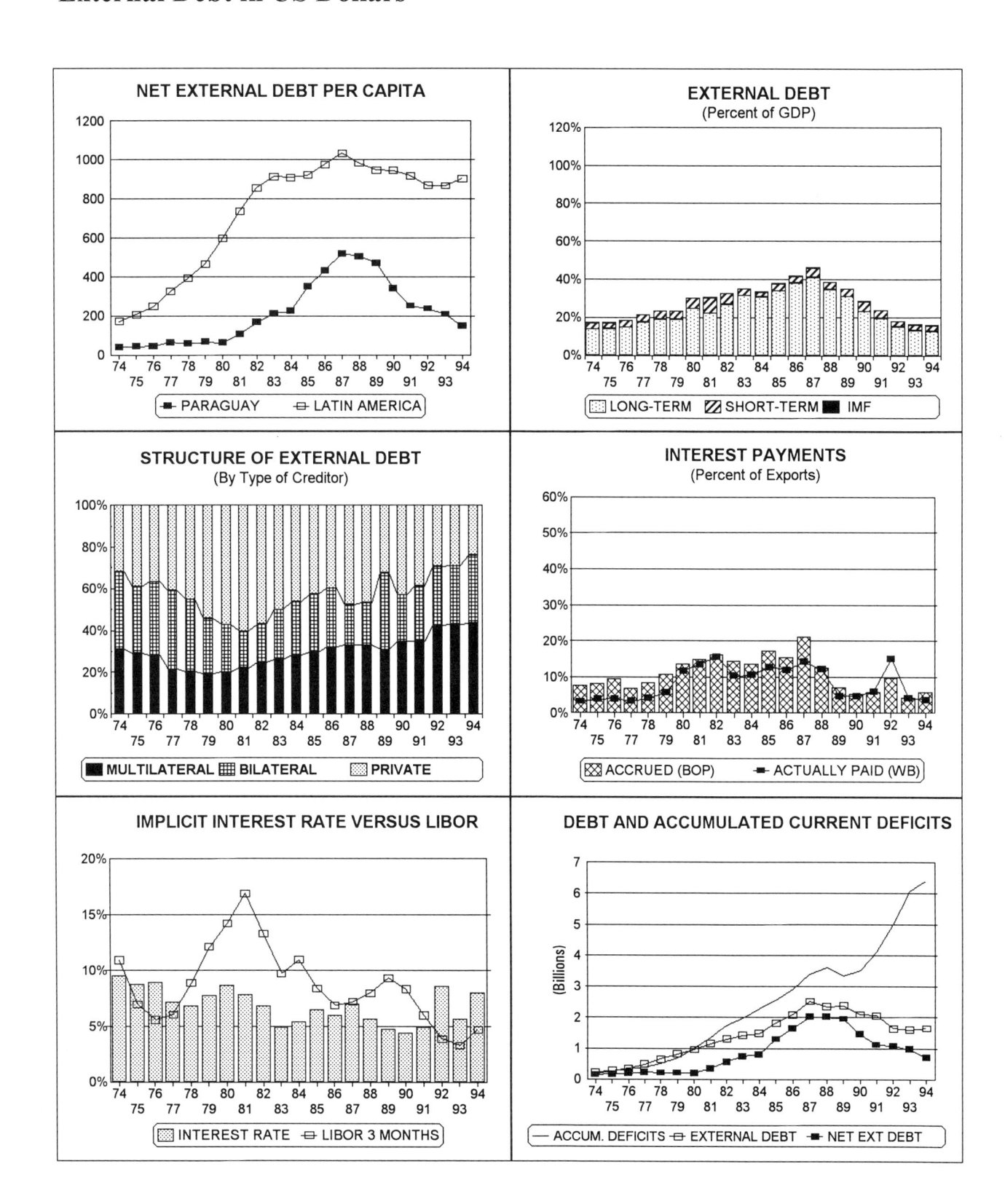

PARAGUAY
External Debt in US Dollars

Statistics and Quantitative Analysis/IDB

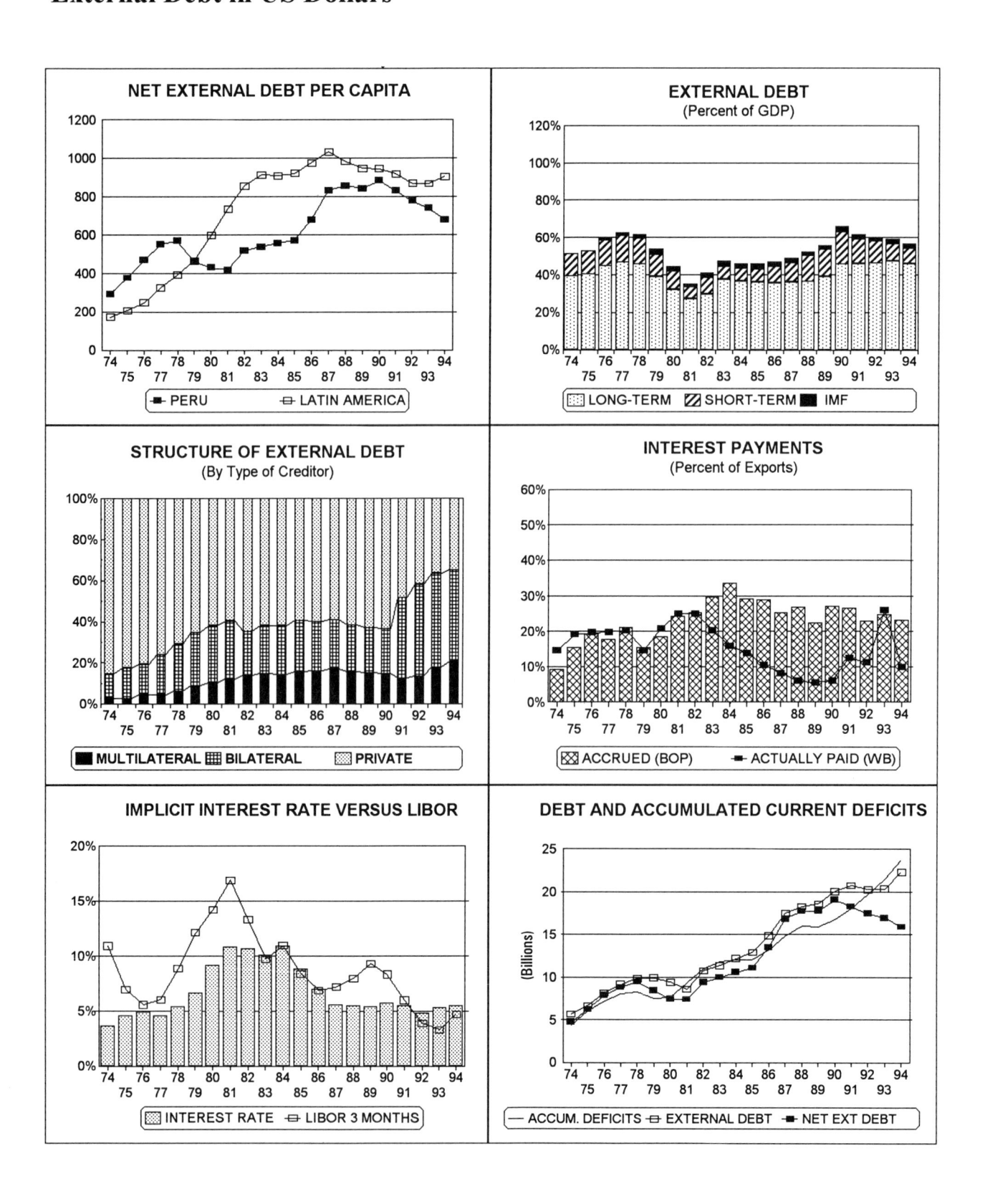

PERU
External Debt in US Dollars

NET EXTERNAL DEBT PER CAPITA
— PERU — LATIN AMERICA

EXTERNAL DEBT
(Percent of GDP)
LONG-TERM, SHORT-TERM, IMF

STRUCTURE OF EXTERNAL DEBT
(By Type of Creditor)
MULTILATERAL, BILATERAL, PRIVATE

INTEREST PAYMENTS
(Percent of Exports)
ACCRUED (BOP), ACTUALLY PAID (WB)

IMPLICIT INTEREST RATE VERSUS LIBOR
INTEREST RATE, LIBOR 3 MONTHS

DEBT AND ACCUMULATED CURRENT DEFICITS
(Billions)
ACCUM. DEFICITS, EXTERNAL DEBT, NET EXT DEBT

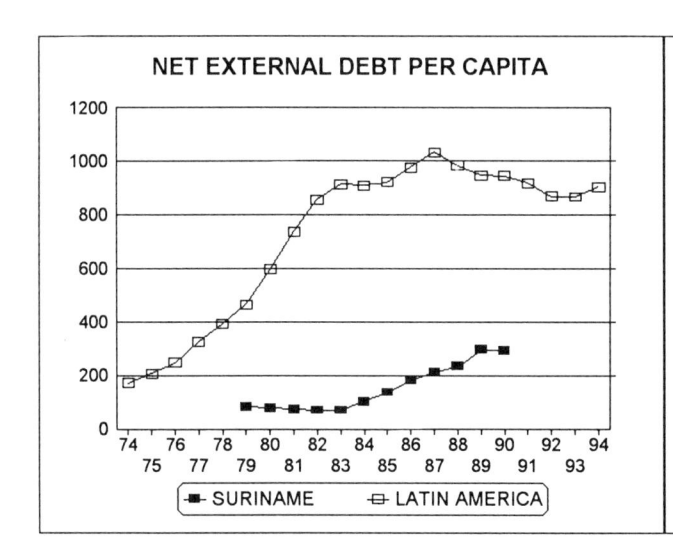

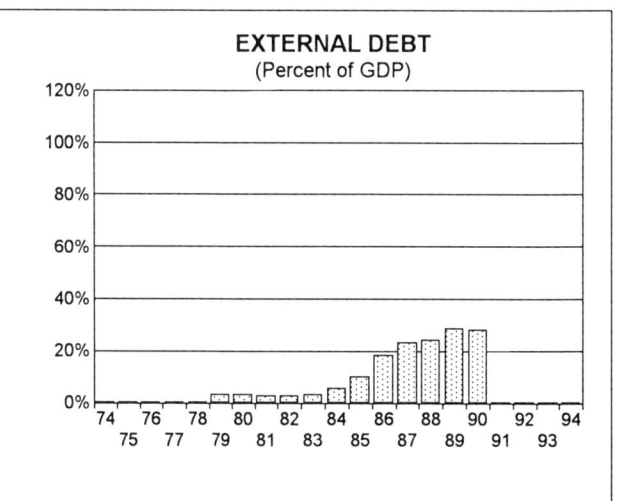

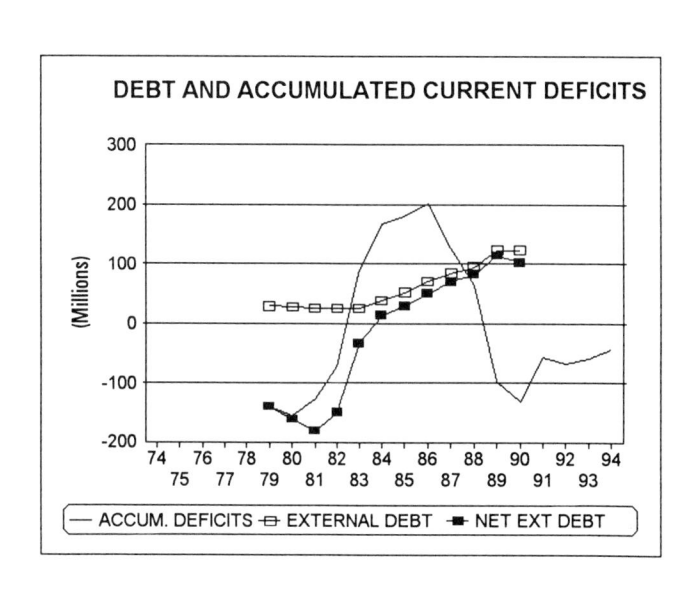

SURINAME
External Debt in US Dollars

Statistics and Quantitative Analysis/IDB

TRINIDAD AND TOBAGO
External Debt in US Dollars

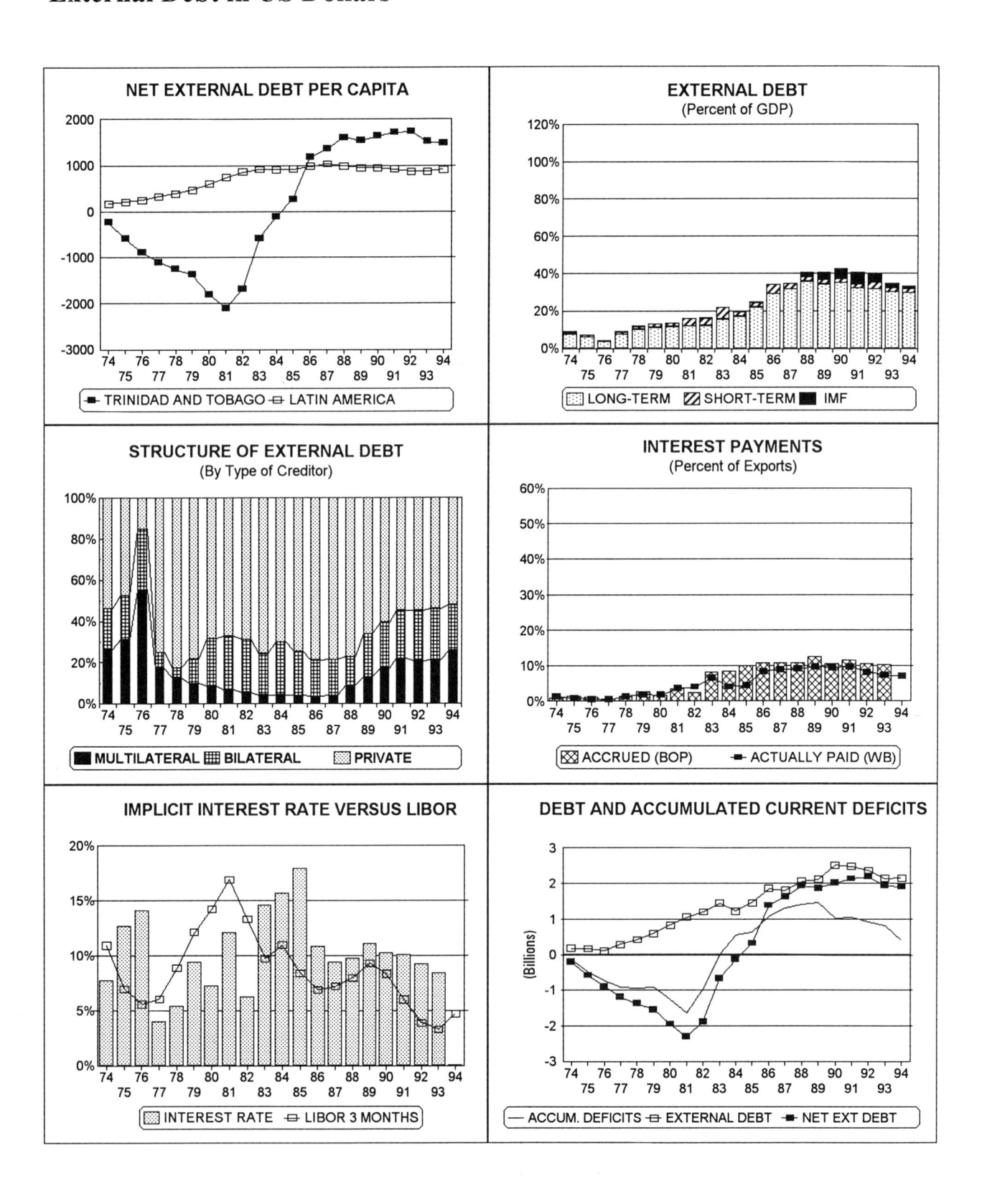

URUGUAY
External Debt in US Dollars

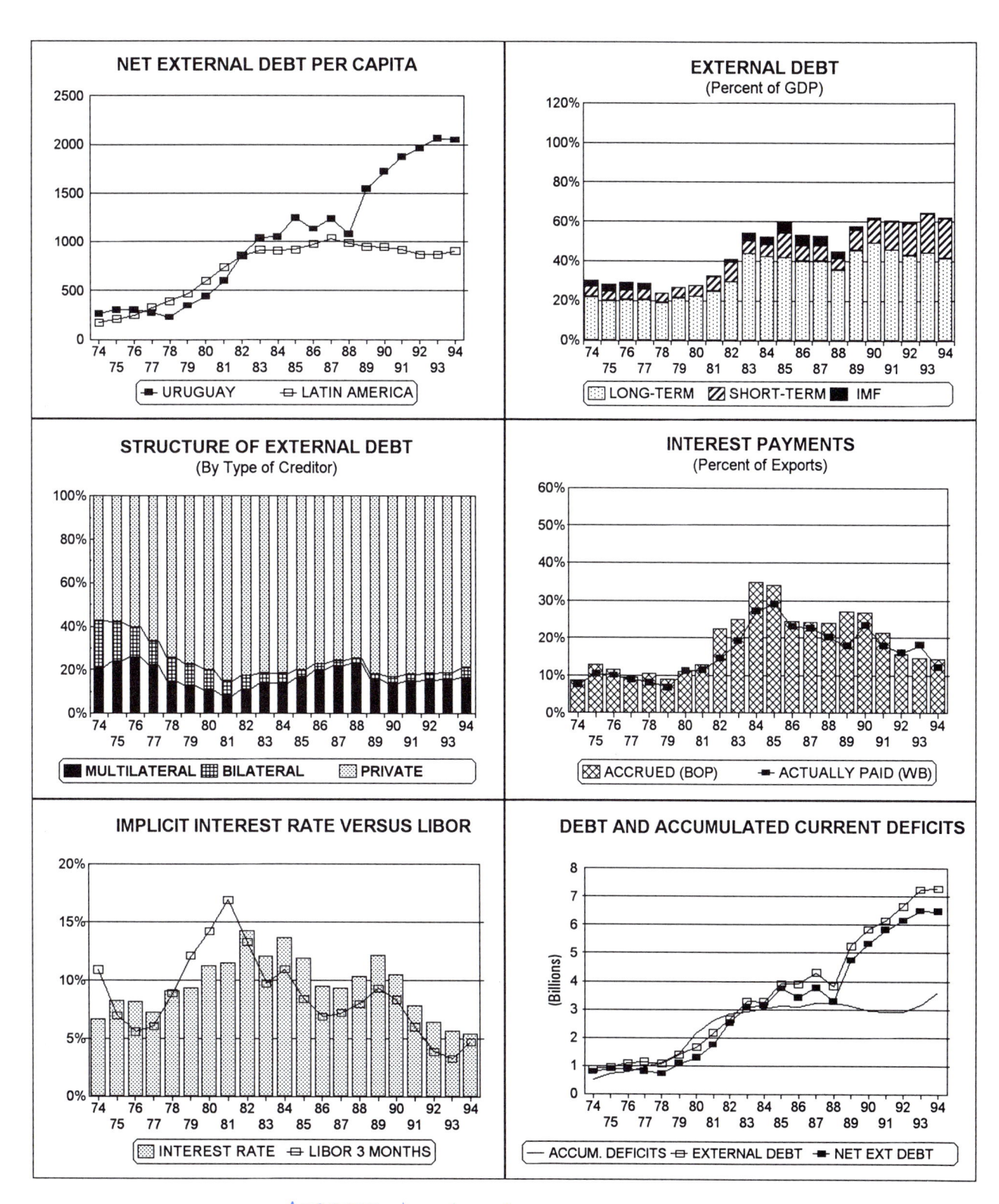

NET EXTERNAL DEBT PER CAPITA
— URUGUAY — LATIN AMERICA

EXTERNAL DEBT (Percent of GDP)
LONG-TERM / SHORT-TERM / IMF

STRUCTURE OF EXTERNAL DEBT (By Type of Creditor)
MULTILATERAL / BILATERAL / PRIVATE

INTEREST PAYMENTS (Percent of Exports)
ACCRUED (BOP) / ACTUALLY PAID (WB)

IMPLICIT INTEREST RATE VERSUS LIBOR
INTEREST RATE / LIBOR 3 MONTHS

DEBT AND ACCUMULATED CURRENT DEFICITS
ACCUM. DEFICITS / EXTERNAL DEBT / NET EXT DEBT

Statistics and Quantitative Analysis/IDB

VENEZUELA
External Debt in US Dollars

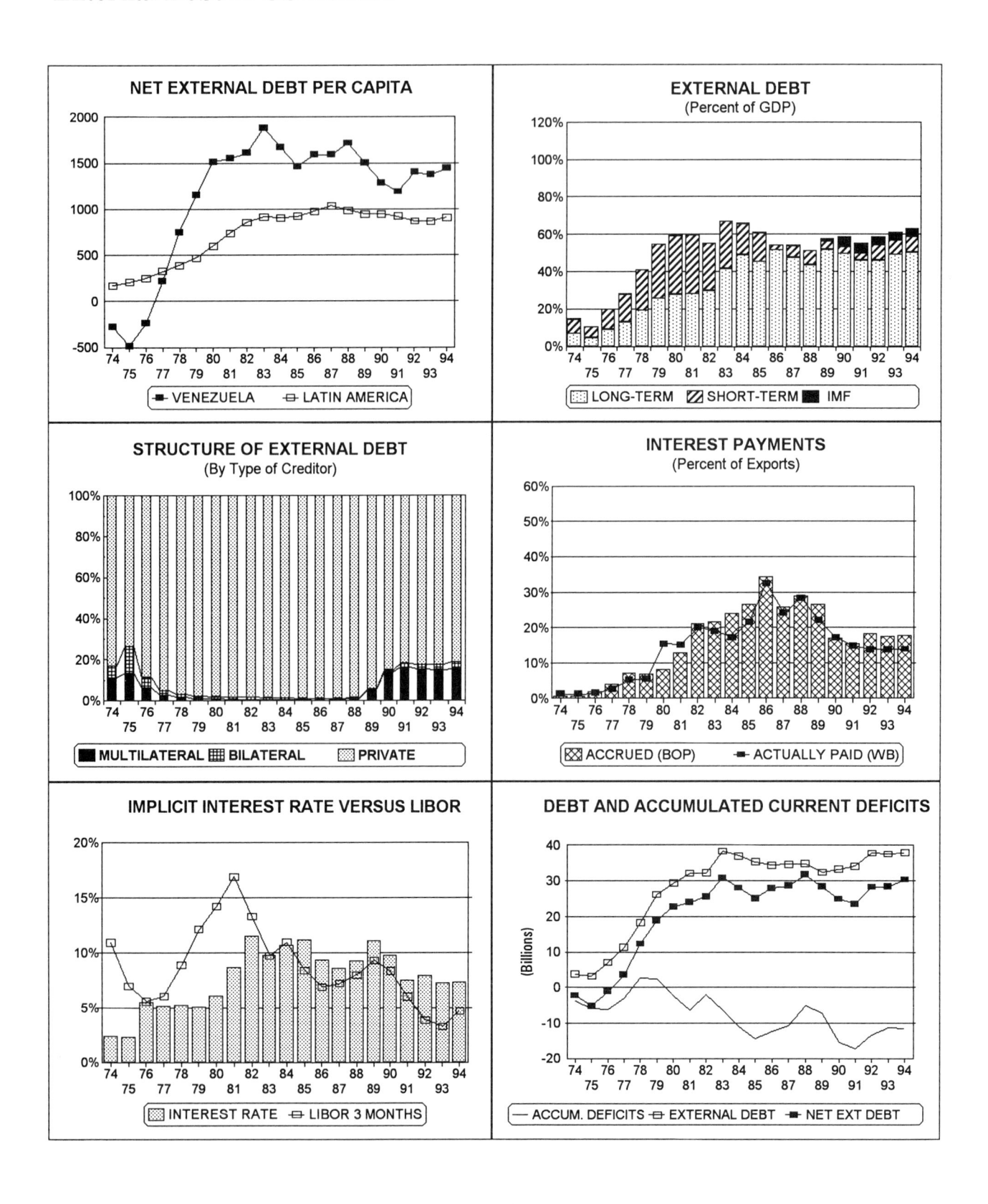